THE CAMBRIDGE COMPANION TO
BRENTANO

Franz Brentano (1838–1917) led an intellectual revolution
that sought to revitalize German-language philosophy and
to reverse its post-Kantian direction. His philosophy laid the
groundwork for philosophy of science as it came to fruition
in the Vienna Circle, and for phenomenology in the work of
such figures as his student Edmund Husserl. This volume
brings together newly commissioned chapters on his important work in theory of intentionality, theory of judgment, the
reform of syllogistic logic, empirical descriptive psychology
and phenomenology, theory of knowledge, metaphysics and
ontology, value theory, and natural theology. It also offers a
critical evaluation of Brentano's significance in his historical context, and of his impact on contemporary philosophy
in both the analytic and the continental traditions.

DALE JACQUETTE is Professor of Philosophy at The Pennsylvania State University. His recent books include
David Hume's Critique of Infinity (2001), *Symbolic Logic*
(2001) and *Ontology* (2002).

MEDIEVAL JEWISH PHILOSOPHY *Edited by*
DANIEL H. FRANK *and* OLIVER LEAMAN
MEDIEVAL PHILOSOPHY *Edited by* A. S. McGRADE
MILL *Edited by* JOHN SKORUPSKI
NEWTON *Edited by* I. BERNARD COHEN *and*
GEORGE E. SMITH
NIETZSCHE *Edited by* BERND MAGNUS *and*
KATHLEEN HIGGINS
OCKHAM *Edited by* PAUL VINCENT SPADE
PASCAL *Edited by* NICHOLAS HAMMOND
PLATO *Edited by* RICHARD KRAUT
PLOTINUS *Edited by* LLOYD P. GERSON
RAWLS *Edited by* SAMUEL FREEMAN
ROUSSEAU *Edited by* PATRICK RILEY
BERTRAND RUSSELL *Edited by* NICHOLAS GRIFFIN
SARTRE *Edited by* CHRISTINA HOWELLS
SCHOPENHAUER *Edited by* CHRISTOPHER JANAWAY
THE SCOTTISH ENLIGHTENMENT *Edited by*
ALEXANDER BROADIE
SPINOZA *Edited by* DON GARRETT
THE STOICS *Edited by* BRAD INWOOD
WITTGENSTEIN *Edited by* HANS SLUGA *and* DAVID
STERN

The Cambridge Companion to
BRENTANO

Edited by Dale Jacquette
The Pennsylvania State University

CAMBRIDGE
UNIVERSITY PRESS

PUBLISHED BY THE PRESS SYNDICATE OF THE UNIVERSITY OF CAMBRIDGE
The Pitt Building, Trumpington Street, Cambridge, United Kingdom

CAMBRIDGE UNIVERSITY PRESS
The Edinburgh Building, Cambridge, CB2 2RU, UK
40 West 20th Street, New York, NY 10011–4211, USA
477 Williamstown Road, Port Melbourne, VIC 3207, Australia
Ruiz de Alarcón 13, 28014 Madrid, Spain
Dock House, The Waterfront, Cape Town 8001, South Africa

http://www.cambridge.org

First published 2004

Printed in the United Kingdom at the University Press, Cambridge

Typeface Trump Medieval 10/13 pt.   *System* LATEX 2$_\varepsilon$ [TB]

A catalogue record for this book is available from the British Library

Library of Congress Cataloguing in Publication data
The Cambridge companion to Brentano / edited by Dale Jacquette.
      p.   cm. – (Cambridge companions to philosophy)
Includes bibliographical references and index.
ISBN 0 521 80980 0   ISBN 0 521 00765 8 (pbk.)
1. Brentano, Franz Clemens, 1838–1917.   2. Philosophy, Austrian –
19th century.   3. Philosophy, Austrian – 20th century.   I. Title: Brentano.
II. Jacquette, Dale.   III. Series.
B3212.Z7C35   2004
193 – dc21   2003053215

ISBN 0 521 80980 0 hardback
ISBN 0 521 00765 8 paperback

Vera philosophiae methodus nulla alia nisi scientiae naturalis est.
— Franz Brentano, 1866

To the memory of Roderick M. Chisholm

CONTENTS

CONTRIBUTORS

WILHELM BAUMGARTNER is Professor of Philosophy and Director of the Franz Brentano Forschung at the University of Würzburg, Germany. He is the editor of *Brentano Studien: Internationales Jahrbuch der Franz Brentano Forschung*, and the author of numerous articles on Brentano, his school, and on philosophy in the phenomenological tradition. He has edited, together with Roderick M. Chisholm, Brentano's *Deskriptive Psychologie*, and has assisted with several translations of works by Brentano into Polish, Slovenian, Italian, and Romanian. He is currently Chairman of the Internationale Franz Brentano Gesellschaft (www.franz-brentano.de), and as Director of the Brentano Forschung preserves the Brentano *Nachlaß* to make it available for research. Baumgartner is currently preparing Brentano's *Lectures on Metaphysics* and *Scientific Correspondence* for publication.

ARKADIUSZ CHRUDZIMSKI is research assistant at the University of Salzburg, Austria, and assistant professor at the University of Zielona Gûra, Poland. He is the author of *Die Erkenntnistheorie von Roman Ingarden* and *Intentionalitätstheorie beim frühen Brentano*, in addition to articles on ontology, epistemology, phenomenology and Austrian philosophy.

ROLF GEORGE is Professor of Philosophy at the University of Waterloo, Canada, where he has taught since 1966. His publications include English translations of Brentano's work on Aristotle, *On the Several Senses of Being in Aristotle*, *The Psychology of Aristotle*, and, with Roderick M. Chisholm, *Aristotle and his World View*. He also edited Brentano's Aristotelian manuscripts, *Über Aristoteles*. He is the author of articles on a variety of topics including logic, Austrian philosophy, eighteenth-century philosophy and distributive justice.

DALE JACQUETTE is Professor of Philosophy at The Pennsylvania State University. He is the author of articles on logic, metaphysics, philosophy of mind, and Wittgenstein, and has recently published *Philosophy of Mind*, *Meinongian Logic: the Semantics of Existence and Nonexistence*, *Wittgenstein's Thought in Transition*, *David Hume's Critique of Infinity*, *Symbolic Logic*, *On Boole*, and *Ontology*, and edited a collection on *Schopenhauer, Philosophy, and the Arts* and the *Blackwell Companion to Philosophical Logic*. He is currently editor of *American Philosophical Quarterly*.

GLEN KOEHN is Adjunct Associate Professor at the University of Maryland, University College. He has taught at South Korean universities, and has had longstanding interests in both Brentano and Aristotle. His recent paper on Aristotelian ethics, "Human Goodness and the Golden Mean," appeared in the *Journal of Value Inquiry*.

SUSAN F. KRANTZ GABRIEL is Professor of Philosophy at St. Anselm College, New Hampshire. She is editor and translator of the English edition of Brentano's lectures on natural theology, *On the Existence of God*, and author of *Refuting Peter Singer's Ethical Theory: The Importance of Human Dignity*, as well as articles on Brentano and other subjects.

JOSEPH MARGOLIS is Laura H. Carnell Professor of Philosophy at Temple University, Philadelphia. He has published widely in a variety of specialities. His most recent books include: *Selves and Other Texts* and *Reinventing Pragmatism: American Philosophy at the End of the Twentieth Century*. He has recently completed *The Unraveling of Scientism* and *The Advantages of a Second-Best Morality*.

LINDA L. MCALISTER is Professor Emerita at the University of South Florida. She has taught at San Diego State University, Brooklyn College, the CUNY Graduate Center, and UCLA. Her dissertation was on Brentano's ethics and she was subsequently engaged by the Franz Brentano Foundation to prepare the English edition of Brentano's *Psychologie vom empirischen Standpunkt*. After publishing other works on Brentano she turned her attention to feminist philosophy. She edited *Hypatia: a Journal of Feminist Philosophy* for several years and she is editor of *Hypatia's Daughters*, a collection of articles about women in the history of philosophy.

KEVIN MULLIGAN is Professor of Analytic Philosophy at the University of Geneva, Switzerland. He has recently edited (with J.-P. Cometti) *La Philosophie autrichienne de Bolzano à Musil: histoire et actualité*, and (with B. Baertschi) *Les Nationalismes*, and is the author of numerous articles on ontology, perception, emotions and values, Wittgenstein and Austro-German philosophies of mind.

CHARLES PARSONS is Edgar Pierce Professor of Philosophy at Harvard University. He has written on logic, philosophy of logic and mathematics, Kant, Husserl, Gödel, and other figures. He is co-editor of volumes III–V of the *Collected Works* of Kurt Gödel and author of *Mathematics in Philosophy* and *Mathematical Thought and its Objects*.

LYNN PASQUERELLA is Professor of Philosophy and Chair of the Institutional Review Board at the University of Rhode Island. She is a Fellow in the John Hazen White Sr. Center for Ethics and Public Service, a past recipient of the University of Rhode Island's Teaching Excellence Award, and has published extensively in the areas of medical ethics, theoretical and applied ethics, public policy, and the philosophy of law.

ROBIN D. ROLLINGER is assistant to the Husserl Archives in Louvain, Belgium. He is the author of two books, *Meinong and Husserl on Abstraction and Universals* and *Husserl's Position in the School of Brentano*, as well as various articles on phenomenology and its background in nineteenth- and early twentieth-century philosophy, psychology, and logic. He is editor of a volume of writings from Husserl's literary remains on transcendental idealism, to appear in the *Husserliana* series, and is currently editing a volume of writings from Husserl's extensive literary remains on the theory of judgment for the *Husserliana*.

KARL SCHUHMANN was Professor of History of Post-Medieval Philosophy at Utrecht University in The Netherlands. In addition to numerous articles on Renaissance philosophy and seventeenth-century mechanism, especially Hobbes, he published many articles on the Brentano school. He was editor of Husserl's *Ideen I*, and, together with Elisabeth Schuhmann, of Husserl's *Briefwechsel*. In 1984, with J. N. Mohanty, he founded the journal *Husserl Studies*. His books include *Die Fundamentalbetrachtung der Phänomenologie*, *Husserl-Chronik*, and *Husserls Staatsphilosophie*.

PETER SIMONS is Professor of Philosophy at the University of Leeds, UK. He is the author of two books: *Parts* and *Philosophy and Logic in Central Europe from Bolzano to Tarski*, as well as over 150 articles, including several on Brentano. His interests include metaphysics, logic, the history of Austrian and Polish philosophy and logic, the philosophy of mathematics, and the application of ontology to engineering and business. He is currently Director of the Franz Brentano Foundation.

BARRY SMITH is Julian Park Professor of Philosophy at State University of New York (SUNY), Buffalo, and Director of the Institute for Formal Ontology and Medical Information Science at the University of Leipzig, Germany. He is the author of *Austrian Philosophy: the Legacy of Franz Brentano*, and has translated Brentano's *Philosophical Investigations on Space, Time and the Continuum*. He has worked extensively in ontology and in the history of German-language philosophy, and his current research is focused on the applications of formal ontology in information science. He was recently awarded the Wolfgang Paul Prize of the Alexander von Humboldt Foundation.

ACKNOWLEDGMENTS

I am grateful first and foremost to the authors for their excellent contributions to this volume of previously unpublished essays on the philosophy of Franz Clemens Brentano. I am indebted also to Hilary Gaskin, philosophy editor at Cambridge University Press, for her professional guidance of this project, and for cultivating an atmosphere of partnership with the press in the book's production. I acknowledge the Alexander von Humboldt-Stiftung for its generous assistance in sponsoring my research at the Franz Brentano Forschung, Julius-Maximilians-Universität, Würzburg, Germany, during my sabbatical leave from The Pennsylvania State University in 2000–1, when the planning and organization of the book was undertaken. I thank Tina (Traas) Jacquette for her love and marathon philosophical conversations. Reinhard Fabian of the Forschungsstelle und Dokumentationszentrum för österreichische Philosophie, Graz, Austria, provided the digital photograph of Brentano which appears on the book's cover, image-enhanced by Scott K. Templeton, to whom warmest thanks are also due. Finally, Karl Schuhmann, contributor to this volume and longtime Brentano scholar of distinction, passed away as this book was in preparation. He is warmly remembered as a philosopher, historian, exacting critic of many philosphical traditions, and admired friend.

Dale Jacquette

ABBREVIATIONS

The following abbreviations are used throughout in referring to Brentano's most frequently consulted writings; publication details are given in the Bibliography.

SNB	*Vom sinnlichen und noetischen Bewußtein: Psychologie vom empirischen Standpunkt III*
UA	*Über Aristoteles*
USE	*Vom Ursprung sittlicher Erkenntnis*
USP	*Untersuchungen zur Sinnespsychologie*
VE	*Versuch über die Erkenntnis*
VPP	*Die vier Phasen der Philosophie und ihr augenblicklicher Stand*
WE	*Wahrheit und Evidenz*
ZF	*Über die Zukunft der Philosophie*

2   STANDARD ENGLISH TRANSLATIONS

AWV	*Aristotle and his World View*
DP-E	*Descriptive Psychology*
EG	*On the Existence of God: Lectures Given at the Universities of Würzburg and Vienna (1868–91)*
FCE	*The Foundation and Construction of Ethics*
KRW	*The Origin of the Knowledge of Right and Wrong*
PA-E	*The Psychology of Aristotle: in Particular his Doctrine of the Active Intellect*
PES-E	*Psychology from an Empirical Standpoint*
SNC	*Sensory and Noetic Consciousness: Psychology from an Empirical Standpoint III*
SSB	*On the Several Senses of Being in Aristotle*
STC	*Philosophical Investigations on Space, Time, and the Continuum*
TC	*The Theory of Categories*
TE	*The True and the Evident*

CHRONOLOGY

16 January 1838	Born, Franz Clemens Honoratus Hermann Brentano, in Marienberg am Rhein (near Boppard), Germany
1855–6	Studies at and graduates from the Aschaffenburger Gymnasiums Studium der Philosophie am Lyzeum
1857–8	Attends Philosophische Fakultät der Universität München (Munich) (three semesters)
1858	Transfers to Bayerische-Julius-Maximilians-Universität, Würzburg, Germany (one semester); studies philosophy and theology; later in the year moves to Berlin and attends two semester lecture courses by Aristotle scholar F. A. Trendelenburg in Berlin
1859–60	Studies medieval Aristotelian (Scholastic) philosophy at Münster Akademie
1862	Completes doctoral dissertation at the philosophische Fakultät Tübingen, *On the Manifold Sense of Being in Aristotle* (*Von der mannigfachen Bedeutung des Seienden bei Aristoteles*); publishes as first book; brief visit to Dominican monastery in Graz, Austria
1863	Begins theological studies in Munich
1864	Enters Theologisches Seminar at the Universität Würzburg; completes

	theological studies and preparation for priesthood
August 6, 1864	Ordained as Catholic priest
1865	Writes Habilitationsschrift in Philosophische Fakultät der Universität Würzburg on *The Psychology of Aristotle, in Particular his Doctrine of the Active Intellect* (*Die Psychologie des Aristoteles, insbesondere seine Lehre vom Nous Poietikos*)
July 15, 1866	Gives public defense of twenty-five *Habilitationsschrift* theses in Würzburg; declares natural science to be the only correct method of philosophy
1866–70	Begins lecturing in philosophy at Würzburg; students during this period notably include Carl Stumpf, Anton Marty, Hermann Schell, Georg von Herling and Ernst Commer
1870	Embroiled in controversy concerning papal infallibility, the outcome of which eventually causes him to give up the priesthood
1872	Appointed Professor Extraordinarius (promoted from Privatdozent) at Würzburg; travels to England and meets Herbert Spencer, Cardinal Newman, and William Robertson Smith; corresponds with John Stuart Mill; Mill dies before their anticipated meeting
April 11, 1873	Renounces holy orders over conscientious objections to doctrine of papal infallibility
January 22, 1874	Appointed Professor Ordinarius at the University of Vienna; students during this period notably include Franz Hillebrand, Edmund Husserl, Alexius Meinong, Alois Höfler, Christian von Ehrenfels, Thomas G. Masaryk, Josef Kreibig, Emil Arleth, Kazimierz Twardowski, Alfred Berger, and

	Baron von Pidoll; lectures also attended by Sigmund Freud
1874	Publishes masterwork *Psychology from an Empirical Standpoint* (*Psychologie vom empirischen Standpunkt*)
1880	Renounces Austrian citizenship in order to marry as former priest, otherwise not recognized under Austrian law of the time; gives up Vienna professorship with the understanding that it will later be restored; afterward allowed to return to lecture at the University of Vienna only as Privatdozent (not permitted as such to supervise Ph.D. theses in philosophy); recovers former German citizenship
September 16, 1880	Marries Ida von Lieben
1888	Birth of son, Johannes Brentano
1894	Death of Ida
1895	Retires as Privatdozent from the University of Vienna; leaves Vienna in April; travels to Switzerland and settles in Florence, Italy; becomes Italian citizen
1897	Marries Emilie Rueprecht
1897–1911	Active period of publication and philosophical correspondence outside academia
May, 1915	Leaves Florence and moves to Zurich, Switzerland, when Italy enters World War I
March 17, 1917	Dies in Zurich and is buried in Sihlfeld Cemetery; later reinterred in family plot in Aschaffenburg, Germany

1   Introduction: Brentano's philosophy

BRENTANO'S SCIENTIFIC REVOLUTION

Brentano is among the most important yet under-appreciated philosophers of the late nineteenth and early twentieth centuries. He led an intellectual revolution that sought to reverse what was then the prevalent post-Kantian trend of German-Austrian philosophy in the direction of an Aristotelian scientific methodology. At the same time, he made valuable contributions to philosophical psychology, metaphysics, ontology, value theory, epistemology, the reform of syllogistic logic, philosophical theology and theodicy, and the history of philosophy and philosophical methodology.

By revitalizing Austrian scientific philosophy, Brentano and his school simultaneously laid the groundwork for twentieth-century philosophy of science as it came to fruition in the logical positivism of the Vienna Circle, for the *Gegenstandstheorie* or object theory of Alexius Meinong and his students in the Graz School, and for phenomenology, notably in the work of Edmund Husserl, and indirectly in such later thinkers as Martin Heidegger, Jean-Paul Sartre and Maurice Merleau-Ponty. Beyond the borders of the German-speaking world, Brentano's philosophy had a profound impact on the course of Anglo-American analytic philosophy, as evinced in tributes to his influence by, among many others, Bertrand Russell, G. E. Moore, Gilbert Ryle, G. F. Stout, and Roderick M. Chisholm.

Brentano was born in Germany to a family of Italian extraction, and spent most of his professional philosophical career in Germany and Austria. After a brief period of lecturing at the Bayerische-Julius-Maximilians-Universität-Würzburg in Germany, he moved to Vienna, where he became a flamboyant and enormously popular university lecturer. During this time, he taught Husserl, Meinong, Anton Marty, Carl Stumpf, Christian von Ehrenfels (the founder of Gestalt psychology), and Kazimierz Twardowski, among numerous others, and his lectures were attended by such interested nonphilosophers as Sigmund Freud. With his prominent beard and electric delivery, Brentano's lectures were standing-room-only events, in which his audience was stimulated, entertained, and infused with the power and excitement of ideas. Brentano made it his philosophical mission to reverse the influence of German idealist philosophy in Austria. He strove to replace romanticism and subjectivism with a scientific philosophy that opposed Aristotle's and John Stuart Mill's empiricism to Kantian and post-Kantian transcendentalism, and especially to Hegel's dialectical idealism and metaphysics of the Absolute.

In the end, Brentano was driven into voluntary retirement after a dispute with the University of Vienna. He conscientiously resigned from the Catholic clergy and gave up Austrian citizenship in order to marry and preserve his right to a university professorship within the letter of the law. The university had promised to reinstate him in his position, but chose instead to offer him a much downgraded position as Privatdozent, in which capacity he was not permitted to supervise doctoral dissertations. After leaving the university in 1895, Brentano continued an active philosophical correspondence in which the vast panorama of his later philosophy was explored in conversations with a close circle of friends.

Why should readers today be interested in Brentano's philosophy? What is its relevance to the philosophical problems that have become urgent in our time? The answer is that Brentano has insightful things to say about most if not all of the philosophical problems that continue to preoccupy philosophers. He made lasting contributions in all the fields of philosophy to which he devoted attention, and in many instances he set the terms and problems for future inquiry while introducing valuable doctrinal and methodological innovations. The propriety of empirical methods in philosophy, the concept of mind and the intentionality or object-directedness of thought, the ideal of correct epistemic and moral judgment, the metaphysics of individuals, and the definitions of intrinsic good and part-whole relations in value theory which he developed have exerted a powerful influence on contemporary investigations in analytic philosophy. At the same time, Brentano is rightly credited as the originator of a scientific phenomenology in the rigorous investigation of first-person psycho-logical thought structure and content. If we want to understand the history of these ongoing philosophical discussions and tap into a rich source of ideas that have yet to be fully exploited, we cannot afford to ignore Brentano's philosophy.

AUSTRIAN PHILOSOPHY AT THE TURN OF THE CENTURY

The flowering of Austrian philosophy at the turn of the previous century is a frequently remarked phenomenon. William M. Johnston, in his landmark study, *The Austrian Mind: an Intellectual and Social History 1848–1938*, offers the matter of fact observation that "It was in Austria and its successor states that many, perhaps even most, of the seminal thinkers of the twentieth century emerged."[1]

When one considers the diminutive geographical portion of the globe occupied by the Austrian empire even during the height of its territorial expansion, this statement is nothing short of astonishing. In the cultural milieu of the intellectually opulent late nineteenth and early twentieth centuries, scholars have puzzled over the rare combination of factors that contributed to the unprecedented pro-liferation of influential philosophical schools at just this time and place.

As a sociological problem, the question of why and how so much interesting philosophy was done in Austria and its political satellites at this time is comparable to the question of why so much excellent painting was centered in seventeenth-century Netherlands. The an-swer, to whatever extent we can satisfy ourselves about such com-plex occurrences, is likely in general terms to turn out to be much the same, but may need to be reformulated in terms of large-scale cultural factors, such as the rise of a merchant class commissioning paintings for their walls during the golden age of Dutch art. A similar socio-economic story can also probably be told with respect to the rise of Austrian philosophy; yet a more philosophical answer can also be given. Gershon Weiler, in his probing essay, "In Search of What is Austrian in Austrian Philosophy," testifies to the inescapable im-pression that there is something special and unique about Austrian philosophy, but also to the difficulty, which many commentators have lamented, in isolating elements that are distinctively Austrian in recent and contemporary philosophy. Weiler adds:

I think there is something interesting and not a little intriguing in the phenomenon of that distinct philosophical style which emerged in Austria,
without the benefit of a language of its own to give it natural distinctness.
To be sure, language retains its primary importance and so what is common
to Austrian philosophy and to the philosophy produced in other regions of
the German-language space far exceeds its distinctive characteristics; the
reason for this is, among other things, that the language-continuum made it
possible for practitioners to move easily about in that continuum. Many of
the most typical Austrians were just other Germans who happened to settle
in Austria. And yet . . . there *is* something about Austrian philosophy that
begs to be given special attention.[2]

Weiler explains the nature and conditions for the emergence of
Austrian philosophy. He tries to account for what is distinctive about
Austrian philosophy and why it gained the prominence it did in
philosophical terms, appealing to specific philosophical reasons that
he infers were probably presupposed by different thinkers in the evolution of Austrian thought. Near the end of the essay, he advances
an hypothesis concerning the ascent of Austrian thought:

Austrian philosophy emerged, as a reaction to romanticism, in that unique
period of time when the inner tensions of the Austrian state began to be
visible for all. This was the time not only of tension but also of immense
cultural activity. Philosophy in Austria at that time was not manned by rev-
olutionaries and would not be oppositional. It could not be expressive since
there was nothing rationally worthwhile to express. So, philosophy turned
neutral, science-oriented, analytic, positivistic and, on the historical map,
Aristotelian and Humean. Not idealist, not ideological and distinctively
lacking in the *Begeisterung* so characteristic of much of German philosophy of the period – philosophy was Austrian at last. Whether Aristotelian or
Humean, Austrian philosophy is typically philosophers' philosophy.[3]

What Weiler means by "romanticism" is the kind of anti-
rationalism he identifies with dominant trends of post-Kantian philosophy in Germany. He agrees with other commentators who have
insisted that this German inspiration never took root in the Austrian
philosophical scene. He sees the evolution of Austrian philosophy
primarily as a reaction against already established Germanic ro-
mantic thought; that is, in a certain sense, as something negatively
perceived. Although his interpretation does not fully explain *why*
Austrian philosophers reacted against German "romanticism" instead of falling in line or being swept along with it, at one level it
takes account of precisely what happened in Austrian philosophy,

with Brentano in the vanguard of thinkers who contributed to the impressive upsurge of scientific philosophy in Germany, Austria, and middle Europe. It is the role of individuals like Brentano and his contemporaries in the movement toward science and away from transcendental metaphysics that we need to understand in order to appreciate how a new philosophy took root in *fin de siècle* Austria.

BRENTANO'S INTENTIONALIST PHILOSOPHY OF MIND

Brentano's first philosophical writings were booklength commentaries on Aristotle's metaphysics and philosophical psychology. His choice of Aristotle as a figure of study in the post-Kantian climate of German idealism at the time is significant, reflecting his interest in empirical, scientifically oriented philosophy, in contrast with the tradition of Hegel, Fichte, and Schelling. These early historical investigations provided Brentano with the background for his most famous and influential treatise, *Psychology from an Empirical Standpoint* (*Psychologie vom empirischen Standpunkt*, 1874). The *Psychology* was originally projected as an overture to a more ambitious multi-volume compendium in scientific psychology that was never completed, and was to have presented detailed applications of Brentano's theory to the psychology of presentations, judgments, emotions and the will, and the relation between body and mind.

Brentano argues in the *Psychology* that psychological phenomena can be distinguished from physical phenomena by virtue of the *intentionality* or object-directedness of the psychological, and nonintentionality of the physical or nonpsychological. This intentionality thesis inspired generations of philosophers and psychologists, some of whom developed Brentano's ideas in a variety of different directions, radiating out from his original investigations. Others devoted their energies to resisting and refuting the concept of intentionality in favor of eliminative or reductive materialist-physicalist, behaviorist or functionalist analyses of the concept of mind, involving treatments of a more narrowly construed model of scientific psychology deriving from the legacy of logical positivism.

Today, Brentano's philosophy remains a focus of interest for specialists in philosophical psychology, philosophy of mind, philosophy of language, theory of knowledge, metaphysics and formal ontology, as well as for philosophers of ethics and aesthetics, theologians and philosophers of religion, and, to a lesser extent, logicians and formal semanticists. His perspectives on the intentionality of mind have deservedly made him an indispensable figure in contemporary philosophical discussions of the nature of thought and of the methodology for the scientific study of mind. Whether or not they agree with Brentano's thesis that the mind is essentially and distinctively intentional, in-depth expositions of the nature of thought in contemporary philosophical psychology generally find it worthwhile to refer approvingly or disapprovingly, and in general to take their bearings relative to Brentano's intentionalist doctrine as a touchstone in modern philosophy of mind.

Brentano's influence on both Husserl's phenomenology and the object theory of the Graz school makes his work equally important to complementary and sometimes diametrically opposed trends in recent philosophy – indeed, he is arguably the most notable bridge figure between the traditions of analytic and continental philosophy. Heidegger reports that Brentano's dissertation, *On the Manifold Senses of Being in Aristotle* (*Von der mannigfachen Bedeutung des Seienden nach Aristoteles*, 1862), was the first work of philosophy he read seriously over and over again when he first became interested in problems of metaphysics. Heidegger claims that Brentano awakened his fascination with what he later articulated as the central problems of his existentialist ontology, in his preoccupation with the question of being that found expression in his *Sein und Zeit* (*Being and Time*, 1927). The irony is that Brentano would undoubtedly have repudiated Heidegger's existentialism, as he did Husserl's later transcendental phenomenology. Meanwhile, in the analytic philosophical world, Russell was extensively reading the seminal writings of Brentano and the new inquiries of Brentano's star pupil Meinong. Russell seems to have followed these Austrian developments for a time, but later reacted starkly against them, thus irrevocably shaping the future course of analytic philosophy in another, extensionalist, rather than intentionalist and intensionalist, direction, to the present day.

THE CHAPTERS IN THIS VOLUME

The chapters in this volume cover all major aspects of Brentano's philosophy. They place his work in historical context, looking to both its antecedents and the subsequent philosophical movements over which Brentano directly and indirectly exerted influence. Collectively, the authors critically assess the strengths and weaknesses of Brentano's lifework and its relevance to contemporary philosophical concerns.

The concept of intentionality in Brentano's early and later philosophy of psychology is center stage in every chapter. Although he made numerous contributions to many different fields of philosophy, his name is most frequently associated with the analysis of psychological phenomena as intentional, and he remained faithful to some version of the intentionality thesis throughout his philosophical career. Although he drastically altered his opinion about the nature of intended objects, as his early doctrine of immanent intentionality or intentional inexistence gave way more resolutely to a strict *reism* or ontology of actual individual existents, he never abandoned his commitment to the intentionality of thought. In his philosophy it is the center around which all aspects of his metaphysics, epistemology, value theory, and philosophical theology find their proper place. Methodologically, the importance of intentionality in Brentano's system is in one way inevitable. Given his empiricist presuppositions, which he shares with John Locke, George Berkeley, David Hume, and John Stuart Mill, and even to a certain extent with the rationalist René Descartes, Brentano needs to give prominence to the subjective contents of thoughts and sensations perceived in immediate experience. The phenomenology of sensation as a play of appearances is all that the strict empiricist can consider knowable; belief in the existence of a corresponding external reality or "body," as Hume says, beyond the phenomena can only be conjectural, however psychologically compelling. The implication for Brentano is that an objective scientific philosophical psychology must take priority over all other branches of philosophy, a perspective that can be seen in every phase and every interconnected component of his work.

In "Brentano's Relation to Aristotle," Rolf George and Glen Koehn recount Brentano's early recognition of his intellectual debt to Aristotle's empiricism. Brentano thought of philosophy historically as moving repeatedly and cyclically through four distinctive phases, the final one of which was supposed to be its "natural" phase, represented in ancient Greek philosophy by the work of Aristotle. He believed that philosophy in his day was on the brink of transition from its most recent third, idealist, phase, reflected in the work of

Immanuel Kant and post-Kantianism, to a neo-natural cycle, in a philosophy modeled on the natural sciences. He saw in Aristotle a precursor to the type of philosophy he wanted to advance. George and Koehn examine in detail the influences, similarities, and divergences between Aristotle and Brentano in areas where Brentano made special contributions to ontology, psychology, and theology, using the lens of Aquinas's twelfth-century interpretations of Aristotle, from which Brentano often took his bearings. The picture of Brentano's relationship with Aristotle that appears in their history shines a light on his methodology and philosophical orientation as a neo-Aristotelianism emphasizing the metaphysics of being and the psychology and epistemology of sensation.

Peter Simons, in "Judging Correctly: Brentano and the Reform of Elementary Logic," explains the role of Brentano's theory of correct judgment in his efforts to improve Aristotelian syllogistic logic. As the only quasi-formal systematization of reasoning available until the middle of the nineteenth century, syllogistic logic had essentially remained unchanged since antiquity. Simons describes the innovations by other contemporary logicians such as George Boole and Augustus DeMorgan as background to a detailed discussion of Brentano's work. Brentano's contributions to logic were largely unsung in his time because they were unpublished. Although Brentano did not sustain a strong interest in logic throughout his career, Simons argues that the early Brentano arrived at an original reconception of logical principles that despite its attractions has failed to gain currency in recent logical analysis. Brentano offers an unorthodox approach to the foundations of logic from the standpoint of the theory of judgment in the psychology of reasoning rather than in terms of the purely linguistic Ur-elements of contemporary logic. According to Simons, Brentano defies the Aristotelian tradition and fails at the same time to anticipate mainstream currents in logic, by holding that the fundamental logical form of judgment is the assertion or denial of an existence claim rather than the predicative association of a property term with an object term. His proposal includes a translation scheme for converting subject-predicate judgments to logically equivalent existence judgments, as in the reduction of "All Greeks are human" to "There are no non-human Greeks." The paraphrase reflects his interest in logic primarily as a vehicle of ontology. Simons explains Brentano's simplified formal notation for expressing existence and nonexistence judgments, introduces primitive Brenta-nian logical inference rules, and offers a series of formal demonstra-tions related to classical valid syllogisms and sentences with exis-tential import. He considers the potential applications of Brentano's logic, which he relates to Stanisław Leśniewski's ontology, taking the measure of its importance for the history of nonsymbolic logic, particularly in the philosophy of Husserl, Meinong, and Twardowski.

The taxonomy of psychological phenomena in Brentano's theory of mind is examined by Kevin Mulligan in "Brentano on the Mind." Mulligan introduces Brentano's analysis of the mind as the most detailed description of mental phenomena, including their parts and interrelations, ever provided before the twentieth century. He admires the minute divisions of the mind's awareness of space, time, sensing, sensory perception, internal perception, presenta-tions, judging, inferring, desiring, feeling, consciousness, and the self in Brentano's phenomenology. He finds Brentano's analyses in-timately connected with his descriptions of the objects of mental phenomena, such as colors, shapes, sounds, and the like, and with ac-counts of intentional relations between mental phenomena and their objects. Such characterizations of the structures and interrelations of thoughts constitute the application of an approach to the philosophy of mind that Brentano alternatively called "descriptive psychology," "psychognosy," and "phenomenology," and which he carefully dis-tinguished from "explanatory" or "genetic" psychology, that seeks to provide causal accounts of psychological phenomena in what is recognized today as cognitive science. Mulligan emphasizes the on-tological framework within which Brentano develops the principles of his descriptive psychology, and the empiricist epistemology to which he is irrevocably committed. He explains Brentano's concept of inner perception as it relates to his philosophical psychology, and looks in detail at Brentano's fundamental distinction between pre-sentations, judgments, and emotions, and considers his phenomenol-ogy of time consciousness, the emotions, crucial to Brentano's value theory, and the self. He concludes that it is impossible to under-stand intentionalist theories of mind from Meinong and Husserl to later phenomenology without understanding Brentano's pioneering philosophical researches in descriptive psychology.

Dale Jacquette in "Brentano's Concept of Intentionality" consid-ers Brentano's early immanent intentionality or in-existence thesis.

Brentano describes intentionality as "the mark of the mental," but does not explain the ontic status of intended objects, which many critics have observed he conflates with internal thought contents. The impact of his concept of intentionality on the course of phenomenology and the philosophy of mind has been substantial, giving rise to several distinct schools of intentionalist philosophy that departed significantly from his own early immanence intentionality thesis. Jacquette considers Brentano's changing view of intentionality, from his early immanence model with its implicit psychologism, against which Brentano vigorously objected, but never seems to have fully understood, to his doctrine of intended real particulars, in light of his empiricist methodology in descriptive psychology and later reist metaphysics. He concludes that Brentano need not be regarded as unmindful of the deeper questions surrounding the ontology of intended objects, but as deliberately avoiding commitment to any particular characterization of their nature other than as the contents of thought in strict observance of his empirical methodology. The problem of psychologism looms in Brentano's philosophical psychology precisely because of his determination to remain agnostic about the metaphysical status of intended objects, refusing to say anything about their existence beyond describing them as the immediate internal psychological contents of thoughts.

Joseph Margolis further thematizes Brentano's doctrine of intentionality in his chapter, "Reflections on Intentionality." Margolis offers insight into the concept of intentionality not only from the standpoint of an historical scholar of Brentano's thought, but as a philosopher who has considered the advantages and disadvantages of several formulations of Brentano's central thesis. He situates Brentano's intentionality thesis historically in relation to Aristotle's psychology, later intentionalism in the medieval period, and modern philosophy, especially the Cartesian tradition. All of these in different ways were vitally important to Brentano's philosophical recovery of the intentional, although his obligations to his predecessors are complex. Touching on key aspects of the aftermath of Brentano's *Psychology*, Margolis tracks subtleties in Brentano's changing conception of intentionality through his writings and as the intentionality doctrine was understood, adapted, and transformed by his students and critics. Margolis raises the problem of the ontic status of intended objects in light of the Appendix "On Genuine and Fictitious Objects" to Brentano's *Psychology* and later reist metaphysics, and explicates the differences between Brentano's and Chisholm's treatments of intentionality. Like most of Brentano's more immediate followers, Chisholm modifies Brentano's concept of intentionality and exploits some of the ambiguities and incompletenesses in Brentano's original account for his own philosophical purposes. The aim of Margolis's comparison is not merely to set the record straight with respect to Chisholm's interpretation, but to clarify what Brentano seems to have meant by intentionality, in view of the fact that Chisholm's analysis of the concept has enjoyed such wide reception. It is worth remarking that the core of Margolis's criticism of Chisholm depends on Brentano's commitment to *Reales* in his later reist ontology, whereas, like most adherents of Brentano's theory of intentionality, Chisholm takes his cues from Brentano's *Psychology*, written many years before his turn toward reism. Margolis finally comments on the value of Brentano's intentionality thesis as the basis for an account of the cultural world and scientific psychology, disagreeing sharply with the way in which Brentano characterizes psychology as a science, his expectations of psychology and psychological explanation, and his convictions about the relative importance of psychology *vis-à-vis* the other natural sciences.

Linda L. McAlister in "Brentano's Epistemology" draws important connections between Brentano's changing attitudes toward the ontology of intended objects and the principles of his empiricist epistemology. She explores some of the difficulties in understanding Brentano's metaphysics of immanent intentionality, and some of the historical interpretations and misinterpretations that have surrounded especially his early theory of intentionality in such commentators as Alois Höfler, Oskar Kraus, Anton Marty, Franzisca Mayer-Hillebrand, and Chisholm. She situates Brentano's theory historically in Aristotelian context, and underscores those aspects of his concept of intended objects relevant especially to his theory of knowledge and epistemology of presentations, judgments, and emotions, with special emphasis on Brentano's later theory of judgment as it relates to the theory of knowledge. Brentano is throughout an empiricist for whom experience is paramount in epistemology, but whose epistemology reflects his ongoing efforts to clarify the meta-physics of intentionality and the ontic status of intended objects.

Charles Parsons's "Brentano on Judgment and Truth" presents a thorough exposition of Brentano's judgment theory. Whereas con-temporary philosophy typically distinguishes between epistemology and semantics, Brentano's concept of judgment combines elements of both disciplines in a broadly psychological framework. Parsons contrasts Brentano's theory of judgment with Frege's analysis of an abstract thought (*Gedanke*) as the sense of a sentence and Russell's theory of propositions. Although conventional analytic philosophy has generally related thoughts and propositions to states of affairs in order to explain their meaning and account for their truth or falsehood, Parsons notes that Brentano combines both of these in-gredients in a single psychological category of judgment. Brentano's view of judgment was at odds not only with those of later major figures in psychology, epistemology, and semantic theory, such as Frege and Russell, but also with those of his own students Marty, Meinong, and Husserl. The ideological rift that opened between these intentionalist thinkers became still deeper after Brentano's eventual avowal of reism. The idea of thought as intending only a concrete individual real particular is evidently incompatible with the theory of propositions or states of affairs, insofar as these are understood as something universal or abstract. Parsons notes that Brentano regards judgment as the affirmation or denial of a presentation (*Vorstellung*). The polarity of judgment values, true or false, affirmation or denial, and love or hate in the case of emotions, turns out to be crucial to his unified psychological analysis of judgment in knowledge and value theory. Parsons explores Brentano's analysis of compound judg-ments as it relates to his recommendations for the reform of syllo-gistic logic and the problem of eliminating term negation from the logic of judgments, linking his discussion to Simons's treatment of Brentano's logical theory. Finally, he traces Brentano's changing at-titudes toward the correspondence theory of truth, which in roughly Aristotelian form he accepts early in his philosophical studies, but later abandons as incompatible with reism. The relation between Brentano's theory of truth as correct judgment in light of evidence, Parsons argues, prevents Brentano's concept of truth from reducing simply to a deflationary or disquotational theory, in which a sen-tence "S" is true if and only if S. As Parsons interprets these themes in Brentano, epistemic evidence is thereby made stronger and more fundamental than truth, on the grounds that truth itself, and not merely correct judgments of what is true, turns out to be logically dependent on whatever evidence justifies judgment.

In "Brentano's Ontology: from Conceptualism to Reism," Arkadiusz Chrudzimski and Barry Smith offer an historical-philosophical excursus into Brentano's major metaphysical crisis, describing the middle and later period of his work when he gave up conceptualism in favor of reism. Beginning with Brentano's Aristotelian distinction between multiple senses of "being," they follow the trail of his pilgrim's progress in ontology, from his theory of judgment and epistemic definition of truth, through the division between different types and categories of judgments in relation to their objects, in both his early and later periods of thought. The topic of mereology or part-whole relations enters into Brentano's ontology as he turns to the problem of real being and the senses in which real beings are composed of different kinds of parts. Chrudzimski and Smith distinguish Brentano's concepts of physical, logical, and metaphysical parts in a resurgence of his Aristotelianism, as an entity's respective substances and accidents. Brentano's theory of relations is described also as largely in agreement with Aristotle's, rejecting the concept of external relations as those that cannot be inferred from the properties of *relata* considered individually, which again is incompatible with Brentano's later reism. Chrudzimski and Smith then take up the difficult subject of Brentano's ontology of intentionality and the problem of immanent intentionality in his early to middle period. By focusing especially on revealing remarks of Brentano's on the identity – or, rather, similarity – conditions for the objects of thoughts, they piece together three conditions for a Brentanian theory of the ontic status of intentional in-existence. They hold that immanent objects must exist, represent the objects of a thought's reference, and remain distinguishable from one another in a sufficiently fine-grained way to preserve an intersubstitutivity principle. In rounding out their account of Brentano's late ontology, they consider his commitment to reism in terms of its implications for parts, wholes, and boundaries, and its paraphrastic adverbial reduction of properties and relations to concrete real particulars.

In "Brentano's Value Theory: Beauty, Goodness, and the Concept of Correct Emotion," Wilhelm Baumgartner and Lynn Pasquerella articulate Brentano's theory of moral and aesthetic value against the background of his later reism. Brentano first accepted a traditional theory of value, according to which an object has value by virtue of possessing a particular type of property or properties. His later reism made such a standard view of value impossible, to the extent that beauty and goodness and their cognates, contraries, and opposites could not be regarded as being among the abstract properties of a valued object. Baumgartner and Pasquerella maintain that, as in other parts of his later philosophy dominated by reism, Brentano is committed to an austere paraphrastic reduction of apparent non-individual entities, properties, relations, and the like, to an adverbial characterization of concrete individual judgments, or, in the case of value, emotions. Value in Brentano's later philosophy thus becomes a function of the concrete individual emotional attitudes that a concrete individual subject experiences in perceiving a concrete individual object. Abandoning the traditional correspondence theory of value in the classification of correct ethical and aesthetic judgment, the later Brentano is compelled by his ontology to reinterpret beauty and goodness respectively as aesthetic and ethical emotions that are experienced as correct; in exact analogy, Baumgartner and Pasquerella remark, with Brentano's theory of truth in which evident judgments are experienced as correct. They close with a critical look at Brentano's objectivism in light of his reduction of value to correct emotion, at least in part as a putatively subjective phenomenon. It is the correctness of the emotion rather than the fact of subjectively experienced emotion in Brentano's theory, in their view, that makes value objective for Brentano in spite of its psychological context.

Susan Krantz Gabriel observes that although Brentano broke with organized religion in the late 1870s, he remained a traditional theist all his life and was still dictating his thoughts on natural theology in 1917. In "Brentano on Religion and Natural Theology," she remarks that Brentano's interests in these topics ranged from Charles Darwin's theory of natural selection and Pierre-Simon Laplace's theory of probability to Auguste Comte's critique of causal knowledge and Georges Cuvier's zoology. At every turn, Brentano shows himself to be conversant with the scientific and philosophical developments of his day, as well as relevant ancient and medieval ideas. Krantz Gabriel argues that the best way to understand Brentano's natural theology is to see it in the context of traditional Aristotelian empiricism modified by his Cartesian outlook. She identifies four main sets of arguments: (1) against skepticism, involving refutations of the view that it can be known a priori that God's existence is impossible to prove; (2) in support of God's existence based on empirical data from the sciences, especially evidence of teleology in nature; (3) in support of the immateriality of the human soul; and (4) in favor of optimism, trying to show that the evil in the world is consistent with the existence of a morally good God. Brentano considers natural theology to be an integral part of philosophy, and Krantz Gabriel holds that his ideas in this area are intimately connected to his work in psychology, metaphysics, and ethics. Brentano's lectures on the proofs of God's existence, she maintains, provide a good sense of how Brentano saw his own philosophy in relation to the thought of René Descartes, G. W. Leibniz, Locke, Hume, Kant, and Mill.

The relationship between Brentano and his best-known student Husserl is thoroughly examined by Robin Rollinger in his chapter, "Brentano and Husserl." Rollinger pursues Brentano's influence on Husserl's founding of modern phenomenology, especially prior to Husserl's so-called "transcendental turn" around 1913. Husserl is known to have followed Brentano's early view of intentionality in his first writings, later developing his phenomenology on the foundations of Brentano's lectures on descriptive psychology or psychognosy, which Husserl attended. The interaction between Brentano and Husserl is complex, and Rollinger examines both the most important phases of Brentano's philosophical transitions insofar as they are relevant to Husserl's early Brentanian philosophy and the vestiges of Brentano's ideas that can be seen even in Husserl's later transcendentalism. Rollinger considers Brentano's researches in psychology, particularly his theory of presentations and judgments in the theory of knowledge and epistemic concept of truth, and finally with respect to the phenomenology of emotions. He delves into Brentano's division between inner and outer perception as a special point of contrast with Husserl's critique of the distinction. Understandably, Rollinger devotes considerable attention to Husserl's first book, *Philosophy of Arithmetic*, written when Husserl was still under the spell of Brentano's immanent intentionality thesis. Husserl's evolving interest in philosophical logic and psychology eventually led to his conception of pure logic in the first volume of the first edition of the *Logical Investigations*, in which he attains what Rollinger describes as his "breakthrough" to phenomenology. The setting of Husserl's inquiry into logical mental processes owes much to Brentano's intentionality thesis, in its original immanence form or as Husserl came to refashion it in his own thinking under the transcendental *epoché*. Working through Husserl's *Logical Investigations* in detail, Rollinger demonstrates the extent to which Husserl's philosophy of logic and phenomenology took shape in part by accepting and in part by rejecting and reacting against certain of Brentano's most salient ideas.

The volume concludes with Karl Schuhmann's assessment of "Brentano's Impact on Twentieth-Century Philosophy." Schuhmann surveys the influence, positive and negative, that Brentano's philosophy has had particularly on contemporary phenomenology and analytic philosophy of mind. He reviews the major figures among Brentano's students and the mark they made on the subsequent history of philosophy, concentrating especially on Marty, Stumpf, and Husserl. His account ranges from the impact of Brentano's psychology on a wide range of thinkers in the continental school, from Karl Jaspers to Paul Ricœur and many others besides, to the importance of intentionality in the later Brentano ambit, the characterization of the distinction between psychological content and object, the concept of states of affairs as truth-makers, the expression of thought in language, and the mereology of part-whole relations, including *Gestalt* phenomena. The content-object distinction is often thought to be confused in Brentano's early immanence theory of intentionality. It was made the special subject of debate among later Brentanians such as Twardowski, Meinong, and Husserl, who launched philosophy in new directions in part by reacting in different ways to problems inherent in Brentano's early coalescence of phenomenological content and intended object. Schuhmann's summary of Brentano's significance for contemporary thought puts an entire century of philosophy influenced by Brentano's original reasoning into philosophical perspective.

BRENTANO, ANALYTIC PHILOSOPHY, AND PHENOMENOLOGY

The story of Brentano's philosophical development requires a large canvas. He was deeply involved in many different philosophical inquiries, and, like Russell – and, one might say, like most scientifically minded thinkers – he was sufficiently open-minded and experimental in his outlook to have changed his mind more than once about many important matters of detail within a broadly continuous philosophical outlook.

Brentano's allegiance to an empiricist philosophical methodology never wavered. Throughout his long and active career, he preserved his most basic moral and metaphysical teachings, some of which were more completely elaborated, while others unfolded in different and sometimes opposing directions at different times. He could be forceful in argument when he believed himself to be in possession of the correct answer to a problem, but never dogmatic. He continually re-examined and rethought, modified, and occasionally radically changed his mind, as he struggled to fit a comprehensive conception of the world into a unified structure defined by his longstanding scientific and epistemological, metaphysical, moral, cultural, and religious values.

The contributors to this volume highlight especially the interesting shifts in Brentano's views concerning the metaphysics of intended objects and the ontology of individuals. Brentano never accepted the existence of universals, but as his thought matured, particularly in his later correspondence, he increasingly gravitated toward reism, according to which only existent individual entities with their particularly instantiated qualities and relations can stand as intended objects of thought. From the theory that intentional states are directed toward "inexistents" of indeterminate ontic status, Brentano thus came to believe that we can only think about particulars. Reism is a noteworthy metaphysical thesis because of its simplicity and extreme ontological austerity, comparable to the varieties of nominalism championed by empirically minded philosophers in medieval philosophy and in the contemporary analytic descriptive metaphysics and calculus of individuals propounded by W. V. O. Quine and Nelson Goodman. Brentano's later reism offers ingenious and instructive if ultimately problematic eliminative paraphrases of ostensible references to nonexistent objects, universals among other abstract entities, and uninstantiated possibilities. It establishes an early standard of exact philosophical analysis in the service of ontological economy that has remained unsurpassed until the advent of the most sophisticated semantic reductions in recent analytic philosophy, for which it continues to provide an edifying model.

It is consistent with Brentano's view of the progression of philosophical movements in his *Die vier Phasen der Philosophie und ihr augenblicklicher Stand* (1895), that he expected the neo-Kantianism he opposed to be replaced by something more "natural" and scientific, in what contemporary metaphilosophy sometimes speaks of as a Kuhnian paradigm shift. He certainly assisted this historical process along in an empiricist direction; yet there are also other explanations for the longstanding impetus of his scientific revolution. The success of Brentano's philosophy is more a matter of the example he set and the uncanny sense of direction with which he made psychology into a respectable empirical science.

Brentano wanted descriptive psychology to occupy a third alternative between conceptual analysis and inductive empiricism as ordinarily conceived. The former approach by itself is inadequate for Brentano's purposes because it is not sufficiently experiential; it is a form of rationalism, which Brentano in his empiricist vein emphatically rejects. The latter, if not appropriately modified for the sake of its special subject matter, cannot soundly support the derivation of universal a priori true generalizations about the nature of consciousness from particular a posteriori phenomenological experience. Brentano's descriptive psychology at the heart of his philosophy is revolutionary in its search for the principles of thinking in the only place they can possibly be found, using specially trained thought to investigate the generalizable features of thought.

Whether Brentano also launched a revolutionary method in philosophical psychology that went beyond its historical influence on such figures as Husserl, Heidegger, Sartre, Merleau-Ponty, and other phenomenologists, and is still a viable program for the philosophy of mind today, remains an open question, subject to conjecture. We cannot overlook the fact that he later disavowed Husserl's transcendental phenomenology in particular, as well as Meinong's *Gegenstandstheorie*, and sought to distance himself from nonexistent intended objects and from the allegations of psychologism with which Husserl charged his former teacher. The reason that Brentano's philosophy has not attracted a large following in scientific psychology would seem to be that what has come to be known as the scientific community in the study of cognitive psychology is firmly in the grip of a narrow conception of empirical science advocated by logical positivism, engaged exclusively in the work of what Brentano would call "genetic" or causally reductive neurophysiological, behavioristic, or computational psychology.

Brentano expects what we would currently refer to as cognitive scientists to be dedicated investigators of the external third-person features of psychological phenomena, and not to involve themselves philosophically with the fundamental questions of descriptive psychology or psychognosy. We need armies of researchers in genetic psychology, given the nature of its tasks, but only a handful of psychognosts investigating the underlying philosophical principles of psychology. We might also say that Brentano's ideas have attained only limited scientific and philosophical popularity because to some extent they have been forgotten or sidelined in recent and contemporary phenomenology, and because they are perhaps still too revolutionary even for recent and contemporary analytic philosophy. "There exist at the present time," Brentano wrote in the Foreword to the original 1874 edition of *Psychologie vom empirischen Standpunkt*, "the beginnings of a scientific psychology. Although inconspicuous in themselves, these beginnings are indisputable signs of the possibility of a fuller development which will some day bear abundant fruit, if only for future generations" (p. xxix). If that day has not yet dawned, it does not follow that Brentano's program will never find a more receptive and enthusiastic audience. Readers of this volume of essays may come to see in Brentano's descriptive psychology the possibility of a radically new philosophy of mind in thought and action, the metaphysics of socially intentional phenomena, and the expression of meaning in culture, a theory whose revolutionary potential has yet to be realized.

NOTES

1. William M. Johnston, *The Austrian Mind: an Intellectual and Social History 1848–1938* (Berkeley: University of California Press, 1972), p. 1.
2. Gershon Weiler, "In Search of What is Austrian in Austrian Philosophy," in, ed., J. C. Nyíri, *Von Bolzano zu Wittgenstein: Zur Tradition der österreichischen Philosophie* (Vienna: Hölder-Pichler-Tempsky, 1986), p. 31.
3. *Ibid.*, p. 39.

2   Brentano's relation to Aristotle

INTRODUCTION

First of all I had to apprentice myself to a master. But since I was born when philosophy had fallen into most lamentable decay, I could find none better than old Aristotle. To understand him, which is not always easy, I enlisted the help of Thomas Aquinas. (ANR, p. 291)

This is Brentano's recollection of his first steps in philosophy, written toward the end of his life. Earlier he had entered a passionate poem in a student's autograph album, portraying himself as brother of Aristotle's famous students, and as his offspring:

> I can even today claim to be of his issue.
> Welcome Eudemus you pious, welcome O brother, and you
> Godlike in speech Theophrast,[1] sweet as the Lesbian wine.[2]
> Since I was given him late, youngest of all his descendants
> Loves my father me most, more tenderly than all the others.
>
> (AWV, p. xii)

The derisive remark about the lamentable decay of philosophy was not aimed merely at philosophers active when he was a student, but at the German Idealist tradition from Kant to Hegel.

Brentano maintained that western philosophy had run through similar four-stage cycles three times.[3] Each time a single period of advance was followed by three stages of decline. The positive phase is characterized by "natural method" and purely theoretical interest. In antiquity it ended with Aristotle. Then practical motives came to the fore in Epicureanism and Stoicism. Philosophy became unscientific, its methods no longer trustworthy, which led to skepticism. But the longing for knowledge could not be stifled and became an

irrational urge. Plotinus and other neo-Platonists invented extravagant and fantastical systems and not only claimed higher inspiration
but were even accorded divine status in their schools.

Four analogous phases occurred in the Middle Ages, beginning
with Albertus Magnus and Thomas Aquinas and ending yet again
in mysticism. In the modern period the upward movement began
with Descartes and Bacon and continued in Leibniz and Locke. The
decline set in with George Berkeley, Voltaire, Rousseau, and other
"popular philosophers," to be followed by Hume's skepticism. The
low point was reached with Kant, who maintained that objects in the
world obey the blind prejudices inherent and innate in our minds.
The work of his successors, Fichte, Schelling, and Hegel, "lacks any
and all value from a scientific point of view" (ZF, p. 125).

In contrast to these philosophers Brentano thought that philosophy must, and in its high periods did, mirror the method of the
natural sciences.[4] He meant by this that all branches of philosophy,
including metaphysics, logic, aesthetics, and ethics, have their foundation in scientific "inner perception," which is necessary and sufficient for all philosophical knowledge (cf. PES bk. 1, ch. 1). In his late
years he thought that he had himself set in motion a fourth cycle of
philosophies and ushered in a new beginning by reconnecting with
Aristotle. He saw himself to be struggling with some of the same
problems that challenged his great predecessor, as well as the other
philosophers of the high periods. Theorizing alongside Aristotle, he
is inclined to attribute many of the same views to him that he himself finds persuasive. His admiration is tempered with criticism, but
he is always happy to find an Aristotelian precedent for a theory he
wishes to maintain. In his interpretation he laid great stress upon
coherence and plausibility as guides (AWV, pp. 9ff.) and was often
prepared to reconstruct the meaning of fragmentary and abbreviated
works by reconciling apparent conflicts, amending the text with
conclusions that Aristotle himself did not explicitly draw. This, he
thought, was as solid a procedure as Cuvier's famous reconstructions
of prehistoric animals from a few fossils (UA, p. 36).[5]

ONTOLOGY

After several years of intensive study of Aristotle and his medieval
interpreters, especially Thomas Aquinas, Brentano submitted his

doctoral dissertation, *On the Manifold Senses of Being in Aristotle*, in 1862. It is not only a significant contribution to Aristotle scholarship, informing much of Brentano's later thought, but had wider influence by helping to shape Martin Heidegger's existential philosophy: "It was the first philosophical text through which I worked my way again and again."[6] It is doubtful that Brentano would have rejoiced in this association, however.

The motto of the book is the first sentence of *Metaphysics* VII, which Brentano translated as "Being is said in various ways" (SSB, p. 3). Taking account of the distinction between using and mentioning an expression we might rephrase this as "The term 'being' has several senses." He argues that the various ways mentioned by Aristotle can be captured by the list of four given in *Metaphysics* V.7 and VI.2:

(1)   Accidental being, when two attributes accidentally meet in a substance, as "when a musical person builds houses . . . In this case to say that one thing *is* another means the same as that the second thing accidentally belongs to the first" (p. 9 *Metaphysics* V.7, 1017^a8). This is an improper [*uneigentlich*] sense of being (p. 26) and not the subject of scientific or metaphysical inquiry. It rates no further attention.

(2)   Being in the sense of being true, as when one says of a judgment that it *is* true (pp. 15–26). This is the concern of logic, rather than metaphysics, and does not introduce a special sort of being different from (3) and (4) below (p. 26). Brentano therefore turns to:

(3)   Potential and actual being – "when this word is applied not only to that which is realised, that which exists, the really-being, but also to the mere real possibility of being" (p. 27). Often a substance is potentially many things, but it can be only one thing actually: *Potentially* the mind can think all things, *actually* only one at a time.

(4)   Being according to the categories. Most of the book (pp. 49–148) is devoted to this last topic with Brentano endeavoring to show that Aristotle's categories, the highest genera, are not simply raked together without any ruling principle, as Kant suggested, but can be systematically deduced. Aristotle lists them in *Categories* IV, giving examples:

Expressions that are in no way composite [and thus, unlike judgements, not capable of truth or falsehood] signify substance [man],
quantity [two cubits long], quality [white], relation [double], place
[in the market], time [yesterday], position [sitting], state [armed],
action [to burn something], affection [to be burnt]. (1^{b}25)

Position and *state* are not as fundamental as the rest. They are absent
from other Aristotelian accounts and Brentano deals only with the
other eight. In each case being is involved: we say that a certain
substance *is* a man, a log *is* two cubits (36 inches) long, a merchant
is in the market, etc. It is not by chance that the same word is used in
different contexts. The "is" is not used equivocally, as when things
"only have a common name while the concepts they designate are
different" (p. 61, *Categories* 1, 1^{a}1). But what do the cases have in
common?

These expressions point to "if not a shared concept, then at least
to a *kinship* of concepts" (p. 63). This kinship is established through
analogies, in Aristotle a figure of the form "as A is to B, so C is to D."
Analogy establishes a kind of unity whenever things "bear to each
other the same . . . relation that another pair has" (*Metaphysics* V.6,
1016^{b}34). For example, Peleus bears the same relation to Achilles as
your father to you (*Metaphysics* XII.5, 1071^{a}20). The set of fathers
has *unity by analogy*; it is *one*, although it is neither species nor
substance. It is, as we would now say, the domain of a relation.

In the same way, "different qualities have the same relation to
distinct subjects, for example when we say that just as this is warm
so that is white" (p. 62, *De Gen. et Corr.* II.6, 333^{a}23). Warmth and
whiteness thus belong together in one domain because they and all
other qualities are related to their subjects in the same way. The
same can be said for quantities, which thus form another domain.
Brentano makes it plausible that in Aristotle's view there are eight
domains, one for each category.

There is a second type of analogy that binds them all together. It is
called "analogy to a common focus." In *Metaphysics* IV.2 Aristotle
illustrates focal meaning with the examples of health and medicine.[7]
The primary meaning of "healthy" is to say that a person is healthy.
But, in virtue of their analogous relationships to the focal point of
health, things that serve to maintain or produce health or are symptoms of it are also called healthy, as when we say that a diet or a

complexion is healthy. When it comes to being, substance is the focal point, whereas qualities, relations, etc., are said to be because they all necessarily involve the primary being of substances. "There are indeed many senses in which things are said to be, but in relation to one thing and to one nature, and not just equivocally" (p. 61, *Metaphysics* IV.2, 1003ª33). This establishes the unity of Aristotle's fundamental ontology:

There should be a single science not only of those things that univocally partake in one name, but also of those that have a name in relation to one nature; for the latter, too, in a sense asserts a common thing. Hence it is clear that it is the concern of one science to investigate being *qua* being. (p. 96, *Metaphysics* IV.2, 1003ᵇ12)

Brentano's project is not finished. He argues against other Aristotle scholars that the categories are real concepts, not just examples or a framework for concepts, and that there are just these eight, and no others. But, "unfortunately, we do not possess such a deduction of the highest genera in Aristotle's writing" (p. 96). Brentano himself will provide this deduction proceeding "in every case from Aristotle's own views" (p. 97). The result is a division represented in the following table (p. 115. The graphics are rearranged, the categories in *italics*):[8]

Being divides into

  I. *Substance*
 II. What attaches to substance; accidents in a broad sense. These are
    A. *Relations*
    B. Absolute (non-relational) accidents, which are
      a. Inherent accidents:
        α. *Quantity*
        β. *Quality*   or else
      b. Operations: accidents with direction:
        α. *Action*
        β. *Affection*   or else
      c. Containment: accidents taken from an external thing
        α. *Where*
        β. *When*

This is Brentano's first reconstruction of an important part of Aristotle's system. As he will often do later, he draws conclusions from what is explicitly said, and relies on the coherence of the picture he has drawn.

In the introduction to his book Brentano speaks approvingly of distinguishing proper from improper senses of being and of excluding the latter from consideration (p. 2). This remark was probably aimed at "accidental being." As for the rest, he accorded existence not only to substances and to attributes, but also to the contents of judgments. He held that there were such objects as abstract states of affairs which either are or are not, as our thoughts are true or false: the *being so* of this or that content of thought. He expressed this by saying that being in the sense of being true is also a form of being.[9] He later changed his mind. In a late letter he said that the apprentice was led astray by the master into thinking that "is" in the sentences "A tree is" and "That a tree is, is" function in the same way.

Yet this youthful study of Aristotle turned Brentano's thoughts toward positing different ways of being as means of solving problems about predication and the highest genera. Such problems include the questions "Do qualities of a thing exist in addition to the thing itself?" and "If they do not, is there some other way that they exist, so that to say 'This horse exists' and 'Its colour exists' is to use the notion of existence differently?" His answers to this sort of question changed in time, ending in the sparse ontology of "reism." In that late phase Brentano remained persuaded that the German words for "is" and "exists" are used in different ways, some of them systematically misleading and that the various forms of the verb "to be" (*sein*) have improper, as well as proper, uses. He then held that expressions that appear to imply the existence of abstract objects involve improper senses of being and came to believe that only concrete substances exist. He thus continued to hold that sorting out uses of the words for being and existence can help us avoid philosophical mistakes. This led him to a notable preoccupation with sentences that have misleading grammatical form and an effort to rephrase such sentences so as to show their content more perspicuously.

PSYCHOLOGY

In 1865 Brentano submitted his *Psychology of Aristotle* to the University of Würzburg as *Habilitationsschrift*, a requirement for the right to give lectures. Many central tenets of his masterwork, the

Psychology from an Empirical Standpoint are prefigured in this second major contribution to Aristotle scholarship. We first report his understanding of the relevant sections of Aristotle's *De Anima.*[10]

Brentano draws attention to a distinction, important for the development of his argument, between two types of change. In the proper sense, the change in a substance is the replacement of an attribute by something opposed to it, as when heat drives out and replaces the cold that was present. By contrast, a *sensation* of heat in the hand is not the replacement of cold by hot, but here "the affection merely makes actual what lay in the subject potentially," and hence is not a change in the first sense (PA-E, p. 54, *De Anima* II.5, 417^{b}2). The hand may be physically cold and yet feel heat, and may then be even more sensitive to the heat. A distinction must thus be made between the physical presence of an attribute in a thing, and the existence of a sensed attribute in an organ of sense when the "sensed object as actuality" occurs in the sense (*De Anima* III.2, 425^{b}25). Using medieval terminology, Brentano calls the first the *physical*, and the second the *objective* presence of the attribute (p. 54). A hand will be said to *be* cold not only when it is physically so, but also when it is cold *objectively*, that is, when it senses coldness.

Organs of sense each have their proper objects, unreachable by other organs. The eye senses colour, but cannot taste, the ear can hear but not feel, etc. (p. 56, *De Anima* II.6, 418^{a}11). This is due to their physical nature, to their being part of the body. There are, as well, common sensibles, like shape and motion, which can be perceived by both sight and touch, but only through the mediation of the proper objects: if the eye could not perceive colour, then also not shape or motion.

Above the special senses a "sense of sensation" or *common sense* has the sensations of the special senses as its proper objects, and makes it possible to know *that* one sees. This cannot be evident to the sense of sight, for then the act of seeing would itself be coloured. So there must be a meta-sense whose own objects are the sensations of sight (p. 58, *De Anima* III.2, 425^{b}12/17), and the objects of all the other special senses. "The *one* final organ of sense, to which the others transmit their sensations" (p. 216) makes it possible to discriminate white from sweet, hot from loud, etc., a feat beyond the capacity of the special senses (p. 59, *De Anima* III.2, 426^{b}8). Neither the special senses nor the common sense, Brentano claims, are in the (immaterial) soul, but in the ensouled *body* (p. 65). When ex-posed to strong physical stimulation they become saturated, tired, or stunned. "This indicates clearly that the sensing subject is some-thing bodily and corruptible, that the sensory faculty is a form that is mixed with matter, a *logos enhylos* [an embodied thinking]" (p. 65). A mental subject, by contrast, would be *stimulated* through intense acts of thought (p. 82, *De Anima* III.4, 429^{a}29). This is one of several arguments meant to show the immateriality of mind. Another rests on the distinction between physical and objective inexistence.

Consider the Aristotelian text "It is not proper to say that the in-tellect is mixed with the body, for then it would be of a certain kind, either hot or cold" (*De Anima* III.4, 429^{a}24). Aristotle does not argue that if the intellect were physically hot by being mixed with body, then it could not be objectively cold, for the two are compatible. Rather, he is here speaking of what is in the intellect objectively, not physically (p. 78–9). In simple terms: if the intellect were mixed with body, then, like the organs of sense, it would have to have a proper object, be hot-or-cold or have some other specific quality *objectively* whenever it thinks. But there is no proper object of the intellect, for potentially the mind is (objectively) *all* existing things (*De Anima* III.8, 431^{b}20). Therefore it is unmixed with body, and because of this it is incorruptible and therefore immortal.

By far the most important part of *The Psychology of Aristotle* is the discussion of the nature of the intellect, and of thought (pp. 74–161). More than forty years after writing this he claimed that no detail of it had been refuted, or even improved (UA, p. 138). His theory, in his own summary, is this:

The thoughts and concepts of the understanding are realised in the exter-nal world [i.e. stem from the attributes of things in the world]. The under-standing does not receive them directly from there, but only through the mediation of the representations of sense. Sense grasps the sensory aspect in things, while the understanding grasps the intelligible aspect in their sen-sory images. Things have an effect upon the organ of sense and the latter similarly upon the understanding. (UA, p. 138)

The formation of concepts requires that, first, *things* should affect the senses, since "no one can learn or understand anything in the absence of sense" (*De Anima* III.8, 432^{a}6). Images are formed, which are necessary for all thought: since the soul "never thinks without an image" (*De Anima* III.7, 431ᵃ16). But this poses a problem: how can the senses and their states, which are in the body, influence an intellect that is "unmixed" with body? Whatever acts upon the mind, the active principle that conveys forms to the mind, cannot be of a lower order than the recipient: "Always, the active is superior to the passive factor, the originating force to the matter which it forms" (p. 119, *De Anima* III.5, 430ᵃ28). Hence it must itself be mental (UA, p. 140). In Brentano's interpretation, Aristotle distinguishes two capacities or attributes of the mental part, namely *active* and *receptive* intellect. Unlike other scholars he does not think of this pair as two distinct *substances*, but as two functions of one and the same entity: intellect *as active*, and intellect *as receiving forms*.

One of the intellectual powers has the . . . property [of being everything potentially] since it becomes everything; but the other is an actual positive property, like light; for in a sense light makes potential colours into actual colours . . . This intellect is by its essential nature activity. (pp. 109ff., *De Anima* III.5, 430ᵃ15)

The active intellect does not think, but makes thought possible (p. 151). It *illuminates* the sensory images, or phantasms, making possible their objective presence in the mind. The intellect as receptive then has images before it, in which it discerns concepts. Brentano summarizes:

We never think a general thought that is not accompanied by a sensory image. Just as the mathematician who wants to prove a general proposition . . . draws in the sand a particular triangle and discovers the general truth by observing this triangle, so also if someone intellectually contemplates some other thing, he always has an appropriate representation in his sensitive faculty. (pp. 95–6)

After thus laying out the different functions of mind, Brentano raises the question how, according to Aristotle, the mind perceives itself, that is, how it can know *that* it is thinking, that an object is present in it? There is no higher level of mind aware of thought at a lower level, as the common sense perceives the sensations of the individual senses. Rather, says Aristotle, "knowledge and perception and opinion and understanding have always something else as their object, and themselves only on the side (*en parergo*)" (pp. 85 and 89ff., *Metaphysics* XII.9, 1074ᵇ35). Brentano not only accepted this, but made it a cornerstone of his own philosophy. It is the root of his famous theory of intentionality. He draws attention to this connection in several later texts:

There is no question that in sensing we have two objects; one is called the external object, the other the inner object. Aristotle said of the latter that we sense it *parergo* and, as a result, the external object was called the primary and the inner the secondary object. (SNC, p. 28)[11]

In thinking, one's mind always relates to two objects, namely, the object of the thought or perception and "himself as the one who sees" (SNC, p. 41).

Brentano acknowledged his debt to Aristotle numerous times. We now discuss the Aristotelian roots of two of his central concerns.

1. In his best known work, the *Psychology from an Empirical Standpoint* of 1874, Brentano outlined the distinction between *mental phenomena* (perhaps better *mental acts*) and *physical phenomena*. Both occur in the mind, the latter exemplified by "a colour, a figure, a landscape that I see, a chord that I hear, warmth, cold, odour that I sense, as well as similar entities that appear to me in imagination" (PES-E, pp. 79–80). By contrast,

Hearing a sound, seeing a coloured object, feeling warmth or cold . . . every judgment, every recollection, every expectation, every inference, every conviction or opinion, every doubt is a mental phenomenon [or act]. Also to be included under this term is every emotion: joy, sorrow, fear, hope, courage, despair, anger, love, hate, desire, act of will, intention, astonishment, admiration, contempt, etc. (PES-E, p. 79)

After dismissing several other suggestions, Brentano concluded that the distinction between the two types lies in the fact that mental acts always have objects that "intentionally inexist" in them, and physical phenomena do not. This view ran counter to much accepted doctrine. It was commonly held that there are certain types of mental occurrence, sensations, where there is no distinction between act and object. Is there a difference between the pain one has, and the feeling of it? Is the pain an *object* of thought or feeling, or does one just *have* it? Is a taste in the mouth the perception of an object? Can there not be joy or dread that is not focused on an object?[12]

The Aristotelian roots of Brentano's theory are plain once it is noted that, for Aristotle the mind is in actuality *nothing* other than the object that it thinks. While the mind is in a way (i.e. potentially) all existing things, it is in actuality only what it thinks (*De Anima* III.8, 431^{b}20). But a mind devoid of actuality cannot be known to itself. Hence there is no state of mind that can be known if there is no inexistent object. Aristotle's view that the object of desire must also be an object of cognition (*De Anima* III.10, 433^{b}10) leads directly to Brentano's position that "representation forms the basis . . . of desire and every other mental act. Nothing can be judged . . . desired, nothing can be hoped or feared if it is not represented" (PES-E, p. 80). If then the objects of desire, etc., are also objects of cognition, it follows from Aristotle's premise that no mental act can be experienced *en parergo*, or even exist, unless an object intentionally inexists in the mind. The mind can know itself only if it knows another thing. Brentano notes "it is apparent that [Aristotle's] conception agrees entirely with our own" (PES-E, p. 132).

In the *Psychology of Aristotle* a deductive argument was offered: Aristotle's conception of the nature and structure of the mind implies that all mental acts have objects. This differs from the reasoning of Book II of the *Psychology from an Empirical Standpoint*, nine years later, where Brentano endeavors to establish the very same conclusion through an enumeration of cases of mental acts, an "inductive procedure" (PES-E, p. 78). This is best seen not as a change of mind, but as buttressing the same conclusion with further argument.

The volume known in German as *Psychologie III*, and in English as *Sensory and Noetic Consciousness*, opens by raising a skeptical question, leading to a new twist in the discussion of the primary knowledge of objects, and the secondary knowledge of the mental activity: Which is more certain? Brentano's answer is unequivocal: "mental activity always includes the evident consciousness of that activity" (SNC, p. 4), and even more strongly "Aside from our knowledge of ourselves as mentally active beings, we have no directly evident knowledge of facts" (SNC, p. 5). To put this in Chisholm's adverbial form of expression:[13] I can be certain that I am appeared to redly, but not that the object, even if described as a sense datum, actually *is* red. "In the final analysis I do not know that a colour exists, but that I have a presentation of that colour" (SNC, p. 5).

Brentano not only argues that the secondarily perceived mental acts are the only entities known with evident certainty, but that *all* acts of the mind are evident to it. In the *Psychology from an*

Empirical Standpoint, Brentano examines and argues against several theories that countenance unconscious mental acts, reaching the conclusion: "The question, 'Is there unconscious consciousness?' . . . is therefore to be answered with a firm *No*" (PES-E, p. 137). Here again an Aristotelian position is supported by further argument: to think is to be affected (*De Anima* III.4, 429^{b}23), and, as noted, until a form enters, the receptive mind is mere potentiality, or, more drastically put, "the mind is nothing actual until it thinks" (*ibid.*).

2. Brentano proposed a challenging reform of syllogistic logic, as it was then taught. His proposal connects with Aristotle's psychology though, oddly, not with his theory of the syllogism.

Brentano avoided the use of metaphor when discussing the mind. It is never described as a theatre, an internal forum, a society, a conversation or the like. Instead, he uses the sparse theory of potentiality, actuality, the presence of forms. In a theatre there can be several actors at the same time, but at any time a potentiality can become only *one* actuality, as a lump of clay can be formed into an egg shape, or a ball, but only one of them at any time. Likewise, "in the understanding, as in any potentiality, there can be only one actuality at any time" (UA, p. 279). If this is so, how can the mind form judgments, which combine two notions, subject and predicate? "As Aristotle says in the books about the soul, predication comes about if subject and predicate are thought one *after* the other" (UA, p. 272). The explanation, according to Brentano, is that the two thoughts meet at a point in time:

But that which mind thinks, and the time in which it thinks, are in this case divisible only incidentally and not as such. For in them too there is something indivisible [according to Brentano this is the point in which the two mental acts meet] . . . which gives unity to the time and the whole of length; and this is found equally in every continuum whether temporal or spatial. (*De Anima* III.6, 430^{b}17)[14]

There is, however, a problem with reasoning. If an argument has two premises, then they join at a common point, but their subjects and predicates do so as well. Brentano did not think that these four thoughts, passing over three dividing points, could become a single actuality. He believed that revising the theory of judgment would solve the problem. A judgment is to be not the joining of one concept, the subject, to another, the predicate, but an accepting or rejecting of a simple or compound thing, an intellectual analogue to acceptance and rejection in the sphere of the affections. The classical categorical judgments are reformulated: "Some S is P" into "[An] SP *is*," "Some S is not P" into "[An] S non-P *is*" "All S are P" into "[An] S non-P *is not*," "No S is P" into "[An] SP *is not*."[15]

The broader aim of this is to make judgments into *simple* thoughts, not combinations of subject and predicate. Once this is accomplished, the two premises of a syllogism will join at a single dividing point and are then, in a sense, in a single time. Brentano summarizes:

Since a syllogism (*Schluß*) contains more than two terms, how can they be brought together if their unification is explained only by the dual nature of the dividing point [which is at once an end and a beginning]? The point in time would have to be a boundary in three ways rather than just two. Evidently, Aristotle allowed the formation of a complex term out of several terms that had been predicated of each other . . . The proposition "A green tree is" is equivalent to "A tree is green" . . . And by virtue of this combination the intellectual achievement we call inference becomes possible despite the Aristotelian law that in the understanding, just as in all other potentialities, there can be only one actuality at a time. (UA, pp. 278–9)

Several decades after developing this new theory of the syllogism, in his reistic phase, Brentano came to think that "be," "is," "are," "is not," etc., function as "synsemantic" words: they are not names or concept words, have no meaning (*Bedeutung*; cf. PES-G, II, p. 57). Rendering sentences into a canonical "SP is/is not" form makes their real structure perspicuous. "A green tree is" indicates *acceptance*, "A blue tree is not" *rejection* of the respective substances, and only substances are now recognized as being: the only sense of being still accepted is the focal meaning of *Several Senses of Being*.

THEOLOGY

Brentano's interest in his teacher's philosophy extended to all parts of Aristotle's writings, and not only to what he could absorb into his own work. It includes, in particular, theology and the problem of God's influence upon, and knowledge of, the world.

The still most common view on this subject is that Aristotle's God contemplates the most perfect thing there is, which is Himself, and nothing else. He therefore knows nothing of the world, perhaps not even that it exists. This line of interpretation goes back to Ibn Sina (Avicenna, 930–1037) and other early Arabic commentators. The French humanist Peter Ramus (1515–72), who had made a name for himself with his dissertation *Whatever Aristotle has Said is False*, revived it in order to illustrate the absurdity of Aristotle's thought. The divine ignorance view was widely accepted, although its textual support is slim, consisting of parts of the seventh and ninth chapter of Book XII of the *Metaphysics*, and specifically the passage: "It must be of itself that the divine thought thinks, since it is the most excellent of things" (1074^b34, Ross's translation). There is only one other concurring text in the *Eudemian Ethics*: "[God] is too perfect to think of anything besides Himself" ($1245^b16–18$). There are, on the other hand, embarrassingly many passages inconsistent with this interpretation. They occur in different contexts and are impossible to refute with summary argument.[16] Traditionally they have been ignored, or dealt with ad hoc. For example, *Metaphysics* I.2 states in plain words that God has knowledge of first principles and causes of all things, saying that such a science "either God alone can have, or God above all others" (982^b20). Ross explains that Aristotle does not here give his own opinion, but speaks of "God as commonly conceived."[17] Even if true, there is no indication that Aristotle disagreed with the common conception.

Brentano's interpretation centers on the last sentence of *Metaphysics* XII.4, to which he gives a reading that differs radically from that of all other commentators. Aristotle distinguished four explanatory factors that determine the state of a thing: matter, form and its contrary, and the "moving principle." For example, to explain the state of health of a person one has to consider bodily matter, the presence of health (in most of the body) and its absence (disease in some parts) and the medical art, which has brought about this state. But the moving cause must itself contain the form: the physician must know what health is, and in natural objects the moving principle, too, must contain the form, since *like* is always generated by *like*. Hence "there will be in one way three explanatory factors, and in another way, four. For the mover (medical art) is in a way also the form of health, and the building art is in a way the form of the house, and man begets man" (1070^b30).[18]

There is thus a list of explanatory factors: matter, form plus moving principle, and privation. This is followed by a list of examples: health, building art and man. Then comes the critical sentence, which is usually translated as

Besides these [several principles] there is that which as the first of all things moves all things.[19]

By contrast, in Brentano's understanding the sentence continues the list of *examples*. Also, the auxiliary verb "to be" is omitted in the text, very common in Greek writing, and must be added to give the following reading:

Besides these [besides medical art, being, health, etc.] there is the way in which that which is the first moving principle of all *is all things*.

This means that in God moving and formal principle coincide, just as in medical art: as medical art is in a sense health, architecture the house, and a man is (the form of) his child, so God *is* all things. Claiming God to be all things is not to subscribe to pantheism. Rather, it means that God is all things *objectively*, in the sense discussed earlier.[20]

Other passages confirm this reading. In a later chapter Aristotle says:

Anaxagoras makes the good a motive principle; for his *nous* [mind] moves things. But it moves them for an end, which must be something other than it, except according to our way of stating the case; for, on our view, the medical art is in a sense health. (*Metaphysics* XII.10, 1075^b8)

Commentators were baffled and unable to explain the reference to medical art.[21] Aristotle is here pointing to a flaw in Anaxagoras' construction where the order of the universe, as an abstract plan, must be the absolute origin of the world. This plan is therefore more noble than God, whose only role is to implement it. But if God is the order of the universe as medical art is health, then the plan is itself the mind of God, who is also the efficient cause of the world. In Brentano's interpretation the Anaxagoras passage connects seamlessly with Aristotle's teaching.

More confirmation is found in *De Anima*. It is understood that in the individual mind as in all natural becoming, potentiality precedes actuality. We saw that the mind is "nothing" until it is appropriately affected, and only after that does it actually become the form it has received. But this does not hold for the universe as a whole: "Actual knowledge is identical with its object. In the individual, potential knowledge is in time prior to actual knowledge, but in the universe as a whole it is not prior even in time" (*De Anima* III.5, 430ª20). Divine thought, as the plan of it all, did not come after, but was at least concurrent with, the existence of form-receiving matter (AWV, p. 60, UA, pp. 275, 325, 350ff., 381).

The nature and extent of God's knowledge of the world has yet to be explained. Ibn Rushd (Averroës, 1128–98), according to Brentano, took the providence of the Aristotelian God to be limited to what is general (UA, p. 222). The great Arabic commentator had maintained, on good textual evidence, that God knows only the forms of things, their genera and species, the laws governing their changes, but not individuals and their states. Like the wise man, God has no knowledge of all things in "in detail" (*Metaphysics* I.2, 982ª10), and the knowledge of general laws is the only kind, or the most appropriate kind, for God to have (*Metaphysics* I.2, 983ª8).

In Brentano's interpretation, God not only has knowledge of the world in detail – "he knows all by knowing Himself" (AWV, pp. 66, 73), but He is also its efficient cause. We are instructed not to import into Aristotle the Humean concept of efficient cause, which supposes that a cause must precede its effect. Rather, "if no condition other than the efficient cause is lacking, then the effect must occur as soon as the efficient cause occurs . . . Thus, if this holds for an eternal and changeless principle, then the effect cannot but exist without beginning" (AWV, pp. 39–40, 62). Hence God can be the efficient cause even of *eternal* features of the world – its laws, forms and the heaven of fixed stars.

There is a stubborn perseverance in Brentano's efforts to make a consistent system out of even the most disparate claims in the Aristotelian corpus. How is one to reconcile, for instance, the law of synonymy with spontaneous generation? The law of synonymy, an unquestioned principle for Aristotle, states that like always comes from like, as a horse from a horse, man from man, etc. (*Metaphysics* XII.3, 1070ª4). But it is also claimed that there is spontaneous generation of organisms like aquatic animals and eels (*Historia animalium* VI.15, 569ª10, VI.16, 570ª2). Moreover, Aristotle "approved of the opinion of others who believed that even the highest kinds of organism arose in this manner in former times" (AWV, p. 60). In these cases, by definition, no namesake has preceded. Here is Brentano's answer:

The law of synonymy must be fully preserved. But it seems to be fully preserved only if we direct our thoughts from the immediate efficient causes, which are so to speak only workers, to the plan in the mind of the eternal master builder at whose behest they work. (*Ibid.*)

Brentano's last book was *Aristotle and his World View*, published in 1911 when he was 73 years old. The book's daring constructions impose on Aristotle's writings a system that reflects Brentano's own views, especially in philosophical theology.[22] He notes a "deeply rooted kinship" between Leibniz and Aristotle (AWV, p. 131) in that both philosophers thought this world the best possible. For Aristotle, and for Brentano, "the world, taken as a whole, is ordered with infinite wisdom and appears as the most perfect possible" (AWV, p. 83). But here the world taken as a whole includes not only the physical world, which has many imperfections, but also the departed immortal souls. Since the summation of goods, in Aristotle, always produces a greater good (AWV, p. 83) the more immortal souls there are, the better.

The number of blessed spirits grows to infinity; each of them leads a life like that of a Leibnizian monad, as a mirror of the universe from its point of view, but a life which, like that of the deity, is without change. (AWV, p. 121)

A possible objection is that the world cannot be the best possible since it is finite. Only a finite number of humans have come into existence and passed away. But every finitude is a limit that can be, and indeed will be, surpassed as more souls depart this world (*ibid.*).

But could God not have created an infinitude of blessed spirits, omitting the imperfect physical world altogether? "Why the whole physical apparatus?" (AWV, p. 122). The answer is that actual infinity is impossible, only unending increments.[23] "If infinite multiplication alone can make God's world the best possible, it is also true that the physical world as an indispensable breeding ground is a peremptory teleological requirement" (*ibid.*).

To put this in context: both Aristotle and Leibniz were "optimists," that is, they believed that this world is the best possible.

But Leibniz did not quite succeed in his argument. He concluded that evil is at a minimum, and that the elimination of any further ill will result in a greater ill elsewhere. This is a dubious claim deserving Kant's sarcastic quip that this god is "like a captain who sacrifices part of his cargo to save the rest and his ship."[24] By contrast, Aristotle's incrementalism is the best a wise and powerful god can do, given that actual infinity is impossible.

Brentano notes that Aristotle never stated explicitly the view here attributed to him (UA, p. 36), but that it "follows with all clarity from general principles" (ibid.). The mind (nous) does not exist from eternity, but is created by God. It survives the body. The surviving spirit is a good. If several goods are summed, a greater good results. Thus the total world, which includes departed souls, gets better and better. Since actual infinity is impossible, the best result can be obtained only through increments, not by a single act of the deity. Brentano remarks that no one had seen this before, but "nothing could be more wrong than to cavil at this result as a baseless fabrication" (UA, p. 36).

CONTROVERSIES

Brentano freely and repeatedly acknowledged his debt to Thomas Aquinas's commentaries on Aristotle. Consulting a scholastic philosopher who had no Greek "seemed so paradoxical to most [Aristotle scholars], that they . . . formed the suspicion, suggested by my position in the Catholic Church, that . . . I had introduced Thomistic doctrine into Aristotle, and that I was less interested in explaining Aristotle than in adding more glory to the reputation of the Doctor Angelicus."[25] Brentano's disagreement with most established Aristotle scholars was summed up in the complaint that (unlike St. Thomas) they did not have the philosophical depth to reconstruct Aristotle's system of thought, however profound their knowledge of Greek language and history.

For example, from antiquity many scholars thought the active intellect to be not a power in the human soul, but identical with God's thought. Eduard Zeller restated this in his important multi-volume history of Greek philosophy (1855–66), in which he also argued that God knows only himself, and that the human soul, if it is to survive after death, must have existed before birth, indeed from eternity.

Brentano took pains to refute all this in his *Psychology of Aristotle* calling these views "absurd (*ungereimt*), wondrous (*wunderlich*), peculiar (*sonderbar*) (PA-E, p. 23, 196). In the next edition of his history (1879) Zeller countered with several polemical footnotes. A "literary feud" ensued, a not very polite academic skirmish rather common in nineteenth-century Germany. Brentano replied in a pamphlet *Über den Creatianismus des Aristoteles* (1882). Zeller responded and after another exchange the contretemps died down.

The two agreed that *nous*, the intellectual part of the human being, is immortal, relying on passages like *De Anima* 430^{b}23. Their disagreement was on the pre-existence of *nous*, Zeller maintaining that if it survived eternally, then it also had no beginning, while Brentano thought that God created each individual mind. The human fetus, after going through a vegetative and sensitive phase, is disposed "at the very end" to receive the intellectual part. At that point "the human foetus, . . . through the special co-operation of the deity becomes like a man" (PA-E, pp. 135–6). Most present scholars would find the opinions expressed on both sides more daring and speculative than the extant texts warrant.

The Zeller controversy was the only public expression of Brentano's disdain for philosophical history as it was then practiced. While continuing to lecture and write about Aristotle, he published nothing on him for more than twenty years.

Brentano repeatedly stressed that only someone knowledgeable in a subject can write its history. A philologist must also be a mathematician to explain Euclid or Archimedes, and the history of chemistry and physics requires appropriate scientific training. So likewise "the inquiry into the history of philosophy demands a philosopher . . . not merely someone who has some philosophical knowledge, but one who is imbued with the spirit of philosophical research" (UA, p. 10). The most scientifically accomplished philosophers, unfortunately, are so absorbed in systematic philosophical research that they rarely take time to concern themselves with history. Other "great names" lacked historical sense or pursued partisan interests. This persuaded many that philosophers are less competent than others to write the history of their subject (*ibid.*), and by default the subject fell into the hands of philologists and other amateurs.

Brentano claimed not to doubt Zeller's philosophical competency. Yet, "without in the least wanting to belittle the man" he had to say that Zeller "always took off and left ashore his philosopher's cloak before diving into the ocean of historical research, as if afraid that it would pull him into the depths" (UA, p. 11).

In an essay on historical method in philosophy[26] Brentano laid down a number of rules, "for all future interpretation of Aristotle" (UA, p. 15). These rules are stated in terms of "prior probabilities," a reference to Bayes's method, which requires a prior estimate of probability, based on "good sense." The data collected afterwards correct this guess and the better the initial estimate the more expeditious the following inquiry.[27] The prior probability related to the interpretation of a philosophical text depends on a preliminary assessment of the philosopher's intentions, competency, habits of argument, etc. Brentano's estimate of Hegel would have been that here everything is possible, so that the prior probability that he meant to be consistent is low. In Aristotle the opposite is the case, so that a verdict of inconsistency must be based on rock solid evidence to override the prior assessment.

He then laid out fifteen rules (UA, pp. 15–20), all beginning with a reference to prior probabilities, e.g. "It is antecedently extremely improbable, nay impossible, that any of Aristotle's statements will contain gross contradictions" or that his statements contradict each other, or plainly observable facts. It is antecedently probable that an interpretation is correct if it explains a doctrine as conforming to Aristotle's methods and world-view, and importantly, given the fragmentary character of the texts, "it is past doubt that much of his teaching is never explicitly stated. Thus it is antecedently highly probable that we sometimes will not understand the coherence of the various doctrines and their compatibility if we do not succeed in filling these gaps" (UA, p. 19). The philological commentators, unable to understand the Aristotelian world order, "rejected some of his most important pronouncements . . . and looked upon the remainder with a disdainful shrug" (UA, p. 38).

The strength of his large-scale systematizing approach is that it can draw out consequences and suggest interpretations of Aristotelian texts that would not be obvious on a piecemeal reading. But it makes Brentano liable to the same error he sometimes disparages in others: that of fathering upon Aristotle conclusions the author would not have acknowledged as his own. He responded to this criticism, which he anticipated (AWV, p. 124; cf. SSB, p. 123), that the views under discussion can be inferred from Aristotle's stated principles and scattered but highly significant remarks and even from the work of his student Theophrastus. And he argues plausibly that responsible interpretation allows or even requires us to attribute implicit views to Aristotle that make coherent sense of dispersed claims. To be fair, it must be said that Brentano's interpretations and interpolations, especially about Aristotle's theology and cosmology, are often extravagant, but they are always challenging, and sometimes unearth striking deep structures. His habit of carefully setting out a range of earlier opinions on a given problem and attempting to reconcile them with each other and with experience is in the Aristotelian spirit. He tried to state the views of his predecessors more clearly than they did themselves before launching objections.

We have noted that Brentano thought he was concerned with the very same problems as Aristotle, St. Thomas and Leibniz, and these philosophical problems could be investigated and solved in the same spirit as those of science. This did not fit well into the philosophical scene after Hegel. The common view, shared by Zeller, was that philosophical systems are expressions of their culture and time, not a progress toward truth but a narrative of shifting paradigms. For Brentano, by contrast, "the study of the history of philosophy is justified only if it stands in the service of systematic [*sachlich*] research."[28]

CONCLUSION

Brentano often and gratefully acknowledged that Aristotle had saved him from errors widely accepted as obvious truths. Here are several issues in which Brentano differed from much of the philosophical tradition he encountered.

1. We mention again the Aristotelian roots of Brentano's theories of intentionality, of judgment and inference already discussed above.

2. It was a common view, profoundly wrong in his opinion, that we never perceive substances, but only their accidents as effects upon the mind. This despite the fact that physical science does not postulate unknowable underlying substances, but deals with observable properties of things. So also psychology: "In inner perception we encounter manifestations of thinking, feeling and willing. But we never

notice a something to which they are attached as properties"(PES-E, p. 11, with slight change of translation). In keeping with Aristotle's views, he maintains that to perceive physical and psychological phenomena *is itself* the perception of substance, and not the *effect* of an unknowable substrate:

The concept of substance in general [Aristotle] takes to be given as part of any perception. Thus it is present both in outer and in inner perceptions, and hence it is clear that nothing real, i.e. no accident, can exist separated from substance. (AWV, pp. 38, 43)

Brentano's claim that the method of philosophy is the method of science underwent various changes.[29] The one constant is that philosophy, like the sciences, investigates the phenomena that lie before us, and does not speculate about causes that are in principle hidden.

3. In much modern philosophy, sensory and noetic consciousness are systematically confused. In British Empiricism, for example, the vehicles of thought are impressions and ideas, images that are colored, shaped, etc. They are also meant to be subjects and predicates of judgments, for which they are most unsuitable candidates. To allow reasoning and asserting there must be mental contents in addition to sensory images. In Aristotle, and in Brentano following him, as we have seen in the example of the geometrician who draws a triangular shape in the sand, conceptual, i.e. noetic, knowledge, although it depends on phantasms, goes beyond them.

4. After Descartes defined mind as thinking, and matter as extended, substance, the mind-body problem came to dominate modern philosophy, resulting in a large number of -isms. How could substances so different from each other interact? Monistic views denying the existence of one or the other were proposed: materialism in Lammetrie and d'Holbach, idealism in Berkeley. Then there were various types of parallelism, like interactionism in Descartes, occasionalism in Malebranche, pre-established harmony in Leibniz, epiphenomenalism in T. H. Huxley. In Aristotle, and in Brentano, the problem does not even arise: thought is not seen as the province of a mind located in, but unconnected with, a body. Rather, mind and body form a single substance, with thought the product of bodily sensation *and* mental activity.

To conclude: Brentano's way of philosophizing and treating the history of the subject really does represent a renewal of style and substance, a more scientific attitude, a profound change from the obscurities of German Idealism.

There are few writers for whom Aristotle was more alive. And even if his interpretations are often speculative and daring, his manner of arguing for them is always challenging, demanding a kind of active involvement that cautious historical accounts seldom manage to produce.

NOTES

1. Theophrastus was originally called Tyrtamos. Aristotle gave him his new name because of his divine gift for speech: *theo-phrastos*: God-speaker (Diogenes Laertius, *Lives of Eminent Philosophers*, bk. 5, ch. 2).

2. Aulus Gellius, a Roman of the second century CE who went to Athens for his higher education, describes how Aristotle appointed his successor as head of the *Lyceum*. The choice was between Eudemus of Rhodes and Theophrastus of Lesbos. "Pretending to dislike the wine he was drinking, he asked for samples from Rhodes and Lesbos and remarked 'Both are very good indeed, but the Lesbian is the sweeter.' When he said this, no one doubted that gracefully, and at the same time tactfully, he had by those words chosen his successor, not his wine . . . And when, not long after this, Aristotle died [in 322 BCE] they accordingly all became followers of Theophrastus." Aulus Gellius, *The Attic Nights*, ed., John C. Rolfe, 3 vols. (Cambridge, MA: Harvard University Press, 1927) vol. 2, pp. 425–6.

3. Brentano sketched this scheme in VPP and followed it in detail in his lectures on the history of philosophy: *Geschichte der griechischen Philosophie* (Bern and Munich: Francke, 1963), *Geschichte der mittelalterlichen Philosophie im christlichen Abendlande* (Hamburg: Meiner 1980), *Geschichte der Philosophie der Neuzeit* (Hamburg: Meiner, 1987).

4. In July 1866 Brentano defended twenty-five Latin theses for his "habilitation" (an advanced doctorate), of which the fourth and most important was "The True Method of Philosophy is None Other than that of the Natural Sciences" (ZF, 1929, p. 138). He always maintained this view, restating it in 1893 (ZF, 1929, p. 30 and pp. 75ff.).

5. Georges Cuvier (1769–1832) was a comparative anatomist and is known as the "father of paleontology."

6. Martin Heidegger, *Unterwegs zur Sprache* (Pfullingen: Neske, 1959), p. 93.

7. See also *Metaphysics*, VII.4, 1030^a27–$^b3$; XI.3, 1060^b31–1061^a10.

8. It is not possible here to run through Brentano's complex argument. We merely give the list of Aristotelian passages he uses. Earlier members of the list go with the higher part of the graph, etc.: 1089^a26, 73^b5, 1089^b23, 1048^b7, 221^a29, 1029^b23, 1022^b7, 83^b16, 225^b5, 1^b25, 103^b21.

9. As he confirmed in a later lecture, "On the Concept of Truth" of 1889, WE, p. 24.

10. A corrected translation of part of PA-E is found in *Essays on Aristotle's De Anima*, eds., Martha C. Nussbaum and Amelie Oksenberg Rorty (Oxford: Clarendon, 1992), pp. 313–42. This collection of essays should be consulted for more recent interpretations of that text.

11. Other references to the Aristotelian origin of his theory of intentionality are found in DP-E and UA.

12. The fountainhead of this view was Etienne Bonnot de Condillac's *Traité des sensations*, Paris 1754. For a brief account of this tradition see R. George, "Kant's Sensationism," *Synthese* 47, 1981, pp. 229–55.

13. Roderick M. Chisholm, *Perceiving: a Philosophical Study*. (Ithaca, NY: Cornell University Press, 1957), p. 57.

14. Another passage of *De Anima* (III.2, 427^a10) suggests that two thoughts can occur at one time in the sense that a stretch of time, like any other continuum, while potentially divisible, is a unit as long as it has not actually been divided.

15. The theory of the syllogism that follows from this is discussed at length in LRU (pp. 21off.), taken from the lecture transcripts of Franz Hillebrand. But the essentials of the theory are already found in PES-E (PES-E, p. 230–1) and in his logic lectures in Würzburg in the winter of 1870. Cf. Carl Stumpf's "Reminiscences of Brentano," in *The Philosophy of Brentano*, ed. Linda L. McAlister (London: Duckworth, 1976), p. 21.

16. Brentano's extensive treatment of these passages is found in the appendix to PA-E. Cf. George, Rolf: "An Argument for Divine Omniscience in Aristotle," *Apeiron*, XXII.1, March 1989, pp. 61–74.

17. W. D. Ross, *Aristotle's Metaphysics* (Oxford: Oxford University Press, 1924) vol. I, p. 123.

18. The translation from Aristotle's *Metaphysics* is by Richard Hope (New York: Columbia University Press, 1952), p. 254.

19. This reading of the first mention of the "unmoved mover" owes much to a generally accepted correction of the Greek manuscripts by the influential Aristotle scholar H. Bonitz. The text found in all manuscripts is *eti para tauta hōs to prōton pantōn kinoun panta*. After Bonitz it became *eti para tauta to hōs . . .* because, he claimed, "Aristotle added a further principle to those already mentioned" (*Aristotelis*

Metaphysica, Commentarius, Bonn, 1849, p. 483). But just this is the doubtful point. The textual change stifles the correct understanding.

20. A more recent commentary notes correctly: "When Aristotle describes the Prime Mover as 'thinking itself,' he is not referring to any activity that could be called self-contemplation; he is simply describing the same activity that humans perform when they engage in abstract thought" (Richard Norman, "Aristotle's Philosopher God," *Phronesis* 14 [1969] pp. 63–74, p. 67). Cf. 1075^{a}4: "Thought and the object of thought are not different in the case of things that have no matter" (Ross translation).

21. Joseph Owens notes that "no further explanation is given of this cryptic remark" (*The Doctrine of Being in the Aristotelian Metaphysics* [Toronto: Pontifical Institute of Medieval Studies, 1963], p. 453).

22. Roderick M. Chisholm called it "a useful introduction to Brentano's own philosophy, in particular, his views about knowledge, the senses of being, the principles of preference, and philosophical theology" (SSB, p. ix).

23. "The infinite exists when one thing can be taken after another endlessly, each thing taken being finite" (*Physics* III.6, 206^{a}25).

24. *Academy Edition* 17.236.

25. Franz Brentano, *Aristoteles Lehre vom Ursprung des menschlichen Geistes* (2nd edn. Hamburg: Meiner, 1980), p. 1. This book also recounts the controversy with Zeller.

26. "On the Method of Aristotelian Studies and the General Method of Historical Research in the Area of Philosophy," written in the late 1880s but not published until 1986, UA, pp. 7–20.

27. Brentano learned about Bayes's principle from E. S. Jevons, *The Principles of Science* (London 1873, 1877). It is treated at length in LRU, part IV.

28. *Geschichte der griechischen Philosophie* (Bern and Munich: Francke, 1963).

29. Linda L. McAlister, *The Development of Franz Brentano's Ethics* (Amsterdam: Rodopi 1982) discusses this issue, pp. 8–18.

3   Judging correctly: Brentano and the reform of elementary logic

In memory of the achievements of Arthur Prior

INTRODUCTION

The nineteenth was logic's breakthrough century. At its beginning, logic had just been claimed by Kant, in justified ignorance of Leibniz's unpublished advances, not to have advanced since antiquity, and the laws of logic were soon to be submitted to the indignities of Hegel and to suffer the scorn of Mill. What started anachronistically in the 1820s with Richard Whately as a modest "back [beyond Locke] to Aristotle" movement in Oxford, trying to reinstate scholastic ways of doing logic after the long dark centuries since Ramus, inspired others lacking the desire to turn the clock back to reconsider logic and its role. This gathered momentum, and what began as a revival turned into a reform and then became a palace-storming revolution. Bolzano's obscurely published and tragically ignored 1837 masterpiece *Wissenschaftslehre* invented modern semantics, while ten years later in 1847 Boole and DeMorgan used mathematical methods and algebraic analogies to propel the study of inference out of the humanities and into mathematics. The twin giants of later nineteenth-century logic, Peirce and Frege, independently made huge strides of innovation: propositional logic, relations, quantifiers all received rigorous treatment. There were many other considerable logicians: Jevons, Venn, Schröder, MacColl, Neville Keynes, and Lewis Carroll all made notable contributions. By the turn of the twentieth century logic had come further in a hundred years than in the preceding two thousand, and was soon to see its flowering at the hands of Whitehead and Russell, Gödel and Tarski, Church and Turing, and many others.

In all this frenetic activity the modest but solid achievements of Franz Brentano rarely get a mention. True, Brentano was not a giant, but he was no pygmy either. In this chapter I outline the simple but effective reforms Brentano proposed for elementary deductive logic, basically syllogistic plus; I then discuss briefly how they can be made the basis of a sensible and pedagogically accessible approach to term logic even today, and finally mention their subtle but important influence on logic in the twentieth century.

Brentano was versed in the logical doctrines of Aristotle, the Scholastics, and the British empiricists. He was not a specialized logician, nor did he have any great interest in logic for its own sake or for its history: his main interests were metaphysical, ethical, and psychological. His logic was a by-product of these interests developed for teaching at the Universities of Würzburg and Vienna. He was an admirer and correspondent of John Stuart Mill, whose 1843 *A System of Logic* for some time held back the tide of mathematization in deductive logic while promoting inductive methods. Brentano did not keep up with contemporary developments in logic. He conceived early in his career an antipathy to mathematical logic, because he associated it with Hamilton's (to Brentano wildly erroneous) doctrine of the quantification of the predicate, and he thereafter ignorantly opposed the idea of treating logic with mathematical methods as if it must always make such an error. That does not prevent Brentano's own ideas from being both astute philosophically and, with a little tidying up, fully amenable to the most rigorous mathematical treatment, but it is deeply regrettable that he ignorantly rejected out of hand most other developments of his time.

TERMINOLOGY AND CONVENTION

In discussing logic, there is a choice which must be made as to whether one is concerned with psychological elements such as ideas, beliefs, and judgments, or with linguistic elements such as words, phrases, and sentences, or finally with abstract meanings such as concepts and propositions. Much ink has been spilled as to which set of items makes the best or most appropriate choice, to what extent the choice matters, what the interrelations are among the various elements and so on. Since that is not our topic here, I shall simply impose a choice. When discussing Brentano, I shall generally use the psychological vocabulary of ideas and judgments. This corresponds to Brentano's own usage and should not prejudice the question whether it is the correct choice for the primary elements of logical manipulation.[1] When discussing how to use Brentano's ideas later I shall use a more standard modern terminology of terms and propositions. A word about the word "idea": Brentano's German word for this is "Vorstellung," which is usually translated "presentation." Not only is this long and cumbersome, it has a different dominant meaning in English, and the German word "Vorstellung" was coined precisely to render service for the English term "idea" and the French word "idée," in Locke or Descartes, so there is every justification in returning to the original in rendering Brentano.

When quoting words or longer bits of language within running text I shall use quotes, as in the previous paragraph. To give within running text an example of an idea (not the word) using a word or phrase, and to give an example of a judgment using a sentence, I shall use the appropriate word, phrase or sentence in italics. If a word, phrase, sentence or formula occurs displayed on a line of its own, it can be taken either way according to context.

THE TEXTUAL BASIS

Brentano himself never published his reforms of logic, which is the main reason why historiographers of the subject have passed them by. The reducibility of judgments to the existential form is argued for in chapter VII of the *Psychology* (PES-E, pp. 201–34) and there are some remarks in the appendix prepared for the 1911 second edition of parts of that book, published as O*n the Classification of Mental Phenomena*. These remarks appear in the English PES-E, pp. 291–301, and Brentano's negative comments on mathematical logic at pp. 301–6. And that, for Brentano's lifetime, is it. Brentano's reform was known directly only to his students. It was given in more detail in his University lectures on Logic, first in Würzburg in 1870–1, then in Vienna, certainly in 1877, 1879, 1884–5, and again in the late 1880s. The Notes of 1879, reused with many amendments in 1884–5, are numbered EL72 in Brentano's papers housed in Harvard, and entitled *Die elementare Logik und die in ihr nötigen Reformen* (Elementary Logic and the Reforms it Needs) while the notes of the later series from the late 1880s, and called simply *Logik*, form EL80. Originally catalogued with EL72 but now separately numbered EL108* and entitled *Alte und neue Logik* (Old and New Logic) are a set of student's lecture notes from the 1877 lectures.[2]

A more detailed account of the reforms was published by Brentano's student Franz Hillebrand in 1891 in his monograph *Die neuen Theorien der kategorischen Schlüsse* (The New Theories of Categorical Inference). How much the material owes directly to Brentano is not clear, but the language and notation are very much his, so we may assume Hillebrand drew heavily on his own and/or Brentano's logic lecture notes from the 1880s. Incomplete efforts to turn the Vienna Lectures EL72 into a book were carried out in Prague between the world wars but the typed transcripts of Brentano's difficult handwritten notes remain unpublished. EL80 was made the basis, by Franz Hillebrand's daughter Franziska Mayer-Hillebrand, of the 1956 book *Die Lehre vom richtigen Urteil* (*The Theory of Correct Judgment*), which appeared under Brentano's name. Although probably nearly every word in that compilation is by Brentano, the result is nothing he ever produced or sanctioned, since Brentano's uncompromising post-1904 reism changed his views on many subjects, and Mayer-Hillebrand cut out passages representing pre-1904 views and pasted in corresponding passages representing the later views. It is almost impossible to disentangle the older from the younger material, so until complete critical texts of EL72 and EL80 appear we still have no definitive edition. Nevertheless, for the purposes of outlining the reform of logic with which I am concerned here, the 1956 book and Hillebrand's 1891 monograph give us enough convergent material to get a fairly clear idea of what Brentano was doing.

EXISTENTIAL JUDGMENTS: THE BASIC FORM

Every logician from Aristotle to Mill held that the basic form of a simple proposition, sentence, or judgment requires two concepts, terms or ideas, a subject and a predicate, to be suitably joined together to form a judgment. In the following judgments

All Greeks are human
Some Greeks are human
No Greeks are human
Some Greeks are not human
Some humans are not Greeks
Socrates is human
Socrates is not Greek

there are always two ideas, taken from the trio *Greek, human, Socrates*. The one whose term occurs first in the English sentence[3] is the subject (idea), the other is the predicate (idea). The binding words or phrases "is," "is not," "are," "are not" are known as "copulae," and are meant to represent the binding or combining of subject and predicate ideas in the mind of the judger when she judges. The words "all," "some," and "no" represent the quantity or *how much* among the things denoted by the subject idea are considered to have the predicate idea attributed to them in the judgment. The ideas *Greek* and *human* are general, being thinkable of many things, the idea *Socrates* is singular, being thinkable of at most one thing.

At an early stage of his development, some time between 1865 and 1870, Brentano came to the view that the fundamental logical form of judgment was not that of subject bound to predicate, as everyone had held since Aristotle, but of affirmations or denials of existence. Quite how he arrived at this view is not known, but presumably the considerations that moved him were partly a reflection of his psychological analysis of ideas and judgments, partly being convinced by examples. Since examples can convince independently of Brentano's psychology, consider them first. In the judgments *God exists, There are neutrinos, It is raining*, there appears in each case to be only one idea, namely *God, neutrino, rain*. The only way a second idea can be brought in is if we take that idea to be *existence*. Now consider the negations of these judgments, *God does not exist, There are no neutrinos, It is not raining*.[4] If the predicate is in each case *exist* and this is taken in the same way as a normal predicate, as in *God does not smoke* or *Neutrinos are not massive* then it seems that we put forward or posit as existent an object or kinds of objects in thinking the subject only to take away the existence again in the predication. That would appear to make negative existential judgments self-contradictory, which most clearly are not, since some are true. A tradition going back through Kant to Hume holds that *exist* or *existence* does not stand for any kind of thing, and rather than attempt to retain the subject–predicate analysis in the teeth of such examples of one-idea judgments, Brentano embraces the existential analysis.

The psychology of judgment bears the analysis out in that according to Brentano all mental acts, including not only judgments (which include perceptions) but also desires, emotions, willings, and feelings, are based on ideas, so all mental acts are either ideas or based on ideas. Simply to have an idea like *red* or *Socrates* in mind is not to take up any cognitive or emotive stance to it. Leaving emotion aside, cognition starts when one takes up an attitude to things. Since things are represented by ideas, and a simple idea like *horse* can represent one or more things, the simplest cognitive attitude one can adopt is to accept or reject things of the kind given by the idea. Accepting *horse* (better: accepting horses) is judging positively that horses exist, that there are horses, rejecting *horse* (better: rejecting horses) is judging negatively that there are no horses. Necessarily, of these two cognitive attitudes, one is true, or, as Brentano usually says, *correct* and the other is false or *incorrect*. The normative aim of cognition is to make correct judgments and to avoid making incorrect ones. The normative aim of logic is to regulate cognition in such a way as to ensure that in reasoning we do not start with true (correct) judgments and through reasoning end up with false (incorrect) ones.

Having established that positive and negative existential judgments (acceptances and rejections) are not reducible to subject–predicate form, Brentano then turns the tables on the tradition by claiming that the standard simple forms of judgment are all in one way or another existential. He can do this by availing himself of compound and negative ideas. The idea *iron mountain* is compounded of two ideas, and means *mountain which is (of) iron*, while the idea *immaterial* is a negative idea opposed to the positive idea *material*. In general one can make a negative idea positive or a positive idea negative by applying the negating modifier *non-* to the idea. This idea-negation switches us back and forth between an idea and its unique opposite or negation, it is a "toggle" between them, and double negation takes us back to the original idea. Compounding ideas in the form *A and B* or *A which is B* or just *AB* is idea-conjunction. An object is an *AB* or an *A and B* if and only if it is at the same time both an *A* and a *B*.

Now Brentano can show how the standard categorical forms of logic, the first four on our list above, can be rendered as positive or negative existential judgments, as follows:

All Greeks are human	is	There are no non-human Greeks
Some Greeks are human	is	There are human Greeks
No Greeks are human	is	There are no human Greeks
Some Greeks are not human	is	There are non-human Greeks

In Brentano's view, the form of words used on the right is a more perspicuous rendering because it brings out clearly the existential nature of the judgment. Notice that all the judgments have two ideas, but that instead of being split up into subject and predicate they are compounded together into a single compound subject, which is accepted or rejected as a whole.

A very vivid if unnatural way to represent how Brentano sees judgments as fundamentally existential is given by Arthur Prior.[5] Take an idea in abstraction from whether it is accepted or rejected as given by a query: *a?*, and its acceptance or rejection by an answer, Yes! or No! So in Prior's rendering the four forms are

A:	Non-human Greeks? No!
I:	Human Greeks? Yes!
E:	Human Greeks? No!
O:	Non-human Greeks? Yes!

With very little qualification, Brentano's sweeping reform of elementary logic, replacing the elaborate rules and arcane terminology of traditional syllogistic with a few simple inference principles, can be traced to his ability to render judgments into existential form. The following section looks at the heart of the reform, before we consider the qualification.

52   PETER SIMONS

NOTATIONS

Brentano has a very simple schematic notation, which I shall briefly explain but not use myself. Positive ideas or terms are given schematic letters like A, B, C, etc., sometimes with subscripts. The negation of a positive term is written (following Jevons) by using the lower-case equivalent, so "a" negates "A," "b" corresponds to "non-B," etc. Term or idea conjunctions are represented by juxtaposition like "AB" or "aBc." A positive existential judgment is represented by postposing a plus sign, so "A +" signifies "A exist" or "There are A." A negative existential judgment is represented by postposing a minus sign, so, e.g., "b −" represents "There are no non-B" or "Non-B do not exist." The four categorical forms in Brentano's notation are

All A are B	Ab −
Some A are B	AB +
No A are B	AB −
Some A are not B	Ab +

Following modern logical practice, I shall put the verb or functor for existence or non-existence *in front* of its idea, using "E . . ." for "there are . . ." or " . . . exist" and "N . . ." for "there are no . . ." or " . . . do not exist." As Charles Parson explains in his essay in this volume, Brentano, unlike Frege and modern logicians, does not take the negation aspect of a negative existential judgment to be part of its content, but to mark a different species of judgment, so for now I shall treat "E" and "N" as two opposed but primitive verbs. Like Brentano I shall represent conjunction by juxtaposition, though I shall use lower-case term variables throughout, and whereas Brentano uses the upper-case/lower-case toggle for term-negation I shall for the negation operator use a preposed minus sign, so −a is the negation of a. Parentheses will be used in an obvious way to group terms, but for the most part they are not necessary. We can represent the judgment *Some a are not b* as "E(a−(b))" but is is both unambiguous and uncluttered to prefer "Ea−b". So the four categorical forms look in this notation as follows

All *a* are *b*	N*a* −*b*
Some *a* are *b*	E*ab*
No *a* are *b*	N*ab*
Some *a* are not *b*	E*a* −*b*

For later use I introduce a "toggle" operator * which operates on terms as follows. If a is a positive term, $*a$ is its negative $-a$. If a is a negative term $-b$ then $*a$ is its positive b and not its double negative $--b$. This toggle corresponds to what Brentano does by switching cases from upper to lower and back.

BASICS

Brentano's one unconditional axiom is the Principle of Non-Contradiction, in its traditional, term-logical form (LRU, p. 202):

TNC $Na -a$ (There is no a non-a)

This is only one version of what has been called the Principle of Non-Contradiction, and it is not needed for syllogistic inference. Brentano lists several other renderings of "the" principle: the favourite in LRU is the following metalinguistic and semantic version:

It is impossible for someone to deny correctly what another affirms correctly, or to affirm correctly what another denies correctly. (LRU, p. 202)

The Law of Excluded Middle is analogously:

It is impossible for someone to deny incorrectly what another incorrectly affirms, or to affirm incorrectly what another denies incorrectly. (LRU, p. 202)

Obviously for us the most straightforward way to render these without using semantic vocabulary or mentioning affirmers and deniers is as theses of propositional logic:

PNC $\sim(p \mathbin{\&} \sim p)$
PEM $(p \vee \sim p)$

This is anachronistic, as Brentano did not have or use propositional logic, but clearly the intended effect is the same. Likewise the opposition of affirmation and denial (acceptance and rejection) is best stated using propositional connectives: the most elegant formulation employs exclusive disjunction, here written "+", so "$p + q$" means "p or q but not both":

OPP $Ea + Na$

OPP shows that one may use propositional negation $\sim$ to *define* one of "E," "N" in terms of the other. Lacking an expression for propositional negation, Brentano treats "E" and "N" as joint but opposed primitives.

Brentano characterizes "correct inference" as follows: "An inference is correct when the assertion of the premises stands in contradiction to the denial of the conclusion" (LRU, p. 203). This is of course a reasonable account, but Brentano is wrong to suppose as he does that it follows from or is a version of the law of non-contradiction as stated by him. Rather it is a *definition* of what is meant by a correct or valid inference. Brentano does not distinguish clearly between "correct" as used of true judgments, and "correct" as used of valid inferences.

Things look better when it comes to inferences. For his first (immediate, one-premise) inferences Brentano gives principles allowing us to strengthen or weaken the content of a judgment. In our notation the slash marks the inference from premises on the left to conclusion on the right and can be read as "therefore":

WEAK   E*ab* / E*a*

I call this the Principle of Weakening, since the content in the conclusion is weaker (less specific) than in the premises. Brentano himself does not give the inference rule a name. His version is more general: "Every correct affirmative judgement remains correct if we leave out arbitrary parts of its content" (LRU, p. 209). For our limited purposes the simpler version turns out to suffice.

STREN   N*a* / N*ab*

I call this the Principle of Strengthening. Brentano has "Every correct negative judgement remains correct if we enrich its content by arbitrarily many determinations" (LRU, p. 209). Brentano's more general formulation allows him to treat valid inferences depending on the non-logical ideas in the inference as instances of this scheme, for example the inferences (LRU, p. 209):

N spatial things / N figures
E horses / E animals

This means that what we would call analytic but non-logical inferences are covered by Brentano's general formulation, because he takes the idea *horse* to be an enrichment of the idea *animal* and so on. This is an intriguing issue worth exploring, but the notion of idea enrichment or analytic containment is notoriously slippery so will not be pursued here. In any case Brentano wisely does not go beyond giving examples.

Here are the two inference rules with two premises stated by Brentano (LRU, p. 210):

REM $\qquad$ Nab, Ea / E$a-b$

EXH $\qquad$ Nab, N$a-b$ / Na

The first rule shows that if there are a but there are no a b, then it must follow that there are a non-b. I call this the *Remainder Principle*: if there are a but one of two possible cases for as is eliminated, the other remains. Brentano is right that it is self-evidently valid. The second rule shows that if there are no a which are b and there are no a which are non-b then it must follow that there are no a at all. I call this the *Exhaustion Principle*: all the cases for there being as are exhausted in the premises. Again it is self-evidently valid, indeed it is more obvious if anything than the previous rule. The names for these rules are again mine, not Brentano's: he does not give them names.

To make the rules work properly we need to provide a little more oil to lubricate the inference engine than Brentano provides.[6] Brentano is an insightful logician but not an exact one, even though his standards of exactness are no worse than average for his time. Interestingly, much of what Brentano says turns on the idea of *identity* of content as distinct from *equivalence* of content. Roughly speaking, ideas which are compounded by conjunction and negation are identical if and only if they differ at most by repetition of conjuncts within a conjunction, rearrangement in order or bracketing of the same conjuncts, or the inclusion or exclusion of double (term-) negation. Judgments which have identical idea content are themselves identical, according to Brentano: all that may happen is that they differ in how they are verbally expressed. For our purposes we may take these principles as read.

IMMEDIATE INFERENCE

The "universal" propositions of the A form (All a are b) and E form (No a are b) are both negative existentials according to Brentano, and can both be true if there is nothing corresponding to one or other of their constituent terms, in particular if the subject term *a* is empty. On the other hand the I form (Some *a* are *b*) and the O form (Some *a* are not *b*) are positive existentials, and to be true must have their constituent terms non-empty. So the subalternation inferences from A to I and from E to O are invalid according to Brentano. Unlike in the traditional square of opposition, A and E are not contraries, because both are true when the subject term is empty, and for the same reason I and O are not subcontraries because they can both be false together. Simple conversions from E*ab* to E*ba* and from N*ab* to N*ba* hardly warrant the name "inference" according to Brentano because the judgments are in each case identical, having the same content differently expressed. Similarly contraposition, from "All *a* are *b*" to "All non-*b* are non-*a*" gives just two ways of saying "N*ab*," and likewise for the O form. (While double negation should be mentioned in that the contraposed A form is mechanically to be rendered "N−*b*−−*a*," recall that Brentano takes −−*a* to be *identical* to *a*, so these are again two ways of saying the same thing.) Conversion applies equally to A and O propositions because their constituent terms can be switched too. *Conversio per accidens* fails for the same reason as subalternation, so the only interesting immediate inferences left from the tradition are those involving the contradictory opposition of A and O, and of E and I (LRU, pp. 203–9), which are just special cases of the opposition stated in OPP.

SYLLOGISMS

Syllogistic inferences are traditionally taken as having three terms, one (the middle term) occurring once in each of the two premises, the other terms (major and minor) once in the premises and once in the conclusion. Of the 128 possible syllogisms recognized as distinct by the tradition, 24 are traditionally taken as valid but only 15 are valid if we accept with Brentano that subject terms may be empty. Given his analysis of the categorical forms, Brentano regards syllogisms as being inferences in *four* terms, one of which is the negation of another. The opposed terms need not be the "middle" term (or its negation) absent from the conclusion.

It turns out that there are just two basic valid syllogistic forms for Brentano. Using our toggle operator * they can be put as follows:

NEG $Na*b$, Nbc / Nac
POS Eab, Nbc / $Ea*c$

For want of more inspiring names, I call them the negative and the positive syllogism respectively, because the first contains only negative judgments while the second contains a positive premise and conclusion.

Let's prove them. Obviously POS rests on the Remainder Principle REM and NEG on the Principle of Exhaustion EXH.

Proof POS (cf. LRU, pp. 212–13)

1	1	Eab	Assumption
2	2	Nbc	Assumption
3	2	$Nabc$	2, STREN
4	1,2	$Eab*c$	2,3, REM
5	1,2	$Ea*c$	4, WEAK

Proof NEG (cf. LRU, pp. 215–16)

1	1	$Na*b$	Assumption
2	2	Nbc	Assumption
3	1	$Na*bc$	1, STREN
4	2	$Nabc$	2, STREN
5	1,2	Nac	3,4, EXH

All the fifteen valid syllogisms of traditional syllogistic logic where subject terms do not necessarily denote are variants of one of these, given by trivial replacements of positive by negative terms or vice versa, by switching the order of term conjuncts in a judgment or by swapping the order of the premises, none of which moves affect validity. Brentano shows that POS yields the syllogisms Darii, Datisi, Disamis, Dimaris, Baroco, Bocardo, Ferio, Festino, Ferison, and Fresison (LRU, pp. 213–15) while NEG gives us Barbara, Celarent, Cesare, Camenes, and Camestres (LRU, pp. 215–17). In addition there are some variants which result in the same way by substitutions and commutation of terms of premises but which are not standard syllogisms.

Those who have battled with gritted teeth through the traditional rules, names, reductions, and other minutiae of traditional syllogistic logic may by now be thinking "Surely it can't be this simple? Just four rules and some housekeeping?" To which the answer is "Make a loud noise, rejoice and sing praise," because it really is this simple.

Well, except for a couple of very minor wrinkles to be discussed in the next section.

EXISTENTIAL IMPORT

The doctrine that A and E propositions lack existential import in the subject, one which Brentano shared with Boole, must have cost Brentano much time in discussion with skeptics and conservatives. In due course he came up with a sop to or compromise with their worries: the theory of double judgment, or, as I should prefer to call it, judgment-and-a-half. Brentano accepts the psychological fact that someone who judges *This a is b* does not feel to herself as though she is making an existential judgment. So he allows a compound kind of judgment which consists in acknowledging or accepting a certain *a* and in addition predicating *b* of *it*. The existential judgment *There is an a* or in this case *This a exists*, which on its own Brentano calls a *thetic* judgment, is supplemented by an act affirming or denying a predicate of the thing or things acknowledged. The second part is dependent on the first, and the whole compound act is called a double or *synthetic* judgment. For the universal judgments of A and E forms we can capture the dependent nature of the second component by using anaphoric reference:

> There are *a* and all of *them* are *b*
> There are *a* and none of *them* are *b*

This has the right sort of feel or ring for what Brentano is trying to explain but I for one have no idea how to capture this vernacular form preserving the feel or ring in addition to the logical force.

Whatever the psychological justification of this complication, logically it is either unnecessary or unhelpful. It is unnecessary for dealing with syllogisms requiring existential import, because, as Brentano himself sees, the shortfall in existential assumptions for syllogisms whose validity requires subalternation or *conversio per accidens* can simply be made up by adding a further existential premise (LRU, p. 221), as we shall see from an example below. In the case of I and O judgments this is logically unnecessary anyway because the acknowledgment of the subject follows from the original judgment by weakening.

The natural way for *us* to treat a double judgment of the A or E form logically is as a conjunction E*a* and N*a* −*b* or E*a* and N*ab* respectively. But Brentano does not have propositional conjunction among his resources so does not take this way. It is thus, as Charles Parsons points out, hard to see what according to Brentano's view could count as the negation of a double judgment. Taking the analyses as conjunctions offered above the negation would be a disjunction, but that is not a single judgment for Brentano as double judgments are supposed to be and as their negations presumably ought to be.

The form of syllogism with an additional simple existential assumption is

| | EXIM | Ea, Nab, N$^*bc$ / Ea $^*c$ |

Proof EXIM

1	1	Ea	Assumption
2	2	Nab	Assumption
3	3	N$^*bc$	Assumption
4	1,2	Ea $^*b$	1, 2, REM
5	3	Na $^*bc$	3, STREN
6	1,2,3	Ea $^*b$ $^*c$	4, 5, REM
7	1,2,3	Ea $^*c$	6, WEAK

This form can be tweaked by substitution and commutation to yield as valid the four "p" syllogisms Darapti, Felapton, Bramantip, and Fesapo, and the five subaltern moods Barbari, Celaront, Cesaro, Camestrop, and Camenop, making up the remainder of the twenty-four valid Aristotelian syllogisms.

SINGULAR IDEAS

A term like "Socrates" and its corresponding idea *Socrates* is said by Hillebrand to have "singular matter" (*Die neuen Theorien der kategorischen Schlüsse*, p. 49). In other words, singularity is not a question of form. This seems to have been Brentano's view as well. In a dictation made shortly before his death and published in the *Psychology*, pp. 311–14, Brentano says: "Thinking is universal, entities are individual." In other words there is nothing in thought which by its nature individuates, and entities being individual have no need of individuation. Whether Brentano held to such a view throughout is not clear but it is not unlikely on the evidence. The distinction between singular and general terms, much made of in post-Fregean logic, is relatively marginal for Brentano, as indeed it was for nearly all pre-Fregean logicians.

Nevertheless the question arises whether in the context of Brentano's logical system as outlined above we are able to *say* or *define* what it is to be singular, or unique. The answer is that we are not. This can be shown by a simple mathematical model. Consider the half-open real interval $J = (0,1]$, i.e. all real numbers x such that $0 < x \leq 1$. Let S be the collection of all sets which consist of unions of half-open intervals $(x, y]$ from J, together with the empty set $\emptyset$. Interpret negation as complementation within J and term-conjunction as set-theoretic intersection of elements from S. S is closed under conjunctions and negations, that is, the conjunction and negation of elements of S are themselves elements of S. The existential judgment Ea is interpreted to be true if a is an element of S other than $\emptyset$, and Na is true if a is interpreted as $\emptyset$. It can be checked that the axioms and principle of Brentano's logic are valid under this interpretation.

What does it mean, logically, to say that a term is singular, or rather, not plural? A term a is plural if it has two or more objects denoted by it, and this is true if there is a way we can distinguish these, i.e. if for some term b some a is b and some a is not b:

$$Eab \ \& \ Ea - b.$$

If there is no such term, then either there are no a at all, or there is only one. In the model given above, every non-empty term is plural by this definition. Take any non-empty term a. Then it must be a union of intervals of the form $(x, y]$. Take any such interval and take a number z within the interval, i.e. such that $x < z < y$. The interval $(0, z]$ represents a term which overlaps with the interpretation of a at least in the interval $(x, z]$, and its complement $(z, 1]$ also overlaps the interpretation of a at least in $(z, y]$. So a conforms to the requirement that it be plural. But a was any non-empty term. So all terms are plural. But Brentano's logical principles are valid in finite models as well, indeed they are valid in the empty model, which I count as a logical virtue because it means logic for Brentano is ontologically neutral, implying nothing about what there is, or indeed whether there is anything. Therefore no resources within the system of Brentano's logic can define uniqueness or singularity.

To do so, we need to make a large conceptual leap, and *quantify* terms, as indeed we did informally above in saying what we mean by plurality. Let us do so and define plurality and uniqueness:

Def. Plur	$\text{Plur}(a) \leftrightarrow_{\text{Def}}. \exists b \, (Eab \, \& \, Ea -b)$
Def. Un	$\text{Un}(a) \leftrightarrow_{\text{Def}}. \sim\text{Plur}(a)$
so	$\text{Un}(a) \leftrightarrow \forall b \, (Eab - Na -b)$

A term is thus *singular* iff it is non-empty and non-plural:

Def. Sing	$\text{Sing}(a) \leftrightarrow_{\text{Def}}. Ea \, \& \, \text{Un}(a)$

It is very interesting that such a simple everyday logical notion as "there is not more than one" should be beyond the expressive power of Brentano's straightforward system – and by implication traditional syllogistic – to define, but should require the relatively modern and sophisticated notion of quantification.

PROPOSITIONAL INFERENCES

Brentano makes a brief foray into the area of what he traditionally calls "hypothetical and disjunctive inference," which is the traditional name for those fragments of propositional inference which had come down from the Stoics and Scholastics through Kant to the nineteenth century, such inferences as Modus ponens and Modus tollens, which two Brentano gives in the respective forms (LRU, p. 223)

MPP	If A is then B is, A is / B is
MTT	If A is then B is, B is not / A is not

It is clear that Brentano did not have a large interest in propositional inference, but his idea can surprisingly be made to work. By indulging the benign fiction that judgments or sentences can be treated as designating special objects such as states of affairs, one can in fact develop within Brentano's general framework a simulacrum of propositional logic, simulating propositional conjunction and negation by term conjunction and negation respectively and turning the whole into sentences using E and N.[7] This is a whimsical exercise in anachronism, but it would doubtless have raised a smile on Brentano's lips.

PUTTING BRENTANO'S IDEAS TO WORK

In my view the combination of existential form, term conjunction and term negation that Brentano uses to capture syllogistic is by no means outdated or odd. It is true that Brentano does not venture far from his traditional basis: his is essentially a *reform* from within, not a revolution. The major developments of the nineteenth century, namely logical treatments of relations and quantification binding variables, remain beyond him. Nevertheless within its limited compass Brentano's views, simply because they so radically simplify syllogistic, are not only elegant but can form the basis of a simple modern term logic with pedagogical virtues. Without going into details,[8] with inessential additions and tidyings up, Brentano's ideas can form the basis of a natural deduction proof theory, the flavor of which is given by the short deductions above, and a semantic tree or tableau system can also be easily developed[9] and be shown equivalent to the natural deduction system. I have used such a system in intermediate logic teaching for several years, and students readily understand it. It is intermediate in complexity between propositional calculus and predicate calculus and is useful for introducing metalogical concepts. A very obvious set-theoretic semantics can be provided. Alternatively, the ideas may be developed axiomatically, piggybacking on a system of propositional logic in the way Łukasiewicz did for Aristotelian syllogistic. Obviously only one of "E" and "N" need then be taken as primitive, and oddly it seems more straightforward to take "N." The resulting system, however formulated, can be given an easy completeness proof and it is decidable by Venn diagrams. I typically introduce a standard universal term "V," read "thing," and a standard empty term "Λ," read as "nonthing" or (with caution) "nothing," and I like to call the associated axiom "NΛ" "Heidegger's Law."

If we introduce term quantification, as we did in the previous system, then the resulting section is equivalent to a kind of logic developed in the 1920s by Stanisław Leśniewski and called by him "elementary ontology." It is a natural Boolean algebra which is as strong a pure term logic as one can attain without introducing relations, and is equivalent to monadic second-order predicate logic, which is complete and decidable. So although Brentano knew nothing of modern logical developments, it says something for his logical instinct and intelligence that his ideas can be slotted smoothly into a throroughly modern and rigorous context.

BRENTANO'S INFLUENCE

Brentano railed against those "mathematical" logicians like Boole and Jevons who proposed to express all categorical propositions as equations. Ironically, psychology aside, Brentano could have done the same. Define term equivalence with Aristotle as mutual containment:

$$\text{Def.} \cong \qquad a \cong b \leftrightarrow_{\text{Def}}. \, \mathrm{N}a -b \, \& \, \mathrm{N}b -a$$

A term is empty if it is equivalent to its own contradiction

$$\mathrm{N}a \leftrightarrow a \cong a -a$$

and we can define all the categorical forms using equivalence, conjunction, and negation, for example the A form All a are b as $a \cong ab$. Of logicians contemporary with Brentano however, one in particular was close to him in his construal of categoricals using assertions and denials of existence, namely Lewis Carroll.[10] Carroll would say "a is an entity" for "There are a" and "a is a nullity" for "There are no a," and his methods of diagrams and elimination and trees employ precisely this understanding. Carroll differs from Brentano only in inconveniently retaining the existential import of A and E forms. Carroll's wonderfully ingenious and humorous sorites (or "soriteses," as he calls them) are all solvable, albeit with some labor, by Brentanian methods.

Although as far as I know neither Brentano nor Carroll influenced the other, many other logicians and logically minded philosophers were influenced, directly or indirectly, by Brentano.[11] Meinong and Husserl both studied with Brentano in Vienna and took seriously his view that logic as the tradition taught it was obsolete. Twardowski, Brentano's last important Viennese student, taught a course on the reforms of logic at Lwów, and his lectures, while rudimentary by later standards, were attended by or at least known to later stars of the Lwów–Warsaw School such as Łukasiewicz and Leśniewski. The former's resurrection of Aristotelian syllogistic, started in the 1920s and brought to fruition in the 1950s, owes much to Brentano's example in showing that modernized methods can be brought to bear on traditional forms of inference without compromising logical rigor. A logician much influenced by Łukasiewicz and like him knowledgeable about the interesting and sometimes obscure corners of its history was Arthur Prior: Prior's writings first taught me that Brentano had interesting things to say in logic. Leśniewski's ontology, as we have seen, is an extension of Brentano's ideas expressed with total rigor, and Leśniewski was aware that his system, especially in its allowance that terms may be empty or plural as well as singular, is closer in some ways to traditional logic than to the predicate calculi of Frege, Russell, and Hilbert. Finally, Brentano's concerns with such philosophical issues in logic as the form of judgment, the notion of truth, existential propositions (positive and negative), influenced Husserl, Meinong, and Twardowski and through them their pupils and grandpupils down to and including Tarski.[12] Brentano may not have been a great logician like Peirce, Frege, or Russell, but he was an astute philosopher with a thorough knowledge of the history of philosophy, and that makes his modest reforms both interesting for their time and of restrained but useful elegance.

NOTES

1. I happen to think it is, but to support that minority view would take a long argument. Like Brentano I also think the ideas and judgments in question are dated individuals (mental tokens), not abstract types or meanings.

2. The numbers refer to a catalogue of Brentano's manuscripts compiled in 1951 by Franziska Mayer-Hillebrand; the starred number is an amendment due to Thomas Binder in 1990.

3. We have to specify the language because a subject term does not have to occur first. Indeed Aristotle, the inventor of logic, in his logical treatises usually rendered the first judgment as if in English we were to say "Human belongs to all Greeks," with predicate before subject. This would have sounded as odd to Greeks as the English does to us: he did it for technical reasons.

4. Brentano considers so-called subjectless sentences in his 1883.

5. A. N. Prior, *Formal Logic* (Cambridge: Cambridge University Press, 1962), p. 166; *The Doctrine of Propositions and Terms* (London: Duckworth, 1976), p. 112.

6. I show in greater detail how to do this in P. Simons, "Brentano's Reform of Logic," *Topoi*, 6, 1987, pp. 25–38.

7. For details see *ibid*. pp. 32–4.
8. See *ibid*. p. 30.
9. For a version for a limited language see P. Simons, "Tree Proofs for Syllogistic," *Studia Logica*, 48, 1989, pp. 539–54.
10. The definitive text is L. Carroll, *Symbolic Logic* (New York: Potter, 1977).
11. See P. Simons, "Logic in the Brentano School," in eds. L. Albertazzi, M. Libardi, and R. Poli, *School of Franz Brentano* (Dordrecht, Boston, London: Kluwer Academic Publishers, 1996).
12. See P. Simons and J. Woleński, *"De Veritate*: Austro-Polish Contributions to the Theory of Truth from Brentano to Tarsk," in, ed., K. Szaniawski, *The Vienna Circle and the Lvov-Warsaw School* (Dordrecht, Boston, London: Kluwer Academic Publishers, 1989), pp. 391–442.

4 Brentano on the mind

INTRODUCTION

Brentano's writings on the philosophy of mind or descriptive psychology have a number of distinctive features, all of which are connected with his understanding of what a part of theoretical philosophy is and ought to be, with his understanding of the relation between the philosophy of mind and experimental psychology, and with the success and thoroughness of his contribution to philosophy. First, his philosophy of mind always makes use of a carefully worked out ontological framework, indeed of at least two such frameworks. Secondly, he invariably argues at some length, sometimes at very great length, for his views. Thirdly, he often takes great pains to relate his views to those of the philosophical tradition, sometimes in order to argue against these views, sometimes in order to make clear just where he is building on the tradition and just where he is departing from it. Finally, Brentano attaches great importance to the fact that the answers to even apparently unimportant or minute questions of descriptive psychology often turn out to be heavy with consequences for all parts of metaphysics and epistemology (cf. USP, p. 79, MWO, p. 39). Failure to notice subtle distinctions in descriptive psychology is often the first step in the construction of metaphysical edifices which turn although nothing turns with them. This conviction, like the role of ontological frameworks in his work, reflects the fact that Brentano was primarily a metaphysician and only secondarily a philosopher of mind.

Brentano's conception of the philosophy of mind owes much to his views about the development of experimental psychology in the last quarter of the nineteenth century. Psychology, he repeats, like many of his contemporaries, is in an immature state, it is a young science. Unlike his contemporaries, he thinks that conceptual confusions and experiments coexist uneasily within psychology. One reason for the immaturity of psychology is the fact that psychology must wait on advances in physiology. But it is the "science of the future." Although the practical activity of rooting out conceptual confusions is an important philosophical task, Brentano thought that it was best carried out by developing a theoretical, descriptive psychology which would underpin explanatory psychology, which Brentano calls "genetic psychology." The latter depends on physiology and physics, whereas descriptive psychology is "relatively free" of this dependence.[1] To say that descriptive psychology is, like explanatory psychology, a theoretical discipline is to say that it consists of a system of interconnected truths. It is not a practical discipline, a collection of truths the unity of which derives from some practical goal external to them – for example that of rooting out conceptual confusions. It is essential, Brentano argued, for descriptive psychology and other branches of philosophy to maintain contact with the natural sciences. Thus descriptive psychology does not exclude experiments.[2] Indeed Brentano devised experiments for scientists to carry out (for the great Prague psychologist Ewald Hering).

What Brentano calls "explanatory" and "genetic" psychology corresponds to what is today called empirical psychology and cognitive science; it seeks to establish empirical laws which report relations of succession between phenomena. What he called descriptive psychology corresponds to what is now called philosophy of mind or philosophical psychology. (Confusingly enough, Brentano says his descriptive psychology is "empirical" since, as we shall see, he thinks it is based on perception, inner perception [PES-E, p. 34, PES-G, I, p. 48].) Descriptive psychology consists in large measure of conceptual truths about and analyses of psychological phenomena in which classifications, the identification of the fundamental types of psychological phenomena, and claims about relations of necessary coexistence are prominent. Descriptive and explanatory questions are clearly distinguished by Brentano in 1874,[3] the labels "descriptive psychology" and "explanatory psychology" followed later.

Descriptive psychology is not only distinct from explanatory psychology it is also prior to it. For theories about the causes and effects of, say, visual perception presuppose some account of the nature of visual perception. Failure to distinguish between descriptive and genetic psychology leads philosophers and psychologists to substitute for analyses of psychological phenomena genetic and often causal claims. Thus philosophical accounts of phantasy invariably emphasize that it is an act which originates in perception (GA, pp. 58, 68). The senses are distinguished from one another by reference to the antecedents of sensory appearances or to bodily organs (GA, pp. 199–201). True or false, such genetic claims make no contribution to an analysis of the mind, to an account of the "inner kinship and difference" (GA, p. 201) between mental phenomena. Description of psychological phenomena yields exact and exceptionless laws, unlike the explanations of genetic psychology which "specify the conditions under which the individual phenomena are bound up causally" (DP-G, p. 1). Although the laws of descriptive psychology "may exhibit a gap here and there, as is indeed also the case in mathematics" "they allow and require a precise formulation" (DP-G, p. 4). One putative example of such a law is that the appearance of violet is identical with that of red-blue. Causal laws – Brentano's example is the claim that the stimulus of a point on the retina by a light-ray with vibrations of a particular frequency produces the appearance of something blue – are subject to exceptions, such as color blindness, the severing of a nerve or hallucinations (DP-G, p. 5).

The first of the two main ontological frameworks employed by Brentano is traditional in its commitments: mental phenomena and acts belong to the category of individual accidents, non-repeatable particulars which are not substances (what are today sometimes called "particularized properties" or "tropes"), their bearers to the category of substances. Brentano frequently refers to psychological phenomena in German by using nominalized infinitives which are best put into English with the help of gerunds. Thus Brentano in English talks of presentings and judgings, loving, and hating – the three fundamental types of psychological accidents. If the effect is that produced by a a list of the novels of Henry Green – the author of *Loving, Living,* and *Doting* – it has at least the advantage of clarity and eliminates the act-object ambiguities to which such expressions as "judgment" and "presentation" give rise.

This first framework is less traditional in its account of the way psychological accidents hang together – via relations of dependence and containment between accidents. Brentano's second framework

mirrors his conviction from around 1905 that the traditional category of individual accidents is empty. Rather, argues Brentano, we
are ontologically committed to substances and only to these, however richly they are qualified. In the language of the first framework,
every affective accident, every liking, loving, or pleasure depends on
some presenting or idea. In the revised version, every liker, lover, or
pleasure-feeler depends on and includes some presenter or ideator.
Since accounts of Brentano's ontological frameworks are available in
this volume and elsewhere, I shall say no more about them and simply employ the first framework, the one which is closer to ordinary
language.[4]

I shall also, for the sake of brevity, put on one side the numerous
arguments Brentano gives for his views, except occasionally when an
argument helps to understand the content of these views, although
these arguments account for an important part of the interest of
Brentano's philosophy of mind. Finally, I ignore Brentano's numerous and remarkable discussions of the history of the philosophy of
mind.[5] What remains? The meat. But even here a choice has to be
made. I omit most of the details of Brentano's account of the different objects of the mind, except where features of these objects are
used to describe mental phenomena. I omit his accounts of the ways
the mind relates to its objects – his theories of "intentionality" –
and his analyses of judgings.[6] After a survey of the main claims and
distinctions made by Brentano in his account of the mind, I consider
in some detail what he says about what he takes to be the ground-
floor and the top floor of the mind – time-consciousness and the
emotions. I then set out his accounts of the self. In view of the difficulties involved in navigating amongst Brentano's texts, changing
views, and opinionated editors, I indicate the main developments of
Brentano's views about the mind. In spite of the fact that, in 1889, he
seems to have thought that descriptive psychology was almost complete (KRW, p. ix, USE, p. 3), these developments ended only with
his death.

PSYCHOLOGICAL PHENOMENA AND INNER PERCEIVING PERSPICUOUSLY REPRESENTED

Presentings, judgings, lovings, and hatings are "psychological" or
"mental phenomena". Brentano sometimes calls these phenomena

"acts" (PES-E, p. 79, PES-G, I, p. 111) and "activities" although every mental phenomenon has a cause and so belongs to the category of undergoings (*passio, Leiden*).[7]

What are psychological phenomena? They are, first, phenomena we are aware of in inner perception. Secondly, they are phenomena which have, relate to, or refer to (*sich beziehen auf*) objects.[8] Physical phenomena, a category which Brentano takes to comprehend colors, sounds, and their ilk rather than explosions, do not have objects. And thirdly, psychological phenomena are either presentings or based on presentings (PES-E, p. 80, PES-G, I, p. 112). Finally, Brentano distinguishes between psychological phenomena and their structures, on the one hand, and psychological dispositions, for example irritability, on the other hand. Such dispositions are bound up with laws, in particular the laws of genetic psychology, and it is important not to lose sight of the relevant laws in talking of dispositions, something it is all too easy to do if one mistakenly takes dispositions to be real entities (GA, pp. 54–6).

What is the extension of the concept *psychological phenomenon*? Brentano's answer appeals initially to the different ways in which psychological phenomena relate intentionally to their objects and asserts that there are three fundamental classes: presentings, judgings, and affective-cum-volitive phenomena. Judgings come in two basic kinds – acceptings and rejectings. To judge that Jules is jubilant is for a presenting of jubilant Jules to be qualified by an accepting. To judge that Jules is not jubilant is for a presenting of the same type to be qualified by a rejecting. Later, Brentano added to the distinction between accepting and rejecting a further distinction between attributing (*Zuerkennen*) and denying (*Absprechen*) something of something. Judging, then, is not a propositional attitude. Throughout all the developments of his analysis of judging he almost always retains the claim that the presentations which provide judgings with their "matter" do not contain negation.[9] Like judgings, affective relations (*Gemütsbeziehungen*) come in polarly opposed kinds – loving and hating. But within the class of presentings no such polarly opposed kinds are to be found.

He seems to have held this view in 1869/70 and, in spite of occasional waverings, held on to it until the end.[10] However, as we shall see (in the next section), he changed his mind about what it means to say that his tripartite classification is "fundamental."

Brentano's third claim about the nature of psychological phenomena – each such phenomenon is a presenting or is based on a presenting – is a consequence of the thesis that there are just three basic
types of mental phenomena and his main claim about the relations
between these – every affective phenomenon and every judging depends on some presenting.

Brentano's first claim about the nature of mental phenomena was
that we are aware of them in inner perception. What, then, is inner
perception? And are inner perceivings not themselves mental phenomena?

We perceive both physical phenomena and the psychological phenomena "in" us. In neither case do we only enjoy presentings. In
each type of perceiving, outer and inner, we judge. But the two types
of perceiving differ so much in cognitive dignity that Brentano often
prefers to reserve the term "perception" (*Wahrnehmung*) for inner
perception.

Inner perception is the first source of knowledge for the psychologist (PES-E, p. 34, PES-G, I, p. 48). It is a piece of knowledge, an
immediate unmotivated apprehension (*Erkenntnis*) that some presented, for example intuited, real and individual entity exists. To
perceive is therefore to judge and the judgment is positive and immediately self-evident. Thus only inner perception, for example my
inner perceiving of my judging or willing, merits the name, neither
"so called external perception nor memory grasp their object with
immediate self-evidence." Inner perception is characterized by "that
immediate, incorrigible self-evidence which it alone posesses of all
types of knowledge of objects of experience" (PES-E, p. 91, PES-G, I,
p. 128). External perception does not give us the right to assume that
physical phenomena exist.[11] On the other hand, external perception
does not tell us that colors cannot exist without being presented
(PES-E, p. 93, PES-G, I, p. 130).

Similarly, in inner perception, mental phenomena are perceived as
having certain properties. But Brentano does not think that if inner
perception does not reveal something to have a certain property, then
it follows that it does not have this property. Inner perception only
"says that what it shows to us is really present, it does not say that
there are no features it hides" (EG §436, DG, p. 416). Thus, although
inner perception does not reveal psychological phenomena to be
spatial, we cannot conclude from this that they are not spatial.[12]

Is inner perception itself not a psychological phenomenon? Is inner perception, for example, of hearing a tone not just as much a psychological phenomenon as the hearing? In 1874 Brentano combines an affirmative answer to this question and his claim that every psychic phenomenon is given in inner perception in the following way:

The presentation of the sound and the presentation of the presentation of the sound form a single mental phenomenon, it is only by considering it in its relation to two different objects, one of which is a physical phenomenon and the other a mental phenomenon, that we divide it conceptually into two presentations. In the same mental phenomenon in which the sound is present to our minds we simultanously apprehend the mental phenomenon itself. (PES-E, p. 127, PES-G, I, p. 179)

When I hear a sound the sound is the "primary" object of the hearing and the hearing is its own "secondary" object:

Apart from the fact that it presents the physical phenomenon of sound, the mental act of hearing becomes at the same time its own object and content, taken as a whole. (PES-E, p. 129, PES-G, I, p. 182)

Since inner perceiving is a judging, there are no judgment-free mental phenomena.[13]

Brentano endorsed the main features of this account of inner perceiving early and late (SNC, p. 7, PES-G, III, p. 8) but changed his mind on two points.

In 1874 he thought not only that whenever a psychological phenomenon occurs a judging and so a presenting occurs, but also that an emotion must occur. He makes this claim in a passage which forcefully states what he took to be the true multiplicity of any mental episode:

Every mental act is conscious, it includes within it a consciousness of itself. Therefore, every mental act, no matter how simple, has a double object, a primary and a secondary object. The simplest act, for example the act of hearing, has as its primary object, the sound, and for its secondary object, itself, the mental phenomenon in which the sound is heard. Consciousness of this secondary object is three-fold: it involves a presentation of it, a cognition of it and a feeling towards it. Consequently, every mental act, even the simplest, has four different aspects under which it may be considered. It may be considered as a presentation of its primary object, as when the act in which we perceive a sound is considered as an act of hearing; however, it may also be considered as a presentation of itself, as a cognition of itself, and as a feeling towards itself. In addition, in these four respects combined, it is the object of its self-presentation, of its self-cognition, and (so to speak) of its self-feeling. Thus, without any further complication and multiplying of entities, not only is the self-presentation presented, the self-cognition is known as well as presented, and the self-feeling is felt as well as known and presented.[14]

Brentano subsequently abandoned the claim that every mental episode involves an affective element.[15]

Brentano's second modification of the above account of inner perceiving distinguishes between inner perceiving in a narrow sense, as above, and in a wide sense. Any account of self-evident inner perception has to deal with the objection that the inner perceptions of even the most fervent fans thereof are not concordant. Brentano thought that such disagreements stem not from inner perception as presented so far but from what he called "inner perception in the wider sense." Inner perception in the narrow sense is essentially confused although self-evident. To perceive is not to notice or distinguish or compare, it is not to apperceive. Confusion is dissipated by apperception, or noticing.[16] To notice is to judge, it is therefore not to be confused with being struck by something, which is an affective state, or with something's being conspicuous. Something can be noticed without being conspicuous. But nothing strikes us without being noticed. Being struck by something is not to be confused with attending or paying heed, which is a desire. Attending or paying heed differs from keeping or bearing in mind. Noticing admits of no degrees, unlike being struck by something and keeping or bearing something in mind (DP-E, pp. 37ff., DP-G, pp. 35ff.).

Brentano's account of apperception or noticing not only allows him to complement his account of inner perception in the narrow sense but also to give a subtle account of what is perceived and noticed or not noticed in sensory perception, in particular in the case of optical illusions (USP, passim). It is also very useful in his campaign to show that mental phenomena – but not the psychological dispositions mentioned above – are always conscious. Some of the phenomena which are said to be unconscious are merely unnoticed but conscious (PES-E, pp. 102ff., PES-G, I, pp. 143ff.).

Inner perception is not inner observation, for the latter modifies where it does not destroy its object, says Brentano in 1874. He seems never to have changed his mind on this point.[17] Is inner perceiving in the wide sense a type of inner observation? Does it modify, not the existence of its object, which is guaranteed by the inner perceiving in the narrow sense on which apperception builds, but the features of its object? It is not clear what Brentano's answers to these questions are.

Six distinctions

Inner perception in the narrow sense, we saw, yields self-evidence and is a piece of unmotivated knowledge. The distinctions *self-evident vs. blind, motivated vs. unmotivated*, like the distinctions *sensory vs. noetic, assertoric vs. apodictic, direct vs. oblique*, and the already mentioned distinction between *primary* and *secondary* objects, make up a family of six distinctions. Together with his ontological frameworks they allow Brentano to provide various perspicuous representations of the mind.

An apodictic judging is always a denying of something as impossible. An assertoric judging is an accepting or denying without any such modal moment. It is either a mere opinion (presumption) or assured (LRU, p. 112). The feature of *self-evidence* is simple and so can only be introduced by means of examples and by contrasting self-evidence with the vastly more frequent phenomenon of the blind, instinctive tendency to believe something which is typical of external perception and memory; the latter but not the former exhibits differences of degrees (SNC, pp. 4ff., 15, PES-G, III, pp. 3ff., 19–20). Both self-evident judgings and assured judgings are often called certain, but the two certainties are very different (LRU, p. 112).

A judging is motivated if and only if it is immediately caused by another psychological phenomenon and this relation of causation is perceived by the judger (LRU, p. 112). Inner perceiving is unmotivated but self-evident. Motivation and self-evidence come together in all those judgings which yield a priori knowledge. In such cases consideration of, for example, certain concepts causes a self-evident judging.[18]

Analogues of these distinctions, Brentano thinks, are exhibited in the sphere of loving and hating. There are blind, instinctive pro-attitudes but also a hating which is characterized as correct (affective self-evidence). A preference for cognition over error which is not only characterized as correct but as necessarily correct is an example of

affective, apodictic self-evidence. Similarly, there is motivated and
unmotivated hating, as when something is hated for the sake of
something else or for its own sake (SNC, pp. 42–3, PES-G, III, p. 55).
It is the contrasts between blind and self-evident judgings and between blind and correct affective attitudes which provide Brentano
with the beginnings of an account of the dynamics of the mind which
involves more than merely causal claims. For, he thinks, many of our
changes of mind are rooted in our coming to notice such contrasts
(FCE, p. 131, GAE, pp. 145–6).

Brentano's distinction between psychological phenomena which
are sensory and those which are intellectual or noetic (SNC, pp. 56ff.,
PES-G, III, p. 77ff.) is skew to his three-way division between types
of mental phenomena. In external perceiving one sees, hears, or otherwise senses a sensory object – something which is colored, a tone,
or something warm (PES-E, p. 9, PES-G, I, p. 13). Brentano follows
the tradition which says that inner perceivings of such sensings are
themselves sensory. Similarly, if such a sensing is the primary object
of memory, the latter too is a sensory act. Sensory objects, then, may
be either physical or psychological. Presentings are either sensory
(intuitions) or conceptual.[19] Brentano mentions that the secondary
object of a sensory presenting is called sensory, that of a conceptual
presenting noetic (PES-G, III, p. 58). As we shall see, some but not
all emotional episodes are sensory.

Similarly, some judgings, both acceptings and denyings (SNC,
pp. 57ff., PES, III, pp. 79ff.), are sensory. For all intuitive presentings
involve blind judging. Brentano sometimes speaks of blind judgings
or certainties as judgings which are the result of a blind instinct. But,
as Kraus (PES-G, III, p. 140 n. 21) points out, this is a merely genetic
characterization of such judgings. It is therefore preferable to say,
with Marty, that

every sensing is originally and indissolubly connected with the acceptance
of what is sensed . . . [T]he child takes to be true whatever appears to him,
instinctively and as a result of innate necessity. Closer considerations show
that this instinctive belief is simply inseparable from sensation. This . . .
sensory belief, on which . . . immediate belief in the external world rests, is
so to speak suspended by the higher cognitive activities but is ineradicable.
It is not a superposed act for one-sided separability belongs to the concept
of superposition. Rather, sensing is an act which contains two mutually
inseparable parts, the intuition of the physical phenomenon and assertoric
accepting thereof.[20]

But if Marty is right, a cardinal principle of Brentano's descriptive psychology, that every presenting of an object is independent of every judging of the same object, is wrong. Non-intuitive, conceptual presentings of an object, it is true, are independent of judgings of the same object. But a sensory presenting of an object is not independent of a judging of the same object.

To imagine is to enjoy presentings which are not the bases of judgings. What is the difference between seeing a man and imagining a man? Sensations and phantasy presentations differ, Brentano thinks, in that they have different objects, although their objects may seem to be the same. Most phantasy presentations are not intuitive but conceptual presentings with an intuitive kernel (GA, pp. 82, 83). In speaking of conceptual presentings, whether or not these are parts of judgings, Brentano often speaks of presentations of noetic objects, of concepts (PES-G, III, p. 59). But this is misleading since he does not actually think that there are concepts. It would be better to say that when we have conceptual presentations we think or operate with concepts.

Within and at the level of presentational activity we find the operation of identification – "we are able to connect the most disparate objects by way of identifications" without the intervention of any judging. Judging intervenes, however, when we compare and distinguish (PES-E, pp. 282–3, PES-G, II, pp. 146–7). In this context Brentano distinguishes between the object of a presenting and the way it is presented, its content (LRU, p. 47, ANR, p. 218) But this distinction is not prominent in his thought.

Presentings are either direct or indirect, *in modo recto* or *in modo obliquo* and thus there are different modes of presentation. Indirect presentings depend unilaterally on direct presentings; they occur whenever what is presented is presented as related to the object of a direct presenting. Thus one may directly present flowers and indirectly present a flower-lover who wants these flowers. To the different types of relations (relations of magnitude, causal relations, the relation between a boundary and what it bounds) and relation-like phenomena (the different intentional "relations") there correspond different types of indirect presentings.[21]

One basic type of sensory presenting is, as we have seen, sensing. How many senses and types of sensing are there? Although his contemporaries were already in the habit of multiplying the senses,

Brentano came to think that there are exactly three senses. The descriptive psychologist should individuate senses by reference to their objects, the sensory qualities. (If the objects of sensing do not belong to the antecedents of sensing, then this way of proceeding is open to the descriptive psychologist.) To all such qualities we apply the distinction between light and dark. Where the opposition applies in the same way we have one sense. There are three analogous applications of the opposition and within each family all the applications are univocal. In addition to the sense for colours and the sense for tones there is one other unified sense which comprehends all the so-called lower senses: the senses of touch, taste, temperature and smell.[22]

Mind, language, and society

Descriptive psychology is the foundation of genetic psychology on which depend not only logic, ethics, and aesthetics but also economics, politics, and sociology (DP-E, p. 78, DP-G, p. 76). How do we get from the mind to social, linguistic, and cultural facts? How does the mental activity studied by descriptive and genetic psychology produce complex social, legal, cultural, and linguistic structures? Brentano's answer resembles that given by Adam Ferguson and other Scottish philosophers.[23] He compares the emergence of the Roman legal system to that of a natural language; a "sort of natural selection" leads from

weak, almost structureless beginnings to the highest types of formation. The law of habit stands in for Darwin's law of inheritance and, since it involves not merely a tendency to preserve and multiply what is similar but also a tendency to produce what is analogous, does so with considerably greater perfection. (ZF, p. 58)

The expression "natural selection" should not make us overlook the fact that in the emergence of language or of a legal system choices are always being made. Should we therefore suppose that some mind oversees the emergence of language, law, or states? Or is it enough to assume that "the felt damage connected with every unsuitable disposition functioned as a powerful regulator?" (ZF, p. 58):

[W]e must imagine the process leading up to the coming into being of the state as very gradual. To be sure, each step towards it requires mental activity, but none of the innumerable participants had a picture of the eventual result . . . Perhaps an analogy will clarify the process: the analogy with the gradual evolution of speech . . . Speech evolved gradually, and innumerable people contributed to its construction, yet here again they did not do it as builders work on a building for which there has all along been a plan. No one had the final product in mind. Each person involved was thinking only of the next step; viz. how he and another man could attain understanding in a concrete case. (FCE, p. 366, GAE, pp. 399–400)

TIME-CONSCIOUSNESS

Brentano's thoughts about time-consciousness in presentations of physical phenomena went through at least four stages.[24] The first account was developed in lectures at Würzburg between 1868 and 1870. "A person who affirms something as past or future," runs Marty's summary of Brentano's lectures, "affirms the same matter but the type of affirmation is in each case different." But Brentano's assumption that present, past, and future are three discrete types of judgment had as a consequence, he thought, that time cannot be a continuum. His second account of time-consciousness, developed between 1870 and 1894, therefore locates time-consciousness within the matter of presentations.[25] Marty summarizes the view as follows:

If you have a presentation of this pencil that I am now moving around in a circle, you do not merely have a presentation of it as at a point (for then you would have a presentation of it at rest), rather you have a presentation of it as being situated at different points on its path, but not as simultaneously so situated (for then your presentation would be of a body as long as the stretch through which the pencil moves) but rather you have a presentation of it as having been at various points on the stretch longer and longer ago. And, to be sure, that the body was there longer and longer ago is something that is, in a peculiar way, *intuitively* present to you. This intuition is a thing pertaining to a peculiar activity of the imagination (*Phantasie*), but not an activity of the imagination in the usual sense of the word, for the latter is not really original, but is productive only through experiences and acquired dispositions; in the presentation of the past, on the other hand, we have something that is *absolutely new*, for which there is no analogue whatsoever in experience . . . Brentano therefore called this activity of the imagination *original association* in contrast to acquired association.[26]

This innate original association Brentano calls "proteraesthesis." Now Marty's account of Brentano's analysis is only a first approximation. Brentano does not think that a moving pencil can be the object of a sensory presentation for it is not a physical phenomenon (which, for Brentano, as we have noted, are colours, sounds, and their ilk). Furthermore, Marty's account here leaves open the question what the object of a presentation of that object as past might be. Brentano seems to have thought at this stage that the attribute of being past is an absolute attribute of a physical phenomenon. It is a temporal determination of, for example, a tone (PES-E, p. 135, PES-G, p. 190). Since intuitive presentations are always of what has or belongs to the same temporal types and since the real temporal types change continuously, what it is for a physical phenomenon to be present and what it is for an event which lies behind the veil of appearances to be present must be two very different things. For the scientific hypothesis of the real world which is to explain the succession of physical phenomena is the hypothesis of a world which develops in a direction Brentano calls time-like (*zeitähnlich*).[27]

Around 1894 Brentano locates time-consciousness once again in modes of judging but allows the temporal modi to form a continuum.[28] In 1905 and 1911 Brentano formulates his fourth account of time-consciousness. He locates it once again in presentations but not, as before, in their objects. Rather, he now thinks, every presentation has a temporal mode and such modes are always modes of presentation.[29] One reason Brentano gives for rejecting the view that the primary objects of presentations have temporal determinations is that it is as big a mistake to think that past and present are differences of objects as it is to think that existence and non-existence are real attributes. He formulates his fourth account of time-consciousness as follows:

If we hear a series of sounds . . . the same sound . . . appears to us first as present, then more and more as past, while new things appear as present whose presentation then undergoes the same modal alteration. (PES-E, p. 279, PES-G, II, p. 143)

The predicate "– appears as present" is too close for comfort to the locution used by Marty to describe time-consciousness as bearing on the objects of presentation ("an object is presented as past"). Brentano's new analysis is perhaps best formulated by saying that the objects of presentations are presented-past, presented-present or presented-future.[30]

One consequence of the fourth view, which Brentano embraces, is that our only awareness of differences in temporal modes of presentation is in inner perceiving.[31]

What is the structure of these presentings in which objects are presented-past and presented-present? Toward the end of his life Brentano claimed that this structure is a special case of the type of structure, introduced above, which is peculiar to those complex presentings in which indirect presentings depend on direct presentings. "Every temporal past-mode or future-mode belongs . . . to the oblique modes."[32] A presenting in a future mode or a presenting in a past mode depends on a direct presenting in a present mode:

> If we say of something that it was a year ago, then we do not in the proper sense accept the event, we accept rather presently existing things as existing one year later than it, and then we may also say that we acknowledge the event as having been a year ago. When something is presented as past or as future it is therefore a matter of its being presented not *in modo recto* but *in modo obliquo*. And everything that holds in general of something presented *in modo obliquo* holds therefore of it, too. (STC, pp. 131–2, RZK, p. 156)

The admission of different indirect modes of presentations and thus of complex modes of indirect-cum-direct presentation and, in particular, the introduction of indirect temporal modes of presentation mean that there are more ways of being psychically related than the three originally envisaged by Brentano. Indeed the "continuous manifold" of temporal modes of presenting infects and so multiplies the modes of judging and of the movements of the heart built on these presentings (PES-E, p. 328, PES-G, II, p. 222). Nevertheless, he points out in 1909, his original three-fold division retains its "preeminent import" because there is no psychic relation to an object without one or more of these three ways of being related and because it is always possible by introducing fictions to treat all our psychological activities as belonging to one of the three basic classes.[33]

Brentano's account of time-consciousness is an account of what he takes to be the ground-floor of the mind. The combination of direct and indirect presentings he appeals to there is also prominent in his account of the first-floor of the mind, our awareness of space, sensory qualities and the spatial centre of of sensory fields in sensory perception. To visually perceive colored regions is to enjoy a direct presenting of a spatial point and an indirect presenting of a colored object "as something from which this point stands apart in a certain direction and to a certain extent" (STC, p. 166, RZK, p. 198; cf STC, p. 97, RZK, p. 117).

EMOTIONS

In his *Psychology*, Brentano notes that language suggests that certain emotions relate to objects – we say we are sad or upset about this or that. In such cases emotions "relate to what is presented in" the presentation they are based on (PES-E, p. 90, PES-G, p. 126). In other words, the intentionality of emotions is inherited from that of their bases, presentations and, in some cases, judgings. Thus remorse, pain, and fear differ in virtue of the temporal modes of their underlying presentations, and positive emotions based on the presenting of some future good fortune will vary as this good fortune is judged to be certain, uncertain, or probable.[34] Because emotions depend unilaterally on presentings and judgings we can conceive of a creature which enjoys presentations and judgments but no emotions (PES-E, p. 267, PES-G, II, p. 128).[35]

Brentano also says that every movement of the heart (*Gemütsbewegung*), or emotion, is a mental phenomenon and gives as examples: joy, sorrow, fear, hope, courage, despair, anger, love, hate, desire, act of will, intention, astonishment, admiration, contempt (PES-E, p. 78, PES-G, I, p. 112,). There are differences between these phenomena, in particular between, say, sadness, and acts of the will but these differences are not as great as the differences between what Brentano calls the class of emotions, on the one hand, and all other psychic phenomena, or between presentation and judgment (PES-E, pp. 235–8, PES-G, II, pp. 83–6).

The class of emotions is unified by a character they all display in their directedness toward objects. In every case there is an accepting or rejecting. Such emotional accepting or rejecting is analogous to the two modes of judging, accepting and rejecting. And Brentano argues that someone who emotionally accepts (rejects) something will, because of this, accept judgmentally its goodness (badness) or value (disvalue). Indeed he thinks that emotionally accepting, attributing

value, and value are related to one another in much the same way
in which judgmental accepting, attributions of truth, and truth are
related to each other.[36]

Not only is every affective phenomenon a case of emotional ac-
cepting or rejecting, it is also a case of loving or hating – a claim
Brentano thinks ordinary language just about allows him to make
(PES-E, p. 246, PES-G, II, p. 98).

Members of the class of emotions differ from one another with
respect to the way they relate to their objects, with respect to the
presentations and judgments they are based on, and in their strength.
A further difference, as we have already seen, is that between loving
or hating something for its own sake and loving or hating something
for the sake of something else (KRW, p. 144, USE, p. 149). Emotions
also differ by having a distinctive hue or coloration (Färbung). The
existence of such qualitative differences sets limits to how much can
be communicated by definitions in this area. But Brentano has great
faith in the project of defining the different emotions by reference to
their underlying bases, provided the definitions take into account the
different oppositions between affective phenomena and differences
of strength.[37] The existence of qualitative differences amongst emotions also entails that there are differences in the way qualitatively
different emotions relate to their objects, differences which do not
affect the claim that such ways have a common character (PES-E,
pp. 250ff., PES-G, II, pp. 104ff.).

Oppositions, Brentano says, "pervade" the class of emotions
(PES-G, II, p. 102, PES-E, p. 248). He mentions joy and sorrow, hope
and fear, desire and aversion, and willing and not-willing.[38] In a note
Kraus says that not-willing, "Nichtwollen," "is not to be understood
as the negation of willing but as a willing that something not exist"
(PES-G, II, p. 290 n. 8). Certainly, Brentano is not here distinguishing
between willing and not-willing. But if willing is to enjoy the polarity which pervades the class of emotions then, in referring to not-
willing, Brentano must have in mind a psychological phenomenon
with its own conative coloring. If Kraus's interpretation were correct
the distinction between willing and not-willing would be a distinction of content. What Brentano has in mind is, rather, a distinction
between conative pro and contra attitudes, for example, striving for
and striving against, or shunning, between willing for and willing
against (as his English translator says) and not a distinction between

contents. This distinction resembles the one he makes between desire and aversion.[39]

Preferring

All the examples of emotions mentioned so far may occur as relations between a subject and the object of his emotion. But in the
Psychology Brentano mentions a phenomenon which always relates
a subject and two objects – "I can say that I love one thing more
than I hate another" (PES-E, p. 252, PES-G, II, p. 107). This is the
phenomenon he came to call preferring (*Vorziehen, Bevorzugen*).[40]
Preferring, unlike "simple loving," is relational; there is simple and
relative loving. Preferrings may themselves be the objects of a preferring (KRW, pp. 143ff., USE, pp. 148ff.). So may other emotions – we
prefer joy to sadness (KRW, pp. 20ff., USE, pp. 21ff.). One of his more
important claims is that simple loving and "preferring which does
not turn into genuine wishing" hold of their objects "in a certain
abstraction from circumstances." Wishing and wanting, by contrast,
take such circumstances into account (KRW, p. 151, USE, p. 157).
Preferring is a much more fundamental phenomenon than willing,
deciding, and choosing because the objects of preferrings may lie
outside our powers (FCE, p. 200, GAE, p. 218). A related distinction which Brentano sometimes makes is that between preferrings
in general and "practical preferrings, that is, acts of choice" where
"choosing is preferential willing."[41]

Brentano seems to have changed his mind about the emotions
as a result of asking himself two questions: What is the relation between pain and love? Do emotions vary in strength? These two problems are aspects of the question whether, and in what sense, higher,
"spiritual" emotions differ from lower, sensory or vital emotions.

Affects

The unified family of affective and conative phenomena is a family
of what Brentano often calls "*geistige*" or spiritual phenomena or
acts. These are not sensory phenomena. There seems, then, to be
no place for sensory pleasure and pain. Furthermore, one very common assumption about such pains and pleasures makes them out to
be psychological phenomena which have no objects, which are not

intentional. This is incompatible with Brentano's view that to be psychological is to be intentional.

Brentano's first attempt to deal with these problems is to be found in his *Psychology*. Each emotion is based on presentations. It is tempting to think that "the lowest feelings (*Gefühle*) of pleasure and pain" do not belong to the same category as joy, sorrow, fear, etc. because they seem to be based on no presentations. But appearances are deceptive. When pain or pleasure are caused in us by tickling, burns, or cuts we have, Brentano argues, feelings based on a presentation of a physical phenomenon with a spatial determination and the object of the feeling is the object of the presentation. We are misled by the fact that we call the physical phenomenon which occurs with the pain-feeling a pain, as when we say we feel pain in one leg.[42] But not every pain or pleasure has as its object a physical phenomenon. If I "hear a harmonious sound, the pleasure which I feel is not actually pleasure in the sound but pleasure in the hearing."[43] This last claim illustrates what Brentano's heirs like to call "*Funktionsfreude*," joy or pleasure in activity rather than in an external object. The claim itself will be rejected by Brentano, although it contains the basic idea of his subsequent thoughts on higher and lower emotions.

Brentano's second attempt to deal with the relation between higher and lower affective phenomena is to be found in a theory set out in 1907. The new theory makes use of Brentano's new account of sensing. "Sensory pleasure (*Lust*) and spiritual agreeableness (*Wohlgefallen*), sensory pain and spiritual disagreeableness" do indeed have a "common character":

sensory pleasure is an agreeing, sensory pain a disagreeing, which are directed towards a sensory act to which they themselves belong. (USP, p. 237)

Brentano's sensory pleasures and pains consist of an act of sensing and a spiritual attitude toward this sensing. To feel pain is to sense and to hate this sensing. But what sort of sensing is involved in pain? What is its object? And how exactly are the sensing and the being disagreeable or hating thereof related?

As we have already seen, Brentano thinks there are exactly three types of sensing. The sensing peculiar to pain is sensing of the third kind, its objects are tactile, taste and temperature qualities. Sensing has both:

a primary and a secondary object. The first is something which is sensory and qualitative, the second is the act of sensing itself which always relates to itself via a presenting and in a self-evident judgement of accepting, and which sometimes relates to itself emotionally. This last case occurs in sensory pleasure and pain and makes the relevant sensing acts, as true affects, differ from other other sensing acts. (USP, p. 237)

Thus once again Brentano is relying on the idea that an act can have itself as an object in many different ways. Brentano rejects two common views:

Not only are pleasure and pain not sensory qualities, they are not psychological relations which would have sensory qualities as objects *in modo recto*. (SNC, p. 59, PES-G, III, p. 80)

If pain were a sensory quality which we sense, then, given Brentano's view that it does not follow from my sensing a physical phenomenon such as a color that there is a color I see, we should expect that my sensing a pain does not entail that there is a pain. This would be an unwelcome result for Brentano since he believes that "we grasp the real existence of pleasure and pain with immediate certainty" (SNC, pp. 16, 59, PES-G, III, pp. 21, 80). But, as we have seen, the sensing of the third kind which is essential to pain is presented and accepted with self-evidence, as is also, we may add, this sensing and the spiritual anti-attitude toward it.

Brentano's new account of what it is *to have a pain* in one leg, then, fits and uses many of his main claims about the mind. But what is involved in having a pain *in one leg*? As we might by now expect, Brentano says that a sensing which finds itself to be spiritually disagreeable has as its direct object, sensory qualities, and as its indirect object, spatial determinations (SNC, p. 59, PES-G, III, p. 81).

Is it true that sensory pleasure and pain involve only sensing of the third kind? Brentano points out that he had not made this restriction in his *Psychology* (USP, p. 239), indeed, as we have seen, he there claims that there is a pleasure in hearing, and the restriction may seem to be obviously false. As Brentano points out, it seems to be incompatible with the facts of enjoyment of music and paintings, not to mention the reaction of the bull to a red cloth. But, he argues at length:

sensations with an emotional character are not given in seeing and hearing themselves but in co-sensations (*Mitempfindungen*) which regularly accompany seeing and hearing in normal cases. (USP, p. 100)

The ability to hear is one thing, the ability of the man who has a musical ear a very different thing (cf. USP, pp. 235ff.). Sensings of the third kind, for example of tactile qualities, which are agreeable or disagreeable may be produced by seeing and hearing. Only in this way do seeings and hearings yield sensory pleasure and pain. But they may, of course, also be the basis for non-sensory pro- and contra-attitudes simply in virtue of their objects. On occasions, Brentano seems also to allow that conceptual activity itself, rather than its objects, may be the objects of non-sensory emotions and he certainly thinks that conceptual activity directed to external objects – good news – can produce agreeable and disagreeable sensings of the third kind. In all these cases, tremblings and other ways of being literally moved, of resonating, are effected. We should, Brentano says, recognize in such "sensory redoundings" "one of the most wonderful teleological features of the order of our psychic life" (KRW, pp. 156–7, USE, pp. 163–4).

Preferrings and emotional intensity

In his *Psychology* Brentano thinks that the relation I may stand in of hating one object more than some other object should be understood in terms of differences of intensity between my simple affective attitudes to these objects. This view, Brentano came to think, is wrong. "More" does not refer to a relation between the intensities of two acts.[44] But he continues to speak of preferring as a type of comparison (KRW, p. 143, USE, p. 148).

THE SELF

Are you, the reader of this sentence, simple or complex? Are you one or many?

You are now visually perceiving physical phenomena and so are aware of your visual perception and you are probably also grasping certain thoughts with interest or boredom and hearing physical phenomena. So you are not, Brentano thinks, simple. Might it be the case that each of the mental phenomena just mentioned belongs to three or four different yous? No. The interest or boredom just mentioned depends on the thinking just mentioned. If each had a different bearer, then the interest or boredom would not depend on the thinking mentioned. Similarly, only the unique bearer of the visual and the auditive perception can compare these, note that that these are numerically distinct phenomena. Thus you are, Brentano thinks, one, complex thing or real unity, and it is your inner perception which reveals to you that this is the case. He also says, rather puzzlingly, that you are, like the mental phenomena mentioned, a psychological phenomenon. The real unity you are at the moment the three phenomena occur does not contain past psychic phenomena. In his *Psychology* he leaves open the question whether the continued existence of the self is the enduring of one and the same unified thing or a succession of different things.[45]

The claim that your psychological acts at a time present themselves to you as a unity which is not the unity of a bundle (PES-E, pp. 96–7, PES-G, I, pp. 135–6) but that of a "unified whole" (PES-E, p. 155, PES-G, I, p. 221) was one Brentano continued to endorse though his arguments in favor of this "unity of consciousness" and his understanding of this unity changed.[46]

You, the reader, knew all along that you are exactly one thing and not two, or three. And Brentano agrees with you. In perceiving physical phenomena produced by the words you are reading you innerly perceive the identity of the inner perceiver and the seer you are: "nothing can be perceived as merely factual with immediate self-evidence which is not identical with the perceiver . . . [No] individual can perceive more than one individual with immediate self-evidence, and this is his self."[47] This might suggest that you know who you are, which thing you are. But, according to Brentano, you do not know which thing you are. Your inner perception reveals that you are exactly one substance but not which substance. It does not, we might say, reveal who you are. If each of us is a man, a substance, with many psychological properties, what makes each such substance the individual man he is is not revealed in inner perception:

If we recognize, however, that in this case [we have a sensory inner perception of ourselves as seeing and hearing beings] we have only a single thing as object, then this also shows that we perceive that thing only in general, because we can, without contradiction, imagine that another being has the very same determination as the being that we perceive. Thus someone else could have the same visual presentations, the same sensory judgements and sensory affects. So these things do not constitute the individuality of that which we inwardly perceive.[48]

All presentings, conceptual or not, Brentano came to think,[49] are general, all "determinations" are "universal" and so presentings do not present us with anything "as individualized" although, as we have seen, they can present us with exactly one object.[50] Since not all general presentations are conceptual, we should not say that Brentano thinks that all presentation is descriptive. But since he thinks that all types of access to selves are general and shareable, we may attribute to him the view that such access has a public dimension. Its private dimension is due to the fact that you cannot perceive any object other than yourself with immediate self-evidence.

In 1874, Brentano's theory that a self at a moment is a unified whole rather than a mere collective was part of his metaphysical theory that a collective is not a substance or thing. He later came to accept that a collective is a thing or substance.[51] It is in his metaphysics also that we find his arguments to show that that "in us which thinks" – that is, sees, hears, judges, loves, desires, etc. – "is not anything material (*Körperliches*) and must be assumed to be spiritual" (EG, §436, DG, p. 428, cf. STC, p. 92, RZK, p. 111; contrast TC, p. 119, KL, p. 158). For, as we have seen, Brentano does not think that inner perception can help us in this connection. It neither reveals mental phenomena to be spatial nor reveals them to be non-spatial.

THE AFTERMATH

The Brentano-effect, inside and outside philosophy, was so great that it is still difficult to appreciate its proportions.[52] A brief look at some of the reactions, witting and unwitting, to claims of Brentano may help to bring these into sharper focus. We may distinguish, first of all, between philosophers who share Brentano's theoretical ambitions for a philosophy of mind and those who reject these.

Some three-quarters of a century after the publication of Brentano's *Psychology* another extraordinarily influential Austrian account of the mind, Wittgenstein's *Philosophical Investigations*, also referred to the apparent immaturity of psychology and the combination of experimental methods and conceptual confusions which characterize it. But, although Wittgenstein, too, attaches great importance to description (to "seeing" the details) and to its priority with respect to explanation and theories, he did not conclude that empirical or experimental psychology required a grounding in a thoroughly theoretical philosophy of mind. It is, nevertheless, a striking fact that many of the views criticized by Wittgenstein and also many of the views he espoused are to be found in the writings of Brentano and his heirs (and hardly anywhere else): endorsement and rejection – of the view that there are private mental objects, of the view that internal relations are normative, of the view that seeing and seeing-as are concept-free, of the view that there are true, synthetic a priori propositions, of the views that there are "spiritual" acts of meaning and ideal propositions, of the view that words are fundamentally tools, of the view that justification may be defeasible and non-inductive, of the view that the traditional questions of epistemology undergo a drastic change of aspect once the pervasive phenomenon of primitive certainty is recognized.

Of the twentieth century philosophers who shared Brentano's ambitions for a purely theoretical philosophy of mind, his pupils and heirs modified Brentano's analyses almost beyond recognition, whereas more recent philosophers have returned to central claims of Brentano.

The intense discussions of Brentano's anatomy of the mind by his pupils and heirs led to modifications and revisions which mainly concerned Brentano's taxonomic claims and, to a lesser extent, his views about the type of analytic framework suitable for analyzing the mind (as opposed to its objects). Brentano's views that time-consciousness is the ground-floor of the mind and emotions its top-floor were both taken over by his heirs but extensively modified.

Perhaps the major source of the revisions was the endorsement by so many of Brentano's scions of three types of object never countenanced, except in passing, by Brentano: *states of affairs* (Husserl, Meinong), understood as wholly distinct from the propositional contents representing them, *Gestalt-qualities* (Ehrenfels) and mind-independent *values* (Husserl, Meinong, Scheler). Since Brentano's students agreed with him that fundamental differences in objects have consequences for the analysis of the acts of which they are the objects, they were led to new analyses of such acts. In particular, to introduce the category of propositional attitudes – a category at the centre of the writings of Bolzano and Frege – under which they brought not merely judging and belief but many other "acts" and attitudes. Thus Ehrenfels and Meinong rejected the thesis that emotions and the will belong on the same continuum because it is incompatible with the fact that although some emotions have things as their objects, to will or desire is to will or desire that some existential state of affairs obtains. Husserl put forward what has become a more popular view: to will or desire is to will or desire that some state of affairs, existential or not, obtains. Similarly, Husserl's view that to see is sometimes to see a thing or a process and sometimes to see that a state of affairs obtains amounts to a substantial revision of Brentano's analysis of seeing, not just because it introduces propositional seeing but because it endorses naive realism about visual perception. Stumpf's influential distinction between functions and acts extends Brentano's distinction between sensory and noetic phenomena but also upsets it by introducing the distinction between propositional and non-propositional acts.

Brentano's emotions have as objects the purely natural objects represented by their cognitive bases and value is understood as a feature of a relation between emotions. Husserl, Meinong and many others came round to the view that emotions directly present mind-independent values of which natural entities are the bearers. Other notable revisions are the arguments of Geiger and Scheler that affective phenomena, both episodes and enduring non-dispositional sentiments, may be unconscious;[53] the rejection, by the early Husserl and Scheler, of the view that inner perception is infallible; the rejection by Stumpf and Husserl of the view that all psychological phenomena are intentional.

Other objections concern important details: Ehrenfels denies that love in the narrow sense of the word, personal love, is any sort of episode; it is, rather, a disposition. Geiger denies that opposition is as pervasive in the affective sphere as Brentano seems to have thought, enjoyment (*Genuss*), he argues, has no opposite.

Brentano, like the grandfather of Austrian philosophy, Bolzano, produced a large number of analyses, logical and psychological. As we have noted, in Brentano's case, there is sometimes a surprising difference between *analysandum* and *analysans*. Thus Brentano tells us that propositions which seem to be about psychological episodes are really about thinkers and about nothing else and that pains are not the non-intentional states they seem to be. This feature of his analyses seems to have led the phenomenologists to distrust analyses which depart very far from appearances.

Although Brentano's structural frameworks, his assumptions about accidents and modal mereology, survive in different forms in the works of his followers, one aspect thereof was to be thoroughly revised. As we have seen, Brentano thinks of a person's psychological complexity at a time as an onion: a hating may be built on a judging which is built on a presenting. One exception to the onion structure is provided by the relation between, say, a presenting of a physical phenomenon and the inner perceiving of this presenting. Here we have something like a relation of reciprocal dependence. Relations of reciprocal dependence play a central role in the philosophies of mind of Husserl, Meinong, and their heirs. Husserl, for example, argues that every token propositional content must be associated with a "mode" which is either a judging or a supposing and that each of these modes requires some propositional content.

This revision of Brentano's framework is intimately connected with what is, together with the introduction of propositional attitudes, the most important revision of Brentano's taxonomy. According to Meinong, there corresponds to every type of "serious" act a non-serious counterpart, a determinate type of imagining or phantasy. Thus to seeing, judging and hating there correspond make-believe seeing, make-believe judging (supposing) and make-believe hating. Husserl and Witasek defend less ambitious versions and variants of the same thesis.

One intriguing feature of the development of descriptive psychology is the way in which theses endorsed early and then rejected by Brentano come to be adopted by his heirs. Thus Scheler revives the doctrine of an inner sense[54] and Brentano's view that in a psychological phenomenon of any type all the other types are co-instantiated. Husserl's oh so appropriately baptized doctrine of the noetic–noematic correlation is structurally similar to Brentano's first account of intentionality. Many of Brentano's heirs, including the early Husserl, rejected his view of the self. But Husserl came to endorse an egology and was followed in this by his many pupils.

Through all the more or less radical transformations of Brentano's analyses of the mind, the vivisections of Husserl, Pfänder, and Scheler, still unfortunately the most thorough descriptions of the mind we possess, it is possible, for those with ears to hear, to discern variations on the Austrian melody initially composed by Brentano.

Much recent work on the nature of the philosophy of mind has taken to heart views like those of Brentano rather than those of Wittgenstein. And even Brentano's specific leads, rather than the modifications of Brentano's theses due to his pupils and heirs, are once again in favor.

Thus Brentano's account of mind combines two now popular claims. The mind is representational and its intentionality is *de se*. Every psychological phenomenon represents according to Brentano's account of inner perception, either itself or something else. Thus Brentano combines the view that there are very many distinct qualia, for example the distinctive hues of different emotions, with representationalism. On his early view, every mental phenomenon contains a representation or presentation of itself. On his later view, every sufferer and lover, for example, is an internal presenter of himself.[55]

All my external perception and all my conceptual thinking is, Brentano thinks, in the first instance, about me. For all such mental activity contains an inner perceiving by me of myself albeit an inner perceiving which involves no direct acquaintance with myself. So what happens when I think of a stone lying in a street in Peking (the example is Brentano's – SNC, p. 7, PES-G, III, p. 7)? Somehow the general concepts employed in such a thinking must be combined with my general grasp of myself. How? At least two remarkable contemporary theories of intentionality provide answers to such questions which are compatible with Brentano's claim that all intentionality is primarily *de se* and secondarily *de re*.[56]

Nevertheless, were Brentano to cast an eye over contemporary philosophy of mind and cognitive science, although he would doubtless salute its severely theoretical attitude, he would also regret that the task of describing the mind has been taken seriously only by those, such as the heirs of Heidegger and Wittgenstein, who have no theoretical goals.[57]

NOTES

1. On psychology's youth and future and its relation to physiology, see PES-E, p. 80, PES-G, I, p. 113, GA, p. 42, ZF, p. 93, PES-E, p. 25, PES-G, I, p. 36, GA, p. 37.

2. MWO, pp. 6, 32, 35. Brentano believes the methods of the natural sci-
    ences, the human sciences and philosophy resemble each other (ZF,
    35ff., 75ff.).

3. PES-E, pp. 7, 44–5, PES-G, I, pp. 10, 62–3.

4. See Arkadiusz Chrudzimski and Barry Smith in this volume; Kevin
    Mulligan and Barry Smith, "Franz Brentano on the Ontology of Mind."
    Critical Notice of F. Brentano "Deskriptive Psychologie," *Philosophy
    and Phenomenological Research*, 45.4 (1984), pp. 627–44; Barry Smith
    and Kevin Mulligan, "Parts and Moments: Pieces of a Theory," in
    B. Smith, ed., *Parts and Moments: Studies in Logic and Formal Ontol-
    ogy* (Munich: Philosophia, 1982), pp. 15–109.

5. On the relation between the philosophies of mind of Aristotle and
    Brentano, see Barry Smith, "The Soul and Its Parts. A Study in Aristotle
    and Brentano," *Brentano–Studien*, 1, 1988, pp. 75–88.

6. See the essay by Charles D. Parsons in this volume.

7. Cf. SNC, p. 11, PES-G, III, pp. 13ff. For surveys of Brentano's philos-
    ophy of mind, see David Bell, *Husserl* (London and New York: Rout-
    ledge, 1990), ch. 1, Chan-Young Park, *Untersuchungen zur Wertthe-
    orie bei Franz Brentano* (Brentano-Studien-Sonderband, I (Dettelbach:
    Röll, 1991); Alfons Werner, *Die psychologisch-erkenntnistheoretische
    Grundlagen der Metaphysik Franz Brentanos* (Hildesheim: Franz
    Borgmeyer, Münster Dissertation, 1931); Roderick M. Chisholm,
    "Brentano's Descriptive Psychology," Akten des XIV. Internationalen
    Kongresses für Philosophie, University of Vienna, 1968, pp. 164–74;
    Barry Smith, "The Soul and its Parts, II: Varieties of Inexistence"
    Brentano-Studien, 4, 1992/3, pp. 35–51.

8. KRW, p. 14, USE, p. 16; SNC, p. 41, PES-G, III, p. 53.

9. On Brentano's analyses of judgment, see Charles Parsons, this volume,
    Johannes Brandl, "Brentano's Theory of Judgement" (Stanford Ency-
    clopedia of Philosophy, http://plato.stanford.edu/entries/brentano-
    judgement/, 2000), Kevin Mulligan, "Judgings: their Parts and
    Counterparts," *Topoi Supplement*, 2, 1989, pp. 117–48, Roderick
    Chisholm, "Brentano's Theory of Judgement," in Chisholm, *Brentano
    and Meinong Studies* (Amsterdam: Rodopi, 1982), pp. 17–36. On some
    manuscripts in which Brentano toys with the idea that negation may
    belong to the matter of a judging, see Arkadiusz Chrudzimski, "Die
    Intentionalitätstheorie Anton Martys," *Grazer Philosophische
    Studien*, 62, 2001, pp. 175–214, *Intentionalitätstheorie beim frühen
    Franz Brentano* (Kluwer, 2001), pp. 62–4, 83.

10. Cf. Carl Stumpf, "Reminiscences of Franz Brentano," in ed., Linda
    McAlister, *The Philosophy of Brentano* (London: Duckworth, 1976),
    pp. 10–46, pp. 21, 37; PES-E, p. 266, PES-G, II, p. 127. Between 1902

and 1906 he was apparently tempted by the view that presentings and judgings should be collapsed into one category; see Oskar Kraus, *Franz Brentano. Zur Kenntnis seines Lebens und seiner Lehre* (Munich: Beck, 1919), p. 25, and Brentano's manuscript "Von der Natur der Vorstellung," edited and prefaced by Johannes Brandl (*Conceptus*, 1987), pp. 25–31.

11.   PES-E, p. 10, PES-G, I, p. 14; SNC, p. 33, PES-G, III, p. 44.

12.   PES-E, pp. 165ff., PES-G, vol. I, pp. 235–6, EG, §436, DG, p. 416, cf. PES-E, pp. 85ff., PES-G, I, pp. 120–4.

13.   PES-E, p. 276, PES-G, II, p. 139; SNC, p. 44, PES-G, III, p. 58. On the (im)plausibility of Brentano's account of inner perception, see David Bell, *Husserl*, pp. 21–3; Hugo Bergmann, *Untersuchungen zum Problem der Evidenz der inneren Wahrnehmung* (Halle: Niemeyer, 1908).

14.   PES-E, pp. 153–4, PES-G, I, pp. 218–19; cf. PES-E, p. 276, PES-G, II, p. 139.

15.   USP, pp. 237, 239; SNC, p. 44, PES-G, III, p. 58; PES-E, p. 276, PES-G, II, p. 139.

16.   SNC, pp. 13, 19ff., 25ff., PES-G, III, pp. 17, 25ff., 33ff.; PES-G, II, pp. 140ff.

17.   PES-G, I, pp. 40, 49, 61; Oskar Kraus, *Franz Brentano*, p. 38.

18.   LRU, pp. 107, 165ff.; FCE, pp. 67ff., GA, pp. 74ff. See, on these distinctions, Charles D. Parsons, this volume, pp. 149–174.

19.   USE, p. 15, PES-G, I, p. 111. Brentano calls intuitive presentings proper presentings. An improper presenting is a conceptual or a mixed conceptual cum intuitive presenting (GA, pp. 80, 166–7, LRU, Part I, C).

20.   This is taken from an 1895 lecture by Marty quoted by Kraus, "Towards a Phenomenognosy of Time Consciousness," in McAlister, *Philosophy of Brentano*, pp. 234–5.

21.   PES-E, pp. 280–3, PES-G, II, pp. 145–7; PES-E, pp. 324ff., PES-G, II, pp. 217ff.; LRU, p. 59.

22.   USP, pp. 157ff., SNC, pp. 45ff., PES-G, III, pp. 60ff.

23.   On the relation between Scottish philosophy and the Brentanian tradition, see K. Mulligan, "Sur l'Histoire de l'approche analytique de l'histoire de la philosophie: de Bolzano et Brentano à Bennett et Barnes," in, ed., J.-M. Vienne, *Philosophie analytique et Histoire de la philosophie* (Paris: Vrin, 1997), pp. 61–103.

24.   See Oskar Kraus, "Toward a Phenomenognosy of Time Consciousness," in McAlister, *Philosophy of Brentano*, pp. 224–39, p. 225 ("Zur Phänomenognosie des Zeitbewusstseins," *Archiv für die gesamte Psychologie*, 75, pp. 1–22, 1930, 2–3). For analyses of Brentano's different views, see Chisholm, "Brentano's Analysis of the Consciousness of Time," *Midwest Studies in Philosophy*, 6, 1981, pp. 3–16;

Chrudzimski, "Die Theorie des Zeitbewusstseins Franz Brentanos im Licht der unpublizierten Manuskripte," *Brentano-Studien*, 7, 2000, pp. 149–61, which, on the basis of unpublished manuscripts, distinguishes six phases in Brentano's thoughts about time-consciousness.

25. Marty's summary is given in Kraus, "Towards a phenomenognosy of Time Consciousness," p. 230. If we rely on the chronology of Marty, a Swiss philosopher, then what Stumpf, "Reminiscences of Franz Brentano," p. 38, calls Brentano's first theory must be his second theory.

26. Marty's summary is given in Kraus, "Zur Phänomenognosie des Zeitbewußtseins," *Archiv für die gesamte Psychologie*, 75, 1930, p. 10, cf. tr. 230; other summaries are Stumpf, "Erinnerungen an Franz Brentano," in, ed., Kraus, *Franz Brentano* (Munich: Beck, 1919), p. 136, tr. 38, Husserl 1980 §§3–5.

27. PES-G, 1924, p. 138 (PES-E, p. 98). Cf. Kraus' Introduction (PES-G, p. lxxxi, PES-E, p. 403), VPP, p. 114.

28. See Brentano's 1895 letter to Marty in Kraus, "Towards a Phenomenognosy of Time Consciousness," p. 227. Brentano also defended this view in 1899, see RZK, p. xxviii n. 15.

29. ANR, pp. 122–4; PES-G, II, pp. 143–5, PES-G, II, pp. 279–81.

30. Chisholm, "Brentano's Analysis of the Consciousness of Time," p. 9, describes the modes of the judgmental theory of time-consciousness as "judged-present, judged-past."

31. SNC, p. 38, PES-G, III, p. 52; PES-E, II, p. 329, PES-G, II, p. 224; STC, p. 100, RZK, p. 121. Two parts of Brentano's account of time-consciousness which I have had to omit are: (1) his account of the temporal relations of earlier–later than and simultaneity, the differences of "transcendent time" and our awareness of these, see STC, p. 157 n.1, RZK, p. 186 note; STC, pp. 89–90, RZK, pp. 107–8; (2) his view that although there is, as we have seen, an external proteraesthesis, there is no inner proteraesthesis, see STC, pp. 87ff., RZK, pp. 105ff.

32. ANR, p. 320; PES-G, II, p. 222, PES-E, p. 328.

33. Brentano's 1909 letter is quoted by Kraus PES-G, vol. I, p. li.

34. KRW, p. 142, USE, p. 147; DP-E, p. 159, DP-G, p. 150.

35. On Brentano's accounts of the emotions, see Chisholm, *Brentano and Intrinsic Value* (Cambridge University Press, 1986), "Brentano's Theory of Pleasure and Pain," *Topoi*, 6, 1987, pp. 59–64; Richard Müller, *Franz Brentanos Lehre von den Gemütsbewegungen*, in, ed., E. Otto, Veröffentlichungen der Brentano-Gesellschaft in Prag, Neue Folge, vol. III, Brünn/Munich/Vienna: Verlag Rudolf M. Röhrer, 1943).

36. PES-E, p. 240, PES-G, II, pp. 88–9. See the contribution to this volume by Wilhelm Baumgartner and Lynn Pasquerella.

37. See, for example, his definitions of willing (PES-E, pp. 248–9, PES-G, II, pp. 103–15, 257; FCE, pp. 200ff., GAE, pp. 218ff.; KRW, pp. 113ff., 150ff, USE, pp. 112ff., 156ff. On these, see Chisholm, *Brentano and Intrinsic Value*, pp. 22ff. On the fact that the way many words for emotions are used lack sharp boundaries, see KRW, p. 152, USE, p. 159.

38. PES-E, p. 251, cf. p. 254, PES-G, II, p. 107, cf. p. 110.

39. See also Chisholm, *Brentano and Intrinsic Value*, pp. 22–4.

40. PES-E, pp. 286ff., USE, §30.

41. KRW, p. 128, USE, p. 130, cf. Müller, *Franz Brentanos Lehre von den Gemütsbewegungen*, pp. 28–33.

42. PES-E, pp. 82–4, PES-G, I, pp. 114–19; cf. PES-E, p. 245, PES-G, II, p. 98.

43. PES-E, p. 90, PES-G, II, p. 127; cf. PES-E, p. 144, PES-G, II, pp. 203–4.

44. KRW, p. 26, USE, p. 25; PES-E, p. 286, PES-G, II, p. 151; USP, p. 80; FCE, p. 133, GAE, p. 147.

45. PES-E, pp. 155–76, PES-G, I, pp. 221–51; cf. PES-G, III, p. 81; EG, §436, DG, pp. 417ff.; STC, pp. 75–6, RZK, pp. 92–3.

46. PES-G, III, p. 82, EG, §436, DG, p. 422. A group of arguments from inner perception is given at PES-G, vol. I, pp. 221ff. These are repeated much later at DG, p. 422, cf. PES-G, III, pp. 81ff. Another such argument is given at PES-G, III, pp. 98ff.

47. PES-G, III, p. 98, cf. p. 6; cf. EG, xxxx, DG, pp. 107–8; AW, p. 53, AWV, pp. 43–4.

48. SNC, p. 60, cf. pp. 72, 79, PES-G, III, p. 82, cf. pp. 99, 112.

49. For his earlier view, cf. VE, p. 33.

50. PES-E, pp. 311ff., 363, PES-G, II, pp. 199ff., 269; TC, pp. 29, 116ff., 188ff., KL, pp. 25, 153ff., 264ff.; EG, §436, DG, p. 417. Cf. Chisholm, *The First Person* (Brighton: Harvester, 1981), ch 3. Since presentings never present us with anything as individualized, Brentano's view – see the end of §3 above – that in visual perception there is direct awareness of a centre of a visual field means that this is merely a direct awareness of a certain point not an awareness of an individualized point.

51. Contrast PES-G, I, pp. 221ff. and PES-E, pp. 341ff., PES-G, II, pp. 240ff.

52. See Smith and Mulligan, "Pieces of a Theory."

53. This sort of position is often ascribed to Freud. But Brentano's erst-while student in fact wrote: "It is surely of the essence of an emotion that we should feel it, i.e. that it should enter consciousness. So for emotions, feelings and affects to be unconscious would be quite out of the question" (Sigmund Freud, "The Unconscious", in, ed., E. Jones, *Collected Papers of Sigmund Freud*, vol. IV (New York: Basic Books, 1915).

54. Brentano accepts the doctrine of an inner sense in 1867 (PA, p. 90) and rejects it in 1874 (PES-G, I, pp. 176ff.).

55. For recent versions of the view that mental phenomena are representational through and through, see Michael Tye, *Ten Problems of Consciousness* (Boston, MA: MIT Press/Bradford Books, 2000).

56. Chisholm, *The First Person. An Essay on Reference and Intentionality* (Brighton: Harvester Press, 1981); David Lewis, "Attitudes *De Dicto* and *De Se*," "Postscripts" thereto (*Philosophical Papers*, vol. I, Oxford University Press, 1983), pp. 133–56, 156–9.

57. Thanks, for their comments, to Johannes Brandl and Barry Smith.

5   Brentano's concept of intentionality

THE INTENTIONALITY THESIS

Among Brentano's most important and philosophically influential achievements is his thesis of the intentionality of mind. To say that thought is intentional is to say that it intends or is *about* something, that it aims at or is directed upon an intended object. Intentionality is thus the aboutness of thought, the relation whereby a psychological state intends or refers to an intended object.

Brentano argues that all psychological phenomena and only psychological phenomena are intentional. He holds that to believe is to believe something; it is for a belief state, a particular kind of mental act, to intend or be about whatever is believed. The intended object of a belief is often a certain state of affairs, that today is Tuesday or that God exists, if the belief is that today is Tuesday or that God exists. The situation is the same with respect to other psychological states, such as desire, hope, fear, doubt, expectation, love, hate. To desire is to desire *something*, to be directed in thought to the object of desire, whatever the object may happen to be. In what is probably the most famous and undoubtedly most frequently quoted passage of his (1874) *Psychologie vom empirischen Standpunkt* (*Psychology from an Empirical Standpoint*), Brentano maintains:

Every psychic phenomenon is characterized by what the Scholastics of the Middle Ages called intentional (also indeed mental) in-existence of an object, and which we, although not with an entirely unambiguous expression, will call the relation to a content, the direction toward an object (by which here a reality is not understood), or an immanent objectivity. Every [psychic phenomenon] contains something as an object *within itself*, though

98

not every one in the same way. *In* presentation something is presented, *in* judgment something acknowledged or rejected, *in* love loved, *in* hate hated, *in* desire desired, and so on.[1]

The intentionality thesis holds out the prospect of understanding the essential nature of thought. If Brentano is right, then an intentionalist metaphysics of mind distinguishes psychological from nonpsychological or extrapsychological phenomena. This, unsurprisingly, is precisely how Brentano proposes to apply the concept of intentionality, which he significantly describes as "the mark of the mental."[2]

Brentano did not invent the concept of intentionality, nor was he the first to recognize the intentionality of mind. References to the intentionality of thought are made by Aristotle, who is Brentano's guiding light for so much of his empirically oriented scientific philosophy. They can also be found in the medieval tradition that took its inspiration from Aristotle's logic and philosophical psychology, particularly in the writings of Thomas Aquinas, through whose commentaries Brentano acknowledges he interpreted Aristotle, but also in the remarks on psychology of other empirically minded medieval thinkers such as Duns Scotus and William of Ockham.[3] Later, in the eighteenth century, in the quasi-empiricist common sense philosophy of Thomas Reid, the intentionality of thought resurfaces as a distinguishing feature of mind.[4]

What Brentano does in *Psychology* is partly to remind philosophers of the historical background of the intentionality thesis, while signaling his participation as the latest in a progression of intentionalists from ancient through medieval to modern times in the late nineteenth and early twentieth centuries. Yet he does considerably more in contributing to this tradition, though arguably in some ways he does not do quite enough. He elevates the concept of intentionality into what he thinks will provide a clearcut criterion for distinguishing thought from nonthought, mind from nonmind, the psychological from the nonpsychological, on the basis of an internally empirically discernible distinction between the intentional and nonintentional. We know as we experience and live through thought in first-person psychological episodes that our thinking is always about something, that it is always directed mentally toward an intended object, which Brentano regards as the distinguishing sign of the psychological.

The intentionality of mind is unequivocally an empirical discovery for Brentano. Empiricism for Brentano is not merely a matter of external sensory perception. He believes that it is equally legitimate to inquire empirically by means of inner perception, when thought examines thought in order to discern its nature. He not only identifies intentionality as the distinctive mark of the mental, but makes intentionality the foundation for an empirical scientific philosophy of mind that far surpasses anything that had previously been contemplated by Aristotle, the medieval thinkers, or Reid.

Brentano thereby sets the stage for some of the most interesting developments in later philosophical psychology, developments that are still very much at the forefront of dispute in philosophy of mind today. He laid the groundwork for his own subsequent discovery of modern phenomenology, inspiring generations of later researchers from Carl Stumpf and Edmund Husserl, to the classical phenomenologies of Martin Heidegger, Jean-Paul Sartre and Maurice Merleau-Ponty, to contemporary intentionalists. In addition, he blazed the trail for the less well-known but equally philosophically important *Gegenstandstheorie* or intended object theory of Alexius Meinong and his students and collaborators, Alois Höfler, Kazimierz Twardowski, Ernst Mally, and others, in the so-called Graz school. The implications of Brentano's intentionality thesis continue to be criticized and elaborated by modern day intensionalist logic and philosophical semantics, and by contemporary philosophical psychology and philosophy of mind of an intentionalist stamp, in which Brentano's concept of thought and its intended objects remain a focus of philosophical controversy.[5]

BRENTANO'S THEORY OF IMMANENTLY INTENTIONAL IN-EXISTENCE

In its simplest form, Brentano's intentionality thesis describes an intentional relation projected from an act of thought to its intended object. It is a kind of pointing or referential connection that singles out whatever the thought is about. The idea in general terms relates a thought to an object in this way, representing the unidirectional projection of intentional relation as an arrow:

ACT OF   ━━━━━━━━━━▶   INTENDED
THOUGHT   OBJECT OF
                                      THOUGHT

An act of thought about an apple is directed toward an apple. The
desire for a houseboat aims at or is directed toward a houseboat,
whether a particular one that is coveted, or any of a class of house-
boats, built or yet to be built, that will satisfy the desire. The belief
that God exists aims at or is directed toward God as the belief's intended object.

This model was eventually complicated by Brentano in several
ways, but even at this stage of general, relatively unsophisticated
elaboration it raises many philosophical questions. From its incep-
tion, Brentano's characterization of the intentionality of mind has
stirred doubts and difficulties, partly because of what he says, but
more especially because of what he leaves unsaid about the nature
of intentionality and the metaphysical status of intended objects.
Brentano further explains that thought involves a double judgment
and reflexive self-intending, as when we think about something and
at the same time are aware of our thinking of it. He describes this as a
"peculiar deflection" or *eigentümliche Verfleckung*.[6] The picture of
intentionality that this concept suggests for self-consciousness can
be represented in this way:

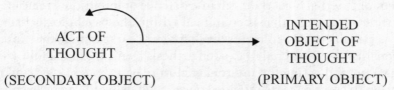

ACT OF   INTENDED
THOUGHT   OBJECT OF
                                      THOUGHT

(SECONDARY OBJECT)   (PRIMARY OBJECT)

Brentano, nevertheless, does not specify what kinds of things
intended objects are supposed to be. Worse, he appears to suggest that the intended objects of thought are actually contained
within, as belonging to, the psychological acts by which they are
intended. This is the so-called early immanence intentionality or intentional in-existence thesis in Brentano's *Psychology*. In the passage
already quoted above, Brentano explains that every "psychic phenomenon" is "characterized" by an "intentional (also indeed mental)
in-existence of an object." Brentano further articulates the relation
of a thought to its intended object as "the relation to a [thought] content" and the "direction toward an object." He is quick to qualify

the intended object with the parenthetical remark "(by which here a reality is not understood)," adding that the intention at issue is the direction toward "an immanent objectivity."

By an immanent objectivity Brentano means an intended object that is contained within an act of thought. In this sense an intended object, if not "a reality," exists in or has "in-existence," existing not externally but in the psychological state by which it is thought, as the thought's internal "content." The sense of "in" in Brentano's phrase "intentional in-existence" is thus locative rather than negative. It specifies where the intended object of a thought is to be located, rather than qualifies it negatively as nonexistent. If there were any residual question about the extent to which Brentano identifies the intended object of a thought as its content or as internal to the mental state by which it is intended, he clinches the case with further emphasis when he writes: "Every [psychic phenomenon] contains something as an object *within itself*, though not every one in the same way. *In* presentation something is presented, *in* judgment something acknowledged or rejected, *in* love loved, *in* hate hated, *in* desire desired, and so on." The intended object of love is contained immanently *in* the act of love, the intended object of a presentation or judgment is contained immanently *in* the psychological act of presentation or judgment, having an internal rather than transcendent or external objectivity, an in-existence or intentional relation to a thought content that is contained within the psychological state. It is possible, then, to represent Brentano's early immanence intentionality or intentional in-existence thesis by means of the following diagram, indicating the internal enclosure of a thought's act and relation to content as its intended object, and using the arrow again to represent the direction of intentionality from an act of thought to its intended object:

THOUGHT

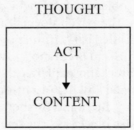

The exposition of Brentano's immanent intentionality thesis left counterintuitive implications and blank spaces to be filled in by others, creating opportunities for a variety of different intentionalist theories to flourish. All such philosophies in the Brentanian vein inherit and modify an interpretation of Brentano's intentionality thesis and carry forward his basic insight in more complete ways and in different directions.

The disowning of intentional in-existence by his students occurred virtually from the beginning, in the aftermath of the publication of his *Psychology*. Many admirers who agreed with Brentano about the intentionality of mind undertook to complete the underlying intentionalist program by addressing aspects of the thesis that they considered to be confused or inadequately developed, or with which they flatly disagreed. The immanent intentionality thesis in Brentano's early philosophical psychology is chiefly responsible for the later charges of psychologism raised against him from several quarters. Brentano afterwards rejected the immanence thesis, and turned to more neutral terminology to discuss the intentionality of mental phenomena.[7] The consequences of his early immanence thesis were far-reaching, and can be found especially in the writings of his students Twardowski, Höfler, Meinong, and Husserl.[8]

What, however, does intentional in-existence mean? What did Brentano intend by the concept of immanent intentionality? The doctrine has been the least popular of his theories in philosophical psychology, and the cause of the greatest and most productive dissent among his students and followers. The majority of later Brentanians have agreed that thought is intentional, but denied that thought is immanently intentional or that its intended objects are intentionally in-existent. And for good reason. The implications of immanent intentionality or intentional in-existence are far-reaching and mostly counterintuitive. If the intended objects are somehow internal to the thoughts by which they are intended, then it appears that no two persons can ever possibly think about precisely the same thing. This is problematic to say the least. It is unclear in that case how thoughts can ever reach beyond their own internal states in order to contact or make reference to entities in the external world, to avoid what Brentano himself referred to as a kind of epistemic idealism, "the mad dance with ideas."[9]

IMMANENT AND TRANSCENDENT INTENTIONALITY

There is unfortunately no coherent unified account of intentionality to be found in or attributed to the early Brentano. His unpublished lecture manuscripts, the 1880 *Logik-Vorlesung* and 1867 *Ontologie* and *Metaphysik-Vorlesung*, have been closely scrutinized for clues, but even these do not explain the ontic status of intended objects.[10]

Consequently, it has appeared to most commentators that Brentano's immanent intentionality thesis posits a new and highly unusual category of objects. Contrary to Aristotelian guidelines for philosophical definitions, most of the available information concerning Brentano's immanently intended in-existent objects is negatively characterized. We know that immanently intended objects are not external objects, that they are not abstract entities like properties or mathematical particulars, and that they are not nonexistent objects or ontically independent extraontologically intended objects of the sort that Brentano's students in the Graz school postulated as beyond being and nonbeing.[11]

Throughout his career, and especially in his later reistic phase after 1904, Brentano was staunchly opposed to a metaphysics of anything other than Aristotelian primary substances and inherent individual qualities. He says unequivocally that immanently intended objects involve a relation to a content. We can nevertheless assume from his later correspondence that he never considered immanently intended objects to be anything like Husserl's *noemata* or phenomenological thought contents.[12] What, then, are Brentano's immanently intended intentionally in-existent objects involving, as he says, a relation to thought content? Brentano's remarks about the nature of intentionality, especially concerning the metaphysics of intended objects in the early published and unpublished writings, are inconclusive, and suggestions about what he might have meant by the concept of intentional in-existence are speculative.

The usual account is that Twardowski, Meinong, and the Graz school adhered more closely to the master's conception of intentionality, and that Husserl, in what has come to be known as his transcendental phase after 1913, marked by the publication of *Ideen I* and the second edition of volume I of the *Logische Untersuchungen* (*Logical Investigations*), strayed farthest from the party line. In his first philosophical publication, *Philosophie der Arithmetik* (*Philosophy of Arithmetic*), which appeared in 1891, Husserl accepted Brentano's immanence thesis of intentionality almost without question, and tried to develop philosophical foundations for arithmetic from the standpoint of a Brentanian doctrine of intentional in-existence.[13] It was not until Gottlob Frege's 1894 criticism of Husserl's *Arithmetik*, in which some of the limitations of the immanence thesis were delineated, that Husserl began to mistrust the psychologism latent in Brentano's theory, and as a result abandoned Brentano's Aristotelian realism and turned toward Kantian transcendentalism throughout the next decade.[14]

In the meantime, Höfler and Meinong in 1890 published their collaborative study, *Logik*. Brentano's immanence thesis is supplanted in their analysis by a conception of intentionality in which a sharp distinction is drawn between the (non-Kantian) transcendent (but not transcendental) intentional object at which thought aims or is intentionally directed, and the thought's immanently lived-through in-existent content.[15] The received history of intentionalist philosophy credits Twardowski's *Zur Lehre vom Inhalt und Gegenstand der Vorstellungen* (*On the Content and Object of Presentations*) as the source of Meinong's distinction between the act, content, and object of a presentation, whereas Twardowski refers to Höfler and Meinong as the source of inspiration for his 1894 treatise.[16] Höfler writes in a characteristic paragraph:

(1) What we above called the "content of the presentation and of the judgment" lies entirely within the subject, like the presenting- and the judging-act itself. (2) The word(s) "object" ["*Gegenstand*"] (and "object" ["*Objekt*"]) is used in two senses: on the one hand it is used for the thing existing in itself [*an sich Bestehende*], the thing-in-itself, the actual, the real . . . to which our presentation or judgment so to speak is directed, and on the other hand it is used for that which exists "in" us psychically [*für das "in" uns bestehende psychische*], the more or less accurate "image" ["*Bild*"] of this reality, which quasi-image (more correctly: sign), is identical with the "content" mentioned under 1. In order to distinguish it from the object taken to be independent of thinking one also calls the content of a presentation and judgment (the same for feeling and will) the "*immanent or intentional object*" ["*immanente oder intentionale Objekt*"] of these psychical phenomena . . .[17]

Höfler and Meinong's study represents a significant departure from Brentano's original immanence or intentional in-existence thesis. The content of a presentation, like the intentional act, is distinguished from the object, but only the content is allowed to be immanent, to belong to or be literally contained within the presentation as a "quasi-image" of the object, while the object itself toward which a thought is intentionally directed is generally assumed to be mind-independent.

Some time in 1905, Brentano experienced what scholars designate as his *Immanenzkrise*, a crisis of increasing disaffection toward his immanence or intentional in-existence thesis of 1874. In the 1911 edition of *Psychology*, titled *Von der Klassifikation der psychischen Phänomene (On the Classification of Psychical Phenomena)*, Brentano rejects immanent objects on the grounds of the reism he had later come to embrace, an ontology according to which only individual things and particular properties exist. Brentano writes in the new Foreword: "One of the most important innovations is that I am no longer of the opinion that mental relation can have something other than a real thing [*Reales*] as its object."[18] In fact, from the very first appearance of the *Psychology* in 1874, Brentano had written explanations and polemical replies that were meant to blunt objections about the psychologism that seemed to be implied by the immanence thesis. He preserved a marked silence toward some of his unorthodox students, especially Meinong and Twardowski, as they reacted in alternative ways first to his immanence thesis and then to its denunciation. He was more vocal in his rejection of Husserl's radical departure from the course he had charted. Husserl evidently wounded his teacher with repeated and by then unwarranted charges of psychologism, and what was worse, abandoned the scientific methodology that Brentano had worked so hard to carve out in philosophical psychology.[19]

By the time Brentano repudiated the immanent objectivity thesis, however, it was already too late. The 1874 immanence theory had made an immediate negative impact on the circle of thinkers that surrounded Brentano, and they responded in a variety of ways, giving rise to object theory in Meinong and the Graz school, and to transcendental phenomenology in Husserl and his later followers. The intellects who were to develop new approaches to the problems of philosophical psychology, epistemology, metaphysics, and value theory, adapting Brentano's empirical methods in psychology, had, before his rejection of immanent objectivity in 1905–11, launched out in several different directions, recognizing that intentionality was somehow the key to the mind and the expression of thought in language and art, but also sharing a profound discomfort with a theory that seemed to seal off the mind from the world by making the objects of thought its own internal immanently in-existent contents. Some kind of transcendence and mind-independence was needed, but what exact form should it take, what new methods would it require, and what implications would it have?

IMMANENT INTENTIONALITY IN A CLOSED CIRCLE OF IDEAS

The main difficulty in Brentano's immanent intentionality thesis is that it seems to place the real world beyond the reach of thought. Intended objects of thought, which with certain qualifications Brentano also characterizes as thought contents, belong to the mental act itself, and as such are contained immanently within it. To take just one of Brentano's examples, *in* desire something is desired; thus, desire has an intentional object. But to what metaphysical categories does the desired object belong, where is it located?

Brentano's official answer is that the desired object is contained in the psychological experience of desire. Suppose I desire a glass of wine. The glass is poured and standing on the table. According to Brentano's immanent intentionality thesis, the desired wine by virtue of its in-existence is immanently contained within the mental act of desire. The dilemma for Brentano is that there either is or is not a bridge from thought to the transcendent objects of intentional attitudes. If there is no bridge, then experience is necessarily cut off from the world, as in the most radical idealism. The theory then implies the counterintuitive consequence that the objects of distinct intentional states are themselves distinct and hence never shared by any other intentional state of the same thinking subject or publicly among different thinking subjects. If there is a bridge, then the link to external reality is more economically made directly from thought to potentially shareable transcendent objects, without positing immanently intentional in-existent objects as intermediaries.

It might be said from an idealist perspective that the glass of wine is equally an immanent object, and that, just as the desired wine is included in the desire for it, so the wine glass on the table is contained in its perception. The perception of the wine for the idealist is after all nothing but another intentional psychological state, and its objects have no existence independent of their presentations. The idealist assumption is nevertheless insufficient for the immanent perceived glass of wine to be identical to the immanent desired glass of wine. The perception and the desire are distinct psychological episodes, which need not occur at the same time, and can even occur one without the other, as when one desires an unseen or nonexistent glass of wine. This implies that the immanent objects of these different mental states have different constitutive properties, so that, by Leibnizian indiscernibility of identicals, the immanent objects of the perception of and desire for a glass of wine are strictly nonidentical. The conclusion is that one cannot desire the very same numerically identical glass of wine that one perceives, remembers, despises, relishes, or eagerly anticipates, since as distinct psychological states, each of these presentations has strictly nonidentical immanent intentional objects. Nor can two different persons desire the same glass of wine, since each person's distinct thoughts will immanently contain their own distinct in-existent intended objects of desire.

This is sufficiently paradoxical to raise doubts about the plausibility of the theory, since it has the consequence that one can only desire what one desires, see, fear, or love what one sees, fears, or loves. The implications are untenable for five reasons:

1. The theory multiplies intentional objects beyond necessity, positing as many different immanent objects as distinct psychological states.
2. There is no suggested explanation of the relation if any between these objects, say, between the glass of wine I see and the glass of wine I desire or fear, though even if distinct these objects must presumably have some intimate connection.
3. Idealism in and of itself embodies an intuitively objectionable segregation of thought and external reality.
4. This version of immanently objective idealism in particular has the further paradoxical result that objects of distinct psychological states are themselves distinct, contradicting intuitive data about the convergence on or directedness of at least some different psychological states toward identical intentional objects.

5.   The immanent intentionality thesis in the idealist frame-
      work finally has the undesirable consequence that different
      subjects can never stand in intentional attitudes toward iden-
      tical objects, no two persons can desire or despise the very
      same glass of wine, for each will desire or despise the dis-
      tinct intentional objects immanently contained within their
      distinct psychological states.

It is interesting if we look at the first horn of Brentano's dilemma
to discover that the immanent intentionality theory is driven toward radical idealism. Such a consequence is intuitively problematic in and of itself, and is moreover inadequate to account for even
the most fundamental widely assumed facts about the intentionality of thought. The theory cuts off experience from contact with the
external world, and precludes the direction toward identical intentional objects by distinct psychological states of the same or different
subjects. The difficulty is not entirely the fault of idealism *per se*,
although the idealist ontology already imposes a barrier between
thought and reality, but specifically of idealism coupled with the
immanent or in-existence intentionality thesis.

The alternative is to deny idealism, positing instead a kind of du-
ality of objects. The modified realist proposal posits external mind-
independent objects, and immanent intentional objects contained
within psychological states by virtue of which mental phenomena
can still be distinguished from nonmental phenomena by the immanent objectivity of the mental. The dual categories of objects can be
related in such a way that when one desires a glass of wine, there is
an immanently desired glass of wine that refers to or stands in some
other relation to the glass of wine on the table in the external world,
so that the subject can intelligibly be said to desire not just the wine
contained within the desire, but the glass of wine on the table in the
extra-mental world that exists independently of thought.

This otherwise more satisfactory compromise is beset by difficulties that make it ultimately unacceptable. Like the idealist approach,
the modified realist proposal multiplies intentional objects beyond
necessity, positing immanent and external or transcendent objects at
least whenever thought is in some sense about existent or subsistent
objects. The relation between the two categories of objects is as mysterious here, in the supposedly improved theory, as under the idealist

assumption. Moreover, the connection linking immanent and transcendent or external objects cannot simply be referential, since reference is itself an intentional feature of a psychological state, and so presumably partakes of the same sort of immanent intentionality that we had hoped to eliminate from Brentano's early intentionality thesis. To paraphrase Brentano, *in* referring, something is referred to.

The proposed modification of the concept of intentionality still provides no outlet from within the closed circle of ideas outward to the external world. How are we then to forge a link between an immanent object of desire, perception, or reference, and the transcendent object to which in some as yet unspecified sense it corresponds? Suppose that the elusive relation could be identified, directly tying immanent to external objects, so that it becomes intelligible to say that an immanent intentionality directed toward the object the thought contains can also bear the same intentional attitude toward the corresponding external transcendent object. If this can be done, then there is no reason for assuming that there are immanently intentional objects in the first place, for then it must suffice to characterize psychological states as bearing the unknown relation directly to transcendent objects without postulating immanently inexistent objects as intermediaries.

In desiring the glass of wine, instead of assuming that there are two distinct objects, immanent and transcendent, strangely related to each other so that both are desired, in which the desire for the transcendent wine is somehow dependent on the desire for the immanent wine, it is evidently simpler and more economical to maintain without qualification that the transcendent wine is directly desired, and that there simply is no immanent in-existent wine qua intended object of desire. The theoretical elimination of immanently intentional objects has the further advantage of avoiding the need to explain the inscrutable relation between immanent and transcendent objects, and of explaining away such counterintuitive consequences as the implication that every intentional state must contain within itself its own immanently intentional objects which are never shared by distinct psychological states.

The problem of duplicating intended objects need not be decisive in overturning Brentano's early immanence or intentional inexistence thesis. Considerations of theoretical economy and the advantages of avoiding counterintuitive consequences suggest that the theory can only be salvaged by adding a few useful distinctions and assumptions. The theory must depart from ordinary ways of thinking about intentional connections between ideas and their objects if immanent intentionality is to remain the criterion of psychological phenomena. Whether it was these exact problems that eventually caused Brentano to abandon the immanent intentionality thesis is not clear and may never definitely be known. The subsequent development of intentionality theory by his students and others influenced by his early work, the reactions against the immanence or intentional in-existence thesis and the solutions their writings contain testify unmistakably to these difficulties in particular as the source of new directions in intentionalist philosophy.

THE CONTENT—OBJECT DISTINCTION AND TRANSCENDENT INTENTIONALITY IN THE BRENTANO SCHOOL

An excellent way to track the reactions of Brentano's own students to the limitations of his original immanent intentionality thesis is to be found in Twardowski's *On the Content and Object of Presentations*. In this milestone in object theory psychology and philosophical semantics, Twardowski distinguishes the mental act, content, and object of every presentation, in somewhat the way Brentano previously distinguished between mental act and immanent or inexistent object. Twardowski does not introduce a new set of philosophical concepts, but reinterprets Brentano's original terminology in a more flexible way.[20]

The concept of a psychological act in which a presentation appears is essentially unchanged from Brentano's discussion. Brentano's theory of the immanent object of an intentional attitude is revised by Twardowski and reinterpreted as the content (*Inhalt*) of the presentation. Brentano had already suggested that objects contained within the psychological states directed toward them were in some sense their contents. Twardowski goes beyond this idea by relegating the immanent component of psychological presentation to the status of content as distinct from object, offering four different arguments to prove that the content of a presentation cannot be identical to its object. The concept of the content of a presentation is already available to Brentano's immanence thesis, but from the standpoint of Twardowski's new categories, Brentano confuses the content of a presentation with its object; the content but not the object of the presentation is immanent, lived-through and contained within the psychological state. The object of a presentation by contrast is transcendent, not in the Kantian sense of a *noumenon* or representationally unknowable thing-in-itself (*Ding an sich*), but simply in the sense of being mind-independent, with an extrapsychological semantic and ontological status, whether existent or nonexistent.[21]

This is importantly different from the modified realism described in the dilemma for immanence theories. Twardowski argues against the possibility that contents could ever be objects, and therefore denies that there could be both immanent and transcendent intentional objects. That in part is his reason for distinguishing content from object, so that although content is immanent, it is in no sense the intentional object of a presentation, which on intuitive grounds remains transcendent. Nor is Twardowski's distinction faced with the problem of explaining the mysterious relation between immanent and transcendent objects, since on his account an immanent thought content mentally represents a corresponding transcendent intentional object. Twardowski nowhere openly accuses Brentano of confusing content with object, but on the contrary lauds him for the important rediscovery of the intentionality of thought. He proceeds immediately, however, to reconstrue Brentano's original categories for his own purposes, turning Brentano's immanently in-existent object into mere content, and positing mind-transcendent objects as the only legitimate intended objects of presentations. Twardowski begins with an homage to Brentano's immanence theory, linking the doctrine explicitly to its author in the footnote:

It is one of the best known propositions of psychology, disputed by almost no one, that every psychical phenomenon is related [*beziehe*] to an immanent object. The existence of such a relation is a characteristic feature of the psychical phenomena which by means of it are distinguished from the physical phenomena . . . One is accustomed on the basis of this relation to an "immanent object," which is peculiar to psychical phenomena, to distinguish between the act and content of every psychical phenomenon, and so each of them is represented under a double viewpoint.[22]

Twardowski argues that the distinction between act and content or immanent object is not enough. It is also necessary, he claims, to distinguish immanent content from transcendent object. He appeals to the authority of Höfler and Meinong's *Logik*, but the distinction occurs in a series of bold pronouncements supported only by an intuitive yearning for objectivity in psychology, and an unexamined denunciation of the idealist alternative.

The conclusion he reaches contradicts Brentano's immanent intentionality thesis. The departure from Brentano is disguised by the fact that Twardowski resituates the immanence of intended objects by interpreting them as contents, and then distinguishing, on the grounds of a perceived ambiguity or confusion, between immanent content and transcendent intended object. He denies that the intended objects of presentations are immanent, and insists for the sake of clarity that they be regarded as mind-independent:

Accordingly, one has to distinguish the object at which our idea "aims, as it were," and the immanent object or the content of the presentation . . . It will also turn out that the expression "the presented" is in a similar way ambiguous as is the expression "presentation." The latter serves just as much to designate the act and the content, as the former serves as a designation of the content, of the immanent object, and as a designation of the non-immanent object, the object of the presentation.[23]

At this stage, Twardowski has clearly renounced if not refuted Brentano's immanent intentionality thesis. What is now "the object of the presentation," in the correct disambiguated sense of the word, is independent of thought, and only the content is immanent and literally contained within the mind. Twardowski offers an apt analogy with the ambiguities surrounding the phrase "painted landscape," on the basis of a distinction between determining and modifying properties. A "painted landscape" can mean either the canvas or the terrain that has been painted, in much the same way that "object of thought" can mean either the representational thought content, or the object of which the content is an image. Twardowski's official terminology for disambiguating these aspects of presentations is to speak of objects as presented *in* (contents) or *through* (objects properly so-called) presentations.[24]

The argument acknowledges Brentano's contribution to philosophical psychology, and perhaps unintentionally also releases Brentano from an untenable position by extending the ambiguity of immanent contents and transcendent objects to Brentano's own statements about the immanence of intentional objects. If, by the immanence of intentional objects, Brentano had meant just what Twardowski describes as the immanence of content, then the threat of idealism would be removed. This, plainly, however, is evidently not what Brentano intended, and Brentano of all thinkers could hardly be expected to follow this way out. Twardowski's failure more directly to criticize Brentano is curious, given that his new distinction between content and object flatly contradicts the immanent intentionality thesis. Perhaps it is a matter of pupil–teacher deference on Twardowski's part, for he shows no hesitation in attacking lesser lights such as Christoph Sigwart, Moritz W. Drobisch, Benno Kerry, and Anton Marty, even though none of them were worse offenders against the content–object distinction than Brentano, and their content–object confusions can be traced directly to his *Psychology*.[25]

The origins of *Gegenstandstheorie* are to be found in Höfler's, Meinong's, and Twardowski's attempts to free intended objects from the closed circle of ideas implied by their immanent in-existence. By indicating a domain of existent and nonexistent mind-independent transcendent intended objects, Twardowski set the stage for the psychological, semantic, and metaphysical investigations of Meinong and the Graz school. Although an object theory domain is suggested in Twardowski's monograph, a full-fledged theory of transcendent, mind-independent existent and nonexistent intentional objects first appears in Meinong's *Über Annahmen (On Assumptions)* in 1902, and in subsequent writings.

It is useful to compare Meinong's technical terminology with Brentano's and Twardowski's. From Twardowski's perspective, part of the difficulty in Brentano's immanent intentionality thesis stems from the ambiguity noted by Höfler in Brentano's use of such philosophically loaded expressions as "object," "thing," and "presentation," a conclusion with which Meinong agrees in following when he does not actually lead the way for Höfler and Twardowski. Having broken with the content–object confusion in Brentano, Twardowski rejects the Scholastic term "immanence" in discussing intentionality, and never uses the word again after its occurrence on the first pages of his treatise to characterize the thesis he is about to correct in Brentano. Meinong, on the other hand, retains the terminology for the distinction between immanent and transcendent intentional objects, but gives the terms a decidedly Twardowskian interpretation.

Meinong's efforts at clarifying his exact use of these expressions is difficult to track, and his repeated attempts to gain precision only confuse things. As a result, one cannot but admire Twardowski's decision to set aside the terminology and proceed only with the newly clarified terms "content" and "object," and the distinction between objects as they are given alternatively in or through presentations. Meinong nevertheless appears to mean by "immanent" object what Twardowski refers to as the content of presentation, that which is part of or contained within the experience, while by "transcendent" object he intends the mind-independent objects a thought intends. In *Über Annahmen*, Meinong explains:

There exists no doubt at all as to what is meant by the contrast of "immanent" and "transcendent" object, and one is so accustomed to the use of the expressions, that one does not as a rule have occasion to worry about the participial form of the word "transcendent." But once one does, it proves difficult enough to justify this form as long as one thinks by "object" only of what is apprehended or apprehensible by means of an affirmative judgment. It is not the table or armchair that "transcends," but rather the judgment, that which in its way apprehends an actuality, in a certain manner reaching beyond itself and "exceeding" the limits of subjectivity.[26]

The important point is that although Meinong preserves Brentano's Scholastic terms "immanence" and "immanent object," he has so altered their meaning that in the object theory he develops they have no more import than Twardowski's "content." Meinong holds with Twardowski, then, that there is an immanent object contained within every psychological state, but that it is the content of the state, not the intentional object toward which the state is directed, by virtue of which the state is psychological rather than physical. The transition to Höfler's and Twardowski's way of thinking about immanent objects is so complete in Meinong's work by 1902 (perhaps even by 1890, depending on the unspecified nature of his collaboration with Höfler), that he complains in an aside that Marty's attacks against the concept of immanence in *Untersuchungen zur Grundlegung der allgemeinen Grammatik und Sprachphilosophie* (*Investigations into the Foundations of General Grammar and Philosophy of Language*) cannot apply to him, but only to those who continue to accept an outdated Scholastic concept of immanently intended objects.[27]

INTENDED OBJECTS IN BRENTANO'S LATER REISM

In his later philosophical psychology, Brentano implicitly rejects the immanent intentionality thesis, but does not follow the path of any of the splinter groups that radiated out from his original concept of intentional in-existence as their point of departure. Instead, he travels to the opposite extreme, adopting the reist view that only concrete physical objects can legitimately be intended in thought or language, and purging his technical philosophical vocabulary entirely of references to immanence and immanent objects.

The development of this final period of Brentano's thought can be seen in his correspondence with Oskar Kraus, Marty, and Stumpf during 1902–16, particularly in the collection of exchanges edited as *Die Abkehr vom Nichtrealen* (*The Retreat from Nonreality*), and the early letters to Marty assembled in *Wahrheit und Evidenz* (*Truth and Evidence*). Intended objects on a reist conception are obviously transcendent, whereby the original immanent intentionality thesis gives place in the later Brentano (as in Twardowski, Höfler, and Meinong) to direct apprehension of objects as mind-independent intentionalities.[28] In a letter to Anton Marty dated March 17, 1905, Brentano responds to Höfler's efforts to preserve the general intentionality of thought while distinguishing between the content and object of thought:

As for what you say about Höfler's remarks, the "content and immanent object" of the presentation was surprising to me . . . When I spoke of "immanent object," I added the expression "immanent" in order to avoid misunderstandings, because many mean by "object" that which is outside the mind. By contrast, I spoke of an object of the presentation, which it likewise is about, when there is nothing outside the mind corresponding to it [*wenn ihr außerhalb des Geistes nichts entspricht*].

It has never been my opinion that the immanent object = "object of presentation" (*vorgestelltes Objekt*). The presentation does not have "the presented thing," but rather "the thing," so, for example, the presentation of a horse [has] not "presented horse," but rather "horse" as (immanent, that is, the only properly so-called) object.[29]

These remarks require careful scrutiny if Brentano's exact meaning is to be understood. Brentano is not saying that he never accepted immanent objects as the intentional objects of thought, but only that he did not regard immanent objects as conceived of *as* contents, or *as* immanent intentional objects. Thus, in thinking about a horse, the immanent object of the thought is a horse, not a thought-of or presented horse.[30]

Brentano's conclusion seems to be that, phenomenologically speaking, when thinking about a horse one simply thinks about the horse, not about the horse *as* thought of – the horse itself, not the presented horse or horse as presented. This part of his clarification agrees fully with common sense, but it does not help to explain how a flesh and blood horse can belong immanently to a psychological state as literally existing within the thought. Brentano's letter to Marty obscures rather than illuminates his position *vis-à-vis* the Höfler–Meinong–Twardowski distinction between act, content, and object. He denies that the immanent object of the presentation of a horse is the horse-as-presented, but the horse itself, except on the most extreme idealism, is not an appropriate candidate as an immanently intended object. What would make sense is to agree with Höfler, Meinong, and Twardowski, by assuming that the immanently intentional component of a psychological state is the content, the contemplated horse or horse-as-presented, which Höfler describes as a quasi-image, and Twardowski likens to a painting or representational artwork that helps thought to intend its object outside of thought.

The object of a thought, as Brentano maintains, is typically not the thought-of object. Those of his distant followers who rejected the immanence thesis would warmly applaud Brentano's claim that only the horse, and not the contemplated horse, is correctly designated an object. That is why the act–content–object distinction was advanced, so that horses rather than presented horses could be regarded as the objects of thought, and presented horses could be understood not as objects, but as the contents of thought. What remains puzzling is not Brentano's claim that horses are the proper objects of thought, but that he should continue to insist even in 1905 that they are the *immanent* objects of thought. The only conclusion to draw is either that Brentano does not understand the content–object distinction, or that he means something significantly different by his own use of the term *"immanentes Objekt"* from what his students and contemporaries, and subsequent traditions, have understood him to mean.

Many if not most of Brentano's arguments for reism emerge only in scattered remarks and correspondence, as piecemeal efforts to show that this or that non-individual cannot be a genuine intentional object of thought. For example, in the draft titled "Entwurf zur Klassifikation der psychischen Phänomene," dated March 1910, Brentano writes:

17. We have only things as objects, all fall under a higher concept.
   The majority of things are also regarded as real. Look at the so-called objective [Objektiv] (contents of judgments such as for example that all men are mortal).
18. Negatives are not objects. Past and future tenses are not objects. Possibilities are not objects. Origin of the so-called concept of possibility . . . Psychic correlates such as that which is acknowledged, that which is denied, the loved, the hated, the presented, are not objects. Truth, error, good, bad, are not objects. That for which the abstract names are signs, are not objects.[31]

In a letter to Kraus on October 31, 1914, he offers a more general argument to establish the truth of reism.

. . . I shall begin immediately today giving you in what I believe to be a simple and rigorous manner a proof that nothing other than things can be objects of our presentations and therefore of our thinking generally.

The proof is founded on the fact that the concept of presenting is a uniform [einheitlicher] one, that the term is therefore univocal [univok], not equivocal [äquivok]. It belongs again to this concept that every presentation presents something, and if this "something" were not itself univocal [eindeutig], then the term "presentation" would also not be univocal. If this is certain, then it is impossible to understand as this "something" at one time a real [Reales] (thing) [(Ding)], and at another time a non-thing [Nichtreales]. There is no concept which could be common to things and non-things.

This proof in my opinion is absolutely decisive. One finds a very expedient manifold verification, and more and more so, in the analysis of cases in which a non-thing appears to be the object of a presentation.[32]

Brentano's proof is anything but decisive. It is unclear what he intends by verifying the proof by means of analyzing situations in which a non-thing appears to be an object of thought, since he does not explain in this short epistle to Kraus – or elsewhere in his writings – what the analysis is supposed to consist in, what direction it should take, and what conclusions it would support. It is worth examining the argument itself in detail. The reasoning has this form:

1. Thinking is thinking about something.
2. The concept of thinking is uniform [*einheitlicher*], so that the term "presentation" is univocal, not equivocal.

---

3. If the term "something" were equivocal, then the term "presentation" would also be equivocal.   (1)
4. Therefore, the term "something" is univocal.   (2,3)
5. In particular, therefore, the term "something" is not equivocal as between designating alternatively either a thing or a non-thing.   (4)

The argument unfortunately is defective. As it stands, the conclusion no more upholds reism than anti-reism, since the deduction at most shows only that "something" cannot mean both sometimes a thing and sometimes a non-thing, and that by itself does not prove that the something toward which a thought is directed is always a thing rather than a non-thing.

Brentano can obtain his conclusion by bringing forward the suppressed assumption that:

2a.   Some presentations are about things.

From this and proposition (5) it follows that:

6. Therefore, only things can be the objects of presentations, to the absolute exclusion of non-things.   (2a,5)

Without assuming that the idealist is wrong to posit "non-things" as possible intended objects of thought, Brentano has no solid foundation for blocking the very opposite conclusion from the equally pre-analytically intuitive assumption that:

2a'. Some presentations are about non-things.

Within his own argument structure, it could then validly be deduced that:

6'. Therefore, only non-things can be the objects of presentations, to the absolute exclusion of things.   (2a',5)

Brentano cannot simply insist on the truth of (2a), and refuse to consider the intuitive merits of (2a'), unless or until he has

satisfactorily established the reist conclusion in (6). The reist conclusion in (6), however, cannot be reached within Brentano's proof
structure unless or until (2a) is sustained and (2a') justifiably with-
drawn. Brentano stoutly asserts that, "There is no concept which
could be common to things and non-things." This again is circular
reasoning against the anti-reist, for whom the very terms "something" and "object of thought" denote a concept that is assumed to
be common to things and non-things. The prospects for a noncircu-
lar defense of Brentano's argument for reism as a result appear rather
bleak.

The circularity objection presupposes the validity of Brentano's
basic argument structure, but this can also be called into question.
The premise in (1) is a modified version of Brentano's intentionality thesis, formulated in more neutral terminology with respect to
its original commitment to the immanence of intentional objects.
There is nevertheless something suspect, almost sophistic, about
the body of the derivation. The fact, if it is a fact, that the word
"presentation" is univocal, and that every presentation is always
about something, may be sufficient to uphold the conclusion in (4)
that the term "something" is also univocal. But the sense in which
"something" is univocal does not imply the final conclusion in (5),
that "something" therefore cannot be ambiguous as between designating alternatively either a thing or a non-thing. To take an obvious
counterexample, consider by immediate analogy that if this mode of
argument were logically valid, then it would be equally correct to
conclude from the claim that the term "human" is univocal, having an unambiguous meaning, that therefore "human" must also be
unambiguous in the sense of not designating alternatively men or
women.

Brentano seems to confuse the univocity or unambiguity of a
concept or term for a concept with the rather different question of
whether the objects falling under a concept or denoted as a set by the
term all belong to the same metaphysical category. The term "something" as Brentano uses it is consistent with its being understood as
a higher-order metaphysical category term (perhaps of the very highest order), subsuming the lower-order metaphysical category terms
"thing" and "non-thing". It may be true that if "presentation" is
univocal and every presentation is about something, then "something" is also univocal in the sense of having a single unambiguous

meaning. But this does not prevent "something" from subsuming ontically diverse lower-order metaphysical categories. There is thus an equivocation in the meaning of the words "univocal" and "not equivocal" as they occur in conclusions (4) and (5) of this reconstruction of Brentano's proof, which renders the argument invalid.[33]

The difficulty with the austere reist ontology which Brentano introduces in this later phase is plausibly accounting for apparent reference to abstract and nonexistent objects, problems for which Husserl's phenomenology and Meinong's object theory were better adapted. Brentano's reism appears in many ways intended to refute the *irrealia* of object theory.[34] Brentano goes to ingenious lengths to tailor intentional objects in these categories to his minimalist reist framework, but from the volume and difficulty of his attempts to reconcile reism with pre-analytic intuition, the high costs of reism, like the high costs of idealism, quickly become apparent. If, on the other hand, from an anti-idealist, anti-reist perspective Brentano's immanence thesis and rejection of abstract and nonexistent objects appear to be metaphysical mistakes, they are undoubtedly among the most interesting, challenging, and theoretically fertile mistakes ever made in the history of philosophy.

EMPIRICISM IN BRENTANO'S IMMANENT INTENTIONALISM AND REISM

Whatever induced Brentano in the *Psychology* to adopt the immanent intentionality or intentional in-existence thesis in the first place? There are several possible explanations, but the complete story may never be told.[35]

If intended objects, according to Brentano's early immanent intentionality thesis, are supposed to be identical to a thought's mental contents, then it is hard to see how Brentano could consistently avoid the charge that his theory of mind is objectionably psychologistic, that it locks meaning and reference within a closed circle of ideas. Despite what he says in the appendix "On Psychologism," which he added to the 1911 edition of the *Psychology* as "Supplementary Remarks Intended to Explain and Defend, as Well as to Correct and Expand Upon the Theory," it is unclear why he takes umbrage at the allegations of psychologism that were raised especially by Husserl.[36] What is remarkable is that in these reflections Brentano responds only to the complaint that his theory of knowledge is subjectivistic, and makes no direct link between it and the immanence or inexistence intentionality thesis.

Brentano's philosophical training inclined him to an appreciation of Aristotle and the Scholastics to an extent that was almost unprecedented among professional philosophers of his time. The dominant trend against which he struggled was woven out of several strands of post-Kantian idealism and Hegelianism.[37] This may explain his affirmation of an immanence theory of intentionality, and his reluctance to embrace the contrary transcendentalist terminology, with its implications of a Kantian thing-in-itself. It cannot be overemphasized that Brentano sought to develop the philosophy of mind on empirical grounds, adapting scientific methods to the study of subjective phenomena. From a strictly empirical point of view, it may appear unnecessary and perhaps even unintelligible to ask whether intentional objects transcend or actually exist beyond or outside of experience. Brentano's main purpose in resurrecting the Scholastic immanence or intentional in-existence thesis was to pin down his subject matter in Aristotelian fashion, articulating a criterion to distinguish the mental or psychological from the nonmental and nonpsychological. With this limited end in view, he may have judged it unnecessary, if not unscientific, to trespass beyond the confines of his strictly empirical discipline into speculative metaphysics.

The idea that a scientific psychology must be both empirical and a priori is a requirement that Brentano consistently states, beginning with the "Foreword" to the 1874 edition of his *Psychology*, where he explains: "My psychological standpoint is empirical; experience alone is my teacher. Yet I share with other thinkers the conviction that this is entirely compatible with a certain ideal point of view."[38] Hardline empiricism might be said to lead to idealism in Brentano's early philosophy just as it does in Berkeley's. The dilemma of respecting both empiricist methodology and common sense pretheoretical beliefs about the mind-independence of objects of experience is dramatically, dialectically played out in the transition from Brentano's acceptance to his rejection of the immanent intentionality thesis.[39]

Guided by the desire to set psychology on the foundations of a firm scientific methodology, Brentano began with an empiricist criterion for distinguishing mental from physical phenomena, perhaps in the conviction that a sound method could not yield incorrect results. Only later, when the theory had achieved sufficient definition, did the nature of the idealistic consequences inherent in its radical empiricism become evident. The choice, at least to those of anti-idealist temperament, was obvious, and meant the abandonment of Brentano's immanence or intentional in-existence criterion of the psychological. Husserl took the inquiry in one direction, leading him toward a phenomenology of *noemata* as subjective quasi-abstract thought contents and corresponding transcendental objects. The founders of object theory took another related but different direction, leading to immanent contents and existent or nonexistent mind-independent intentional objects beyond being and nonbeing.

Alternatively, if we consider David Hume's empiricism as a model for Brentano's, a different picture might be painted of the philosophical motivations for the immanent or in-existence intentionality thesis. In *A Treatise of Human Nature* (1739–40), Book I, Part II, Section VI, "Of the idea of existence, and of external existence," Hume argues that:

[no] object can be presented resembling some object with respect to its existence, and different from others in the same particular; since every object, that is presented, must necessarily be existent. A like reasoning will account for the idea of *external existence*. We may observe, that 'tis universally allow'd by philosophers, and is besides pretty obvious of itself, that nothing is ever really present with the mind but its perceptions or impressions and ideas, and that external objects become known to us only by those perceptions they occasion.[40]

Later, in Part IV, Section II, "Of scepticism with regard to the senses," Hume concludes that philosophy cannot rigorously prove the existence of external reality, even if the passions and in particular the imagination are psychologically compelled to accept the existence of a real world beyond the contents of impressions and ideas. "We may well ask," he writes, "*What causes induce us to believe in the existence of body?* but 'tis in vain to ask, *Whether there be body or not?* That is a point, which we must take for granted in all our reasonings."[41]

It is a possibility, in the light of these interpretive obstacles, that Brentano may not have reasoned through all the relevant implications of immanent intentionality. In his concern to balance a neo-Aristotelian metaphysics with a sharp distinction between psychological and nonpsychological phenomena, and in his desire to recognize that intentionality from the standpoint of an empirical discipline needs to be neutral about the ontic status of the many different kinds of objects that thought is capable of intending, he may not have recognized that the intentional in-existence of intended objects had landed him deeply in incompatible theoretical desiderata. A Humean model, in contrast, might have led Brentano to see it as a requirement of strict empiricism not to venture beyond what can be known in immediately inner experience about the intended objects of thought. Such a methodological commitment limits intentionality to the contents of thought; at least an empirical psychology cannot confidently say more than that about the real ontic status of intended objects.

The only factor that could cause Brentano to abandon a strict empiricist agnosticism concerning the ontology of intended objects would be an independent line of reasoning that positively excludes the possibility of reference to nonindividual, merely psychologically intended objects. Brentano's later reism provides just the kind of metaphysical considerations that could pressure him, from an equally principled empirical standpoint, to say something more definite about the nature of intended objects than that they are immanently or in-existently related to thought contents. Although Brentano never acknowledges the psychologism latent in his early immanence or in-existence concept of intentionality, his reism introduces an exclusive ontology of particulars that implicitly addresses the psychologism problem by limiting intended objects to mind-independent external existent entities transcending the contents of thoughts. If the only metaphysically permissible candidates for intended objects are existent particulars, then Brentano is finally in a position to conclude as a consequence of a modified intentionality thesis coupled with his later reist ontology that the only conceivable intended objects of thought are mind-independent existent particulars.[42]

NOTES

1. PES-G, p. 115 (my translation; emphases added).
2. See PES-G §5; especially, pp. 115–17.
3. Klaus Hedwig, "Der scholastische Kontext des Intentionalen bei Brentano," in, eds., R. M. Chisholm and R. Haller, *Die Philosophie Franz Brentanos* (Amsterdam: Rodopi, 1978), pp. 67–82. Hedwig, "Intention:

Outlines for the History of a Phenomenological Concept," *Philosophy and Phenomenological Research*, 39, 1979, pp. 326–40. Herbert Spiegelberg, "Der Begriff der Intentionalität in der Scholastik bei Brentano und bei Husserl," *Philosophische Hefte*, 5, 1936, pp. 72–91. Spiegelberg, "'Intention' and 'Intentionality' in the Scholastics, Brentano and Husserl," trans. and ed., Linda L. McAlister, *The Philosophy of Brentano* (London: Gerald Duckworth and Co. Ltd., 1976), pp. 108–27; Spiegelberg, *The Phenomenological Movement: a Historical Introduction*, 2nd edn. (The Hague: Martinus Nijhoff, 1978), vol. I, pp. 27–50. Ausonio Marras, "Scholastic Roots of Brentano's Conception of Intentionality," ed., McAlister, *Philosophy of Brentano*, pp. 128–39.

4. Thomas Reid, *An Inquiry into the Human Mind, on the Principles of Common Sense* [1764], ed., Timothy J. Duggan (Chicago: University of Chicago Press, 1970), Chapter 5, §3, especially pp. 65–7.

5. The crucial passage is PES-G §5. The later edition is titled *Psychologie vom empirischen Standpunkt* (rather than "*Standpunkte*"), ed. Oskar Kraus, 1924, pp. 124–8, in which Brentano declares intentionality the "mark" or "characteristic" (also "sign" or "indication") (*Merkmal*) of the mental. Brentano begins by asking, p. 124: "*Welches positive Merkmal werden wir nun anzugeben vermögen?*" The final paragraph of §5, p. 128, reads: "*Die intentionale Inexistenz eines Objekts dürfen wir also mit Recht als eine allgemeine Eigentümlichkeit der psychischen Phänomene geltend machen, welche diese Klasse der Erscheinungen von der Klasse der physischen unterscheidet.*" The passage is often said to contain two distinct theses. The first is an assertion about the ontological status of the objects of thought, and the second offers the intentional in-existence criterion of psychic phenomena. We are equally concerned with both of Brentano's theses, with the idea that the intentionality of thought distinguishes the psychological from the nonpsychological, and with the problems raised by Brentano's obscure discussion of immanent intentionality, relation to content, or intentional in-existence. Spiegelberg in the sources referred to in note 3 above maintains that Brentano's two theses are philosophically unrelated, while Marras argues, perhaps more convincingly, that they are logically and conceptually intimately connected in Brentano's thought. Brentano regards intentional in-existence as a unique characteristic psychical phenomena, but further distinguishes between physical and psychical phenomena on the grounds that psychical phenomena alone are encountered in inner perception ("*innere Wahrnehmung*") and physical phenomena alone are encountered in outer or external perception ("*äussere Wahrnehmung*").

6. See PES-E, pp. 29–30, 112–13, 118–19 and 405–8. See also SNC, pp. 28–38.

7. Kraus, "Einleitung des Herausgebers," in Brentano, PES-G, I, pp. liv–lv, lxii; PES-G, 2nd edn., vol. II, pp. 179–82.

8. For example, Reinhardt Grossmann, *Meinong* (London: Routledge and Kegan Paul, 1974), pp. 48–56.

9. See Jan Srzednicki, *Franz Brentano's Analysis of Truth* (The Hague: Martinus Nijhoff, 1965), especially pp. 3, 27, 50–51.

10. Brentano's unpublished manuscripts were cataloged in 1951 by Franziska Mayer-Hillebrand in *Verzeichnis der Manuskripte Franz Brentanos* (Innsbruck, typescript). The most extensive philosophical survey of the unpublished manuscripts as they relate to the problem of Brentano's early intentionality thesis and the ontic status of intended objects under the immanence or intentional in-existence thesis is offered by Arkadiusz Chrudzimski, *Intentionalitätstheorie beim frühen Brentano*, Phaenomenologica Series 159 (Dordrecht, Boston, London: Kluwer Academic Publishers, 2001).

11. I develop these themes at greater length in Dale Jacquette, "The Origins of *Gegenstandstheorie*: Immanent and Transcendent Intentional Objects in Brentano, Twardowski, and Meinong", *Brentano Studien*, 3, 1990–1, pp. 277–302.

12. Edmund Husserl, *Ideen zu einer reinen Phänomenologie und phenomenologischen Philosophie, I (Allgemeine Einführung in die reine Phänomenologie)* [1913] (Halle: Max Niemeyer, 1922; 1928), Chapter 9, N. 88–135.

13. Husserl, *Philosophie der Arithmetik* [1891], Husserliana edn., ed., L. Eley (The Hague: Martinus Nijhoff, 1970). See Maurita J. Harney, *Intentionality, Sense and the Mind* (The Hague: Martinus Nijhoff, 1984), pp. 24–5, 122–5; David Woodruff Smith and Ronald McIntyre, *Husserl and Intentionality: a Study of Mind, Meaning, and Language* (Dordrecht: Dr. Reidel Publishing Company, 1982), pp. 171–4.

14. Gottlob Frege, "Review of Dr. Husserl's *Philosophie der Arithmetik*," trans., E. W. Kluge, *Mind*, 81, 1972, pp. 321–37 (from *Zeitschrift für Philosophie und philosophische Kritik*, 103, 1894, pp. 313–32).

15. Alois Höfler, in collaboration with Alexius Meinong, *Logik* (Vienna: Tempsky Verlag, 1890), pp. 6–7.

16. Kazimierz Twardowski, *Zur Lehre vom Inhalt und Gegenstand der Vorstellungen: Eine psychologische Untersuchung* [1894] (Munich and Vienna: Philosophia Verlag, 1982), p. 4. See John N. Findlay, *Meinong's Theory of Objects and Values, Edited with an Introduction by Dale Jacquette*, from the 2nd edn., Oxford University Press, 1963 (Aldershot: Ashgate Publishing, 1995) (Gregg Revivals), pp. 7–8.

17. Höfler, *Logik*, p. 7 (my translation). Twardowski, *Zur Lehre vom Inhalt und Gegenstand der Vorstellungen*, p. 4.

18. Brentano, "Vorwort", KPP, reprinted in Brentano, PES-G, 2nd edn., II, p. 2 (my translation).

19. Brentano, PES-G, 2nd ed., vol. II, pp. 179–82, 275–7 ("Vom ens rationis. Diktat vom 6. Januar 1917"). See also Franziska Mayer-Hillebrand, "Einleitung der Herausgeberin," Brentano, *Die Abkehr vom Nichtrealen: Nur Dinge sind vorstellbar und können existieren: Briefe und Abhandlungen aus dem Nachlaß, mit einer Einleitung* (Bern: Francke Verlag, 1966), pp. 33–92; Letter from Brentano to Anton Marty, April 20, 1910, ibid., pp. 225–8. For a different picture of the later relations between Brentano and Husserl, see Spiegelberg, "On the Significance of the Correspondence Between Franz Brentano and Edmund Husserl," in *Die Philosophie Franz Brentanos: Beiträge zur Brentano-Konferenz*, Graz, September 4–8, 1977, edited by Roderick M. Chisholm and Rudolf Haller (Amsterdam: Rodopi, N.V., 1978), pp. 95–116. James C. Morrison, "Husserl and Brentano on Intentionality," *Philosophy and Phenomenological Research*, 31, 1970, pp. 27–46. Herman Philipse, "The Concept of Intentionality: Husserl's Development from the Brentano Period to the 'Logical Investigations,'" *Philosophy Research Archives*, 12, 1986–7, pp. 293–328.

20. Twardowski, *Zur Lehre vom Inhalt und Gegenstand der Vorstellungen*, §6, "Die Verschiedenheit von Vorstellungsinhalt und -Gegenstand," pp. 29–34. Meinong, as might be expected from his collaboration with Höfler and the influence of their *Logik* on Twardowski's categories, accepts Twardowski's content–object distinction, but rejects his third and fourth arguments. Meinong, "Über Gegenstände höherer Ordnung und deren Verhältnis zur inneren Wahrnehmung," *Zeitschrift für Psychologie und Physiologie der Sinnesorgäne*, 21, 1899, pp. 181–271. See also Husserl, "Besprechung von K. Twardowski, *Zur Lehre von Inhalt und Gegenstand der Vorstellungen*," in Husserl, *Aufsätze und Rezensionen (1890–1910)*, ed., Bernhard Rang, *Husserliana*, 22, 1979, pp. 349–56.

21. Twardowski, *Zur Lehre vom Inhalt und Gegenstand der Vorstellungen*, pp. 24–5, 27, 36.

22. *Ibid.*, p. 3 (my translation). Grossmann gives a somewhat different translation of Twardowski's term "*beziehe*" as "intends." See Twardowski, *On the Content and Object of Presentations*, trans., Reinhardt Grossmann (The Hague: Martinus Nijhoff, 1977), p. 1: "It is one of the best known positions of psychology, hardly contested by anyone, that every mental phenomenon *intends* an immanent object" (emphasis added). This gives a misleading impression of Twardowski's careful attempt to say only that an immanent component of every presentation is in more neutral terminology "related" (as his further references to the "*Beziehung*" also make evident) to a psychological phenomenon.

Grossmann's choice of "intends" here suggests on the contrary that the immanent component of thought is the one everyone agrees is *intended* or toward which the thought is *directed*. But this would contradict most of Twardowski's subsequent discussion, since it makes the immanent component of thought the intentional object rather than merely the content. Twardowski says only that there is general agreement about every psychological phenomenon being *related* to an immanent object, which permits him to lean heavily on Brentano's intentionality thesis without commitment to immanent objectivity.

23. Twardowski, *Zur Lehre vom Inhalt und Gegenstand der Vorstellungen*, p. 4 (my translation).

24. *Ibid.*, §4, "Das 'Vorgestellte,'" pp. 12–20.

25. *Ibid.*, especially pp. 55–102.

26. Meinong, *Über Annahmen*, 2nd edn. [1910], *Alexius Meinong Gesamtausgabe*, eds. by Rudolf Haller and Rudolf Kindinger in collaboration with Chisholm (Graz: Akademische Druck-u.-Verlagsanstalt, 1968–78), vol. IV, p. 229 (my translation); see also p. 237. Meinong, *Über Gegenstände höherer Ordnung und deren Verhältnis zur inneren Wahrnehmung, Gesamtausgabe*, vol. II, pp. 382–3; *Sach-Index zur Logik und Erkenntnistheorie, Gesamtausgabe, Ergänzungs Band* (VIII), pp. 61–3.

27. Meinong, *Über Annahmen*, pp. 85–6, n. 3. Anton Marty, *Untersuchungen zur Grundlegung der allgemeinen Grammatik und Sprachphilosophie* (Halle: Niemeyer Verlag, 1908), p. 761.

28. See Tadeusz Kotarbinski, "Franz Brentano as Reist," in, ed., McAlister, *Philosophy of Brentano*, pp. 194–203. Stephan Körner, "Über Brentanos Reismus und die extensionale Logik," in, eds., Chisholm and Haller; *Die Philosophie Franz Brentanos*, pp. 29–43.

29. ANR, pp. 119–20 (my translation; author's emphases). (Compare the translation of this letter in TE, p. 77.)

30. Brentano, Letter to Kraus, November 8, 1914, ANR, pp. 250–2; "Worterklärungen", January 27, 1917, *ibid.*, pp. 390–1.

31. Brentano, "Entwurf zur Klassifikation der psychischen Phänomene," March 1910, ANR, pp. 219–20 (my translation).

32. Brentano, Letter to Kraus, October 31, 1914, ANR, p. 249 (my translation). See Brentano, DP-G, p. 131: "*Die Realitäten, die in unsere Wahrnehmung fallen, sind psychische, d.h. sie zeigen eine intentionale Beziehung auf ein immanentes Objekt.*"

33. For another assessment of the proof, see D. B. Terrell, "Brentano's Argument for Reismus," in, ed., McAlister, *The Philosophy of Brentano*, pp. 204–12.

34. Brentano, Letter to Kraus, September 14, 1909, ANR, pp. 201–2; Letter to Anton Marty, April 20, 1910, ANR, pp. 225–8; Letter to Marty, December 28, 1913, ANR, pp. 240–1; Letter to Kraus, November 16, 1914, ANR, pp. 255–9; Letter to Kraus, January 10, 1915, ANR, pp. 274–5; Letter to Marty, März 17, 1905, Brentano, WE, pp. 87–9.

35. The best accounts are found in Chisholm, "Brentano on Descriptive Psychology and the Intentional," in, eds., E. N. Lee and Maurice Mandelbaum, *Phenomenology and Existentialism* (Baltimore, MD: Johns Hopkins University Press, 1967), pp. 1–23. J. M. Howarth, "Franz Brentano and Object-Directedness," *The Journal of the British Society for Phenomenology*, 2, 1980, pp. 239–54. See also Rancurello, *A Study of Franz Brentano: His Psychological Standpoint and his Significance in the History of Psychology* (New York: Academic Press, 1968).

36. Husserl's critique of psychologism with evident reference to Brentano is found throughout his *Logische Untersuchungen, erster Band: Prolegomena zur reinen Logik* [1913], ed., Elmar Holenstein (The Hague: Martinus Nijhoff, 1975). Brentano, in the Appendix "On Psychologism" to *Von der Klassifikation der psychischen Phänomene*, writes: "The charge of psychologism has been made against my theory of knowledge. This is a word which has lately come into use and when it is spoken many a pious philosopher – like many an orthodox Catholic when he hears the term Modernism – crosses himself as though the devil himself were in it." Although Brentano explicitly mentions Husserl as the source of objections to psychologism in his philosophy, he casts the criticism as directed obliquely at his theory of knowledge rather than specifically at the immanent intentionality or intentional in-existence thesis in his philosophy of mind, about which Brentano seems oblivious.

37. See Chisholm, "Editor's Introduction," *Realism and the Background of Phenomenology* (New York: Free Press, 1960), pp. 4–6. Srzednicki, *Franz Brentano's Analysis of Truth*, pp. 10–11, 114.

38. Brentano, PES-E, p. xxvii. Also, p. 71: "Accordingly, we can best establish laws for complex mental phenomena by taking as our model the method used by natural scientists, in particular by physiologists, to investigate more complex phenomena in their field of research. The physiologist is not satisfied with having derived the laws for more complex phenomena from higher laws; he takes pains to verify these laws by direct induction from experience. In the same way, the psychologist must seek an inductive verification of the laws which he has discovered deductively. Indeed, such a verification seems especially advisable in his case because, as we have seen, the higher laws which constitute

the premises of his deduction often leave much to be desired in the way of precision. In such circumstances, even being able to point to individual outstanding cases is welcome corroboration, especially in the absence of other cases which appear contradictory. If the latter is the case, then a statistical confirmation will give the desired proof. Thus, psychology will be rich in examples which furnish an excellent illustration of deductive method in the empirical field, and of the three stages which the logicians have distinguished in it: induction of general laws, deduction of special laws, and verification of these laws by means of empirical facts."

39. See Jacquette, "Brentano's Scientific Revolution in Philosophy," Spindel Conference 2001, *Origins: the Common Sources of Analytic and Phenomenological Traditions, Southern Journal of Philosophy*, Spindel Conference Supplement, 40, 2002, pp. 193–221. Jacquette, "*Fin de Siècle* Austrian Thought and the Rise of Scientific Philosophy," *History of European Ideas*, 27, 2001, pp. 307–15.

40. David Hume, *A Treatise of Human Nature* [1739–40], ed., L. A. Selby-Bigge, 2nd edn. rev. P. H. Nidditch (Oxford: Clarendon Press, 1978), p. 67.

41. *Ibid.*, p. 187.

42. AW. See Rolf George, "Brentano's Relation to Aristotle," in, eds., Chisholm and Haller, *Die Philosophie Franz Brentanos*, pp. 249–66. Stephen Körner, "On Brentano's Objections to Kant's Theory of Knowledge," *Topoi*, 6, pp. 11–19. Massimo Libardi, "Franz Brentano (1838–1917)," in, eds., Liliana Albertazzi, Libardi, and Roberto Poli, *The School of Franz Brentano* (Dordrecht: Kluwer Academic Publishers, 1996), especially pp. 32–8.

6   Reflections on intentionality

The topic of "intentionality" is a well-known quagmire. There seems to be no doubt that the Scholastic *intentio* had fallen into disuse in modern philosophy until it was recovered by Franz Brentano in an arresting way in the original edition (1874) of *Psychology from an Empirical Standpoint*.[1] There, Brentano recovers intentionality – or, adhering to the text, "intentional inexistence" – as the essential nerve of an empirical psychology centered on describing the various kinds of "presentations [*Vorstellungen*] and other activities which are based upon presentations and which, like presentations, are only perceivable through inner perception." These activities, Brentano says, belong to their "substantial bearer," the soul (in Aristotle's sense of a certain "form of life" [*physis, morphé*], which Brentano follows), "the subject of consciousness" (as Oskar Kraus adds, without prejudging whether it is "spiritual or material" in being a "substantial substrate").[2] Hence, Brentano means to avoid the Cartesian account here (though, in other respects, he is sympathetic to Descartes's *res cogitans*) and, following the example of Aristotle, takes himself to be recovering the ancient science of psychology in an up-to-date way, since the themes of that discipline have become unfamiliar. Although, as he adds, psychology (thus construed) is nothing less than "the crowning pinnacle" of all the sciences, depends "on all of them," may even be said to "exert a most powerful reciprocal influence upon them" – in fact, becomes "the basis of all scientific endeavor as well, reviewing the whole of human life and serving as the basis of society and of its noblest possessions."[3]

The best-known feature of Brentano's work in this regard is, of course, his famous disjunctive contrast between the "mental" and the "physical." But if you take seriously the unresolved question of the "metaphysics" of the soul and the role of the body, then, speaking as Brentano does, the distinction between the "mental" and the "physical" does not yet resolve the very different question of the adequacy or inadequacy of materialism.[4] Brentano is noticeably careful here, though he explores various refinements of, and departures from, the views offered in the *Psychology* in later essays, in indicating what he is not claiming or addressing.

He advances certain formulations at the start, however, that we should have before us, nevertheless, in thinking further about intentionality. For one thing, he explicitly says: "psychology is the science which studies the properties and laws of the soul, which we discover within ourselves directly by means of inner perception, and which we infer, by analogy, to exist in others."[5] This raises at once the profound question of the adequacy of the "argument by analogy" (regarding knowledge of other minds), the question of presentational doubt, as well as the skeptical question about the external world and about our knowledge of the external world, and the question about the relationship between "natural science and mental science."[6] Whatever Brentano's later speculations may be, it seems strategically unwise (given his useful caution about how to follow Aristotle) to complicate the analysis of intentionality with the instant introduction of questions of the sorts just mentioned. (I return to these worries toward the end of this discussion.)

In fact, Brentano provides a masterly clarification of his account of intentional "activities" in the Appendix to *The Classification of Mental Phenomena* (in effect, the new title for Book Two of the *Psychology*), which was prepared for inclusion in the 1911 edition (and is included in the English translation of the *Psychology*). This was the principal source, for instance, on which Tadeusz Kotarbinski was led to affirm (in his generous way) that "Brentano was the first to develop a reistic philosophy, more than a decade before the system had a name."[7] Kotarbinski was right in what he says here: the matter is quite important, as we shall see, in simplifying Brentano's general account in the best sense, as well as in distinguishing Brentano's best view (by my own persuasion) from the views of a bewilderingly diffuse army of subsequent discussants who have taken the notion into extravagant conceptual thickets.

Kotarbinski himself draws attention to the very useful distinction between the "two" groups of those who are the most important "followers" of Brentano: the "reists," who include Oskar Kraus (and in effect himself) and Brentano's better-known followers who include Alexius Meinong, Edmund Husserl, Anton Marty, and Kazimierz Twardowski (who was a student of Brentano's and who was also Kotarbinski's teacher). Kotarbinski favors a physicalist reading of "reism" and Brentano (to the extent he is a reist) nevertheless allows the admission of some version of *res cogitans*. This also suggests a useful constraint on a full-blown metaphysics to which the analysis of intentionality would (in time) have to be reconciled. The two issues should remain distinct, however.

In fact, if we keep them distinct, it is entirely possible to consider enlarging the range of contributions to the analysis of intentionality to include the work of figures like Husserl, Heidegger, Merleau-Ponty, Sartre, Gadamer, and others insofar as they do not veer off in a number of problematic directions: in particular, (a) in pretending to distinguish between "being" and "existence"; (b) in claiming to identify mental "objects" apart from mental (or intentional) "activities," which are themselves said to include such "objects" inseparably; (c) in inventing *sui generis* mental "disciplines" such as non-empirical phenomenology or transcendental "reflection"; and (d) in failing to distinguish properly between actual relations between existent things and analogous uses of the relational idiom in speaking, say, of the "relationship" between someone's thinking about this or that and the "this or that" being thought about. In all of these respects, Brentano may be reasonably said to be a "reist" in a sense close to Kotarbinski's. There are other difficulties with Brentano's account which may also be flagged, whether ultimately to be set aside or not – in the interest of affording a defensible account of intentionality along the lines of Brentano's own analysis: most notably, Brentano's insistence on the self-evidence of our knowledge of "mental phenomena."

As a general rule, it pays to examine quite separately the matter of what to count as the "intentional" as opposed to whether the "presentation" of mental phenomena is "self-evident" (either the "activity," which Brentano features, or what is "presented," which intrudes grammatical miscues about what exists), as well as the question of what to include as "mental phenomena." For example, Brentano says very plainly: "When someone is cut he has no perception of touch, and someone who is burned has no feeling of warmth, but in both cases there is only the feeling of pain. Nevertheless there is no doubt that even here the feeling is based upon a presentation. In cases such as this we always have a presentation of a definite spatial location which we usually characterize in relation to some visible and touchable part of our body."[8] What needs to be noticed here is Brentano's ready acknowledgment of psychophysical linkages (tempting us to formulate psychophysical laws) between the mental and the physical and the separation of the question of the range of the "intentional" and "presentational" from the "self-evidence" of mental phenomena.

Apart from all this, it needs to be borne in mind that, in introducing his account, in the *Psychology*, Brentano notes that "we usually call soul the substance which has sensations such as fantasy images, acts of memory, acts of hope or fear, desire or aversion."[9] This introduces two of the most vexed matters that bear on intentionality, which Brentano clarifies in what appears to be the most promising way, in the Appendix mentioned: namely, (i) whether the "analysis" of intentionality is primarily a question of analyzing various kinds of "mental activity" or of identifying certain separable mental "objects" – sensations, images, propositions, activities of thinking, fearing, and the like, including thinking about thinking – *to which* further kinds of mental activity can be applied; and (ii) whether the "objects" of thinking are "real" (whether "existent" or not) and could be said to be before the mind (as "mental" objects), so that thinking could be said to enter into a certain "relationship" with "intentional" objects.

BRENTANO'S REIST THESIS AND OTHER CURRENTS

There is no quicker way to get clear about Brentano's seemingly best account of intentionality than to cite a few lines from Section IX of the Appendix (titled "On Genuine and Fictitious Objects") – Brentano has in mind here our thinking of a centaur:

All mental references refer to things.
In many cases, the things to which we refer do not exist.

. . .

A content is never presented in the sense of being object of the presentation [the non-existence of a centaur, say], nor is it ever affirmed, in the sense in which an object is affirmed, not even by those who believe that it is to be affirmed . . . But absolutely the only thing which is presented is a person who is making the judgment concerned, and we judge that insofar as we are thinking of such a person, we are thinking of someone who judges correctly . . . We ought rather to say we deny that anything exists for which the word "content" is a name, just as words like "of" and "but" have no meaning by themselves and do not name anything . . . But it does, indeed, make sense to say, "There is no thing which is named by the preposition 'of' or the conjunction 'but.'"

Hence we are certain that one cannot make the being or non-being of a centaur an object as one can a centaur; one can only make the person affirming or denying the centaur an object in which case the centaur, to be sure, becomes an object in a special *modus obliquus* at the same time. And so it holds true generally that only that which falls under the concept of a thing (*Reales*), can provide an object for mental reference. Nothing else can ever be, like a thing, that to which we mentally refer as an object – neither the present, past, nor future, neither present things, past things, nor future things, nor existence and non-existence, nor necessity, nor non-necessity, neither possibility nor impossibility, nor the necessary nor the non-necessary, neither the possible nor the impossible, neither truth nor falsity, neither the true nor the false, nor good nor bad.

When we depart from the analysis indicated, "surely [Brentano says] we are dealing . . . with mere fictions."[10] This is his clearest "reist" formulation. (But, of course, he may well disagree with Kotarbinski and others about the "realist" import of his reism.)[11]

The widening reception of Brentano's views, largely overshadowed in European philosophy by Husserlian phenomenology, was notably facilitated by Roderick M. Chisholm, whose efforts at promoting the translation and discussion of Brentano's work in the English-speaking world also affected the substantive analysis of intentionality itself.

The record has become extremely tangled: partly because Brentano kept reworking his account in ways that are not easily collected in a single consistent final summary (for instance, through personal correspondence); partly because Edmund Husserl, originally heavily indebted to Brentano's account, struck out on his own in launching the distinctive discipline of phenomenology, which Husserl strenuously contrasted with empirical psychology and which therefore took "intentionality" in an entirely new direction, one that very quickly mushroomed in bewilderingly diverse ways;[12] partly because Chisholm himself is at pains to contrast Brentano's view and Husserl's, to favor the former's over the latter's in epistemological ways – although it must be said that (in presenting Brentano's account), Chisholm seems to have been mistaken, at times, about important details regarding Brentano's view of intentionality;[13] partly because the theory of intentionality is now often presented from a Husserlian point of view – or, even further afield, from a Heideggerean point of view, which, then, predictably, finds Brentano's pointedly psychological approach inadequate;[14] partly because both Brentano's account of intentionality and that of his Husserlian commentators (Spiegelberg, for instance) are sometimes said to have failed to grasp the full play of the original Scholastic account(s) from which they derive;[15] partly because contemporary analytic philosophers who pursue the intentionality question have almost no interest in the detailed subtleties of either Scholastic or Brentano's or Husserl's accounts[16] and prefer the linguistic to the psychological; partly because, with due respect to the pioneer efforts of both Brentano and Husserl, very few discussants of empirical psychology and/or phenomenology would be willing nowadays to be bound by Brentano's or Husserl's conceptions of their respective "sciences"; partly because of the utterly different directions in which the analysis of intentional phenomena has been pursued more recently, particularly in Europe, for instance by Martin Heidegger and Maurice Merleau-Ponty;[17] and partly because, quite frankly, many now give evidence of recognizing the entire artifactual world of human culture as a distinct intentional domain – or, "Intentional" domain, as I prefer to say, meaning by that to emphasize that the cultural world is not confined to mental life, that it has its distinctive public structures, and that the *sui generis* mental life of enlanguaged persons is itself formed and transformed by the Intentional or enculturing processes of the institutions of societal life.[18]

This last development has obvious affinities with the inquiries of the hermeneutic tradition spanning Friedrich Schleiermacher and

Hans-Georg Gadamer (though not necessarily their particular doc-trines) as well as Husserl's fledgling (nearly aborted) inquiries into the *Lebenswelt* (which never quite matched the robustness of the cultural world but was, instead, regarded as a pre-theoretical space of experience from which divergent cultures and histories were said to be formed).[19] In any case, on my own reading, emphasis on the cultural manifestations of intentionality (the "Intentional," as I suggest) distinguishes between what may be characterized as the biologi-cally grounded psychology of *Homo sapiens* and the culturally trans-formed "second-natured" mental life and activity of human persons; abandons transcendentalism in every form (psychological or phe-nomenological); and features the distinctive (Intentional) structures of the public world of the arts, technology, history, action, science, and language, which (I claim) cannot be adequately characterized in physical, biological, or biologically confined psychological terms, or solely in psychological terms of any kind at the level of human culture.

Here, the study of Intentionality promises to bring together the master themes of late eighteenth-century studies regarding the di-versity of language, Hegel's innovations, hermeneutics, and the flow-ering of the human sciences and related currents down to our own time.[20]

DIFFERENCES BETWEEN BRENTANO'S AND CHISHOLM'S ANALYSES

Chisholm's analysis of Brentano's account of intentionality has been enormously influential; and yet there do seem to be a number of problematic summary remarks of Chisholm's that are less than reli-able. These have been flagged very early on by Linda McAlister, the editor and (often) translator of Brentano's works into English. Here it pays to have before us Brentano's best-known summary from the *Psychology*:

Every mental phenomenon is characterized by what the Scholastics of the Middle Ages called the intentional (or mental) inexistence of an object, and what we might call, though not wholly unambiguously, reference to a content, direction toward an object (which is not to be understood here as meaning a thing), or immanent objectivity. Every mental phenomenon includes something as object within itself, although they do not all do so in the same way. In presentation something is presented, in judgment something is affirmed or denied, in love loved, in hate hated, in desire desired and so on.

This intentional in-existence is characteristic exclusively of mental phenomena. No physical phenomenon exhibits anything like it. We could, therefore, define mental phenomena by saying that they are those phenomena which contain an object intentionally within themselves.[21]

Certain cautions need to be borne in mind. For one thing, Brentano is speaking quite informally here (for instance about "content" and "object," a "mental phenomenon['s] includ[ing] something as object within itself," and so on: Brentano himself warns us that he is speaking informally. Second, we must not hold Brentano too closely to what, in various accounts, the Scholastics may have meant by "the intentional (or mental)." For a third, the sense of "in-existence" is little more than a grammatical convenience; it does not signify existence, non-existence, reality, "object" (*Reales*), or any peculiar kind of existence or reality; it seems to mean only what, ulteriorly, by paraphrase, is able to be referred to (where it is) as an "object," whether existent or not: a unicorn as well as my (actual) horse C — what Brentano calls a *Reales*, within the "content" of my intentional activity (thinking of my horse or a unicorn). When someone thinks of a unicorn, *he* exists and is actually thinking of a unicorn; and in that sense (*modus obliquus*) "the unicorn" is an "object" *in* his intentional activity, though there is no existent object in his mental activity and though the unicorn is not real or existent in any sense at all, either *in* his thinking or in the real world. Finally, insofar as it is "intentional," thinking enjoys no referential or "presentational" *relation* to its intentional (or in-existent) "object": it enjoys no relationship at all. For Brentano, then, a unicorn is a *Reales*, an individual thing, though it is not real, does not exist.

When he speaks of "presentation," Brentano explicitly means "the act of presentation," not "what is presented." Hence, "every judgment, every recollection, every expectation, every inference, every conviction or opinion, every doubt, is a mental phenomenon. Also to be included under this term is every emotion: joy, sorrow, fear, hope, courage, despair, anger, love, hate, desire, act of will, intention, astonishment, contempt, etc." Physical phenomena, by contrast, include "a color, a figure, a landscape which I see, a chord which I hear, warmth, cold, odor which I sense; as well as similar images which appear in the imagination."[22] Physical phenomena need not, therefore, take the form of *realia* (individual things): these *phenomena* do not.

Speaking of this contrast, Chisholm says:

Brentano's criterion of the psychological or mental might be put in this way: From the fact that a certain thing is the object of an intentional act or attitude, one cannot infer either that that thing exists or that it does not; from the fact that a proposition is the object of an intentional act or attitude, one cannot infer that the proposition is true or that it is false; everything that is psychological involves what is thus intentional; but nothing that is physical can similarly "contain its object intentionally within itself"; intentionality, therefore, may serve as a criterion of the psychological or mental.[23]

Now, I have the highest regard for Chisholm. But with the best will in the world, his summary of Brentano's account is strangely inapt. First of all, on Brentano's view of the intentional, "object" can only mean "something" within the presentation of an intentional act that may be characterized in terms appropriate to a *Reales*, a particular thing. Second, as an intentional "object," "it" cannot exist: Chisholm's question cannot rightly arise. In fact, Chisholm says so elsewhere.[24] Third, it's not clear at all *what* Chisholm is saying about the physical: does he mean that, according to Brentano, the "object" (whatever it is) "contained" in the physical (whatever that means) cannot be inconclusive on the matter of its existence or nonexistence (whatever that means)?

It's not quite right to say that no comparable question arises with regard to the physical – because the question doesn't arise with regard to the intentional *either*! It's rather that to talk about the "object" that an "intentional" presentation "has" is not to talk about an object in the sense in which the physical domain includes actual objects! That is precisely why intentionality *is* the mark by which to distinguish the mental and the physical. Fourth, *that* propositions may be true or false hearkens back to the correspondence theory of truth, which Brentano repudiates.[25] Hence, fifth, Brentano rejects all theories of truth that depend on the admission of *irrealia*, such as propositions. In conformity with his reist tendencies, truth depends, for Brentano, on "evidence" regarding *realia*. Chisholm could not be further from the mark.

This is not to endorse Brentano's theory of truth and evidence or what he would include among real "things." But it is to affirm the

splendid economies Brentano has achieved in the analysis of intentionality. Furthermore, I am entirely willing to admit that Chisholm
has indeed provided a very reasonable (*alternative*) account of
intentional sentences, distinct from Brentano's analysis of *the
mental*. Read that way, everything Chisholm has worked out in the
way of intentionality deserves another inning. But it needs to be
noted that what Chisholm means by "objects" and "propositions"
are conceived very differently in Brentano's account.

What, then, Chisholm offers as a near-paraphrase of Brentano's
view are three criteria of intentional *sentences*: (1) that "a simple
declarative sentence is intentional if it uses a substantival expression – a name or a description – in such a way that neither the sentence nor its contradictory implies either that there is or that there
isn't anything to which the substantival expression truly applies";
(2) that "any noncompound sentence which contains a propositional
clause . . . is intentional provided that neither the sentence nor its
contradictory implies either that the propositional clause is true or
that it is false"; and (3) that, in effect, in intentional contexts, co-
designative terms (names or descriptions) cannot be substituted in
the same sentence, *salva veritate*. Chisholm then shows that we
can "re-express Brentano's thesis – or a thesis resembling that of
Brentano, by reference to intentional sentences."[26] The matter regarding whether Chisholm's account *is*, rightly, an analysis of the
mental remains unanswered. If, for instance, we consider Quine's
specimen argument regarding "9 is greater than 4," "necessarily 9
is greater than 4," "the number of planets is 9," therefore "necessarily the number of planets is greater than 4," it looks very much
as if the intensionality of sentences may not always be paraphrased
in terms of the intentionality of the mental.[27] (Quine specifically
notes the resemblance of such "modalities" to the behavior of the
"propositional attitudes.")

THE "INTENTIONAL" AND THE "*INTENTIONAL*"

I turn, finally, to a consideration of an altogether different sort,
the one I've flagged as the "Intentionality" of the cultural world.
Brentano's analysis of intentional phenomena strikes me as a most
excellent contribution to the launching of a scientific psychology. I
have no doubt about that. But I cannot agree with Brentano about
the right characterization of psychology as a science, or with all that

Brentano expects psychology to describe and explain (for instance, the immortality of the soul), or his belief in the "clear knowledge and complete certainty which is provided by immediate insight [or mental phenomena]," or his conviction about "the great advantage of psychology over the natural sciences."[28]

All of this is a sign of a serious need to detach Brentano's important contribution from his own conception of the structure and conditions of the very discipline he is at pains to define. If I ask myself, therefore, what, given Brentano's emphasis on the analysis of intentionality, should be expected to play a role in organizing Brentano's own investigations, I find that what is needed is very nearly completely ignored or, in a way, positively disallowed by Brentano himself (and by Chisholm). I agree that the intentional is crucial to the analysis of mental phenomena; but I also believe that neither Brentano nor Husserl rightly grasped the full import of their common theme (though for very different reasons).

That is a serious charge, and I realize I must defend it. But I rise to do so here only as part of a preliminary assessment of Brentano's account of the intentional and of what more is needed in order to avoid the inevitable distortion of restricting the intentional to "mental phenomena." The intentional, Brentano asserts again and again, yields a form of certainty and immediate knowledge superior to anything the physical sciences could possibly claim. Let me offer, therefore, a slim set of theorems sufficient for a large correction of Brentano's vision that would secure his own work well enough but would place it in the larger field of investigation to which it rightly belongs. I won't try to argue for these theorems here. I have explored them in different ways frequently enough.[29] They are hardly unreasonable or problematic; and many readers will probably find them entirely obvious.

They include at least the following: (i) psychology is not an autonomous discipline, certainly not a discipline whose phenomena are likely to be explained in exclusively physical or biological terms or in terms grounded in the "mental phenomena" Brentano thinks are immediately known with certainty or in any terms separated from the societal life of persons uniquely formed and transformed through the processes of historical enculturation; (ii) the paradigm of the mental is indisputably linked to the self-conscious ability of human persons to report, avow, and describe the content of their own mental life in accord with (i): where, that is, the detailed description and explanation of the mental life of prelinguistic children and sublinguistic animals is conducted heuristically, unavoidably, in terms of the same paradigm, with whatever adjustments are theoretically needed; (iii) persons or selves, the apt enlanguaged agents that we are, are themselves "second-natured," culturally artifactual, transforms of the members of *Homo sapiens*, made capable of self-conscious thought, experience, deliberate choice and action, the manufacture and creation of cultural artifacts of all kinds (as by art and technology), changes in their own enculturing culture, and the raising of offspring on the way to becoming new selves; (iv) the mental life of persons is, however diverse qua "mental phenomena," generated by internalizing (and thus sharing) a public culture, so that even first-person knowledge of mental phenomena is a function of a public culture: in that sense, there can be no final privilege accorded first-person knowledge of mental phenomena; and (v) there is no principled difference between the analysis of the intentional "activities" of persons or selves (in Brentano's sense) and what, thereby, is publicly "presented" (or "uttered," as I would rather say): that is, in speech, behavior, action, art, technology, manufacture, or the like, and all such public "utterances" (collected as literature, science, history, documents, buildings, computer programs, and so on) are intrinsically interpretable as "Intentional" (in the sense suggested).

On the view I recommend, the Intentional does not include the intentional in all its manifest forms (specifically prelinguistic intentionality, for instance, unless by theoretical analogy[30]); but the pre- or sublinguistic intentional is ineluctably modeled on the Intentionally transformed intentional life of humans – simply because no purely physical or behavioral analysis has proved adequate to the task. Furthermore, the Intentional is primarily collective, as in language, tradition, institutions, history, ideology, and the like; although actual Intentional agency is exhibited only by individual selves (singly or aggregatively), who exhibit their "idiolectic" variants of the common culture they share. (There are no collective agents, except by way of legal fictions and the like.) The profound limitation in Brentano's and Husserl's accounts of intentionality is betrayed (at a considerable distance from their own work) in, for instance, the account of societal life advanced by John Searle (and many others): Searle, who, of course, has himself analyzed intentionality, plainly thinks of language and the intentional artifacts of societal life as (somehow) generated by aggregates of persons.[31] But Searle's view (a fortiori, Brentano's) is simply a variant of the paradox Rousseau offers in *The Social Contract*.

There are all sorts of important distinctions regarding intentionality (or Intentionality) to be made out here: in the arts, for instance, regarding expressiveness and representationality; in language and other forms of communication, regarding semantic, syntactic, pragmatic, and semiotic attributes; in history, regarding horizonal interpretation and the ongoing reinterpretation of what has already been interpreted.[32] But the single most decisive consideration for our present purpose is this: (a) that a scientific psychology, one that features the paradigm of the mental, cannot be an autonomous discipline, cannot be separated from the analysis of the world of human culture; (b) that "mental phenomena" cannot be epistemically privileged, cannot even be separated from the analysis of a publicly shared world; and (c) that the analysis of intentionality, in the paradigm form of Intentionality, cannot separate or privilege the mental over the non-mental or vice versa. What this means is simply that Brentano has brought us to the threshold of the full range of intentionality (and that Husserl misperceived what more was needed).

Some who follow Brentano broadly here – Donald Davidson, for instance – wrongly hurry to conclude: "we have the resources needed to identify states of mind, even if those states of mind are, as we like to say, directed to nonexistent objects, for we can do this without supposing that there are any objects whatever before the mind."[33] Davidson does not pause long enough, however, to consider how we should treat mental images, after-images, hallucinatory images, pains, itches, tickles, and the like normally caught up in intentional "states." The fashion nowadays is to try to eliminate all "objects whatever before the mind," but that's hardly to explain how it's to be done.[34]

It is true that Heidegger and Gadamer saw more clearly than either Brentano or Husserl what more would need to be supplied (in the Intentional direction), but they have preferred to air these further complications in ways that show no interest in building on Brentano's pioneer clarity. And yet, of course, if we allow the enlargement of the intentional in favor of the Intentional (in the sense proposed) then Brentano's plausible scruple, formulated along reist lines (where, as Brentano supposes, "mental phenomena" play a decisive evidentiary and epistemological role) begins to founder. For, for one thing, in favoring the Intentional, we cannot fail to deny the epistemic and evidentiary advocacy of first-person foundations (without disallowing first-person reports of mental phenomena); and, for a second, in acknowledging the paradigmatic model of enlanguaged thought and experience, we are led to deny any privileged paraphrastic program of the "content" of intentional phenomena.

By extending the scope of the intentional, therefore, we greatly simplify its analysis. It would not be too much to say that Chisholm's preference for characterizing the intentional in terms of the analysis of sentences now appears more than reasonable, if it is not cast as a straightforward summary of Brentano's thesis; although to confirm its contribution would inevitably call into doubt Chisholm's own program favoring the certainty and self-evidence of "self-presenting states."[35]

If I understand him rightly, Chisholm does believe that "some beliefs or statements," those that "concern appearances or 'ways of being appeared to,'" are "self-justifying" and that they are self-justifying because they are about "self-presenting properties" (or states): that is, on the thesis that "the presence of such properties is also evident to the subject who has them."[36] Chisholm is perfectly aware that he is advocating the doctrine of "the Given" (in some form) and that he is open to the familiar criticism formulated as the "Myth of the Given."[37] This is a much-debated question. But I don't find that Chisholm actually addresses the sense in which "self-presenting properties" (or "states") are to be characterized (rather than merely identified, by way of instances: "being sad," "thinking about a golden mountain," "believing oneself to be wise," "'[being] appeared redly to'"[38]) in that respect in which they serve as evidence for relevant beliefs and statements because (being what they are) they are "evident" in a very strong or "foundational" sense.

I have no doubt that *experience* can serve as evidence for particular beliefs and statements, which implies the epistemic relevance of intentional complexities. But *if* it were the case that "experience" in Chisholm's or Brentano's sense were not "given" (on a benign reading of the term) *as* already conceptually and (indeed) linguistically structured, then the entire argument would instantly be rendered more than problematic. We may gather from this that the inclusion of the "intentional" within the scope of the "Intentional" (admitting the Intentional modeling of the "intentional" among prelinguistic children, sublinguistic animals, and the theoretical abstraction of the non-propositional or non-conceptually structured "sensory," if wanted) will very seriously challenge the doctrine of the self-evident. What we must appreciate, dialectically, is this: that *if* experience plays an evidentiary role with regard to beliefs, then (a) experience must be able to be "before the mind" in some sense, (b) will be intentional for at least that reason, (c) may be problematic as to whether it involves "objects," and (d) plays the role it does even if we reject the notion of the self-evident.[39]

In any case, the analysis of intentionality would be substantially altered by the adjustment I am proposing, along the following lines at least: (a) that the "Intentional" = the "cultural" (or culturally significant and significative), in a way that would allow for the initial inclusion of all the forms of "aboutness" or "reference to" that Brentano, Husserl, and those they have influenced have ever proposed; (b) that the Intentional is the paradigm of the intentional (in the sense already supplied); (c) that the Intentional presupposes the *sui generis* epistemic competence and "mental phenomena" of encultured selves, but is not restricted to the mental at all: may be instantiated in the public artifacts of cultural life (what I have called "utterances": speech, behavior, technology, art); and may, correspondingly, be invoked for modeling intentional attributions to analogous structures in the sublinguistic biological world (for instance, with regard to the functional structures of termite mounds); (d) that the Intentional (a fortiori, the intentional) has realist standing; (e) that the Intentional affects the work of the physical sciences as much as the human sciences, even though the descriptive and explanatory vocabulary of the former may explicitly preclude the use of intentionally or Intentionally qualified terms; (f) that the Intentional is intrinsically interpretable and that the objective standing of any statements or beliefs will be affected by the historicized processes of interpretation and conceptualization; and (g) that, accordingly, there can be no prioritizing of any single model for analyzing the structure of the Intentional or intentional, except relative to one or another kind of inquiry and interest. Adjustments of these sorts would enlarge by an enormous factor our sense not only of the ubiquity of the intentional but also of the unexpected diversity and complexity of its structural entanglements. To admit all that would be to admit, therefore, just how much Brentano actually missed.

NOTES

1. PES-E, especially "The Distinction between Mental and Physical Phenomena"; see, also, TE.
2. *Ibid.*, p. 5.
3. *Ibid.*, p. 3.
4. *Ibid.*, p. 5.
5. *Ibid.*
6. *Ibid.*, pp. 9–10.
7. Tadeusz Kotarbinski, "Franz Brentano as Reist," in, ed., Linda L. McAlister, *The Philosophy of Brentano* (Atlantic Highlands, NJ: Humanities Press, 1976), p. 200.
8. PES-E, pp. 82–3.
9. *Ibid.*, p. 5.
10. *Ibid.* (Appendix): "Supplementary Remarks Intended to Explain and Defend, as well as to Correct and Expand upon the Theory," pp. 291–4.
11. On the argument in "Supplementary Remarks . . ." Brentano finds himself in substantial agreement with Leibniz's view of concrete things (pp. 294–5).
12. See, for instance, Edmund Husserl, *Cartesian Meditations*, trans., Dorion Cairns (The Hague: Nijhoff, 1967); and *Ideas: A General Introduction to Pure Phenomenology*, trans., W. R. Boyce Gibson (London: Allen and Unwin, 1931).
13. See Roderick M. Chisholm, "Editor's Introduction," *Realism and the Background of Phenomenology* (Glencoe: Free Press, 1960), particularly pp. 20–2; Chisholm, *Perceiving: a Philosophical Study* (Ithaca, NY: Cornell University Press, 1957), ch. 11; and Linda L. McAlister, "Chisholm and Brentano on Intentionality," in, ed., Linda L. McAlister, *The Philosophy of Brentano* (Atlantic Highlands, NJ: Humanities Press, 1976).
14. See, for instance, Herbert Spiegelberg, " 'Intention' and 'Intentionality' in the Scholastics, Brentano and Husserl," in, ed., McAlister, *Philosophy of Brentano*; see, also, Edmund Husserl, "Phenomenology," trans. C. V. Salmon, *The Encyclopedia Britannica*, 14th edn. (1929), vol. XVII.
15. See, for instance, Ausonio Marras, "Scholastic Roots of Brentano's Conception of Intentionality," in, ed., McAlister, *Philosophy of Brentano*.
16. For specimen views, See John R. Searle, *Intentionality: an Essay in the Philosophy of Mind* (Cambridge: Cambridge University Press, 1983);

Jerry A. Fodor, *A Theory of Content and Other Essays* (Cambridge: MIT Press, 1990); Daniel C. Dennett, *The Intentional Stance* (Cambridge: MIT Press, 1987); and William Lyons, *Approaches to Intentionality* (Oxford: Clarendon, 1995).

17. See Martin Heidegger, *Being and Time*, trans., John Macquarrie and Edward Robinson (New York: Harper and Row, 1962); and Maurice Merleau-Ponty, *Phenomenology of Perception*, trans., Colin Smith (London: Routledge and Kegan Paul, 1962).

18. See Joseph Margolis, *Historied Thought, Constructed World: a Conceptual Primer for the Turn of the New Millennium* (Berkeley, CA: University of California Press, 1995); *Interpretation Radical but Not Unruly: the New Puzzle of the Arts and History* (Berkeley, CA: University of California Press, 1995).

19. See, for instance, Edmund Husserl, *The Crisis of European Sciences and Transcendental Phenomenology; an Introduction to Phenomenological Philosophy*, trans. David Carr (Evanston, IL: Northwestern University Press, 1970); and Hans-Georg Gadamer, *Truth and Method*, 2nd edn., trans. Joel Weinsheimer and Donald G. Marshall (London: Sheed and Ward, 1989). An instructive sense of Heidegger's very different (and more promising) turn, along hermeneutic lines, may be found in Martin Heidegger, *Ontology – the Hermeneutics of Facticity*, trans. John van Buren (Bloomington, IN: Indiana University Press, 1999).

20. To mention some further specimen inquiries to fix our sense of the possibilities, see Ernst Cassirer, *The Philosophy of Symbolic Forms*, 3 vols., trans. Ralph Manheim (New Haven, CT: Yale University Press, 1953, 1955, 1957); Thomas S. Kuhn, *The Structure of Scientific Revolutions*, enlarged edn. (Chicago, IL: University of Chicago Press, 1970); and Michel Foucault, *The History of Sexuality*, 3 vols., trans. Robert Hurley (New York: Pantheon, 1978, 1985, 1986).

21. PES-E, pp. 88–9.

22. *Ibid.*, pp. 78–80; see Oskar Kraus's notes 1 and 2, pp. 79–80: Brentano means the objects of direct sense-perception, not external objects – so "a landscape" is "sensible *per accidens.*"

23. Chisholm, "Editor's Introduction," *Realism and the Background of Phenomenology*, p. 4.

24. Chisholm, *Perceiving*, p. 169. Oddly, the *Perceiving* book antedates the *Realism* anthology. Compare McAlister, "Chisholm and Brentano on Intentionality."

25. See TE.

26. Chisholm, *Perceiving*, pp. 170–3. Chisholm gives an alternative formulation of criterion (3); but the sense of it accords with the familiar formulation I've given.

27. See W. V. Quine, *Word and Object* (Cambridge, MA: MIT Press, 1960), §41.
28. See PES-E, Bk. I, Ch. 1 (pp. 10, 14, 20).
29. See, for example, Joseph Margolis, *Historied Thought, Constructed World*; and *Culture and Cultural Entities: toward a New Unity of Science* (Dordrecht: D. Reidel, 1984).
30. Compare Roderick M. Chisholm, *Theory of Knowledge*, 2nd edn. (Englewood Cliffs, NJ: Prentice-Hall, 1977), Ch. 4; and Fred I. Dretske, *Seeing and Knowing* (Chicago, IL: University of Chicago Press, 1969).
31. See John R. Searle, *The Construction of Social Reality* (New York: Free Press, 1995).
32. For a sample of my own way of pursuing these matters, see Margolis, *Interpretation Radical but Not Unruly*.
33. Donald Davidson, "What is Present to the Mind," in *Subjective, Intersubjective, Objective* (Oxford: Clarendon, 2001), p. 67. Davidson correctly offers this rejoinder as an answer to Michael Dummett's belief that Brentano did not solve the problem of nonexistent objects before the mind. Davidson refers to Brentano's *Psychology* by way of Dummett's reference, but does not actually seem aware of Brentano's having addressed the question. In fact, Dummett himself seems to have missed the point. See Michael Dummett, *The Interpretation of Frege's Philosophy* (London: Duckworth, 1981), p. 57.
34. Probably the most insouciant offender in this regard is Dennett. See Daniel C. Dennett, *Explaining Consciousness* (Boston, MA: Little, Brown, 1991).
35. See Chisholm, *Theory of Knowledge*, Ch. 2; also, *The Foundations of Knowing* (Minneapolis, MN: University of Minnesota Press, 1982), particularly pp. 126–47.
36. Chisholm, *Foundations of Knowing*, pp. 147, 11; see, further, pp. 9–13.
37. The term is Wilfrid Sellars's. See Wilfrid Sellars, "Empiricism and the Philosophy of Mind," in *Science, Perception and Reality* (London: Routledge and Kegan Paul, 1963).
38. Chisholm, *Foundations of Knowing*, p. 10.
39. This bears directly on one of the strongly contested questions of the day in analytic philosophy. See, for instance, John McDowell, *Mind and World* (Cambridge, MA: Harvard University Press, 1994, 1996).

7   Brentano's epistemology

MENTAL AND PHYSICAL PHENOMENA

In this chapter, I will set out what I take to be the basic tenets of
Franz Brentano's epistemology. This seemingly simple task is a crucial one because virtually every other aspect of Brentano's philosophy uses his epistemology as a starting point and is structured in
the same way. As the title of his major published work, *Psychology
from an Empirical Standpoint*, suggests, Brentano saw himself as an
empiricist; his account of knowledge, belief and other epistemological concepts is therefore constructed from the building blocks, so to
speak, of the phenomena of experience.

According to Brentano, these phenomena are of two kinds, mental and physical, and he believes all human experience is experience of one or other of these phenomena. So we first have to see
how he differentiates between mental and physical phenomena, between the mental and the physical. He lays out this distinction in
the first chapter of Book 2 of his *Psychology*, entitled "On the Distinction Between Mental and Physical Phenomena." Brentano first
surveys several ways of laying out the distinction between these
two classes of experiential phenomena. He then enumerates examples of mental and physical phenomena, and then tries to find the
defining characteristics of mental phenomena. He identifies several
characteristics which he thinks all mental phenomena have and all
physical phenomena lack. Far and away the most important of these
in his estimation, and the one which has aroused the most interest on the part of later philosophers, is what he calls "intentional
inexistence."[1]

INTENDED OBJECTS OF KNOWLEDGE

Brentano's first example of mental phenomena is presentations (*Vorstellungen*), either sensory or issuing from the imagination. By "presentation" he says he means not the object which is presented, but the condition, or what he broadly speaking calls the act, of having such a presentation.[2] Thus, the acts of hearing, seeing, or otherwise perceiving something would be mental phenomena regardless of whether the object which is, for example, seen is perceived through the visual organs or seen, so to speak, in the mind's eye. Other examples are acts of judgment such as remembering, inferring, believing, doubting; and emotions such as being happy or sad, loving and hating, as well as willing, intending, and the like.[3]

Examples of physical phenomena that Brentano mentions are "a color, a figure, a landscape which I see, a chord which I hear, warmth, cold, odor which I perceive; as well as similar images which appear in the imagination." It appears from the examples, then, that mental phenomena are all mental acts, in a broad sense, while physical phenomena are, strictly speaking, all instances of sensible qualities. As I mentioned above, Brentano thought that there is one particular mark of mental phenomena which characterizes them better than any other. He writes:

Every mental phenomenon is characterized by what the Scholastics of the middle ages called the intentional (or mental) inexistence of an object, and what we might call, though not wholly unambiguously, reference to a content, direction toward an object (by which you should not take me to mean a thing), or immanent objectivity. Every mental phenomenon includes something in itself as an object, though they do not all do so in the same way. In presentation something is presented, in judgment something is affirmed or denied, in love loved, in hate hated, in desire desired and so on.[5]

Critics, perhaps not surprisingly, have disagreed as to precisely what Brentano is saying in this passage. Some, such as Alois Höfler, have supposed that since one can think of, hate, judge, etc., things which do not exist, such as Pegasus, then the immanent object which Brentano speaks of is not Pegasus, but a "thought-of Pegasus" (*gedachtes Pegasus*) that exists in one's mind whenever someone thinks of Pegasus.[6] In the light of some passages from Brentano's early writings this appears to be a plausible interpretation. Consider, for example, the following passage:

There cannot be anyone who contemplates an A unless there is a contemplated A; and conversely. . . . The two concepts are not identical but they are correaltive. Neither one can correspond to anything in reality unless the other does as well. But only one of these is the concept of a thing – the concept of something which can act and be acted upon. The second is the concept of a being which is only a sort of accompaniment to the first; when the first thing comes into being, and when it ceases to be, then so too does the second.[7]

Such a passage might well lead one to think that the mental act in question is "someone's contemplating A" and that the object or immanent object which Brentano spoke of is a "contemplated A," i.e., a mental entity distinct from any A outside the mind. But this is a strange view from which it would seem to follow that one can only love, desire, think of, judge, etc. one's own mental contents, never anything external to the mind to which those mental contents might correspond. Brentano knew, however, that such a view would be incorrect. He says:

It would, of course, be clearly ridiculous to say that someone who wanted to know something, achieved the knowledge he wanted by coming to comprehend something else rather than that which he wanted to know.[8]

So we may suspect that Höfler has misinterpreted him, though he is certainly not alone in this. In fact, Brentano explicitly repudiates this interpretation in a letter to his former student, Anton Marty.[9] Though written during Brentano's later philosophical period, the crucial parts of this letter refer back to his earlier position, which he attempts to clarify by saying:

[I]t has never been my view that the immanent object is identical with "thought-of object." What we think is the object or thing and not the "thought of object." If, in our thought, we contemplate a horse, our thought has as its immanent object – not a "contemplated horse," but a horse. And strictly speaking only the horse – not the "contemplated horse" – can be called an object. But the object need not exist. The person thinking may have something as the object of his thought even though that thing does not exist.[10]

Brentano remarks that by "immanent" he never meant to imply that the object is an entity which is different from the transcendent object (if there is one). He meant only to indicate that the object need not actually exist in order to be the object of an intentional act; intentional existence suffices. For him, the term "immanent object" means not that the object exists but that it is an object whether or not there is anything which corresponds to it. Its being an object, however, is merely the linguistic correlate of the person having it as object, as in thinking of it in his experience.[11]

How can this assertion be reconciled with the passage quoted above, where he seemed to be saying that, for example, what he meant by "immanent object" or "intentional object" was a thought-of object? Is Brentano mistaken when he says that he has held the same view all along? Commentators Oskar Kraus and Franzisca Mayer-Hillebrand seem to think so, for they say that by the time this letter to Marty was written, his earlier view had become so foreign to him that he questioned whether he had ever even held it.[12] Roderick M. Chisholm follows Kraus in this interpretation of Brentano's position, though he at least seems to recognize the awkwardness of attributing a position to Brentano which he quite explicitly says he never held.[13] It seems unlikely, though, to say the least, that Brentano would have forgotten having held a view which he is supposed to have held for twenty or more years.

The only point on which the letter specifically departs from the earlier view is this: Brentano had earlier maintained that "someone's contemplating A" and the "contemplated A" were correlative concepts, while in the letter he calls the "contemplated A" a linguistic, that is, a grammatical, correlate. The grounds for this change were that he came to believe that concepts can only be of things, and while both A and the person contemplating A may be things in Brentano's sense, a contemplated A is not. In the letter to Marty, however, Brentano nowhere denies that he had once said that the two were conceptual correlates. He denies rather that he ever held that anything such as a "contemplated A" is the immanent or intentional object of a mental act. Hence, I see no compelling reason for saying that Brentano had forgotten his earlier view. He also gives us a further clue which seems to confirm that he saw no difficulty about saying, simultaneously, that there is a correlative concept or a perceived object whenever there is an act of perceiving and that such an entity is not the immanent or intentional object of the perceptual act. He tells us that his view of the matter is the same as Aristotle's; in the *Metaphysics*, we find Aristotle saying:

Knowable and thinkable things are relative because something else is referred to them. For something to be thinkable indicates that there is a thought to refer to it; but it is not the case that the thought is relative to what is being thought, for this would be saying the same thing twice. Similarly, seeing is seeing some thing, not just seeing what is seen, although it is of course true to say this; but seeing is relative to color or to some other thing of the sort, for it would be saying the same thing in two ways to say "seeing the seen."[15]

Brentano and Aristotle are in general agreement that whenever someone thinks of X, it is true that there is a correlative thought-of X, but they view this as trivially true, and they both deny that a thought-of X is the object of the act of thinking. The object is, rather, just X. What Aristotle does not mention here, and what Brentano adds, is that X can be referred to in this way even when it does not actually exist. Brentano reiterates his affinity with Aristotle on this point elsewhere in this letter in an attempt to further elucidate his position. This reference to Aristotle helps to explain how the object of a thought, for example, could at the same time be something which, if it exists at all, is external to the mind, and yet still be related to the mind which thinks it. He notes that Aristotle says that in sense perception the form of the object is received by the senses without the matter, and likewise the intellect receives the intelligible form in abstraction from the matter. Brentano here remarks to Marty, "Wasn't his thinking essentially the same as ours?"[16]

As Brentano seems to have understood the doctrine, when someone sees or thinks of a horse, the immanent object is a horse, but as an immanent object it has a different "mode of being" than it has when it is completely unrelated to a mind as the object of a mental act. The similarity between Brentano's doctrine and the intentional inexistence of the Scholastics comes to mind here as well. Compare the following passage from St. Thomas Aquinas's commentary on the relevant passage in Aristotle's *De Anima*:

[S]ense receives the form without the matter, since form has a different mode of being in sense perception than it has in the sensible thing. For in the sensible thing it has natural being; but in sense perception it has intentional being.[17]

Thus, we have here to do with two different modes of being which objects may have: actual existence and intentional existence (or inexistence if one prefers the Scholastics' term; as mentioned in note 1, the prefix "in" is locative rather than negative), which is, as Chisholm puts it, "short of actuality, but more than nothingness . . ."[18] I may, for example, think about a white horse and there may actually be a white horse which I am thinking about. If so, this horse has actual existence, but it also has intentional existence because when I think about him he acquires, in addition to his actual existence, a kind of existence in my mind which he did not have previous to anyone's thinking about him. And what is more, even if there were no actually existing white horses at all, a white horse could still be the object of my thought, for a white horse begins to exist intentionally the instant I begin to think of it.

This interpretation of Brentano's doctrine of intentional inexistence differs from that of Kraus, Höfler, and Mayer-Hillebrand. Chisholm is inclined to follow them on this point. It is perhaps presumptuous to disagree with those such as Kraus, who had close personal contact with Brentano. On the other hand, it would be even more presumptuous to reject Brentano's own testimony as to what his position was in favor of theirs. Chisholm was aware of this dilemma, and suggested an alternative interpretation in an attempt to reconcile Brentano's early writings with his later explications of them. The interpretation is as follows:

(1) an actual intentionally inexistent unicorn is produced when one thinks about a unicorn; (2) one's thought, however, is not directed upon this actual intentionally inexistent unicorn; and yet (3) it is in virtue of the existence of the intentionally inexistent unicorn that one's thought may be said to be directed upon a unicorn.[19]

I do not believe this interpretation will do either, for although it is correct insofar as it says that the object of thought is a unicorn when one thinks of a unicorn, it still mistakenly assumes that "actually intentionally inexistent unicorn" means "thought-of unicorn," and is somehow different from the unicorn that is thought. This then leaves Chisholm wondering "what point would there be in supposing there is the inexistent unicorn" if the object of thought is the unicorn, simpliciter.[20] The fact of the matter is, Brentano pointedly denied that "intentionally inexistent unicorn" means "thought-of unicorn." He says "it has never been my view that the immanent object is identical with the thought-of object," and he regarded such a view as utter foolishness.[21]

ACTUAL AND NONACTUAL INTENDED OBJECTS IN RELATIONS

The solution to this problem of interpretation and an explanation of why Brentano thought the views his students attributed to him were so absurd is to be found in a consideration of his views concerning relations. In these passages, Brentano advances the thesis that a defining characteristic of mental phenomena is that they are relational. Brentano then believed that a necessary condition for there being a relation, xRy, is that both x and y exist.[22]

How can these two views be reconciled when it is patently obvious that we often think of centaurs, unicorns, and the like, which do not exist? Kraus and the others have interpreted Brentano's early solution to this objection to the relational character of mental phenomena to be as follows: if "y" stands for a centaur, then there can be no relation xRy, for the object term in relation must stand for something that exists. It must be the case, therefore, that the mental act of thinking about a centaur is really a relation of the form xR(thought-of y), because though y does not exist, a thought-of y surely may. Brentano, however, could not have held such a view, even though he thought that there do exist entities such as "thought-of y's" because, on his account, a thought-of y comes into being as a correlate of the act of thinking b of y. But if y itself does not exist, then, on his theory of relations, there can be no act of thinking of y which would produce the correlative thought-of y.

Chisholm's alternative interpretation seems to ignore the strictures which Brentano's view of relations imposed upon him, and would have him saying that xRy can be a relation even though y does not actually exist, somehow in virtue of an actually existing thought-of y. Rather, what I believe Brentano meant was this: in the case of, for example, someone thinking about a centaur, xRy is a genuine relation because, even though the centaur does not have actual existence, he does have another mode of existence, that is, intentional inexistence, but existence nonetheless, and hence the requirement that relations obtain only between existent entities is satisfied.

I do not mean to deny that Brentano also thought, at this time, that entities such as "thought-of centaurs" do indeed exist. He believed that they do, as a matter of fact, acquire actual existence whenever centaurs, etc., are thought of, just as Aristotle did. This fact nevertheless has no bearing at all on the present question. Confusion over the role played by such entities has been responsible, it seems to me, for the repeated misinterpretation of Brentano's intentionality thesis. They certainly are thought by Brentano to be objects of mental acts in some situations, but these are special cases, and not simple, straightforward mental acts in which one subject thinks of, judges, or loves a single object. Rather, these would be cases, for example, in which I think of Jones thinking of a centuar. Then my objects of thought are Jones and a thought-of (by Jones) centaur. Furthermore, Brentano thought that once I have the concept of a thought-of centaur I can think of it without thinking of the person who thinks it. But such cases are dependent upon one's (for example Jones) being able to have centaurs, simpliciter, as objects of mental acts, and this in turn depends upon centaurs, etc., having intentional existence if mental acts are relational as claimed.

Later, a transformation in Brentano's views about relations goes hand in hand with a transformation of his intentionality doctrine. So we see that mental phenomena are acts which refer to objects whether those objects have both actual and intentional existence or intentional existence only; they are acts which either bestow a kind of existence on an object which has no actual existence, or add a second mode of existence to an object which does actually exist already. It is Brentano's contention that all mental phenomena have this characteristic, and no non-mental, that is, no physical phenomenon shows anything like it. This is certainly true when one restricts physical phenomena to mere sensible qualities as Brentano does. Whether the notion of intentionality provides any adequate means of differentiating the mental from the physical when it is removed from the context of Brentano's epistemological and ontological assumptions is a question which has been widely discussed among twentieth-century philosophers.[23] I have entered into this long discussion of Brentano's original doctrine of intentionality because I believe it has been misinterpreted in the past and I wished to offer what I think to be the correct interpretation. This is, however, by no means a mere digression. The underlying assumptions behind Brentano's early theory of truth, the fact that he believed the defining characteristic of mental acts to be that they always intend an object, is one of the things which led him, during the earlier period, to believe in the existence of a realm of independently existing states of affairs.

In addition to intentional inexistence Brentano suggests several other features that are characteristic of mental phenomena. It is not always clear what the logical status of these other characteristics is supposed to be, since, presumably, intentionality is meant to be both a logically necessary and sufficient condition for something's being a mental phenomenon. The first of these other characteristics is that all mental phenomena are either presentations or are based upon presentations.[24] Secondly, mental phenomena are the exclusive objects of inner perception and, therefore, they alone are directly perceived and yield self-evident knowledge. This characteristic is closely tied up with another which Brentano expresses by saying that mental phenomena are the only phenomena which have actual existence in addition to having intentional existence. It is clear from the text that Brentano does not mean this characteristic to be a logically necessary one, however; he does not mean that it is logically impossible for a physical phenomenon to have actual existence as well as intentional existence, and, in fact, he argues strenuously against Bain who took this view.[25]

Physical phenomena may actually exist, but, because Brentano refuses to say that we know something unless it is an evident truth or derived from an evident truth, we can, according to him, never really know whether or not they have actual existence. We cannot help instinctively believing that they do, but nonetheless we are not entitled by our experience to assume that they have anything more than intentional existence. So, to be on the safe side, Brentano makes it a policy to refuse to say that physical phenomena have actual existence in addition to intentional existence.[26] The passage quoted above is a somewhat misleading way of expressing this idea. Finally, Brentano maintains that when we perceive a mental phenomenon, regardless of its complexity, it always manifests itself as a unity. On the other hand several, or complex, phenomena may be perceived simultaneously but they do not appear as parts of a whole in the same way.[27]

THREE-FOLD CLASSIFICATION OF MENTAL PHENOMENA

Once Brentano believes he has explained the difference between mental and physical phenomena, the next step is to describe and classify the various sorts of mental phenomena. To make such a classification, one needs some principle to go by; but what sort of a principle should it be? Not surprisingly, Brentano says it should be a "scientific" or a "natural" principle which orders its objects in a way which is useful for purposes of investigation and which classifies naturally similar things together. He also says that under no circumstances should a classification be made a priori but only after the objects which are to be classified have been studied. In his search for the best principle for the classification of mental phenomena Brentano surveys several possibilities and concludes that one based upon the fact that there are different kinds of intentional relations, i.e. different relations which mental phenomena can have to objects, is the best principle.[28]

By applying this principle, Brentano developed a three-fold classification of mental phenomena. This in itself is nothing new, for many philosophers since Descartes have favored a three-fold division, but the usual way of classifying mental phenomena was into thought, emotion, and will. Brentano, however, divides thought into two classes, presentation and judgment, and combines emotion and will into a single class. Of his first class, that of presentation or idea (Vorstellung), he says:

We speak of a presentation whenever we perceive anything. When we see something we are presented with a color, when we hear something we are presented with a sound, and when we imagine something we are presented with a fantasy image. In virtue of the generality with which we use the word, we can say that it is impossible for a mental act to refer to something in any way if that thing is not presented.[29]

Judgments make up Brentano's second class of mental phenomena. Every judgment is either an affirmation (Anerkennung) or denial (Verwerfung) of an object. Brentano uses the word "judgment" (Urteil) to cover a broad range of mental acts; of course it includes belief, opinion, and knowledge, but some others as well: ". . . this sort of affirmation or denial occurs as well in cases where many people do not use the term 'judgment', as, for example, in the case of mental acts and in the case of memory. But naturally we will not let ourselves be deterred from classifying these cases too as judgments."[30]

Brentano's third class of mental phenomena is that of what he calls the phenomena of love and hate. He is using these two terms in a special technical sense, such that "love" encompasses all pro- or positive attitudes and favorable feelings, emotions, and positive acts of will, while "hate" refers to all negative attitudes, feelings, emotions, and acts of will. This class of mental phenomena is said to contain all mental phenomena not already included in the first two classes, and, as Brentano describes it, the class consists of the emotions in the widest sense of this term, including not only the simplest forms of inclination and disinclination which may arise from the thought of an object, but also the joy or sorrow that is grounded in the beliefs that we have, as well as the highly complicated phenomena that are involved in ends and means.[31]

Brentano thinks that the direct testimony of inner perception shows this to be the correct classification because it shows that there is a basic difference between the way one is related to an object in presentation and in judging: judging involves either an affirmation or denial of an object, whereas nothing of the sort occurs in a mere presentation.[32] On the other hand, inner perception also shows that there is no crucial difference (though there are, of course, differences) between emotions and acts of will that warrant their being placed in separate categories. It shows us that they are both, broadly speaking, acts of love or hate toward an object and there is no sharp break between them. In fact, there is, according to Brentano, a continuum of mental phenomena from pure feelings to acts of will, so that if one were to try to separate them into two distinct classes, one would not know where to draw the line between them.[33]

Even though all of this is learned through inner perception, which is in itself a source of infallible knowledge, other philosophers, also presumably relying on inner perception, have made different classifications. This, Brentano explains, is because there is still room for error in remembering, reporting, and interpreting the data of inner perception. Hence, he sees that he must offer independent arguments designed to show that his view is correct and the others are mistaken; he also offers explanations of why various other philosophers have made such mistakes.

JUDGMENTS

Brentano's views about judgments were highly innovative in his time, rejecting, as they do, both of the prevalent analyses: the view that judgments consist of mere combinations of ideas and the view that judgments are especially intense presentations. On Brentano's analysis, the distinctive thing about judgments is that, in addition to there being an idea or a presentation of a certain object, there is a second intentional relation that is directed upon that object. The relation is one of affirmation or denial – either acceptance or rejection. If a man says, "God," he gives expression to the idea of God, but if he says, "There is a God," then he gives expression to his belief in God.[34] Implicit in saying that judgment is a different kind of relation toward an object from that involved in a presentation is the rejection of both the view that judgments are simply very intense presentations, and the view that judgments are merely a combination of ideas or presentations. The latter view is, according to Brentano, a gross misconception of the nature of judgment:

We may combine and relate presentations at will – as we do when we think of a green tree, or a golden mountain, or a father of a hundred children, or a friend of science – but if we have only combined and related we have made no judgment. (To be sure, every judgment is based upon some presentation or other and so, too, is every desire.) And on the other hand, we may make a judgment without thereby combining ideas or relating them as subject and predicate.[35]

Judgments such as "God exists" or "It is raining" are the ones which Brentano thinks prove that there are judgments which involve no combining of ideas or combining of a subject with a predicate (except grammatically).[36] People who think that a judgment must always involve the combining of a subject with a predicate would say that in judging that God exists, you are affirming the combination of the predicate, existence, and the subject, God. Brentano thinks, however, that such judgments are merely affirmations of a simple object, such as God, rather than of a combination. To support his view, he argues as follows:

[W]henever someone affirms a whole, he also includes in his affirmation every part of that whole. Thus whoever affirms a combination of attributes affirms every particular element of that combination. Whoever affirms that a learned man exists, i.e. affirms the combination of a man with the attribute "being learned," affirms thereby that a man exists. When we apply this to the judgment "A exists," if this judgment were the affirmation of the combination of the predicate "existence" with "A," then it would include the affirmation of each individual element in the combination and therefore would include the affirmation of A. We would not have succeeded in avoiding the assumption that a simple affirmation of A is involved. But how does this simple affirmation of A differ from the affirmation of the combination of A with the attribute "existence" which is supposed to be expressed in the sentence "A exists"? Clearly it does not differ at all. So we see rather that the affirmation of A is the true and the whole sense of the sentence and nothing but A is the object of the judgment.[37]

Brentano recognizes many distinctions within the class of judgments. For example, he distinguishes between simple and compound judgments. Simple judgments are said to be genuinely unitary; that is to say that they contain only one affirmation or denial. Compound judgments, on the other hand, may have more than one affirmation or denial included in a single proposition. He adds:

[I]n ordinary life we often use the categorical, subject-predicate form to express a multiplicity of judgments, one built upon another. The proposition, "That is a man," is a clear example. Use of the demonstrative already presupposes belief in the existence of the thing in question; a second judgment then ascribes to it the predicate "man."[38]

Brentano believes that all simple judgments, as well as those compound judgments whose full meaning can be expressed by a conjunction of simple judgments, can be translated without change of meaning into existential judgments of the form "A is," where something such as "AB," which can symbolize a modified object such as "a learned man," is a permissible substitution instance for "A." That is to say, all such categorical judgments are equivalent to mere affirmations or denials of an object.[39] This suggestion does not sound revolutionary today, but at the time, the notion that perhaps the majority of judgments which we make do not involve the affirmation or denial of a combination of the idea of existence with some other idea was a great departure and met with considerable resistance from John Stuart Mill and others.[40]

According to Brentano, universal categorical judgments such as "All men are mortal" are translatable, without change of meaning, into judgments of the form "There is no immortal man," i.e. "AB is not." Negative universal categorical judgments such as "No stone is living" are equivalent to "AB is not," i.e. "There is no living stone." Note that on this account all universal judgments reduce to negative existential judgments, which is to say they reduce to denial of an object. Simple particular categorical judgments are all said to be equivalent to positive existential judgments, that is, to affirmations of objects. "Some man is ill" becomes "There is an ill man," i.e. "AB is," while "Some man is not learned" becomes "There is an unlearned man" or "AB is."[41]

Brentano believes, however, that there are some compound judgments that cannot be expressed without change of meaning by simple judgments and thus cannot be put into existential form. For example, "The rose is a flower" is not equivalent to "There is no rose which is not a flower."[42] Thus, he distinguishes between both predicative and existential forms of judgment. The important thing is that he has tried to loosen the grip that the subject/predicate theory of judgment has had on philosophers, and he emphasizes that most judgments are, logically speaking, existential in form. It is quite clear from what has already been said that Brentano recognizes, too, a qualitative distinction between judgments; there are positive judgments, i.e. acts of affirmation or acceptance, and negative judgments, acts of rejection or denial. The concepts of existence and truth are closely tied to affirmative judgments and those of non-existence and falsity to negative judgments. Brentano held, during this early phase of his career, that if I make a judgment of the form "A is," as in "There is a tree," my judgment is correct or true if there is a tree, false if there is not. With respect to the connection between affirmative and negative judgments and existence and non-existence Brentano says the following:

The concepts of existence and non-existence are correlatives to the concepts of the truth of (simple) affirmative and negative judgments. The judgment is correlative with that which is judged, the affirmative judgment with that which is judged affirmatively, the negative judgment with that which is judged negatively. So, too, the correctness of the affirmative judgment is correlated with the existence of that which is affirmatively judged, and that of the negative judgment with the nonexistence of that which is negatively judged. One may say that an affirmative judgment is true, or one may say that its object is existent; in both cases one would be saying precisely the same thing. Similarly for saying that a negative judgment is true, and saying that its object is non-existent. We may say that for every (simple) affirmative judgment, either it or the corresponding negative judgment is true; and we may express precisely the same logical principle by saying that, for every such affirmative judgment, either its object is existent or its object is non-existent.[43]

There remain two further important distinctions Brentano draws among judgments: the distinction between assertoric and apodictic judgments and that between blind and evident judgments. Traditionally speaking, the distinction between affirmative and negative judgments is one of quality, while the distinction between assertoric and apodictic judgments is one of modality. To judge assertorically is to judge something to exist or not to exist, as a matter of fact. To judge apodictically is to judge something to be logically necessary or logically impossible. Brentano believed that this distinction and the distinction between blind and evident judgments pertains to the act of judging itself, and not, for example, to its object.[44]

Finally, Brentano distinguishes between blind and evident judgments. Clearly not all judgments are true: some are based on prejudices that we acquire in our infancy that may take on the appearance of indubitable principles. All men by nature have an impulse to trust other judgments that are equally blind – for example, those judgments that are based upon so-called external perception and those that are based upon memories of the recent past. What is affirmed in this way may often be true, but it is just as likely to be false, for these judgments involve nothing that manifests correctness. So the defining characteristic of a blind judgment seems to be that it is not "manifestly correct" or "experienced as being correct" ("als richtig characterisiert"). So-called "evident" or "insightful" judgments, on the other hand, do have this characteristic. Brentano's attempts to clarify what it is to be "experienced as being correct" are less than illuminating, because he believes that in the final analysis a person can only learn what an evident judgment is by experiencing one. Thus, he repeatedly turns to examples to make the notion clear. He can tell us some things about the distinction, however, as, for example, in the passage below from the Ursprung, where he maintains that the distinction between blind and evident judgments is not merely a matter of degree of conviction. After all, we can be so firmly convinced of some blind judgments that we do not doubt them at all, and we sometimes hold such a belief so firmly that we cannot rid ourselves of it even when we know there is no justification for it.

But . . . [such judgments] do not have the clarity that is characteristic of the higher form of judgment. If one were to ask, "Why do you really believe that?" it would be impossible to find any rational grounds. If one were to raise the same question in connection with a judgment that, is immediately evident, here, too, it would be impossible to refer to any grounds. But in this case the clarity of the judgment is such as to enable us to see that the question has no point; indeed the question would be completely ridiculous. Everyone experiences the difference between these two classes of judgment. As in the case of every other concept, the ultimate explication consists only in a reference to experience.[45]

One choice of examples of so-called evident judgments contains judgments of inner perception, such as first-person judgments of one's own psychological states at the moment they are occurring, as in "I am now experiencing sound and color sensations," or "I am now thinking," or "I now want something." Brentano recognizes another sort of evident judgment as well, which he likes to exemplify by the law of contradiction. He has in mind judgments whose truth is assured by the very concepts employed in the judgment. For example, that a door cannot be both open and closed at the same time would be evident because it is true in virtue of the very meaning of the concepts "open" and "closed" as they apply to things like doors.[46] What these two different kinds of evident judgment have in common is their infallibility, their incorrigibility; they cannot but be true when they are made. First-person psychological judgments are true because they are, to use Chisholm's term, "self-presenting,"[47] while the others are analytically true. Clearly, the distinction between blind and evident judgments is different from the distinction between assertoric and apodictic judgments, for there may be evident factual (assertoric) judgments – exemplified by the judgments of inner perception – as well as evident apodictic judgments, that is, axioms or analytic truths. Brentano holds that evident judgments are universally valid:

[A]ny judgment which is . . . seen by one person to be true is universally valid; its contradictory cannot be seen to be evident by any other person; and anyone who accepts its contradictory is ipso facto mistaken. What I am saying here pertains to the nature of truth: anyone who thus sees into something as true is also able to see that he is justified in regarding it as true for all.[48]

Brentano's epistemology depends throughout on his theory of intended objects of presentations, judgments, and emotions. In all three categories, a corresponding state of mind can turn out to be correct or incorrect. The task of a Brentanian epistemology is, first, to analyze the meaning of such possibilities and explicate their consequences, and, second, to describe an appropriate methodology whereby correct states of mind expressing truths can be recognized, justified, attained, and increased, for the sake of enhancing empirical knowledge of the world. The complications in Brentano's epistemology can be traced historically through the major periods of transition in his philosophy as efforts to refine his understanding of the theory and practical applications of his theory of knowledge in light of modifications in his metaphysics of the intended objects of thought. Empirical psychology, differently interpreted at different stages in the development of his thought, is always primary; its implications for the ontology of intentionality and the ontic status of intended objects nevertheless reflects back in characteristic ways on his project to articulate the theoretical principles of epistemology.[49]

NOTES

1. PES-E, pp. 88–94. Brentano also refers to the concept as "intentional in-existence"; the prefix "in-" does not indicate negation but rather location, indicating immanent existence "in" our minds.
2. PSE-G, I, p. 112.
3. Ibid. Oskar Kraus notes that Brentano included "a landscape which I see" in this list by mistake, for his actual view of the matter was that, strictly speaking, the only things we perceive are instances of sensible qualities, so only they are entitled to be called physical phenomena.
4. Ibid., pp. 266–7. Compare PSE-G, II, p. 34, where Brentano says: "*Wenn wir etwas sehen, stellen wir uns eine Farbe, wenn wir etwas hören, einen Schall . . . vor.*" Brentano's view is thus like that of a sense-data theorist who says, strictly speaking, the only things we perceive are patches of color, sounds, shapes, and the like. It requires a further act of judgment to say, for example, that the colors which I see constitute a landscape. It should be pointed out, however, that "a chord which I hear," is subject to the same difficulty as is "a landscape which I see," for it is not a single tone, but several tones which are judged to combine into a harmonious unit. Landscapes, chords, and so on, nevertheless

can be the objects of judgments and other mental acts. And since, in a way, they are "constructions of" sensible qualities, which in turn are physical phenomena, one could, speaking somewhat more loosely, call them physical phenomena too, and Brentano does adopt this usage here and in several other places; for example, he speaks of tasting a piece of sugar, thinking about a horse or a tree, and the like.

5. PES-G, I, pp. 124–5; PES-E, p. 88. I follow Roderick M. Chisholm in translating *"Realität"* as "thing"; see TE, p. vii.

6. Apparently, some people misunderstood this passage so thoroughly as to think that Brentano meant by "objects" purposes or ends, and by "acts" the impulses which strive toward those ends. See PSE-G, II, p. 8, and John Passmore, *A Hundred Years of Philosophy*, 2nd edn. (London, 1966), p. 180.

7. TE, p. 27.

8. PA-G, p. 135.

9. The letter is dated March 17, 1905. It can be found in TE, pp. 77–9, and it is also reprinted in ANR, pp. 119–21.

10. TE, pp. 119–20. Translation adapted from that of TE.

11. TE, pp. 77–8; TE, p. 78; ANR, p. 120.

12. WE, p. 177; TE, p. 154; ANR, p. 407.

13. Chisholm, "Brentano on Descriptive Psychology and the Intentional," in, eds., Maurice H. Mandelbaum and Edward N. Lee, *Phenomenology and Existentialism* (Baltimore, MD, 1967), p. 11.

14. TE, p. 79; ANR, p. 121.

15. Aristotle, *Metaphysics*, 1021^a29-$^b4$.

16. WE, p. 68: *"Hat er nicht wesentlich gedacht wie wir!"*; TE, p. 78. Mayer-Hillebrand has deleted this remark, with no explanation whatsoever, from the text she published in ANR.

17. St. Thomas Aquinas, *Aristotelis Librum de Animna* (Taurini, 1948). 3rd edn., No. 55.

18. Chisholm, "Intentionality", in, ed., Paul Edwards, *Encyclopedia of Philosophy* (New York, 1967), vol. IV, p. 201.

19. Chisholm, "Brentano on Descriptive Psychology and the Intentional," p. 11.

20. Chisholm, "Brentano on Descriptive Psychology and the Intentional," p. 11.

21. TE, p. 77.

22. For a further discussion of Brentano's theory of relations see below.

23. For an outline of the issues that have been raised on this topic and a selected bibliography, see Chisholm, "Intentionality," p. 204.

24. PES-G, I, p. 136.

25. *Ibid.*, p. 137.

26. PES-G, pp. 124–32.

27. PES-G, I, p. 132.

28. *Ibid.*, p. 137.

29. *Ibid.*, pp. 32–3; 81.

30. *Ibid.*, II, p. 34.

31. *Ibid.*, p. 34.

32. USE, p. 18.

33. PES-G, II, pp. 38–9.

34. *Ibid.*, pp. 83–4; 87–8. USE, pp. 17–18. English translations from the *Ursprung* are by Chisholm and Schneewind throughout.

35. See LRU, p. 35.

36. USE, p. 17.

37. See Brentano's "*Miklosich über subjektlose Sätze,*" reprinted in PES-G, pp. 11, 183–96.

38. PSE-G, 49.

39. "*Miklosich über subjektlose Sätze*", USE, II, p. 194 (Chisholm–Schneewind translation).

40. PES-G, II, pp. 53ff. In this passage Brentano did not stress the fact that he meant to be speaking only of simple categorical judgments, and this led to misunderstandings on the part of some critics. He clarifies his position in a footnote to the *Ursprung*, which does not appear in the 2nd through 4th editions, but which is reprinted TE, pp. 33–7.

41. See J. P. N. Land, "Brentano's Logical Innovations," *Mind*, I, Old Series (1876), pp. 289–92. John Stuart Mill was willing to accept Brentano's suggestions for formal improvements in logic which this new view of the nature of judgment yielded, but he could not accept the notion that there could be a judgment in which only one presentation or idea is affirmed. See his letters to Brentano of December 18, 1872, and February 6, 1873 in, ed., Francis E. Mineka, *Mill's Later Letters* (Toronto: University of Toronto Press).

42. PES-G, II, pp. 56–7; 95. WE, p. 45; TE, p. 39.

43. TE, p. 34.

44. USE, pp. 20–1.

45. USE, p. 21.

46. *Ibid.*

47. Chisholm, *Theory of Knowledge* (Englewood Cliffs, NJ: Prentice Hall, 1966), p. 28

48. TE, p. 55.

49. His onetime student, Edmund Husserl, is an obvious example.

8   Brentano on judgment and truth

I   INTRODUCTION

It is well known that Brentano classified "psychical phenomena" as presentations, judgments, and phenomena of love and hate. Presentations are presentations of objects, although their objects may not exist. One might say roughly that presentations are the vehicles of content, but a presentation is not propositional in form and does not embody any stance of the subject toward the content in question. Judgments are affirmations or denials of presentations. Thus they are based on presentations but are not a species of them. It is of course judgments that are true or false. Phenomena of the third class are also based on presentations, and, like judgments, also embody a stance of the subject toward the content in question. Brentano sometimes characterizes this as *Gefallen oder Mißfallen*, which might be rendered roughly as a pro- or con-attitude. Such attitudes can also be correct or incorrect, an idea that is the starting point of Brentano's ethics. However, phenomena of love and hate will play almost no role in what follows. The three-fold classification is presented in *Psychology from an Empirical Standpoint* in 1874 and Brentano held to it for the remainder of his career.

The common-sense idea of a judgment is that it is an instance of someone judging something; where what is at issue is truth or falsity, the agent comes to a belief one way or the other.[1] It should follow that a judgment would incorporate what Frege called force, in this case the agent's stance toward the truth or falsity of the proposition judged to be one or the other. But it follows that many sentences that occur as parts of other sentences, for example antecedents of conditionals, do not express judgments. Suppose that Smith judges:

(1)   If it rains tomorrow, the game will not be played.

In a typical case, where Smith is uncertain about tomorrow's weather, he does not judge that it will rain tomorrow; even if it happens that he does, (1) does not express such a judgment.

Frege's view of this situation was an early version of a view that became standard in the twentieth century, although it has been subjected to many challenges. According to him, one should distinguish judgments from what he calls thoughts, which are roughly what is commonly called propositions. A thought does not embody any force; to say that a sentence expresses a certain thought says nothing about whether someone uttering it takes that thought to be true. In a suitable context, (1) combines two thoughts, that it will rain tomorrow and that the game will not be played, in order to form a single compound thought. Smith judges that thought to be true, but he makes no judgment at all concerning the two thoughts of which it is composed.

By a "propositional object" I mean an object that (according to one or another theory) is expressed or designated by a sentence. Judgments might be taken as one kind of such objects. Frege's thoughts and the propositions of the early Russell and of many other English-language writers are another. One might add states of affairs (Sachverhalte) or situations, as well as facts. In much logical literature from early modern times into the twentieth century, judgments are the principal propositional object, but the term has significant ambiguities. The suggestion derived from common sense is that there is a judgment only if an agent judges something. That would suggest viewing a judgment as an event and thus doubtfully a propositional object at all. But logical writers used the term to do the work of the term "proposition," with the effect of detaching the idea of a judgment from judging or assertion.

In contrast, Brentano holds consistently to the conception of a judgment as the outcome of an actual judging and thus as embodying a commitment as to truth or falsity. Judgments are thus clearly distinguished from the thoughts or propositions that, on another view, might be their constituents but about whose truth or falsity the agent takes no stance, such as the antecedent and consequent of (1). Judgments appear to be the only propositional objects Brentano admits.

Brentano differs in this respect from some of his principal pupils, in particular Marty, Meinong, and Husserl.[2] In later writings, written after he had adopted the position called reism, according to which an object of thought has to be a *Reales* or a thing (something concrete), Brentano argues frequently against propositions or states of affairs. However, as we shall see in §6, "Questions about Truth as Correspondence," he did accept them from the 1880s until his adoption of reism. In his late phase Brentano is probably best interpreted as rejecting even judgments as propositional objects, in the sense of objects expressed by sentences. What he admits are subjects who affirm or deny presentations.[3] However, we will for much of our discussion abstract from Brentano's later reism. It will be discussed in §5, "General Presentations and Reism."

Brentano argues for his view that judgment is a distinctive form of mental phenomenon, and thus a distinctive intentional relation to an object, in chapters 6 and 7 of the 1874 *Psychology*. Much of the argument is directed at theories of judgment current at the time, in particular the idea that goes back to Aristotle that judgment consists of combination or separation of presentations. Brentano's underlying idea is that the object of a presentation can be the object of a judgment affirming or denying it. Since a presentation need not be a combination or separation, judgments, such as simple existential judgments, affirming or denying presentations that are not are counterexamples to the Aristotelian account.[4]

According to Brentano, judgments are affirmative or negative, so that negation belongs to the judgment and not to the structure of the presentation judged. This is another place at which Brentano disagrees with Frege, where Frege's view has become the received view in later times. Brentano's is a traditional view, and against it Frege argued forcefully that negation is not a mode of judgment but belongs to the content, so that a sentence like "it will not rain tomorrow" expresses a thought that is the negation of the thought expressed by "it will rain tomorrow."[5] A judgment that it will not rain tomorrow does not differ in force from a judgment that it will rain tomorrow; where they differ is in the thought that is judged to be true. In Brentano's view, in contrast, "rain tomorrow" might well express a certain presentation; the judgment that it will rain tomorrow affirms this presentation, while the judgment that it will not rain tomorrow denies it.[6]

To carry through Brentano's view, it would be necessary to represent all complexity of content as belonging to the presentation judged. Brentano's theory of judgment can be viewed as a brave attempt to carry through a view of this kind. Much of his effort in discussion of judgment is in attempts to do justice to the various forms of complexity that arise from the complex logical form of sentences.

In its original form, Brentano's view of judgment implies that in a sense all judgments are existential judgments or negations of existential judgments. This peculiarity of his view of judgment influenced his thought on truth at an early point and led to a particular line of questioning of the traditional idea of truth as *adaequatio rei et intellectus*, the root of what has come to be called the correspondence theory of truth, already adumbrated in the 1889 lecture that is the opening essay in the compilation *Wahrheit und Evidenz*. Brentano was not the only or even the most influential philosopher to question the correspondence theory at the time, but his criticisms had distinctive features. In late writings he sketched as a positive view an epistemic conception. The discussion below of Brentano's views on truth will concentrate on these aspects.

2   THE PROBLEM OF COMPOUND JUDGMENTS

Presentations as Brentano conceives them are what in traditional logic was expressed by terms, singular and general. Since the object of a presentation need not exist, singular as well as general presentations can be either affirmed or denied. What we would express as someone's judging that Pegasus does not exist would be in Brentano's language his denying or rejecting Pegasus; the case is exactly parallel to that of unicorns.

The difficulty an account such as Brentano's faces is how to represent judgments that involve compounding, particularly sentential combination such as that embodied by (1). This issue already arises in Brentano's first development in the 1874 *Psychology*, where he sketches an explanation of the syllogistic forms. Brentano's view immediately gives a distinctive place to existential statements, "A exists," where A is a term, since to judge that is just to affirm A. Thus his view immediately removes the temptation to treat "exists" in such statements as a predicate, even a "logical" but not "real" predicate, as Kant did.[7]

The most direct way of looking at the syllogistic forms from the point of view of modern logic yields the result that categorical propositions are equivalent either to existential propositions or negations of such, since we have:

'All A are B' is equivalent to 'There are no As that are non-Bs.'

'No A are B' is equivalent to 'There are no As that are Bs.'

'Some A are B' is equivalent to 'There are As that are Bs' or 'There are ABs.'

'Some A are not B' is equivalent to 'There are As that are non-Bs' or 'There are A non-Bs.'

These readings can go directly into Brentanian terms: To judge that all A are B is to deny As that are non-Bs; to judge that no A are B is to deny As that are Bs; to judge that some A are B is to affirm As that are Bs; to judge that some A are not B is to affirm As that are non-Bs.

Essentially these readings are given by Brentano in *Psychology* (KPP, pp. 56–7, PES-E, pp. 213–14). He draws a number of conclusions that modern logicians have drawn, such as that the inferences from A to I and from E to O are not valid, and that certain traditionally accepted syllogisms are not valid, although they become so if an existential premises is added.[8] (See the essay by Peter Simons in this volume.)

Second, the readings make clear that already at this level Brentano's account requires some principle for the combination of terms or presentations. The first is basically conjunction, so that given A and B we have 'As that are B.' A second would be negation applied to terms: as they stand, the readings involve an "internal" negation in addition to the negation embodied in negative judgment, i.e. denial. Some of the neatness of the theory is lost by admitting term negation in addition to denial. Brentano does not address this issue in *Psychology*, but as we shall see he was uncomfortable with term negation and did develop some ideas for eliminating it.

Brentano in one place at least (KL, p. 45, TC, p. 42) admits disjunctive terms, so that we can also allow judgments that affirm or deny A-or-Bs. At any rate, if term negation is applicable to compound terms, then any truth-functional combination of terms can be expressed as a term.

Two problems would remain before Brentano's theory could yield the expressive power of first-order logic. First, one would have to accommodate truth-functional combination of closed sentences. If we make the assumption about terms of the last paragraph, that would be sufficient to generate a logic with expressive power equivalent to that of monadic quantificational logic, since in monadic logic nested quantification can be eliminated. Second, one would have to have a treatment of many-place predicates and polyadic quantification.

If Brentano had developed the second, he would have been one of the founders of mathematical logic, which he neither was nor claimed to be. The question whether this can be done in the framework of a Brentanian theory of judgment is one external to Brentano himself. Term logics that are equivalent to first-order logic have been developed, but they involve devices that were not thought of in Brentano's time even by mathematical logicians. It would have been necessary for Brentano to consider many-place predicates on the same footing as one-place predicates. His remarks on relations take in only binary relations, and there he holds the unusual view that only the first place of a binary relation is direct or referential (*modo recto* in Brentano's terminology); on this subject see §4 ("Modes of Presentation") below.

We can remain closer to Brentano in considering how the first question might be addressed. This has been treated in some detail by Roderick M. Chisholm.[9] Consider first the simplest case, judging that p and q. One might say that S judges that p and q if he (simultaneously) judges that p and judges that q. But as Chisholm points out, that would not be sufficient, since S might not put the two together. Suppose first that both judgments are affirmative, so that S accepts A and accepts B. Brentano admitted conjunctive objects, objects consisting of an A and a B. Call them A-and-Bs. S's accepting A-and-Bs has the requisite property of committing S both to As and to Bs in a single judgment. One might object that S is committed to more, to another object, precisely the A-and-B. That would be so if we think of it as a set having an A and a B as elements. If these objects are distinct non-sets, then the pair set must be distinct from both of them.

Brentano did not think of conjunctive objects as sets, at least not as set theory has come to think of them. It is well known that given either the empty set or a single individual, one can generate an infinite sequence of sets by successive application of the forming of pair sets. Brentano considers and rejects an argument for such generation beginning with two apples. A key step that he rejects is that a pair of apples is something "in addition" to the original two apples:

Someone who has one apple and another apple does not have a pair of apples in addition, for the pair which he has simply means the one apple and the other taken together. *So what people wanted to do was to add the same thing to itself, which is contrary to the concept of addition.* . . . The pair is completely distinct from either of the two apples which make it up, but it is not at all distinct from both of them added together. (KPP, p. 253, PES-E, p. 352)[10]

Particularly the last remark suggests that Brentano thinks of the pair as the mereological sum, and some of his remarks about pluralities parallel claims made by defenders in later times of mereological sums. That would serve to block the generation of an infinite sequence out of only one or two individuals. However, elsewhere Brentano writes in connection with the question of the relation of such a whole and its constituents that "there are things that compared with others have revealed themselves neither as wholly the same nor as wholly other, that are partially the same" (KL, p. 50, TC, p. 46). Mereology plays a larger role in Brentano's work, so that he could claim that the introduction of *conjunctiva* in the present context is not *ad hoc*.

Now consider the disjunction of two affirmative judgments, again one affirming As and one affirming Bs. Admitting disjunctive terms, one can render the judgment as one that affirms $(A$ or $B)s$. We would say that this works because '$\exists x Ax \lor \exists x Bx$' is equivalent to '$\exists x(Ax \lor Bx)$.' It is for that reason that the solution is simpler than that concerning conjunctions of affirmative judgments.

This simple solution is also available for the case of conjunction of two negative judgments. To judge that there are no As and that there are no Bs would be simply to deny $(A$ or $B)s$.

The idea used for conjunctions of affirmative judgments will clearly work for disjunctions of negative judgments. Judging that either there are no As or that there are no Bs would be to judge that there are no $(A$-and-$B)s$. For let a be an A and b be a B. Then a and b "taken together" constitute an A-and-B. So if there are no A-and-Bs, then either there are no As or there are no Bs. Conversely, since any

A-and-B has an A as a part, if there are no As, then there cannot be any A-and-Bs, and likewise if there are no Bs.

There remains the problem of binary combination of an affirmative with a negative judgment. How might Brentano analyze the judgment that either there are no As or there are Bs? Chisholm's proposal is that such a judgment would reject As that are not part of A-and-Bs.[11] For suppose that judgment is true, and it is likewise true that there are As. Then any such A must be part of an A-and-B, and so there are Bs. Hence either there are no As or there are Bs. Conversely, suppose there are no As. Then clearly there are no As that are not part of A-and-Bs. Suppose that there are Bs. Then let b be such. If there are As, then any such A will combine with b to form an A-and-B and hence is part of an A-and-B. So if there are Bs, then there are no As that are not part of A-and-Bs. The symmetry of disjunction implies that we can handle in the same way a judgment that either there are As or there are no Bs.

Consider now the case of a mixed conjunction, a judgment that there are As and there are no Bs. Chisholm proposes that such a judgment be viewed as accepting As that are not part of $(A$-and-$B)$s, and this is evidently correct since it is equivalent to 'It is not the case that either there are no As or there are Bs.'

One might also ask about conditional judgments, such as the judgment that if there are As, then there are Bs. Brentano's suggestion about hypothetical judgments (LRU, pp. 122–3) seems to me to amount to reading the conditional in the now familiar truth-functional way. Thus this case is reduced to cases already considered. 'If there are As then there are Bs' is the mixed disjunctive judgment 'Either there are no As or there are Bs.'

It thus appears that the judgments Brentano is able to handle are closed under truth-functional combination and, assuming the truth-functional interpretation of the conditional, under the formation of conditionals. The price of this, however, is high. To handle simple conjunction, he needs to introduce mereological sums or some other conjunctive objects, thus introducing possibly contestable ontology in order to handle one of the simplest logical operations. To handle mixed binary compounds he needs in addition the notion of being part of an A-and-B. This in fact generates a more serious problem. Clearly the statement 'x is part of an A-and-B' means that x is part of *some* A-and-B. Thus there is an implicit quantifier that seems not to be captured by Brentano's reduction of existential quantification to affirming a presentation, universal quantification to denying one. We shall consider in §3 how Brentano might deal with this without accepting the idea of being a part of some A as simply primitive.

3   CAN ONE ELIMINATE TERM NEGATION?

Let us now step back and consider how Brentano might avoid admitting negative terms and so reduce all negation to denial. In order to address this issue, we turn to his conception of double judgment. A double judgment affirms an object and then affirms or denies something of it. Brentano characterizes them as judgments that "accept something and affirm or deny something of it" (KPP, p. 194, KRW, p. 107).[12] In the essay "On Genuine and Fictitious Objects," added to the 1911 edition of *Psychology*, Brentano deploys this idea to analyze the categorical forms of judgment.[13]

With respect to our problem about negation, it offers a solution to the problem of the O form. 'Some S is not P' affirms an S and denies of it that it is P (KPP, pp. 165–6, PES-E, p. 296). Brentano also proposes that a psychologically more accurate rendering of the I form would also view it as a double judgment, affirming an S and affirming of it that it is P (KPP, p. 165, PES-E, p. 295).

However, the notion of double judgment has the limitation that it *affirms* an S (for some S or other) and then affirms or denies some predicate P of it. There is no negative counterpart. Indeed, it is hard to see what sense it could make to *deny* an S and then affirm or deny something of it. Thus, while the notion of double judgment elegantly eliminates the negative term from the O form, it does not seem to solve the corresponding problem about the A form. Thus Chisholm, who claims about as much as could be claimed for Brentano on this issue, seems to give up at this point on trying to eliminate term negation from Brentano's theory.[14]

The notion of double judgment might be applied to a problem we encountered concerning truth-functional combination. For example, a mixed conjunction, affirming As and denying Bs, was analyzed as an affirmation of As that are not part of $(A$-and-$B)$s. That would be represented as a double judgment affirming an A, and denying an A-and-B of which it is a part. We have, however, simply exploited the strategy for dealing with the O form, and the same problem that we met with in connection with the A form prevents us from extending this to other cases, in particular that of mixed disjunctions, which are in Brentanian terms negative judgments.

The weakness of double judgments for Brentano's purposes is that they do not have straightforward negations. In particular, if they are introduced in order to handle truth-functional combination, the iteration that such combination involves will not be available.

A device that Brentano uses in order to give analyses in accord with his later reism is to introduce the idea of someone thinking of an A, for some A, or someone making a judgment with respect to As. That suggests another solution to the problem of the A form. Brentano writes:

> If the O form means the double judgment 'There is an S and it is not P,' then the proposition 'Every S is P' says that anyone who makes both of these judgments is judging falsely. I think of someone affirming S and denying P of it, and say that in thinking of someone judging in this way, I am thinking of someone judging incorrectly. (KPP, pp. 168–9, PES-E, p. 298)

It is not clear that this is offered as a way of eliminating the negative term in the rendering of the A form. Still, we might, following Peter Simons, derive from it the paraphrase of 'Every S is P' as 'Whoever affirms S and denies P of it judges incorrectly.'[15] Simons states that this is still in the A form and so does not advance the case. But it is perhaps better viewed as of the E form 'No one who affirms S and denies P of it judges correctly' and so as denying a correct acceptor-of-P-denying-P-of-it. Still, introducing what is effectively the concept of truth, and applied to a double judgment, seems a very questionable move in order to analyze one of the simplest and most traditional logical forms.

The notion of double judgment itself raises some questions. First of all, for a given presentation S, to affirm an S is not in general to affirm any particular S; for example one can believe that there are cows without there being any particular cow in whose existence one believes. This is particularly true on Brentano's scheme, since he thinks of existence as tensed. To accept cows is to accept cows as existing now. But suppose I have not been near a farm for a number of years. I'm confident that there are cows, but the only ones I can point to are from the past. I can't rule out the possibility that all of them have by now died, even though the supply of milk in the supermarket assures me that, if so, they have been replaced by others. So there's no particular cow that I accept. However, it seems that, say, judging that some cows are not white involves accepting a cow and denying *of that cow* that it is white. How can that be if there is no particular cow that I accept, and so a fortiori none that I judge not to be white?

We could render such a double judgment as affirming an x that is a cow and denying of x that it is white. The x would have to be in some way indeterminate. Brentano does not put the matter this way, and I am not sure that it accords with his views; for example it represents even the subject term in such a judgment as a predicate. What he says that bears on the question is obscure, as for example this explanation of the I form:

> Looked at more closely, it signifies a double judgment, one part of which affirms the subject, and, after the predicate has been identified in presentation with the subject, the other part affirms the subject which had been affirmed all by itself in the first part, but with this addition – which is to say that it ascribes to it the predicate P. (KPP, p. 165, PES-E, p. 295)

What is it for the predicate to be "identified in presentation with the subject"? It appears that Brentano means what is explained in his last dictation, included in the 1924 edition of *Psychology*. There he states that there are presentations

> which are unified only through a peculiar kind of association, composition, or identification, as, for example, when one forms the complex concept of a thing which is red, warm, and pleasant-sounding. (KPP, 206, PES-E, 316)

A little later he elaborates by saying, "When we say, 'a red warm thing', the two things presented in intuitive unity are not totally identified but identified only in terms of the subject" (pp. 207, 317).[16] What seems to be needed is some version of the content–object distinction: In a double judgment, the predicate is identified with the subject in being affirmed or denied of an *object* that the subject is presupposed to apply to. But that would restate the formulation of the last paragraph and not clarify it.

We have concluded that Brentano's ideas for reducing negation to denial and thus for avoiding Frege's conclusion that negation belongs to the content of a judgment rather than being a mode of judgment itself are inadequate for the purpose and not entirely clear in themselves. Before leaving the subject I will comment on some remarks about term negation in the same essay from the 1911 *Psychology* that we have been considering. If negative terms are admitted, then it seems that negation is simply allowed as an operator on terms. Nonetheless Brentano regards term negation as introducing a kind of fiction, the fiction of "negative objects." He seems to think such a fiction involved in the everyday understanding of negative terms:

This fiction . . . is a commonplace to the layman; he speaks of an unintelligent man as well as an intelligent one, and of a lifeless thing as well as of a living thing. He looks on "attractive thing" and "unattractive thing," "red thing," and "non-red things," equally, as words which name objects. (KPP, p. 169, PES-E, p. 298)

One might well ask, why not? In the sense in which "red thing" names anything, it names those things that are red, and then surely "non-red thing" names those things that are not red. Brentano does not give an argument, but it is very likely that "red thing" names a general presentation, and he may think that such a general presentation as would be named by "non-red thing" would be a negative object. The general background is discussed in §5 below.

4   MODES OF PRESENTATION

A quite different aspect of Brentano's treatment of complex judgments belongs actually to his account of presentations. That is how he distinguishes modes of presentation (*Modi des Vorstellens*[17]). The major distinctions subsumed under these headings are what he calls temporal modes and the distinction between direct and oblique (*modus rectus* and *modus obliquus*). The latter, although it is applied in the first instance to presentations rather than to linguistic contexts, is essentially the distinction that is familiar to us. A simple, straightforward presentation will represent its object *in modo recto*; in particular, if a judgment affirms such a presentation, it commits one to the existence of the object. He says that the direct mode "is never absent when we are actively thinking" (KPP, p. 145, PES-E, p. 281). Oblique reference arises primarily in two cases: where one is thinking of a "mentally active subject," where a thought of such a subject *in recto* will involve thought of the objects of his thought *in obliquo*. Thus a presentation of Kant thinking of the pure intuition of space will present Kant *in recto* and the pure intuition of space *in obliquo.* That is what we would expect since thought of an object is a "referential attitude" in contemporary terminology. Brentano allows that something thought of *in recto* might be identified with something thought of *in obliquo*:

. . . as for example when I have a presentation *in recto* of flowers and of a flower-lover who wants those flowers, in which case flowers are thought of both *in recto* and *in obliquo* and are identified with one another. (KPP, p. 147, PES-E, p. 282)

The other case is more surprising: "Besides the fundament of the relation, which I think of *in recto*, I think of the terminus *in obliquo*" (KPP, p. 145, PES-E, p. 281). In other words, in a thought to the effect that *aRb*, only *a* is presented *in recto*, so that the second term of the relation is an oblique context. I don't know of an argument Brentano gives for this somewhat strange view. He does distinguish relations where if the first term of the relation exists, the relation implies that the second does as well; his example is 'taller than' (KPP, p. 218, PES-E, p. 325). Cases of this kind are not as frequent as one might think. But the reason for this lies in Brentano's view of temporal modes.

Brentano holds that the existence and properties of objects are essentially tensed. So he denies that being past, present, or future represent differences in the objects. A presentation thus has a temporal mode of presentation, in the simplest case present. To say that something exists, without qualification, is to say that it exists now; therefore Brentano says of figures from the past that they do not exist. It also follows that a relation like 'earlier than' does not require the existence of both terms (KPP, pp. 218–19, PES-E, pp. 325–6). Of course, it follows that it doesn't require the existence (now) of either. The battle of Blenheim was earlier than the battle of Waterloo, although both are past and so do not exist on Brentano's view.

What is relevant to his view of judgment is that a temporal mode is an additional complication to the logical form of a judgment. If I judge that the battle of Waterloo occurred, I affirm it in a past mode. If I judge that the US presidential election of 2008 will occur, I affirm it in a future mode. Clearly much more complex combinations are possible. However, it is only affirmation of present existence that is affirmation "in the strict sense" (KPP, p. 221, PES-E, p. 327). He seems to hold that other temporal modes are varieties of the oblique mode. I will not, however, pursue the question how Brentano develops or might have developed the conception of temporal modes.

5   GENERAL PRESENTATIONS AND REISM

As is well known, shortly after the turn of the century Brentano abandoned the whole idea of objects other than things except as sometimes useful fictions, adopting the view called reism, according to which an object of thought must be a *Reales* or thing. This raises a question how Brentano would understand general terms or predicates occurring in judgments, even the simplest ones affirming or denying *P*, where '*P*' replaces a general term. If a judgment affirms horses, it would naturally be taken as, in our terms, making reference to horses, that is the animals with which we are familiar, and not to anything further such as a property or attribute of being a horse.

We must ask, however, what the presentation is that is affirmed in such a case. What we might expect from Brentano's reism is that he would hold that a general horse-presentation would have many objects, just those that are objects of individual horse-presentations. However, Brentano distinguishes sensory from noetic or intellectual consciousness; the latter includes what we would describe as the exercise of concepts. He seems rather firmly to reject the view I have suggested:

> . . . a term can only be called general, if there is a general concept that corresponds to it. If we deny this and say that a term is general if many individual presentations are associated with it, then we would misinterpret the difference between ambiguity and generality, and would fail to see that the statement that many individual presentations are associated with one and the same term, in itself expresses a general proposition concerning these individual presentations. (SNB, pp. 86–7, SNC, p. 63)

> The beliefs that we cannot think of universals, and that so-called general terms are only associated with a multitude of individual presentations, have also been refuted.(SNB, p. 89, SNC, p. 65)[18]

In fact, Brentano's view is that all presentations are in a way general, that none can by virtue of its content fully individuate an object, although in some cases, such as presentations of inner perception referring to the self, it can be argued that they can have at most one object (SNB, p. 98, SNC, p. 72). Although he makes a distinction of intuitions and concepts parallel to Kant's, he denies that intuitions have a content that individuates their objects (KPP, pp. 199–200, 204, PES-E, pp. 311–12, 315). In the first of these texts (supplementary essay XII to PES) he justifies this by a rather intricate argument concerning perception and space. That need not concern us here; the question is how this view comports with his reism (which is in evidence in this text and even more in the following one).

An answer is suggested by some passages in *Die Lehre vom richtigen Urteil*, which, however, often does not give the *ipsissima verba* of Brentano. Brentano often speaks of the use of language as introducing fictions; many of his examples are mathematical, and some are logical (e.g. KPP, p. 215, PES-E, pp. 322–3). In LRU, p. 41, it is explicitly stated that concepts are fictions; however, in one place (§29), the language clearly comes from Kastil, and in the other (beginning of §30), this also appears to be the case.[19] However, the view of general thought presented is plausibly Brentanian. Thinking of something as a man, a human being, and a living thing are increasingly general ways of thinking of a thing. But the thing referred to is an individual, even though thinking of it in any of these ways fails to single it out as an individual. Brentano himself says elsewhere that a thing (*Reales*) is always determinate, but is object of a presentation "in a now more, now less differentiated way, without therefore ceasing right away to be thought of in a certain way generally and indeterminately" (ANR, p. 348). In this passage he uses 'concept' without any comment but denies that universals are things. "Every such universally thought thing is, if it is, completely individualized."

A less Brentanian way of putting the point is that thought of something as, say, a man is the thought of an x that is a man. What we have said in §3 ("Can One Eliminate Term Negation?") about double judgments indicates that some such perspective is essential for Brentano's treatment of rather simple judgments. We can't eliminate the x by taking the thought as of a definite particular object, which the thought represents as being a man. That would run afoul of Brentano's claim that the content of our thought never yields a genuinely individual representation, and furthermore in the cases considered in his treatment of syllogistic, the x is bound by a quantifier. It is somewhat awkward because, if one takes seriously the doctrine that all presentations are general, it implies that all presentations have in some sense the form of predicates. I am not at all sure that that is a consequence that Brentano would have embraced. And it is undoubtedly uncomfortably close to nominalism, even from the point of view of the later Brentano.[20]

6   QUESTIONS ABOUT TRUTH AS CORRESPONDENCE

Brentano's substantial publication on truth during his lifetime was a lecture of 1889, "On the Concept of Truth,"[21] reprinted in the posthumous *Wahrheit und Evidenz*. It shows a characteristic of much of his reflection on truth. His point of departure is the traditional characterization of truth as *adaequatio rei et intellectus*. His inclination is to defend it but much of the discussion concerns what it means, and some points are made that suggest real criticisms of the correspondence theory as it developed at the time and later. The line of thought then inaugurated leads him to be more definitely critical of the traditional formula in the later writings first published in *Wahrheit und Evidenz*. But even later, he shows some reluctance to abandon it altogether.

Brentano's thought on truth develops out of his thought on judgment, in particular the central role that (affirmative and negative) judgments have in his view and his criticism of a traditional view of judgment as a combination of presentations. The discussion of truth in the 1889 essay begins with a formula of Aristotle:

He who thinks the separated to be separated and the combined to be combined has the truth, while he whose thought is in a state contrary to that of the objects is in error. (*Metaphysics* 1051b3)[22]

After some discussion of subsequent history and examples, Brentano offers a corrected version:

A judgment is true if it attributes to a thing something which, in reality, is combined with it, or if it denies of a thing something which, in reality, is not combined with it. (§33)

He makes no difficulty about the case of affirmative subject–predicate judgments. But he immediately asks about judgments of existence: What is combined if I judge that a dog exists?[23] Clearly, on Brentano's view such a judgment affirms a dog, so that *dog* is the only presentation involved. A little later he says that in the case of a negative existential judgment like "There is no dragon" there is no object to which the judgment corresponds if it is true. It could not be a dragon, since *ex hypothesi* dragons do not exist. "Nor is there any other real thing which *could* count as the corresponding reality" (§42).

Brentano goes on to find a similar difficulty in negative predications.

> Suppose I say, "Some man is not black." What is required for the truth of the statement is, not that there *is* black separated from the man, but rather that on the man, there is an absence or privation of black. This absence, this non-black, is clearly not an object; thus again there is no object given in reality which corresponds to my judgment. (§43)

At this point one might well expect him to reject the correspondence theory or at least to admit that it has significant exceptions. He introduces a contrast between things (*Dinge*) and "objects to which the word 'thing' should not be applied at all" (§44). As examples he mentions "a collection of things, or . . . a part of a thing, or . . . the limit or boundary of a thing, or the like" (§45). He also mentions things that have perished long ago or will only exist in the future as well as "the absence or lack of a thing," an impossibility, and eternal truths. Because none of these are things, "the whole idea of the *adaequatio rei et intellectus* seems to go completely to pieces" (§45).

That is, however, not the conclusion that Brentano draws. Instead he says that we must distinguish between the concept of the existent and that of thing, and so he says:

> A judgment is true if it asserts of some object that is, *that* the object is, or if it asserts of some object that is not, *that* the object is not.
>
> And this is all there is to the correspondence of true judgment and object about which we have heard so much. To correspond does not mean the same as to be similar; but it does mean to be adequate, to fit, to be in agreement with, to be in harmony with. (§§51–2)

Brentano's formulation is reminiscent of another much-quoted Aristotelian formulation:

> To say of what is that it is not, and of what is not that it is, is false; to say of what is that it is, and of what is not that it is not, is true.[24]

Aristotle, however, undoubtedly has the 'is' of predication in mind, while Brentano is thinking in terms of his early doctrine that all judgments are (affirmative or negative) existential judgments.

Brentano has saved a version of the traditional formula, but apparently at the cost of introducing "objects" that are not "things." He does think that in cases where the presentation underlying a judgment does not have a thing as its object, in cases other than judgments of necessity and possibility, there is an indirect dependence on things (§55). He also suggests that there is something trivial about the definition (§57) but responds that it still offers useful conceptual clarification.

Brentano does not make clear here how far he is prepared to go in admitting objects that are not things, what he later calls *irrealia*. Without more explicitness, it is not clear that he has answered even his first sharp question about the traditional version: To what object does a negative existential truth like "There are no dragons" correspond? He suggests that he would admit absences or privations as objects, but this is clearer in the case of absences relating to things, such as the absence of black in a man who is not black. Alfred Kastil reports Brentano as having said in 1914 that he had thought he had to extend the *adaequatio rei et intellectus* to negative judgments, "as if in this case as well an objective correlate corresponded to the judgment, the nonbeing of what is correctly rejected" (WE, p. 164, TE, p. 142). In later writings reflecting his turn to reism, he frequently criticizes the claim that if it is true that there are no As, then there must be "the nonbeing of As". This would, apart from other objections to it, introduce a new kind of object to correspond to a true judgment, a state of affairs or perhaps fact.[25]

7   VIRTUAL ABANDONMENT OF THE
       CORRESPONDENCE FORMULA

The discussion of the last section should show that with the adoption of reism (see §5) Brentano effectively gave up the basis of his continuing to defend a conception of truth as correspondence. And that is indeed what one finds in the late letters and essays in *Wahrheit und Evidenz*. However, he seems still to have been reluctant to abandon the formula.

Thus much of Brentano's letter to Marty of September 2, 1906 is devoted to arguing against admitting such states of affairs as "the being of A" as had been accepted by Marty and, as we have just seen, earlier by Brentano. Against the idea that they are useful, Brentano writes:

Where someone might say, "In case there is the being of A, and someone says that A is, then he is judging correctly," I would say, "In case A is and someone says that A is, he judges correctly." Similarly instead of "If there is the non-being of A and someone rejects A, he judges correctly," I would say "If A is not and someone rejects A, he judges correctly," and so on. (WE, p. 94, TE, p. 84)

Thus he seems to think states of affairs not necessary to state basic truth-conditions. He also offers a regress argument against them: Suppose someone wishes to judge with evidence that A is. But he could not affirm A with evidence unless he could also affirm the being of A. Otherwise "he would be unable to know whether his original judgment corresponds with it." But then by parity of reasoning he would also have to be able to affirm the being of the being of A, and so on (WE, pp. 95–6, TE, pp. 85–6).

This argument might be generalized to an argument against any form of correspondence theory: Suppose that its being true that p consists in the correspondence of p with something, call it P. Then to determine whether it is true that p, it would be necessary to determine whether p corresponds with P. But the correspondence theory implies that that consists in a correspondence of the proposition that p corresponds with P with something, call it P'. Then the same question arises again.[26] One might reply that to judge that p, or determine whether p, is one thing, to judge that it is true that p or determine whether it is true that p is another. If the sentence 'p' is, say, 'Tame tigers exist,' it does not refer to a proposition, thought, or judgment, whereas 'it is true that tame tigers exist,' in the sense that is being interpreted by correspondence, does so refer since it predicates truth of one of these entities. To determine whether tame tigers exist we do not have to investigate judgments or other propositional objects. If we find that tame tigers exist, then some logical principle leads us to the conclusion that it is true that tame tigers exist, but only then is reference to a propositional object introduced. Thus we can reject Brentano's claim that to accept tame tigers, we must *simultaneously* accept the being of tame tigers. However, it seems likely that even if Brentano had accepted this objection, he would still have objected to the infinite sequence that is generated by passage from 'p' to 'it is true that p'.

Whatever the conclusion about the regress argument, the conception against which it is directed, that of truth as correspondence to a state of affairs, seems unmotivated unless a sentence *designates* a state of affairs, or at least a true sentence does. But Brentano, both in the 1889 essay and later, offers characterizations of the truth of a judgment without any such assumption. And he seems to be rejecting this suggestion even if states of affairs are admitted when he writes:

But if we were to suppose that the non-being of the devil is a kind of thing, it would not be the thing with which a negative judgment, denying the devil, is concerned; instead it would be the object of an affirmative judgment, affirming the non-being of the devil. (WE, p. 134, TE, p. 117)

At the end of the dictation (of May 11, 1915) from which this passage comes, Brentano says that "we may stay with the old thesis" (WE, p. 136, TE, p. 119). But his reading of it is clearly deflationary. The next item in the compilation, a dictation from two months earlier, makes this deflationary reading more explicit, by emphasizing not only the kind of example with which he has raised difficulties previously but also bringing up oblique, modal, and temporal contexts. If I judge that an event took place 100 years ago, "the event need not exist for the judgment to be true; it is enough that I who exist now, be 100 years later than the event" (WE, p. 138, TE, p. 121). He concludes that:

the thesis [that truth is *adaequatio rei et intellectus*] tells us no more nor less than this: Anyone who judges that a certain thing exists, or that it does not exist, or that it is possible, or impossible, or that it is thought of by someone, or that it is believed, or loved, or hated, or that it has existed, or will exist, *judges truly* provided that the thing in question does exist, or does not exist, or is possible, or is impossible, or is thought of . . . etc. (WE, p. 139, TE, pp. 121–2)

From our own perspective, we might summarize what Brentano says as that someone who judges that p judges truly if and only if p. Brentano lacks two things in order to come up with the familiar truth schema: some sort of general schema for judgment and seeing the predicate 'true' as a device of disquotation applied to linguistic items.

Brentano was far from being the only philosopher of his time to question the correspondence theory of truth. After all, the coherence theory was a staple of British idealism, whose main exponents were contemporaries. And the pragmatists' distinctive ideas about truth were advanced during Brentano's lifetime, even though it was late in Brentano's career that William James's views on truth led to considerable debate. Nonetheless Brentano's line of questioning seems to me of continuing interest, and the ideas discussed above have more in common with those of Alfred Tarski and his successors than with those advanced in the debates on truth at the turn of the century. His coming close at least to the propositional form of the now standard truth schema is not duplicated by another writer of the time known to me except Frege. Frege went further than Brentano in claiming in a few texts that the thought that p is true is just the same thought as p. That claim is bound up with Frege's particular conception of judgment; he would reject the idea advanced above in connection with the regress argument, that 'the thought that p is true' introduces content additional to that of 'p,' namely reference to the thought that it expresses. Although what appears to be a regress argument by Frege has been criticized, once the context in Frege's theory of judgment is recognized it may be defensible.

Where Brentano comes a little closer to Tarski is in suggesting the idea that the condition for the truth of a judgment should parallel its structure. To be sure, Frege does, in explaining the language of *Grundgesetze*, give compositional truth conditions that are more rigorous than anything Brentano offers, but he does not make the connection that Brentano does with the *explanation* of the notion of truth. Just what the connection should be between compositional truth conditions and explanations or definitions of truth has continued to be a disputed matter in our own day.

8   TRUTH AND EVIDENCE

If Brentano had stopped his account of truth with remarks like the last one quoted, he might count as an ancestor of what is nowadays called deflationism. But instead he continues and offers a characterization of truth in terms of evidence, that is in terms of evident judgment. If a judgment is evident, then it constitutes certain knowledge. Evidence is therefore clearly a much stronger notion than truth. Although judgments of inner perception can be evident, and they would count as empirical for Brentano, his concept of evidence is for practical purposes rational evidence, since if a judgment is evident no reason can override it. Although he is critical of Descartes's particular formulation (WE, pp. 61–2, TE, pp. 52–4), Descartes's clear and distinct perception seems to have provided a model for Brentano's conception of evidence. In his late writing evidence seems to have been treated as a more basic notion than truth. Thus he follows his deflationary rendering of the import of the *adaequatio* formula with what reads as a definition of true judgment in terms of evident:[27]

Truth pertains to the judgment of the person who judges correctly – to the judgment of the person who judges about a thing in the way in which anyone whose judgments were *evident* would judge about the thing; hence it pertains to the judgment of one who asserts what the person whose judgments are evident would also assert. (WE, p. 139, TE, p. 122, emphasized in the German)

Thus, if an agent x affirms A with evidence, and an agent y affirms A, whether or not with evidence, then y judges truly. Brentano held that an evident judgment is "universally valid"; in particular no other evident judgment can contradict it. Thus any other evident judgment with respect to A will agree with x's, so that the truth-value of y's judgment is uniquely determined. If a third agent z denies A, then z judges falsely, as one would expect. Evidently this definition requires the possibility of comparing the content of the judgment of different agents or of agents of different times; it must make sense to say of y that his judgment affirms or denies what x's judgment affirms or denies.

The definition faces a pretty obvious difficulty, which was pointed out by Christian von Ehrenfels.[28] Suppose that an agent y affirms A. If it is possible for there to be an agent x who judges with evidence with regard to A, then by the above there is at most one possible result of his judgment, and if it is affirmative then y judges truly; if it is negative then y judges falsely. But suppose that it is not possible for an agent to judge with evidence with regard to A. Then it seems that Brentano's characterization does not give an answer as to whether y's judgment is true. Or, if one holds that a vacuous contrary-to-fact conditional is true, then both the affirmation of A and the denial of A will be true.

Brentano's disciple and editor Oskar Kraus offers another formulation: y's affirmation of A is true if no possible evident judgment can contradict it, i.e. deny A (WE, pp. xxvi–xxvii, TE, pp. xxv). But, as Ehrenfels seems to have pointed out, if no evident judgment is possible one way or the other with respect to A, it seems that by Kraus's criterion both a judgment affirming A and a judgment denying A will be true. To this objection Kraus replies that supposing that A exists, then even if knowledge about A were possible, it could not be negative (i.e. an evident negative judgment). But an evident affirmative judgment is impossible only because it is assumed that the existence of A is unknowable. This does not seem to me to avoid the conclusion that according to the definition, a negative judgment with regard to A is true.

This type of objection touches Brentano particularly, because according to him the scope of evident judgment (for humans at least) is limited to the deliverances of inner perception and analytic judgments. Hence even simple common sense statements about the outer world have the property that neither they nor their negations can be affirmed with evidence.

The above remark expressing an epistemic criterion of truth was dictated by Brentano some years after Husserl had already published in the *Logische Untersuchungen* an account of truth in which there is an internal connection of truth and evidence.[29] Husserl's account is embedded in his intention-fulfillment theory of meaning and thus has a quite different context from Brentano's. It would be distracting to engage in a detailed comparison of the two accounts. However, it is instructive to see how Husserl deals with problems similar to those posed by Ehrenfels's objection to Brentano. In the *Prolegomena* he asserts an equivalence between 'A is true' and 'It is possible that someone should judge with evidence that A' (vol. I, §50, p. 184). But he denies that they mean the same. More relevant to our present problem is that he insists that the possibilities in question in such statements are ideal possibilities, so at least many examples that come to hand of statements we cannot know to be true or false become irrelevant, as is presumably the case with the example in Kraus's discussion of the existence of a diamond weighing at least 100 kilograms. Husserl is willing to assert the ideal possibility of knowledge of a solution to a problem in a case where the reason for thinking there is one is purely mathematical and he concedes that to find it may be beyond human capabilities; the example he gives is the general n-body problem of classical mechanics (vol. I, p. 185).

In the fuller discussion of truth in the Sixth Investigation, Husserl discusses in general terms what he calls the ideal of final fulfillment (§37). An act is fulfilled to the extent that its content is presented in intuition.[30] Final fulfillment involves the presence in intuition of the object, complete agreement of intuition with what is intended, and in addition the absence of any content in the fulfilling act that is an intention that calls for further fulfillment. Thus in final fulfillment the object itself is given, and given completely.

Husserl illustrates these ideas by means of perception, although he insists that fulfillment by outer perception is always incomplete. That, however, serves his purpose in bringing out that in general final fulfillment is an *ideal*. The concept of evidence applies to "positing acts" of which judgments would be an instance (although Husserl also regards normal perception as positing its object).[31] In the case of judgments, the object is a state of affairs (*Sachverhalt*); Husserl's view about propositional objects is closer to that of the pupils with whom Brentano disagreed than to that of the later Brentano. The epistemologically significant concept of evidence applies to positing acts that are adequate in the sense of leaving no unfulfilled components, in which, again, the object is given completely (§38).[32] Such evident positing has an objective correlate, which he says is "being in the sense of truth" (*Sein im Sinne der Wahrheit*), an echo of Aristotle that is no doubt derived from Brentano. This reliance on a strong concept of evidence to explain the notion of truth makes Husserl vulnerable to the type of objection made by Ehrenfels. What his reponse to it amounts to is that with respect to any positing act final fulfillment (or cancellation through conflict between what is intended and what is given) is "in principle" possible.

Husserl's own view of outer perception created a difficulty for this view. Even in the *Logische Untersuchungen* his position was that outer perceptions always contain unfulfilled intentions, because in perception the object is always incompletely given. At the time he seems to have thought that the impossibility of complete fulfillment of outer perception was only impossibility for *us*, and that in an appropriately ideal sense complete fulfillment is possible. By the time of *Ideen I* in 1913, he had changed his mind, and he states there that it belongs to the essence of *outer objects* that they can be given only from a perspective and thus incompletely (§§43–4); not even God could overcome the inadequacy of outer perception. Nonetheless he writes that complete givenness of the object is "predelineated as an Idea in the Kantian sense" (§143); complete givenness is approached as a kind of limit by an infinite continuum of perceptions of the same object in harmony with one another. It seems that truth itself will have to be adjusted to the fact that evidence in the strong sense also has the character of a Kantian idea.[33]

Let us return to Husserl's statement of *Prolegomena* §50 that 'A is true' is equivalent to 'It is possible that someone should judge with evidence that A.' This formulation is somewhat more perspicuous than the formulations of Brentano and Kraus. If we accept that it might be impossible to judge with evidence either that A or that not-A, then what we have is a violation of the law of excluded middle. Since the intuitionist challenge to classical mathematics of L. E. J. Brouwer, of which the first steps were taken during Brentano's lifetime, the idea that the law of excluded middle might be given up or qualified has become familiar to us, and it is one of the possibilities that has to be considered in developing an epistemic conception of truth. The most straightforward way of carrying this out would be to adopt something like the Husserlian formulation and declare that, if it is not possible to judge with evidence with regard to A, then A is neither true nor false. If evidence is interpreted as entailing the degree of certainty that Brentano takes it to, and we measure possibility by the actual capabilities of the human mind, that will lead to a counterintuitive result, for example that ordinary empirical judgments are neither true nor false.

The development of epistemic conceptions of truth in the twentieth century has proceeded differently. Intuitionism, which offers the most rigorous and thorough development, is primarily a view about mathematics. We could translate Brouwer's view into Brentano's language by saying that A can be said to be true only when one judges with evidence that A. Unlike Brentano, Brouwer does not think it makes sense to talk about truth with regard to "blind" judgments. But rather than allow truth-value gaps, Brouwer interprets negation so that one can judge that not-A if one knows that an absurdity results from the supposition that one has a proof of A, i.e. that one can judge with evidence that A.[34] It follows that it is impossible for neither A nor not-A to be true, but it does not follow that either A or not-A is true.

Although the idea has been advanced of extending the intuitionistic approach to logic and truth in general, this program has not been carried out, and the problem of certainty that we have been discussing is a serious obstacle to it. In intuitionism, possession of a proof of A guarantees the truth of A. But in most domains of knowledge even very strong evidence for a statement A might be called in question by additional evidence. The result is that although epistemic conceptions of truth have been found attractive by many philosophers, there is no canonical development of it for the empirical domain corresponding to intuitionism for the mathematical. Many writers have, following Charles Sanders Peirce and Husserl, taken what is true to be what is evident under highly idealized conditions.

In Brentano, the epistemic characterization of truth is offered after a deflationary reading of the correspondence formula. In the writing about truth in our own time, some writers have been led to some version of an epistemic conception by what is nowadays called deflationism, the view that the equivalence of '"p" is true' and 'p' represents the whole content of the concept of truth, and perhaps in addition that the concept of truth serves no purpose beyond that of "disquotation," that is of passing from statements in which linguistic items are mentioned to statements in which they are used, and perhaps of generalization as in statements like "Everything Dean says about Watergate is false." Although Brentano's meditation on the *adaequatio* formula led in a deflationary direction, it would be overintepretation to describe him as a deflationist in contemporary terms. He does not explain the transition from his deflationary remarks to the epistemic criterion. But he evidently thought that there is a connection, and in this respect he is a precursor of one strand of contemporary deflationism.

NOTES

* I am indebted to Dagfinn Føllesdal, Kai Hauser, Peter Simons, and the editor for helpful comments.
1. It is this case that Brentano calls judgment, although in ordinary language judging is often appraisal as to value, as for example the judging of figure-skating or other performances.

2. For a wide-ranging treatment of judgment in the Brentano school, see Kevin Mulligan, "Judgings: their Parts and Counterparts," in *La scuola di Brentano, Topoi Supplements* 2 (1988), pp. 117–48.

3. It might seem that the idea of judgments as events, i.e. someone's judging, would be congenial to Brentano's reism. However, I have not found a place where he admits events as *Realia*.

4. Brentano summarizes his argument in §8 of chapter 7 (KPP, pp. 64–5, PES-E, pp. 221–2). I am indebted here to Kai Hauser.

5. For example "Die Negation," *Beiträge zur Philosophie des deutschen Idealismus*, vol. I (1919), pp. 143–57, 152–5. (Original page numbers are given in *Kleine Schriften*, ed., Ignacio Angelelli [Hildesheim: Olms, 1967] and *Collected Papers*, ed., Brian McGuinness [Oxford: Backwell, 1984].) There is no reason to think that Brentano individually is Frege's target; he is not referred to in Frege's extant writings.

6. Apparently Brentano does not distinguish terminologically between affirming a presentation and affirming its object, so that affirming rain tomorrow and affirming the presentation are expressed by the same word, generally *anerkennen*.

7. Brentano credits Herbart with treating existential propositions as distinct from categorical subject–predicate propositions (KPP, p. 54, PES-E, p. 211). Kai Hauser has suggested (in correspondence) that treating affirmative judgment as judgment of existence may have arisen from Brentano's reflection on Aristotle; cf. the remark that Aristotle recognized that the concept of existence is obtained by reflection on affirmative judgment (WE, p. 45, TE, p. 39).

8. In reading categorical propositions in this way, Brentano was anticipated by Boole. An elegant decision procedure for syllogisms so interpreted was devised in the 1880s by Charles Peirce's student Christine Ladd-Franklin. In response to criticism by J. P. N. Land, Brentano admitted that one might read the categorical propositions as presupposing the nonemptiness of the subject concepts.

9. "Brentano's Theory of Judgment," in *Brentano and Meinong Studies* (Amsterdam: Rodopi, 1982), pp. 17–36.

10. Brentano reveals that the example of the two apples comes from Cantor, who is said to have claimed before a meeting of mathematicians to generate an infinity of objects starting with two apples.

11. Clearly this paraphrase involves a negative term.

12. Translation modified. This remark occurs in a footnote added in 1889 to *Miklosich über subjektlose Sätze* (1883).

13. So far as I know Brentano does not address directly the problem how to understand simple judgments of the form "there are non-*A*s" or "there are no non-*A*s." The obvious idea is to take them as judgments

of the form "there are [are no] *things* that are non-As." Then in the negative case, the elimination of the term negation would pose the same problem as that noted in the text for the A form.

14. "Brentano's Theory of Judgment," p. 24.

15. "Brentano's reform of logic," p. 43 of the reprint in *Philosophy of Logic in Central Europe from Bolzano to Tarski* (Dordrecht: Kluwer, 1992).

16. It is puzzling that Brentano speaks here of intuitive unity, since the case is essentially the one that on the previous page he has contrasted with intuitive unity. Kraus appends to "intuitive unity" a note, "Read: presented things." This is not very clear, but it is likely that he thought "intuitive unity" in the quotation in the text a slip.

17. The English phrase reminds one of Frege, but Frege's term is *Art des Gegebenseins*, and it should be clear from the text that the meaning is quite different. See "Über Sinn und Bedeutung," *Zeitschrift für Philosophie und philosophische Kritik* 100 (1892), pp. 25–50, p. 26.

18. The second of these passages undoubtedly comes from Brentano's reistic period, and although the editor of SNB is not explicit about its date, it seems very likely that the first does as well, since nearly all the texts in the volume for which he gives dates are from the last years of Brentano's life. The mention of "association" suggests that Brentano's target is a view like Berkeley's. Deborah Brown argues that Brentano's rejection of the view I suggest rests in considerable part on (mistaken) identification of medieval nominalism with views like Berkeley's. See "Immanence and Individuation: Brentano and the Scholastics on Knowledge of Singulars," *The Monist* 83 (2000), pp. 22–47; see esp. pp. 36–38.

19. See notes 36 and 37, LRU, p. 312. Note 37 intimates that §30 comes from supplementary essay XII of PES, but that is accurate only for the last part.

20. For a historically informed and much more detailed treatment of Brentano's views on individuation and his relation to nominalism, see Brown, "Immanence and Individuation."

21. Section numbers in the text below refer to this essay; this will enable the reader to locate a passage either in the German (WE) or the English (TE).

22. Translation by W. D. Ross quoted in §11 (in TE).

23. Brentano states that Aristotle too recognized that this was not a case of combination.

24. *Metaphysics* 1011^{b}26–27, Ross trans.

25. Peter Simons comments that the admission of such objects was an innovation in the 1880s. Since it was abandoned with the turn to reism, it would be characteristic only of the middle period of Brentano's thought.

It should be noted that the "problem of nonbeing" to which Brentano responded at this point is one concerning judgment (or on other theories or propositions), roughly the problem how something could be true without there being anything in virtue of which it is true. It should thus be distinguished from the problem posed by *presentations of objects* that do not exist, which led to Meinong's theory of objects. Cf. the chapter by Dale Jacquette in this volume.

26.　Such an argument is intimated by Frege, "Der Gedanke," *Beiträge zur Philosophie des deutschen Idealismus* 1 (1918), pp. 58–77, p. 60.

27.　Oskar Kraus, Brentano's disciple and editor, clearly reads this as a reductive definition; see WE, pp. xxiii–xxv, TE, pp. xxiv–xxv. I would wish for more evidence before taking it that way, but for convenience I will refer to it as a definition.

28.　See WE, p. xxvii, TE, pp. xxv–xxvi.

29.　*Logische Untersuchungen* (Halle: Niemeyer, 1900–1, 2nd edn. 1913–21) Investigation VI, ch. 5; cf. *Prolegomena* (i.e. vol. I), §§49–51. The page references given will fit either the first or the second edition.

30.　Or "represented" in imagination; however, this case is excluded by the idea of final fulfillment.

31.　Husserl's positing acts correspond to Brentano's affirmative judgments, in which an object is posited in Husserl's language, affirmed or accepted in Brentano's. Brentano regarded perception as involving a judgment. Husserl denied this, but the issue is at least initially terminological: according to Husserl, the simple positing of a perceived object is not yet a judgment.

32.　In the same section Husserl allows that evidence admits of levels and degrees, but this applies to what he calls the more lax and less epistemologically significant concept of evidence.

33.　We do not deal here with the later evolution of Husserl's views on these matters, which move further from the view of the *Logische Untersuchungen*. See Dagfinn Føllesdal, "Husserl on evidence and justification," in, ed., Robert Sokolowski, *Edmund Husserl and the Phenomenological Tradition: Essays in Phenomenology* (Studies in Philosophy and the History of Philosophy, vol. xviii, Washington: Catholic University of America Press, 1988), pp. 107–29.

34.　Curiously, Kraus's rendering of Brentano's criterion for the truth of A amounts in Brouwerian terms to the truth-condition for not-not-A. That is not surprising given Brentano's tendency to paraphrase judgments apparently not involving negation by negative judgments.

9 Brentano's ontology: from conceptualism to reism*

CONCEPTUALISM (1862–1874)

It is often claimed that the beginnings of Brentano's ontology were Aristotelian in nature; but this claim is only partially true. Certainly the young Brentano adopted many elements of Aristotle's metaphysics, and he was deeply influenced by the Aristotelian way of doing philosophy. But he always interpreted Aristotle's ideas in his own fashion. He accepted them selectively, and he used them in the service of ends that would not have been welcomed by Aristotle himself. The present paper is an exposition of the development of Brentano's ontology, beginning with the *Lectures on Metaphysics* first delivered by Brentano in Würzburg in 1867 and concluding with his late work from 1904–17.

Being and truth

Aristotle distinguished various ways in which being can be predicated.[1] There is first of all the ontologically serious use of the word "is": being in the sense of the categories, also called "real being" in what follows. The two other ways of saying "is" relate respectively to what Aristotle called "purely accidental being" and "being in the sense of being true." It is especially the notion of being in the sense of being true that will concern us in what follows.

We often say that something *is* simply because the judgments reporting or describing that something are true. (Compare: "There is a fictitious detective who is more famous than any existent detective.") It is not clear whether for Aristotle this being in the sense of being true has any genuine ontological import. On the one hand

Aristotle contrasts the truth of judgments with the being of things,[2] and he claims explicitly that being in the sense of being true pertains to the realm of judgments and thus does not belong to the subject-matter of metaphysics. On the other hand one should not forget that, according to Aristotle, for each true judgment there must be some (composite) entity which makes it true;[3] and such truthmakers certainly belong to the subject-matter of metaphysics. The claim that the being true of a judgment is something very different from the being of a thing is thus by no means the end of the ontological problems invoked by Aristotle's theory of truth.

For the young Brentano, in contrast, such a claim *is* the end of such problems. As he points out, even a non-existing entity is, in the sense of the word "is" here at issue, since it is *true of* each putative non-existent that it does not exist. That Brentano takes this line follows from his adoption of a reading of the Aristotelian concept of being in the sense of being true in terms of the Scholastic doctrine of *ens objectivum*.[4] According to the latter, when a subject is thinking of an object *A*, he is said to have that object *objectively* (i.e. *as object*) in his mind. At the same time, however, this mode of speech is designed to have no special ontological consequences. Brentano often uses the Aristotelian concept of being in the sense of being true and the Scholastic concept of *ens objectivum* as mutually interchangeable tools of philosophical analysis, both of which he supposes to be ontologically innocent.

A further reason why being in the sense of being true has no ontological import for Brentano lies in his conception of truth itself, which is an epistemological conception. The notion of the truth of a judgment is elucidated by Brentano not by reference to an entity which makes the judgment true, but rather by reference to certain epistemological peculiarities of true beliefs or assertions.

Aristotle's explanation of the notion of truth by reference to the idea of "connecting what is connected" and "separating what is separated" makes sense at best for *categorial*, not however for those *existential* judgments (of the form "*A* is" / "*A* is not") which Brentano had pointed to already in 1867 as constituting the basic form of judgment. The element "is" / "is not" of such existential judgments expresses, according to Brentano, not a kind of predicate but rather only a mental attitude of acceptance or rejection in relation to whatever is referred to by the mental presentation corresponding to the term "*A*." It is, then, not the judgment as a whole which is in the market for standing in a relation of correspondence to reality, but rather only its constituent *presentation*.[5]

An affirmative existential judgment (of the form "*A* is") is true, if such a correspondence exists, i.e. if there is in the world an object which is *A*. A negative existential judgment is true if there is no such object.

Even for many affirmative existential judgments, however, the issue of correspondence with an object can be quite problematic. Consider judgments about the past and the future ("*A* was" / "*A* will be"). If a judgment of this kind is to be true, then there need not *be* any object which corresponds to its constituent presentation. *A* must *have been* or it must be such that it *will be*, but it need not exist in the present moment.

Time, and all that exists in time (which means for the young Brentano everything), is, properly speaking, only in that punctual boundary which is the present moment. This view however conflicts with what he takes to be a conceptual truth, namely that no boundary can exist alone, separated from the continuum which it bounds – in this case a continuum extended beyond the present moment along the temporal dimension.[6] Brentano resolves this problem in his early period by allowing also a looser mode of speech, which allows us to refer to time as something which exists also as an extended whole, as a kind of unfinished reality.

The claim that an existential judgment about the past or future corresponds to reality can then be translated as: "If time were a finished reality like space . . . then there would be a reality corresponding to [the given judgment's] presentation."[7]

The young Brentano operates here essentially with counterfactuals whose ontological force is not further explained. He does however suggest that tensed judgments need no special truthmakers of their own.[8]

For many other types of judgment, too, the formula *adaequatio rei et intellectus* has no clear sense. Consider for example a disjunctive judgment such as "Either *A* exists or *B* exists." Such a judgment is true if and only if at least one of its constituent presentations corresponds to reality. And the truth-conditions for a hypothetical judgment of the form "If *A* is not, then *B* is" are exactly the same. Such compound judgments thus involve no relation of correspondence of their own. Rather, their truth-conditions are specified recursively, as functions of the truth-conditions of their constituents.

Finally we have apodictic judgments such as "It is necessary that A exists" or "It is necessary that A does not exist." Such judgments are accounted for by Brentano epistemically. They are true, if and only if the existence or non-existence of A is evident "on the ground of the concepts involved." Later, Brentano insisted that the only apodictic judgments whose truth can be known by human beings are such negative truths as: "Necessarily, there is no triangular circle." Even then, however, he does not exclude the possibility that positive apodictic knowledge might be accessible to more sophisticated minds. In particular, he believed that, if we were only able to grasp the concept of God in an adequate way, then we would recognize that a version of the Anselmian ontological argument is valid.[9]

Given this variety of cases Brentano concludes that, to the extent that the *adaequatio* notion of truth can be defended at all, there is not one but a whole series of correspondence relations at work, and the truth theorist must construct the relation anew for each new kind of judgment. From this, however, Brentano concludes that it cannot be this relation that is at the core of our concept of truth. Rather we must already have some prior concept of truth which we use in constructing the relevant type of *adaequatio* in each successive case. This primary concept of truth is, according to Brentano, precisely the *epistemic* concept outlined above. At one point he even states that "truth and knowledge are one and the same."[10]

This formulation could hardly be accepted as it stands, however, not least because truths can be produced by chance, without any epistemic justification. In his later manuscripts, accordingly, Brentano defines a true judgment as one which *could* be judged by a subject who is acting in an epistemologically correct way, which in turn means: by a subject who is judging with evidence, i.e. with maximal epistemic justification (which according to Brentano involves infallibility). His final definition of truth might thus be formulated as: "It is true that *p*" means: "*p* could be judged with evidence."[11]

It is commonly believed that this epistemological (and thus evidently anti-Aristotelian) definition of truth is characteristic only for the late Brentano. We see however that it is present already in the Würzburg *Lectures on Metaphysics*.

Real beings and their parts

There are of course many problems with Brentano's epistemic definition of truth. The central notion of evidence and the modal force of "could be" both remain obscure. For our purposes here, however, it is important to note only that the young Brentano believed himself to have shown that the explanation of the concept of truth requires no special entities or modes of being which would need to be postulated for specifically semantical reasons.

When Brentano turns to the topic of real being in the Würzburg lectures, therefore, he does this independently of any reference to semantics, seeking to establish the structure of being in light of the classical questions of ontology. What is the relation between a thing and its properties? Can properties be shared in common by a plurality of things? Are there essential and accidental characteristics? What is the correct analysis of change, persistence, coming into being and passing away?

PHYSICAL PARTS.   The core of Brentano's ontology lies in his treatment of the different kinds of *parts* of things. He distinguishes first of all *physical* parts, which are those detachable pieces of things that are governed by the basic principles of mereology. The treatment of the mereological composition of the world was one of the points in which the young Brentano was a faithful disciple of Aristotle. This means that pieces not actually detached – for example your arm or my leg – and wholes not actually connected exist only potentially. The only things that exist actually, for Brentano and for Aristotle, are complete substances, whether physical or mental.[12]

The young Brentano had a place, too, for the Aristotelian concept of *boundary*,[13] though while he sees the physical parts of things as being at least potentially real, the mode of being of boundaries is for him something still weaker. This is because, while the physical parts of real things can in principle be isolated, so that they can become real things in their own right, boundaries cannot even in principle be isolated from the extended substances which they bound. Boundaries are, as Brentano puts it, fictions *cum fundamento in re*. Their foundation consists in the fact that real things can be measured, and measurements are expressed by reference to corresponding boundaries.[14]

LOGICAL PARTS. Brentano distinguishes also what he calls the *logical* parts of an entity, which he conceives *via* an analogy with the parts of a definition in Aristotle's sense. In a concrete human being there are, according to Brentano, at least two logical parts: an animal nature and a rational animal nature. Like the parts of an Aristotelian definition they are arranged in the manner of a Chinese box, with general parts (like the animal nature) being included within less general parts (like the rational animal nature).[15] The coloredness of a patch of red is included in this sense in the corresponding redness. The underlying idea here is that a proper part of something can remain the same even if the something as a whole ceases to exist. A speck in the visual field need not be red; but it must have some color.

There are some who accept logical parts as special denizens of reality, conceiving each concrete individual as comprehending an onion-like hierarchy of universal constituents of decreasing grades of generality. This picture is embraced specifically by those immanent realists who hold that it is certain universal constituents of individual things which serve as the semantical correlates of general terms.[16] This is not however a picture which Brentano himself was able to accept. At no stage in his career did Brentano believe in universals, no matter how rich his ontology was in other respects.

Brentanian logical parts are, rather, fictions in a sense which is best explained by reference to the following semantico-ontological theory.[17] Words refer to objects in the world by means of presentations. The latter are themselves accidents of the soul or mind. Individual terms are associated with presentations specifying exactly one object. General terms (and predicates) are associated with presentations which specify only those characteristics of the object of reference which could be shared by many objects (as for example the presentation of a horse specifies only one characteristic shared by its putative objects, namely that of being a horse).

Yet Brentano insists that the correlate of a general term is still, ontologically speaking, exactly the same thing as the correlate of an individual term. What corresponds to the general term "man" is always this or that individual human being, exactly as in the case of a proper name like "John" or of a definite description like "the only woman in this room."

Brentano thus postulates no special semantical values for general terms. How, then, is the role of general terms to be explained?

Brentano's answer is that, while the division of a real thing into its logical parts is a fiction, this fiction is *cum fundamento in re*, as is seen in the fact that some divisions of this sort reflect *correct*, and others *incorrect*, presentations. We can make this distinction between correct and incorrect, Brentano holds, even though there exist in the underlying structure of reality no corresponding special entities (called "universals") which would legitimate it.[18]

Normative terms are thus employed in the same way both in Brentano's treatment of the concept of truth and in his treatment of generality. Just as he needs for the former no truthmakers but rather only a notion of correct and incorrect judgments, so he needs for the latter no universal entities but rather only a notion of correct and incorrect general presentations.

METAPHYSICAL PARTS.   Brentano distinguishes, finally, the notion of *metaphysical* parts, which he introduces for the purpose of giving an analysis of the Aristotelian notions of substance and accident. Among properties one can distinguish two groups: the essential and the accidental. The properties of an object are essential if they could not be lost without bringing about the destruction of the object itself. Examples of essential properties are: *is a man, is a horse*. Accidental properties, in contrast, are those properties which can be gained and lost at will with no effect on the existence of their bearer. Examples are: *is hungry, is a student*. Only substances (which, according to Aristotle, are constituted by their essential properties) are ontologically independent, in the sense that only they can exist without requiring some other entity which serves as their ontological support. Accidents, in contrast, must be *in* a substance in something like the way in which an electric charge is in a conductor or a smile is in a human face. Substances are concrete; accidents are abstract: they do not exist in and of themselves but only in the sense that they can be isolated within their respective bearers by abstraction.

Aristotle spoke both of individual and universal accidents,[19] but according to Brentano both substances and accidents are individual entities. Brentanian accidents are analogues of what some nowadays call "tropes" or "individual properties." They are individual in the sense that they cannot be shared by a plurality of substances. Each red apple must have its own individual accident of redness and the issue of shared properties is to be explained by reference to the similarity obtaining between the accidents in question.

Brentano's conclusion is that such metaphysical parts (substances and accidents) are not to be counted as denizens of reality in the fullest sense of the word. Like logical parts they, too, are fictions *cum fundamento in re*,[20] and their "foundation" is, again, explained in normative terms. It is not that there is some inner structure in each thing involving both a substantial core on the one hand and its accidents on the other. Rather each real thing is such that it is correct to consider it as being such that it would remain the same even if it lost some of those accidents which are now correctly predicated of it, as a man may lose a headache and as a mind that is seeing and hearing may cease to see or hear.[21]

Relations

Aristotle regarded relations as the weakest form of being. He calls them the least of all realities,[22] and Brentano agrees with this statement.[23]

The first point to note is that Brentano never believed in external relations in Russell's sense, i.e. relations whose obtaining cannot be inferred from truths about the terms of the relation taken separately. According to Brentano it is a conceptual truth that each relation must have its basis in the constitution of the terms involved, or in other words that all relations supervene on certain monadic properties of their terms, a principle which we can express as follows: If there is a relation R between the objects a and b, then there must be monadic properties F and G which are such that (i) a is F and b is G, and (ii) for each x and y, if x is F and y is G, then, necessarily, the relation R holds between x and y. It follows from the fact that John is six feet tall and Mary is five feet tall that Mary is smaller than John.

Since monadic properties themselves are fictions, it becomes clear that relations could only be still more fictitious.[24]

ONTOLOGY OF INTENTIONALITY (1874–1904)

From around 1870 Brentano concentrates on psychological questions. In the *Psychology from an Empirical Point of View* (1874) he introduces the notion of "having something immanently as an object" as the defining feature of mental phenomena. Every such phenomenon, we read, "includes something as object within itself."[25] Such objects are called by Brentano "immanent objects," "contents," or "intentional correlates." The most important aspect of the "immanence" of an immanent object is its undetachability from the corresponding mental act. This is the sense in which an immanent object is "in" the mind.

It is not clear whether in 1874 this mode of speech was intended to carry any ontological commitment. It is not excluded that at this time Brentano still wanted to construe all apparent reference to special entities as a mere *façon de parler* in the spirit of the medieval doctrine of objective existence referred to already above.[26] In light of the way Brentano's analysis of intentionality developed after the *Psychology*, however, the reference to such immanent objects must be interpreted as signifying the introduction of a new ontological category with all the ontological commitments that go together herewith. In the following we will thus project this ontologizing interpretation of immanent objects also on those passages of the *Psychology* in which Brentano introduces his doctrine of intentionality, passages which in and of themselves are, notoriously, difficult to interpret.

The role of immanent objects

It seems that the main factor leading Brentano in the direction of accepting immanent objects as forming an ontological category in their own right was his growing awareness of the important role which such objects would have to play in his theory of intentionality. The main goal of the latter is of course to give an account of mental directedness in a way which does justice to the phenomenological homogeneity of such directedness in both veridical and nonveridical cases. The latter are marked by the failure of the principle of existential generalization, so that from a sentence like:

(A)   "John believes that Santa Claus is bald"

we cannot infer that there is something which John believes to be bald.

Sentences expressing mental directedness are marked also by a failure of the principle of substitution, so that from:

(B)   "John believes that the victor at Jena was a Corsican,"

together with the true identity of the victor at Jena with the vanquished at Waterloo, we cannot infer that John believes that the vanquished at Waterloo was a Corsican.

The first inference is invalid, as Brentano would have it, because
it is only the existence of an *immanent* Santa Claus which can be
deduced from (A). The second is invalid because the *immanent* victor
at Jena, which is the object of (B), is not identical with the *immanent*
vanquished at Waterloo.

Ontological theories of intentionality – theories committed to special entities in addition to acts and objects in external reality – can
be divided into two groups, which can be labeled *object theories* and
mediator theories, respectively. An object theory situates the entities
it postulates in the target-position of the relevant intentional acts.
Such entities thus serve as objects of reference. A mediator theory
postulates entities which function instead as structures mediating
our intentional access to external objects.

Frege's theory of sense and reference is clearly a case of a mediator
theory. That the theory outlined by Brentano in the *Psychology* is
an object theory becomes clear when we see how he uses the medieval conception of *ens objectivum* in presenting his ideas. Recall
that whenever a subject thinks of an object *A* we are entitled, on the
objectivum-conception, to say that *A* is, objectively, in the subject's
mind. Where Brentano had earlier seen this reference to an object in
the subject's mind as being free of any ontological commitment, in
the *Psychology* he moves toward the view which grants a genuine ontological status to the postulated entity. Talk of the "immanence"
of an immanent object means now not that the ontological commitments putatively associated with terms like "object" have to be
suspended but rather, quite to the contrary, that they are to be embraced to the full: an immanent object exists in every case of mental
directedness, whether veridical or non-veridical.

This full-fledged object theory of intentionality dominates the
lectures on *Descriptive Psychology* of 1890/1 in which the immanent object is referred to by Brentano as an "intentional correlate."[27]
Along the way, however, Brentano considers also a theory of intentionality which uses immanent objects as mediating structures. In
his *Logic Lectures* from 1877 and from the second half of the 1880s he
proposes a semantical theory according to which a name refers to an

external object while the corresponding immanent object functions as a mediating meaning.[28]

Yet the theory of the *Logic Lectures* also contains some elements of an object theory. While investigating the problem of names without designata, Brentano writes that "signifying (naming) nothing should not be confused with signifying (naming) something which does not exist."[29] It is, however, not clear, whether Brentano is here committed to a view according to which every presentation would have, besides a mediating immanent object, also its own (existent or non-existent) referent.[30]

It seems thus that in his middle period, which is to say from 1870 to 1904, Brentano did not formulate any truly consistent theory of intentionality. Rather, he oscillated between an object theory and a mediator theory.

The ontology of immanent objects

Immanent objects were conceived by Brentano as satisfying three conditions: (i) for each mental act the existence of the appropriate immanent object must be guaranteed, so that a suitably modified principle of existential generalization can be accepted; (ii) each immanent object must be able either to substitute for or to represent the object of reference (depending on whether we assume an object- or a mediator-theoretic interpretation of Brentano's views); (iii) immanent objects must be distinguished from each other in a sufficiently fine-grained way to save some form of the principle of substitutivity.

That Brentano's doctrine of immanent objects satisfies condition (i) follows from the fact that an immanent object is no less a part of the structure of every mental act than is the moment of inner perception (that in virtue of which we are conscious of our mental acts as we have them). The mental act and its immanent object are called by Brentano "parts of the intentional correlate-pair." These parts are separable, as Brentano puts it, "only in the distinctional sense," i.e. only in our thoughts, and not in reality.[31]

Condition (ii) follows from the fact that an immanent object is defined as having exactly those properties which would be possessed by a corresponding real transcendent object, though it has these properties only *in a modifying sense*.[32] Thus immanent objects are for example red or green or warm or cold only in a modifying sense (compare the modifying sense of the world "healthy" used in phrases like "healthy drug" or "healthy bicycle").

A conception along these lines is consistent with both readings of Brentano's theory of intentionality. According to the object-theoretic reading, one could claim that each subject in fact refers only to immanent objects, though he has before his mind exactly the same properties which he would have if, *per impossibile*, he were able to refer directly to the corresponding transcendent object. The fact that the immanent object has these properties only in a modifying sense is then not apparent to the subject in the act itself.[33] A partisan of the mediator-theoretic interpretation, in contrast, could claim that for an object to have a certain property in a modifying sense means precisely for it to represent an object which has (would have) this property in the normal sense.

Condition (iii) is satisfied by virtue of the fact that an object such as the immanent victor-at-Jena may be construed as having only one property, namely that of being victor at Jena, and as thus being distinguished from (for example) that immanent object which has the single property of having been vanquished at Waterloo.[34]

We can see also that the Brentanian version of the principle of substitutivity must speak, not of identity, but rather of a kind of similarity between the immanent objects of distinct acts. Since every immanent object is an inseparable correlate of a particular mental act, it follows that there could be no two mental acts with numerically identical immanent objects. There could, however, be two immanent objects which do in a sense have "the same content," namely immanent objects which have (in a modifying sense) the same properties. Since Brentano does not believe in universals, "same" means here that each immanent object would then have (in a modifying sense) its own collection of individual properties which are pairwise strictly similar.[35]

Propositional contents, temporally modified objects and truth

Brentano's official theory of judgment was at every stage a non-propositional theory.[36] A judgment consists in the acceptance or rejection of a presented object, and this acceptance or rejection needs no objectual correlate in addition to the object itself. In the *Logic Lectures* from the second half of the 1880s, however, Brentano toys with a refinement of this view according to which judgments have, in addition to the correlates of their underlying presentations, special immanent and transcendent correlates of a quasi-propositional sort. The special immanent correlate is referred to by means of the phrases: "accepted object" or "rejected object," the special transcendent correlate, at least in the case when the judgment in question is true, by means of the phrases: "being/non-being of the presented object." Compare the following passage from the *Logic Lectures*:

Like names, assertions too have a double reference:
(a) to the content of a psychical phenomenon as such;
(b) to a putative external object.
 The first is the meaning.
 The phenomenon at issue in this case is however not a presentation, but a judgement. The judged as such is the meaning. Similarly in the case of the request: the desired as desired is the meaning.
 Because [in the case of a judgment] that which mediates the reference to the putative object is a different type of phenomenon, we designate it differently, calling it not a naming, but rather an announcing [*ein Anzeigen*]. The announced [*das Angezeigte*] is that which is accepted or rejected. We can call it indication [*andeuten*] or counter-indication [*abdeuten*] (and for the latter we can speak also of an indication of non-being).[37]

Brentano thus anticipated later ontological doctrines of *Sachverhalte* and *Objective* proposed by Stumpf and Meinong.[38]

 These special judgment-correlates are "propositional" in the sense that they are composite entities involving as parts correlates not only of the constituent presentations but also of the moment of acceptance or rejection on the side of the judgment. Their introduction thus amounts to giving an ontological interpretation of judgmental acceptance and rejection (which, according to the young Brentano, needed no such interpretation).

 Another group of entities that rose to prominence in Brentano's middle period are temporally modified objects. Such objects *exist* in the fullest sense, Brentano now holds, which means that they exist *now*. Each time we judge something about the past or future our judgment consists in a (temporally neutral) acceptance or rejection of such a temporally modified object. The deep logical form of the sentence "Yesterday the weather was beautiful" is "The-yesterday-beautiful-weather *is*." An ontologically perspicuous language must then situate all tenses in the role of modifiers of nominal expressions.[39]

With this rich ontology, Brentano was able to formulate the version of the correspondence theory of truth which we find in his lecture "On the Concept of Truth" of 1889. In this work Brentano sees every true positive existential judgment as being correlated with an appropriate existing object: the transcendent correlate of the underlying presentation. To every true negative existential judgment, on the other hand, there corresponds an appropriate non-existing transcendent object, namely the object which is rejected in the judgment. Consequently, the ontological universe divides smoothly into two parts. On the one hand we have existing entities, which can be correctly accepted, and on the other hand we have non-existing entities, which can be correctly rejected.[40]

Yet Brentano hastens to add that the sphere of existing entities should not simply be identified with the totality of real things. For there are, according to his theory at this stage, many non-real existents.[41] He lists in addition to immanent and temporally modified objects also aggregates, properties, relations, boundaries, *negativa*, *privativa*, simple and modalized propositional contents (such as the existence of a horse or the necessary non-existence of a triangular circle). Analogically, among non-existents there are both non-real as well as real entities (or entities, that *would* be real, if only they existed) such as for example a centaur.[42] In general, the non-reality of an entity no longer signifies that it is ontologically without standing, i.e. that it is merely fictitious.

Properties and relations

In particular, between 1874 and 1890 Brentano classifies individual properties as non-real parts and at the same time treats them as entities to be taken ontologically seriously. A property (metaphysical part) such as an individual blackness is still an abstract individual part of its concrete individual bearer (the pertinent black thing) but it is no longer construed as a fiction. The pairs consisting of a property and its bearer are called "correlative pairs." The members of such a pair are neither really, nor conceptually, independent,[43] but nonetheless they are distinct entities, both of which are to be taken ontologically seriously. A property is no longer a fiction, the shadow of a conceptual construction or of a mere mode of speech. The correctness of a property attribution now has its objective correlate on the side of the truthmakers in the world.

The majority of relations are still classified as non-real entities which supervene on the monadic properties of their terms. In his *Logic Lectures* from 1884/5, however, Brentano points to certain special relations which he wants to call *real*.[44] These are the relations which hold among the metaphysical and also among the logical parts of real things, relations which cannot be construed as supervenient on the monadic properties of their terms. The fact that two metaphysical parts (two individual abstract properties) – say, *whiteness* and *triangularity* – are united in one thing, amounts to an external relation in Russell's sense. There are no characteristics of the whiteness and triangularity in question from which we could infer this fact. And similarly, the fact that the logical parts *color* and *redness* are united in one thing is not implied by the nature of the logical part *color*, though it is implied by the nature of the logical part *red*. Some colored things are not red, but every red thing must have some color. The relations between logical parts are thus external, as it were, only in one direction.

Notice that the relations among logical and among metaphysical parts of things are very different from the relations between concrete individuals. All of the latter are still seen by Brentano as supervening on their monadic properties.

REISM (1904–1917)

As is well known, the rich ontology of the middle period was not Brentano's last word. It seems that the overpopulated universe of non-real entities was something that Brentano felt himself forced for a time to accept, but something with which he was never really happy. In the final period of his life a house-cleaning took place on a number of different fronts. Some types of non-real entities (including physical parts, aggregates, boundaries, and accidents) are reinterpreted as real entities; others (including immanent and temporally modified objects as well as propositional entities) are rejected as the product of an inadequate interpretation of language. The world of

212 ARKADIUSZ CHRUDZIMSKI AND BARRY SMITH

the late Brentano thus contains only real entities, and as he calls all real entities "things" or "*res*," his late ontology is commonly labeled "reism."

The transitory period 1893–1904

In the period between 1893 and 1904 the rich ontology of the middle period was gradually deflated. In a letter to Marty of November 24, 1893 Brentano reports an idea which had occurred to him in "a dreamless night": that what is common to all putative non-real entities is that they involve a hidden reference to some mental activity. What he means by this can be made clear if we examine its implications for the treatment of the past and the future.

Instead of introducing special temporally modified objects, Brentano suggests, we should operate with temporally unmodified objects but let them be apprehended in mental acts of certain specific *temporal modes*.[45] The main idea is then that talk of entities of the given sort can be replaced without loss by talk of a certain special mental activity operating with "normal" objects. Ontological categories are eliminated at the price of added psychological complexity.

In 1901, Brentano uses this technique to bring about the elimination of the category of properties. He criticizes his earlier theory and claims that to say that a thing *a* has a property *F* is in principle nothing other than to say that *a* could be correctly presented as an *F*. To be sure, a presentation which presents its object merely as *F* (as a horse, as a human being, etc.) presents its object in an incomplete way, but even incomplete presentations can be correct.[46] The similarity with the Würzburg conceptualist position is then apparent.

Wholes, parts, and boundaries

The official late ontology of Brentano, as presented for example in the manuscripts collected by Alfred Kastil in 1933 under the title *Theory of Categories*, is very different from his Würzburg position.

The first reason for this lies in the fact that Brentano has become much more permissive in relation to mereological questions. After 1900 he moves to a conception according to which all aggregates and physical parts of things exist as things in their own right. In 1904 it is absolutely clear that not only is each physical body and each non-material soul or mind a thing, but so also, on Brentano's new dispensation, is every physical part of a thing and every aggregate of things.[47]

The second reason for Brentano's move to reism relates to the fact that the reduction of properties along conceptualist lines itself faces internal difficulties. If to say that an object a has a property F is nothing other than to say that a could be correctly presented as an F, and if a presentation is construed as an accident (and thus as a property) of the soul, then it seems that the problem has only been shifted to another level. The having of properties has been analyzed in terms of possible correct presentation, but presentation itself turns out to be a *property* of a certain kind, namely an accident of the mind. According to the young Brentano, even such mental accidents are fictitious, i.e. explainable only in terms of the possibility of their being correctly presented. Now, however, it seems to have occurred to Brentano that an explanation along these lines threatens an infinite regress.

The new proposal is to construe an accident as a whole which contains its substance as a part.[48] Accidents, too, are things, exactly like the substances which they include as parts. Yet the relation of parthood involved in this theory is a very special one. An accident is a whole which is "something more" than the underlying substance; the former "enriches" or "enlarges" or "modally extends" the latter. Yet Brentano insists that an accident adds to its substance nothing which would be "entirely different" from the substance itself. The main idea is that there is nothing (no thing) in the accident which would remain if the substance were somehow removed.[49]

One of the principles of classical mereology is the so-called remainder principle. This affirms that if an individual has a proper part, then it has a further proper part, disjoint from the first and constituting, as it were, the difference between the two.[50] As we see, this principle does not hold for the parthood relation to which appeal is made in Brentano's theory of accidents, and this means that his mereology is of a non-standard type.[51]

Brentano's late ontology includes also a new and interesting treatment of the category of boundaries. The objects which are presented to us in the most typical cases of outer perception are spatial continua. It was Brentano's firm belief that no such continuum could ever be constructed out of discrete points. A continuum is, rather, such as to involve what Brentano calls a coincidence of boundaries.

Each boundary can continue to exist even if a part of the continuum which it bounds should be destroyed (as the surface of an apple can continue to exist even though parts of the inside have been eaten away by maggots), but no boundary can exist except as part of *some* larger extended whole, which it serves as the boundary of.[52]

After 1904 we might expect that boundaries would be classified as things. After all, a reistic world consists exclusively of things. Brentano himself sometimes classifies boundaries as substances;[53] but they would have to be a very strange kind of substance indeed, given that they are in each case ontologically dependent on some other, larger substance of which they form a part.[54] Chisholm claims that Brentanian boundaries ought most properly to be construed as constituting a *sui generis* category of entities, which are neither substances nor accidents.[55]

Relations

The category of relation finds an extensive treatment in Brentano's late philosophy. On the one hand he speaks of one-sided relations, which means: relations which require for their existence only the existence of one of their terms.[56] Intentional and temporal relations (for example: is thinking of, being before) he now sees as being of this kind. We can conceive such one-sided relations also as monadic properties of their only term. The apparent reference to the second term is then just the reflection of a particular mode of describing the situation, perhaps the only possible one for subjects with cognitive powers like ours, but one having, as such, no ontological consequences.

Indeed, in the case of temporal relations Brentano asserts that there must be absolute temporal positions which from the ontological point of view are nothing other than the monadic properties of objects. Still, these absolute temporal positions are cognitively inaccessible to us. All we can do is to describe temporal positions relationally, e.g. "before the Second World War," "100 years before Christ," etc.[57]

On the other hand other relations require the existence of both of their terms; this holds for example of every spatial relation between physical parts of a compound substance. Such relations are now referred to by Brentano as "collective determinations";[58] they are monadic properties of the corresponding aggregates.

Each relation is thus either an accident of one of its (putative) terms, or it is an accident of an aggregate of things; and since all accidents and all aggregates are things, the late Brentano can claim that the world consists of things exclusively.

Intentionality

The late Brentano has an ontologically robust theory of mental accidents. They are concrete individual things constituting modal extensions of their substances (minds) and thus containing the latter, somehow, as parts. Consequently, he can speak of mental presentations as genuine entities, and the conceptualist reduction of non-mental properties in terms of "being correctly presentable in such and such a way" no longer appears flagrantly circular.

The theory of intentionality which seems at first glance to be suggested by this reduction is an *adverbial* theory. If the only ontological building blocks out of which we can reconstruct our world are concrete individuals, including those accidents which are modally extended concrete individuals, then the only way in which we could speak of (possibly non-existent) objects of presentation is to translate such talk into the adverbial idiom. To have a presentation of a triangular object is to present triangularly. "To present," here, refers to a certain accident of the soul and "triangularly" specifies the kind to which this accident belongs. The adverbial complement thus refers in a sense to an accident of an accident, an accident of second order.[59]

On the other hand Brentano needs to consider more than just the modes of presentation. He stresses very often that if we want to specify a presentation we can do this only by referring to its object, and indeed, it seems that an adverbial specification such as "triangularly," "bluely," "dogly," or "horsely" is understandable only by a kind of linkage to the objects whose properties the given terms would convey. We understand what it means "to present bluely" only because we know what it means for the object of the presentation involved to be blue. This raises a problem for those champions of the adverbial theory who see it as providing a method for the elimination of objects of intention.

This conception suggests another picture of Brentano's ontology of intentionality. In place of a simple adverbial theory in the frame of which one would speak only of mental substances (minds) and their monadic accidents, we obtain a theory which introduces an intentional relation which is irreducibly non-extensional in the sense that for the sentences describing this relation the principles of existential generalization and substitution simply fail.[60]

Now, it is clear that the adverbial interpretation concurs better with the general reistic attitude of the late Brentano. For it is unclear, to say the least, where in a reistic world such irreducibly non-extensional intentional relations could find their place. The solution that we propose is to assume that the true Brentanian ontology of intentionality is indeed an adverbial ontology as outlined above, but to insist at the same time that the only specification of the meaning of the corresponding adverbial determinations which a human being would be able to give is in terms of putative objects of presentation. According to this interpretation, the ontology of intentionality is at bottom adverbial, but the "ideology" of intentionality must for cognitive agents like ourselves refer to the putative objects of intentions.[61]

Brentano's ontology of intentionality thus remains, in the end, at least compatible with solipsism, and with the view that we have no evidence that there exist entities other than ourselves.

NOTES

* We should like to thank Wilhelm Baumgartner (Würzburg), Johannes Brandl (Salzburg), and Guido Küng (Freiburg/Switzerland) for granting us access to Brentano's unpublished manuscripts. We also thank Johann C. Marek (Graz) for pointing out the importance of the manuscript EL 108*. The work of Arkadiusz Chrudzimski was supported by the Austrian Foundation for the Promotion of Scientific Research (FWF).

1. Cf. *Categories* and *Metaphysics*, 1117^a7–32.
2. *Metaphysics*, 1028^a25–7.
3. Cf. *ibid.*, 1051^a34–1051^b9.
4. This identification is to be found already in MBS, pp. 31–7; (SSB, pp. 20–5. Cf. also PES-G, p. 80 PES-E, pp. 54–5).
5. M 96, XXXVIII. (Roman numerals refer to the individual lectures into which the manuscript is divided.)
6. The formal implications of Brentano's ontology of boundaries are presented in Smith, "Boundaries: an Essay in Mereotopology," in, ed., L. H. Hahn, *The Philosophy of Roderick Chisholm* (Chicago, IL, and LaSalle, IL: Open Court).

7. M 96, XXXVIII.
8. Brentano often resorts to counterfactuals when he wants to eliminate entities of some unwanted category, and it seems that he believes counterfactuals to be ontologically innocent. See for example WE, p. 139 (TE, p. 122) and ANR, pp. 357f. He thus stands in marked conflict with those who believe that a philosophical explanation of counterfactuals must involve something like an ontology of possible worlds.
9. Cf. DG, pp. 48–52, 58; EG, pp. 43–46, 49f.
10. M 96, XXXVIII.
11. Cf. WE, p. 139; TE, p. 122.
12. Cf. *Metaphysics*, 1019a 8–10, 1039a 3; M 96, L; and Barry Smith, *Austrian Philosophy: the Legacy of Franz Brentano* (Chicago, IL: Open Court, 1994), pp. 76–9.
13. Cf. *Physics*, 220a 22, 221a 25, 234a 1f., 251b 20–28.
14. M 96, XXV.
15. Cf. *Metaphysics*, 1018b 34–37.
16. Cf. Barry Smith, "On Substances, Accidents, and Universals: in Defence of a Constituent Ontology," *Philosophical Papers*, 26, 1997.
17. M 96, XLI.
18. M 96, XXXI.
19. Cf. *Categories*, 1a 20–1b 9.
20. M 96, XLIII.
21. Cf. M 96, XXVI.
22. *Metaphysics*, 1088a 30–31.
23. Cf. M 96, XLVII.
24. The only exception that Brentano allows are certain relations to God, particularly the relation *is-a-creature-of*. Cf. M 96, XLVII.
25. PES-G, p. 124; PES-E, p. 88.
26. Cf. Münch, *Intention und Zeichen*; Antonelli, "Franz Brentano und die Wiederent deckung der Intentionalität;" Antonnelli, *Seiendes Bewußtsein*.
27. DP-G, p. 21; DP-E, pp. 23–4.
28. Cf. the copy of Brentano's lectures *Alte und neue Logik* from 1877 (manuscript EL 108*, p. 21) and his *Logic Lectures* from the second half of the 1880s (manuscript EL 80, pp. 34f.). Cf. also Arkadiusz Chrudzimski, *Intentionalitätstheorie beim frühen Brentano*, Phaenomenologica Series 159 (Dordrecht, Boston, MA, London: Kluwer Academic Publishers, 2001), pp. 33–46. Brentano's mediator theory was almost certainly the (unacknowledged) source of the theory of intentionality presented in Alois Höfler (in collaboration with Alexius Meinong), *Logik* (Vienna: Tempsky Verlag, 1890). This book was written together with Meinong, and the theory presented there was later developed by Twardowski

and then also taken further by Meinong and Husserl. See Jacquette, "Origins of *Gegenstandstheorie*."

29. EL 80, p. 35.

30. In this case Brentano could be regarded as a true forerunner of Twardowski and Meinong.

31. DP-G, p. 21; DP-E, pp. 23f. Cf. also Barry Smith, "The Soul and its Parts II: Varieties of Inexistence," *Brentano Studien*, 4, 1992–3, p. 43.

32. DP-G, p. 27; DP-E, pp. 29–30. Cf. also Smith, "The Soul and its Parts," p. 45 and Smith, *Austrian Philosophy*, pp. 129–30.

33. It is plausible to assume that this aspect of the ontological structure of the immanent object presents itself only from the perspective of inner perception. Cf. Chrudzimski, *Intentionalitätstheorie*, pp. 104–11.

34. Cf. manuscript *Abstraktion* (1889 or 1899), Ps 21, p. 4. Cf. also Chrudzimski, *Intentionalitätstheorie*, p. 155.

35. Cf. Chrudzimski, *Intentionalitätstheorie*, pp. 35, 218–26.

36. See R. Chisholm, *Brentano and Meinong Studies* (Atlantic Highlands, NJ: Humanities Press, 1982) and Peter Simons, *Philosophy and Logic in Central Europe from Bolzano to Tarski* (Dordrecht, Boston, MA, London: Kluwer Academic Publishers, 1992).

37. Manuscript EL 80, p. 36. Cf. also Chrudzimski, *Intentionalitätstheorie*, pp. 62–6.

38. Cf. Smith, "The Soul and its Parts."

39. For further details of Brentano's theory, its influence and the objections raised against it, see Barry Smith, "On the Phases of Reism," in, ed., Jan Woleński, *Kotarbiński: Logic, Semantics, and Ontology* (Dordrecht, Boston, MA, London: Kluwer Academic Publishers, 1990). On Brentano's theory of time consciousness see A. Chrudzimski, "Die Theorie der Intentionalität Franz Brentanos," *Grazer Philosophische Studien*, 57, 1999.

40. Cf. WE, p. 24; TE, p. 21.

41. Cf. WE, p. 23; TE, p. 20.

42. Brentano's disciple Marty developed this ontology in great detail. Cf. Smith, *Austrian Philosophy*, ch. 4.

43. Cf. manuscript Ps 21, pp. 9ff.

44. Manuscript EL 72, pp. 218–20.

45. Cf. BAM, p. 7.

46. Cf. WE, p. 74; TE, p. 64.

47. KL, p. 4; TC, p. 16.

48. KL, p. 11; TC, p. 19.

49. KL, p. 108; TC, p. 85. See also Chisholm, *Brentano and Meinong Studies* and Smith, *Austrian Philosophy*, pp. 69–71.

50. This principle has been called by Simons the *Weak Supplementation Principle*. In point of fact classical mereology assumes much stronger principles. Cf. Peter Simons, *Parts* (Oxford: Clarendon Press, 1987), pp. 25–37 and S. Leśniewski, *Collected Works*, 2 vols., eds. S. J. Surma, J. T. Srzednicki, D. I. Barnett, and V. F. Rickey (Warsaw, Dordrecht, Boston, MA, London, 1992), pp. 230–2, p. 316.

51. Cf. Wilhelm Baumgartner and Peter Simons, "Brentanos Mereologie," *Brentano Studien*, 4, 1992/3, p. 68.

52. Cf., e.g., RZK, p. 14; STC, pp. 10 f. Cf. also Smith, "Boundaries," pp. 248–9.

53. Cf. KL, p. 249; TC, p. 179.

54. "Brentano's thesis runs: if something continuous is a mere boundary then it can never exist except in connection with other boundaries, including those which possess no dimension at all, such as spatial points and moments of time and movement: a cutting free from everything that is continuous and extended is for them, too, absolutely impossible" (Smith, "Boundaries," p. 536).

55. Chisholm, *Brentano and Meinong Studies*, p. 13.

56. Cf. KL, pp. 167–70; TC, pp. 125–7.

57. Cf. PES-G, p. 118; PES-E, p. 86.

58. Cf. KL, p. 57; TC, p. 50.

59. The late Brentano accepted such accidents of accidents. See Smith, *Austrian Philosophy*, pp. 72–3.

60. This interpretation is assumed in Arkadiusz Chrudzimski, "Die Theorie der Intentionalität bei Franz Brentanos," *Grazer Philosophische Studien*, 57, 1999.

61. This solution is argued for in Chrudzimski, *Intentionalitätstheorie*, pp. 243–7.

10 Brentano's value theory: beauty, goodness, and the concept of correct emotion

Auch Gutes kann schön sein, aber die
Begriffe decken sich darum nicht.

(GA, p. 136)

Brentano's theory of value, derived from his philosophical psychology, attempts to locate an objective basis for the intrinsic value of both aesthetic and ethical contemplation through the intentional objects of emotions and desires. As theories of intrinsic value, Brentano's aesthetics and ethics are concerned with what is good and bad, beautiful and ugly, pleasurable and displeasurable, in and of themselves, and not merely as a means to an end. As objective theories, Brentano presupposes that our aesthetic and ethical evaluations, like our judgments or beliefs, are either correct or incorrect. In what follows, we will set forth some of the basic principles involved in Brentano's aesthetics and ethics and elucidate how Brentano attempted to provide a foundation for these disciplines using his descriptive psychology.

BRENTANO'S REISM

Traditionally, objectivist theories of value maintain that certain objects possess properties that give them their value. Subjectivist theories, in contrast, assign value solely on the basis of the observer enjoying or valuing an object. In the earlier stages of his philosophy, Brentano defended a type of traditional objectivist theory. Aesthetic and ethical value were essential properties of the objects upon which contemplation was directed. Intrinsic beauty and ugliness, along with goodness and badness, were properties possessed by and predicated of certain objects. Thus, attributing the characteristics of beauty or goodness to an object consisted of objective reference involving a thinker as the subject, a property, which was the content of thought, and an intentional relation between the subject and the content. The correctness or incorrectness of aesthetic and ethical judgments depended upon the correspondence of these judgments with the nature of the object to which these properties were attributed.

However, in the final stages of his philosophy, beginning in 1905, Brentano took a metaphysical stance which led him to adopt reism. This had a profound impact on what was involved for him in attributing aesthetic and ethical value to an object. Brentano's reistic ontology eschewed abstract objects, such as properties, propositions, and states of affairs, as mere fictions. According to this new theory, strictly speaking, there are only concrete individual things. Consequently, the terms "beauty" and "goodness" no longer could be understood as referring to a necessary property of that which we call "beautiful" or "good." Given Brentano's rejection of beauty-making and good-making properties, what is the basis of aesthetic and ethical evaluation? To understand Brentano's response, it will be useful to turn first to Brentano's philosophy of mind, or descriptive psychology, which he believes serves as the foundation for our knowledge of the concepts of the good and the beautiful. Within his descriptive psychology, he outlines a classification of mental phenomena in relation to an analogy that he posits between acts of judgment and emotion.

BRENTANO'S PHILOSOPHY OF MIND

In his *Habilitationsschrift* on *Die Psychologie des Aristoteles*, Brentano undertakes an investigation into the acts of the thinking person and the intellective powers of the human mind. His objective is:

exactly to determine the influence of all factors which constitute our thoughts in order to clarify the power of the mind (*nous*). . . . In order to grasp the influence of the sensitive part [of the intellect] upon the intellectual one, we have to accept a new active power in the very intellectual part. . . . This power is the active mind (*nous poietikos*), which additionally accompanies the intellective faculties of the mind . . . (PA-G, pp. 162, 164)

Brentano tells us here that there are "parts" (*energia*) of the intellect, or the mind, respectively. There is both a sensitive part and an active one. The sensitive part is receptive in character. Nevertheless, Brentano refers to it as "an instrumental cause for our thinking" (*ibid.*, p. 167) because it relates to outer objects in such a way that they "are presented to us in the thoughts of the mind or in phantasms" (*ibid.*, p. 158). Brentano asserts that the "dependence of thinking on phantasms" (*ibid.* pp. 162 and 171) is known to us because the mind (*nous dynamei*) is present in them as a "material principle."

The active part of the mind (*nous poietikos*) is characterized as an "actual property of our mind," which meets and accompanies the receptive mind, "is present in the sensitive part," evidently and consciously acting upon it, "modifying its vital functions" (*ibid.*, pp. 57, 159–60, 164–5, 200). The active part of the mind operates, then, as a "mental principle" in contrast to a "material principle;" and presents us with mental states that are intentional, evident, transitive, and self-relating (*ibid.*, pp. 137 and 192). This actual faculty, principle, and subject of mind is the "cause of our thinking" (*ibid.*, pp. 175–80) and such that it does not undergo "substantial change," but only "accidental change." Thus, Brentano remarks, "an accidental change, as for instance a change of thoughts is no contradiction to it" (*ibid.*, p. 168 n.).

In summary, the following can now be stated with respect to the mind:

1   The two parts of the mind, according to its material and formal principles, may be found in the mind or soul itself. There is "no alien substance in it" (*ibid.*, Cf. Aristotle, *Metaphysics* 1050^b16, 1069^b24).

2   The active mind is intentionally "directed upon" the receptive mind and its objects and at the same time self-relating.

3   As shown by Descartes, the difference in the actual mind between its substantial immutability and accidental changeability involves no contradiction, but is rather to be taken as *modi cogitandi* of the mind.

4   The active mind and its properties rest upon the "passive," receptive mind, whose singular data it transforms into presentations and judgments and acts of will.

Brentano's *Habilitationsschrift* can be interpreted as a harbinger of his philosophy of mind as carried out in his *Descriptive Psychology* and *Psychologie vom empirischen Standpunkte*. There he analyzes conscious mental phenomena, their interrelations, and the tasks and methods of psychology as completely as possible. Brentano highlights three fundamental classes of psychological phenomena: (1) ideas or presentations; (2) judgments (affirmations and negations); and (3) emotions, including love and hate, positive and negative interests, desires, acts of will, and choices. Presentations (*Vorstellungen*) function as basic or "fundamental" parts of the mind on which the other two kinds of functions, judgments and emotions, are superimposed. It is important to note that for Brentano, the term "presentation," which we acquire through sense perception or imagination, does not mean "that which is presented," but rather the *act* of presentation. It is this act of presentation that forms the foundation not merely of "the act of judging, but also of desiring and every mental act. Nothing can be judged, desired, hoped, or feared unless one has a presentation of that thing." (PES-E, p. 80; cf. DP-E, pp. 89–109)

Moreover, according to Brentano:

Each act of consciousness, directed primarily to its given object, is at the same time directed to itself. In the presentation of a color there is at the same time a presentation of this presentation. Even Aristotle held that in the psychic phenomenon itself there is contained the consciousness of the phenomenon. (DP-E, p. 22)

In addition to first-order presentations, or presentations simpliciter, then, Brentano maintained that there are second-order presentations. These "presentations of presentations" occur as a result of the fact that in every mental act, including presentations, the inner experience itself becomes the object of consciousness. Thus, if I judge that some object, A, is good or beautiful, it is immediately obvious to me that I am judging A to be good or beautiful. The act of judging becomes an object of consciousness in this way.

As soon as one has an emotional attitude toward something, there is an implicit presentation of it. Nothing is an object of desire which is not an object of presentation. Yet, desire constitutes a second, entirely new and distinctive type of reference to the object and a second, entirely new way in which it enters into consciousness. When someone desires an object, the object is immanent both as presented and as desired at the same time. Likewise, nothing is an object of judgment which is not an object of presentation, and when the object of presentation becomes the object of an affirmative or negative judgment, our consciousness enters into a completely new kind of relationship with the object. This object is present in consciousness in a two-fold way – first as an object of presentation, then as an object to be affirmed or denied. This feature of judgments and emotions is revealed to us in inner perception. (PES-E, p. 201; cf. USE, p. 16).

The classification and description of psychic phenomena or acts Brentano offers show again that the substantial mind appears in its accidental functions. Indeed, Brentano describes this relationship between mental phenomena and the thinking subject in terms of the relationship between a substance and accident. He uses the term "accident" in the traditional Aristotelean sense to mean "something which requires another being as its subject." Yet, he goes on to contradict Aristotle by countenancing accidents of accidents. For Brentano, judgments and emotions are accidents of presentations, which are themselves accidents. Using his reistic terminology, one-who-judges is an accident of one-who-thinks, and one-who-thinks is an accident of the subject.

While presentations, judgments, and emotions have their status as accidents in common, presentations are different from the phenomena presented in the other two categories in that one can have a presentation without the presentation being accompanied by a judgment or emotional attitude toward it. If the accident falls away when the individual is no longer judging or taking pleasure in some object, A, the presentation nevertheless continues to exist. Just as one could stop judging or taking pleasure in an object, one could stop having a presentation. The individual wouldn't thereby cease to exist. The substance underlying the accident survives the change in mental phenomena. The same independence cannot be attributed to judgments and emotions, however, since a presentation necessarily underlies an act of judging or emotion. If the subject ceases to think about A, it follows that there can be no judging or valuing A.

Brentano viewed the relationship between substances and accidents as that of a part to a whole. The relationship has an unexpected twist, though. For Brentano, the accident is the whole which has the subject as its one and only proper part. One-who-judges or one-who-takes-pleasure is the whole, which has one-who-thinks as its only proper part. The whole cannot exist without its underlying part, yet the part can survive the loss of the whole. Therefore, Brentano further characterized presentations as being one-sidedly separable from the acts of judging or emotions that are dependent upon them. Conversely, he referred to judgments and emotions as "one-sidedly dependent" upon presentations. Viewing matters this way is consistent with Brentano's mereological essentialism. Wholes have each of their parts necessarily. If the part ceases to exist, so does the whole. On the other hand, the part is capable of existing independently of the whole.

ANALOGY BETWEEN JUDGMENTS AND EMOTIONS

According to Brentano, beauty and goodness are to be understood by reference to the emotions, the third class of psychological phenomena, and not judgments. With respect to attributions of beauty, Brentano says:

One speaks sometimes of judgments of taste, but this can be approved only in a metaphorical sense. Taste is no judgment, but a feeling, and of course, a preference in the feeling (for the beautiful as opposed to the ugly and for the more beautiful as opposed to the less beautiful) or rather a disposition for such preference. (GAE, p. 32)

Again following Aristotle, Brentano contends that there are certain similarities that can be identified between acts of judgment and acts of higher emotions. First, as has already been noted, both judgments and emotions include acts of presentations as basic "parts." When one judges something to be the case, or takes pleasure or displeasure in an object, a presentation is at the basis of that judgment or emotion. Judgments and emotions are indeed "motivated" by the "material of presentation."

Second, Brentano points out that judgments and emotions go beyond simple presentations or ideas in involving either an affirmation or a denial. Both are of either a positive or negative character. Just as judgments are either affirmations or negations, Brentano regards acts of emotion as either pro-attitudes or anti-attitudes that can be divided into love and hate, being pleased or displeased. (Cf. Roderick

226 WILHELM BAUMGARTNER AND LYNN PASQUERELLA

M. Chisholm, *Brentano and Meinong Studies* [Atlantic Highlands, NJ: Humanities Press, 1982], pp. 17–36.)

Finally, just as an affirmation or denial of some object may be correct or incorrect in the act of judging, an act of loving or hating may be correct or incorrect in the realm of emotions. In fact, as we have seen, the concepts of "the beautiful" and "the good" are such that in both cases we can speak of "correctness" and "incorrectness" if we judge something to be "beautiful," or "good," respectively.

Yet, there are also certain disanalogies between judgments and emotions. Since every judgment is either true or false, when something is affirmed as correct, it is necessarily implied that it would be incorrect to deny that which was affirmed. There is no middle between true and false, as we know from the Law of Excluded Middle. On the other hand, to say that it is not correct to love an object does not imply that it is correct to hate it. Some things are such that they are neither correctly loved nor correctly hated. Rather, they are indifferent.

In addition, there is another distinction that can be drawn between truth and goodness. Within the dichotomy between good and bad, there are what we may call "comparative middles" – the concepts of better and worse. No such comparative middles exist in the sphere of judging. No one act of judging is more true than another.

THE STANDARD FOR AESTHETIC AND ETHICAL JUDGMENTS

Whereas Brentano had previously considered an aesthetic or ethical judgment correct if there was a correspondence between the assignment of aesthetic or ethical value and the object of the valuing possessing certain properties, he came to abandon the traditional correspondence theory of value. His rejection of this view followed from the fact that determining whether an ethical or aesthetic judgment was correct would require knowledge of the correspondence and a comparison between a mental act and an *ens irreale* or "nonthing." This personal turn in Brentano's philosophy and his move toward reism becomes evident when he speaks of the task and "correct method of the psychognostician" in Part I of his *Descriptive Psychology*. Instead of using propositions, Brentano refers directly to the individual person, the psychognostician. The procedure of the descriptive psychologist is psychological analysis personalized. Concrete persons and concrete or genuine terms are used instead of predicates. The use of language is transformed into a reistic description. The reasons for this are to be found throughout Brentano's theory of intentionality. Of the "pair of intentional correlates," only the intentional act, not its object correlate has to be real. Instead of describing the human mind, he describes the acts of the thinking person, herself – the psychic relations of a thinker who is evidently aware of intentional relations which are explicitly noticed and analytically described. These intentional relations are ascribed to oneself and analogously to other persons. The consequence for Brentano's later view is that there are no states of affairs and aesthetic objects with which our acts of judging and emotions correspond.

Therefore, the reism promulgated by Brentano prompted his move away from a correspondence theory in favor of a form of coherence theory. On this new view, the standard for beauty and goodness becomes the evident judger. Brentano was convinced that just as the concept of truth can be derived from evident judgments which are experienced as correct, the concepts of the good and beautiful can be derived from emotions which are experienced as correct. Our understanding of the concepts of "good" and "beauty" originates from our concept of the evident, which is experienced in inner perception, in the following manner. Within the class of judgments, certain ones are known to be true directly and immediately. Such evident judgments fall into two categories. They are either "truths of reason" or judgments about the judger's own intentional acts. The correctness of these judgments is a self-evident concept we acquire as a result of reflection upon our own mental states. Therefore, a true judgment is "correctly characterized" (*richtig charakterisiert*) by reference to inner experience and evidence. By contrast, an incorrect judgment would be missing these characteristics. In addition, when a good desire, love, or will is "correctly characterized" it becomes evident that its intention is worthy of desire, love, or will. Again, an incorrect desire, love, or will would be missing these characteristics. The same holds, *mutatis mutandis*, for the anti-attitudes, aversion and hate, respectively.

Immediately evident judgments are regarded as the standard of truth for other judgments which are not experienced as correct. According to Brentano's coherence theory, if a judgment that is not evident agrees with an evident judgment's object, quality, and mode, the judgment is true. If it does not agree with the evident judgment or is in "disharmony" with it, it is false.

Acts of emotion ascribing aesthetic and ethical value, as intentional acts, are given in inner perception. As previously indicated, there is no psychic phenomenon, according to Brentano, which does not transitively refer to something, a "primary object" as object, and intransitively to itself, as the "secondary object" of that relation. Hence, all psychic phenomena are immediately evident. The objects that are perceived, however, the sense-data, come to us in outer perception. Strictly speaking, they have no reality in and of themselves. Thus, Brentano asserts,

Every mental phenomenon is characterized by . . . the intentional (or mental) inexistence of an object, . . . reference to a content, direction toward an object (which is not to be understood here as meaning a thing), or immanent objectivity . . . This intentional in-existence is characteristic exclusively of mental phenomena. No physical phenomenon exhibits anything like it." (PES-E, pp. 88–9; cf. DP-E, Part II, D.2)

The much debated "in-existence" or inherence of an "object," e.g. the beloved (content; correlate) in the act of love, is not to be dealt with here in detail, but only insofar as to show that intentional relations bear an anomaly. When one-who-loves directs the act of love upon an object, the actual lover exists and apparently knows when she loves. The beloved, or desired, however, needn't exist at all (needn't mean a thing but a metaphorical "the beloved in my heart").

One consequence of the nature of aesthetic objects, then, is that judgments about the causes of our aesthetic experiences will never be directly evident. For this reason, Brentano must recognize the existence of an evident judger for whom all judgments are directly evident. Otherwise, there would be no coherence between our judgments about the external world and an evident judgment. The implication would be that no knowledge of the external world would be possible.

THE MEANING OF "BEAUTY" AND "GOODNESS"

"Beauty" and "goodness," when applied to objects in the world, are now considered by Brentano to be syncategorematic terms meaning "pleasure experienced as correct" or "love experienced as correct" (Chisholm, *Brentano and Intrinsic Value* [Cambridge, Cambridge University Press, 1986], p. 51). To say that an object is good means that it is correct to love that object. To say that an object is bad means that it is correct to hate the object. With the standard for beauty and goodness becoming the evident judger, there is no property inhering in these objects which causes the emotion and in virtue of which our acts of love or hatred become correct or incorrect. The concepts of the good and the beautiful can be derived from emotions experienced as correct. The same is true for our desires. Desires are wrong if individuals desire instinctively and intensively according to their inclinations. A correct desire is characterized by a "higher form of valuation," which is analogous to an evident judgment (Cf. USE, pp. 20–1, 23). For this reason, Brentano concentrates specifically on the act itself, as opposed to "that which is presented," and asks, for instance, what makes an act of judging a "correct judgment," an act of loving a "correct love," an act of preference a "correct preference," and an act of desiring a "correct desire." The results should be clear. Brentano's theory of value places mental states as primary in analyzing aesthetic and ethical value.

BRENTANO'S THEORY OF SENSATIONS

In characterizing "beauty" and "goodness" in terms of pleasure and love experienced as correct, Brentano's theory of value draws upon his analysis of sensations. This analysis distinguishes between two types of pleasure and displeasure – sensory and nonsensory. While aesthetic experiences may result from physical sensations, they are themselves examples of nonsensory pleasure and displeasure. This nonsensory pleasure or displeasure is an emotion directed upon the act of sensing the aesthetic object.

Nevertheless, there is an intimate connection between sensory and nonsensory pleasure and displeasure that must be explored in order to understand fully Brentano's theory of value. According to Brentano, acts of sensation are intentional acts that are given in inner perception. As we have seen, the objects of sensation, sense-data, are given in outer perception and as such exist only in an extended sense as intentional objects. Sensory pleasure and pain consist neither in these acts of sensation nor in the objects of sensation. Instead, they are emotional affects directed upon acts of sensation. In fact, certain acts of sensation, in addition to affirming the existence of various objects of sensation, present themselves as objects of emotion. The objects of sensory pleasure and pain, then, are not the sense qualities, but the experiencing of these qualities. The emotional relationship that characterizes the experience of sensory pleasure and displeasure consists in an act of love or hatred directed upon an act of sensation.

BRENTANO'S OBJECTIVISM

The primacy of the intentional and the fact that the terms "beautiful" and "ugly" are now construed as merely the expressions of an emotion toward an object should not lead to the conclusion that Brentano abandoned his objectivist theory in favor of subjectivism. The difference between Brentano's theory and subjectivist accounts can be illustrated by considering the following. Suppose you and a friend attend an artist's reception. Walking around the room, you look at works of art, listen to the festive music playing in the background, and taste the wine, cheese, and fruit set out as refreshments. You are the subject of a variety of sensations and aesthetic experiences. Imagine now that you and your friend converge in front of a striking piece of art. It is a painting that you find breathtakingly beautiful. Your friend, on the other hand, experiences genuine displeasure at its sight. On a subjectivist account of this story, genuine aesthetic disagreement between you and your friend is not possible. Your attributing beauty to the painting is simply a report of your own mental states. Your friend's attribution of ugliness to the painting is similarly a report of her own mental states. The phrase "That painting is beautiful" uttered by you means simply "That painting is beautiful to me." The fact that your friend doesn't like the painting doesn't contradict the fact that you do like it. Thus, there is no genuine disagreement, just an expression of subjective mental states.

Yet, for Brentano, the emotions directed toward an object that are a constituent of aesthetic experience will be either correct or incorrect, such that your judgment that "x is beautiful" and your friend's judgment that "x is not beautiful" cannot both be correct. Two individuals making contradictory judgments in aesthetic, logic, and ethics alike cannot both be judging correctly at the same time.

While Brentano takes the evident judger, and so certain mental states, as primary in determining the correctness of aesthetic preferences, these intentional states are not what determine the aesthetic quality of the work. The correctness of one of the judgments is determined by direct and immediate insight into the correctness of judgments and emotions. In certain cases, we are able to grasp a judgment as being correct with immediate evidence. Analogously we can, in certain cases, grasp an emotional relation as being correct with immediate evidence. (ANR, p. 186; cf. USE, p. 152; GAE, p. 146–7.) In fact, for Brentano, psychic acts are all conscious and evident in character. The immediately evident knowledge is to serve as the criterion for the correctness of my present and further judgments and emotional relations. It also has to serve objectively as the criterion for the decision, whether judgments and emotional states of others are correct (cf. GAE, pp. 202ff.). If certain judgments and emotions prove to be correct, they also exemplify the meaning ("*Sinn*") of a correct judgment and emotion.

The statement "x is good" expresses love directed at an object. If the love is experienced as correct, the statement is known to be true. An individual loves or hates correctly if these feelings are adequate to their object in the sense of being appropriate, fitting, or suitable. The same account of objectivism applies to Brentano's theory of aesthetics. "X is beautiful" expresses pleasure experienced in an object. If the love or pleasure taken in an object, x, is experienced as correct, the hatred of that object or displeasure taken in it is incorrect. Ethical and aesthetic judgments are either correct or incorrect and if opposite judgments are made regarding the value of an object, at least one judger is wrong in her assessment.

In proposing his theory, Brentano wants to draw upon the analogy between the correctness of intellectual phenomena and emotive phenomena. Thus, he remarks that a judgment is considered "true" if it is:

"self evident" or if it can be concluded from an immediate evident judgment . . . with which it has, except for the evidence, all other parts in common . . . There would be no proof and no science, if there were no evident judgments. Together with the evidence, the general validity

(*Allgemeingültigkeit*) of the judgment is given . . . The investigation of the concept of truth had the end of shedding light on the hitherto unclear concept of the good. I mean the light of analogy, with which we now are able to set forth our investigation on the topic. (GAE, pp. 142–3)

We now know what it is to be a correct judgment or correct emotion. Any judgment or emotion which fits with these directly evident judgments and emotions is itself correct. On a correspondence theory, one fittingness is understood to mean that if an object possesses the property of being beautiful, it is appropriate or fitting to take pleasure in the object. But, exactly what does it mean to say that an attitude is appropriate or fitting when there are no such properties? Chisholm suggests a plausible way of interpreting Brentano. According to Chisholm, "To say that a pro attitude is fitting or appropriate to an object A, is to say that the contemplation of A requires a pro attitude toward A. And analogously for anti attitudes" (Chisholm, *Intrinsic Value*, p. 52).

PRAXIOLOGY

In further analyzing the concept of the good, Brentano points out that

Some goods as objects of our desire are not good in themselves, but for something else, i.e. a useful means for an end. This end in turn can be useful for a higher end. In the end we reach something we call good, not because it is useful for something else but per se. If we call the latter "good" we herewith say nothing else than: The lover of it loves correctly. (GAE, p. 144; cf. USE, p. 19)

What is made explicit here is that some goods are higher or preferable to others. Thus, Brentano takes on defining the concept of "highest practical good" because he believes that ethics, in a practical manner, should be able to "teach us the highest end" (*ibid.*, pp. 4–5). Notice that the phrase, "highest end" implies both a "good end" and a "better end," however. In endeavoring to provide a new foundation for ethics, Brentano offers a formal exposition of "ethical knowledge," dialectically investigating the concept of the "correct end." He says:

. . . we shall describe as completely as possible the cases in which we know something as good or better than something else, on the ground of correctly characterized interest acts. Only when the fundament is laid this way it is possible to build up ethics in a logical stringent way. (GAE, p. 152)

We have already seen what "good" means for Brentano. What now is the meaning of "better" and of correct preference? Brentano maintains that the meaning of preference of a good A to a good B does not consist simply in a higher quantity or higher intensity.

When I love A more than B, this does not mean that I love A more intensively, but that I prefer it. . . . "Better" in this respect says nothing else but something preferable to something else, i.e. what can be preferred correctly. (GAE, p. 147)

Still, the preferability is not to be seen as real predicative determination of a thing, but rather the knowledge of correct preference. Hence, a correct preference is characterized not by inclination or belief, but by the very evidence that correct preference is in itself normative ("as it ought to be," *ibid.*, § 87) and that an opposite preference therefore would be incorrect. Correct preference stems from an inner experience of correct intention. In order to know something as good or worthy to be loved, one has to have loved it correctly. Correct preference is also determined from knowledge *ex terminis* (all acts of correct love and preference are general in the respect that we think them in general terms). This term is applied to higher emotional states as their fundament and functions as an "analogue of apodictic, not just assertoric knowledge" (*ibid.*, p. 150).

Among the examples of preferences experienced as correct, Brentano includes the following:

1   The existence of something, if it is good, is preferable to its non-existence.
2   A presentation of something good is better than presentation of something bad.
3   Joy, as long as it is not "*Schadenfreude*" or joy in the bad, is preferable to sadness.
4   A love of the good is better than a love of the bad.
5   The object of higher love, knowledge, is worthy of more love than its opposite.
6   An evident judgment is preferable to a blind one.
7   Insight is preferable to error.

In essence, Brentano's preference sentences reflect a Leibnizean *bonum progressionis* and *bonum summationis*. The principle of the summation of goods holds that a summation of a good is to be preferred to a partial good and a partial bad is to be preferred to the summation of a bad. Thus, a good that lasts longer than another good is to be preferred, the summation of mental states is to be preferred to a single one, some good known to be real is to be preferred to a probable or presumed one, and the preference of the more probable good is to be preferred to an equivalent but less probable good.

His principle of *bonum progressionis* asserts that if we think about a process leading from a good toward something bad, or from something known to be a higher good toward a lesser good, each of the former is to be preferred. In addition, the emotions of pleasure and displeasure have certain qualities based on the qualities of their intentional objects. One pleasure is better than another if the object of the former is better than the latter. Displeasure is such that one act is better than another if the object of displeasure is worse. Thus, pleasure in the bad is worse than pleasure in the good, and displeasure in the bad is better than displeasure in the good. The value of pleasure may be defeated if it is pleasure in the bad, but it must be clear that Brentano would not allow for this emotion to be considered both good and bad. Pleasure in the bad is bad, pleasure in the good is good, displeasure in the good is bad, and displeasure in the bad is good.

With this, Brentano develops a theory of correct practical preference based on a correct choice in respect to a direction towards a correct end:

From correct preference, as in the case of the *bonum summationis*, it follows that it is clearly the correct end of life to convey the good in the broadest possible range . . . in the entire *Lebewelt* . . . in the entire sphere of our reason . . . as far as a good can be realized in it . . . This is the highest commandment: . . . Choose the best which is attainable! (USE, pp. 16 and 30; cf. GAE, §§ 64 and 65; GA, pp. 153–68)

How do we know what is preferable?

Surely not as a real determination which sticks to the objects. As "being" is not a predicate which would meet other predicates of a thing, so "good" is not such a predicate, too. And like "good," "better" is no real determination either. Of someone who evidently affirms something, we say he knows about the existence of something; of someone who loves something with a love characterized as correct and who is aware of his correct loving, we say he knows something as good. The meaning of knowing something as "better" is nothing else but to be aware of oneself as someone who prefers it with a preference characterized as correct. (GAE, p. 148)

For Brentano, if we know what it is to choose or prefer correctly, there is no question that everyone of us personally is enabled to find out the correct practical preference in a given case, the correct choice and decision with respect to its direction towards a correct end and its fulfillment and to do her part in the realization of the highest practical good.

A CHALLENGE BASED ON VALUE'S INTRINSIC NATURE

One of the challenges for Brentano's theory of value as it is outlined is to maintain its character as a theory of intrinsic value in the absence of essential properties. Given Brentano's revised ontology, both the objects valued and the emotions directed upon these objects are internal acts. While Brentano rejects properties as abstract entities in an effort to avoid making a comparison between the act of external perception of the value of an object and an internal emotion, he does not want to deny that the objects valued are objectively good or beautiful.

On Brentano's earlier theory of value, he considered goodness and beauty essential properties of the objects possessing them. With the elimination of properties, Brentano would have to regard beauty and goodness as accidents. Yet, accidents by their very nature are not essential to the things possessing them. Hence, though Brentano would like to avoid being committed to non-reistic entities, there is ostensibly no way for him to accomplish this and at the same time maintain a theory of value that is a theory of intrinsic value.

CONCLUSION

According to Brentano, aesthetics and ethics are both practical disciplines, as opposed to sciences. As such, Brentano considers ethics and aesthetics to be dependent upon a theoretical science, the philosophy of mind, for their foundation. This foundation, Brentano believes, is necessary in order to achieve several interrelated objectives – to define the concepts of the good and the beautiful, to gain empirical knowledge of these concepts using concrete examples, and

to gain a scientific character for aesthetics and ethics, the purpose
of which is in teaching how to achieve aesthetic and ethical knowledge and to act accordingly. In addition, Brentano maintained that an
investigation into the fundamental mental phenomena of aesthetics
(phantasy and presentations) and ethics (emotive phenomena) will
require following certain methodological rules, which are supplied
by the laws of descriptive psychology and by the "logic of proof."

The impact of Brentano's theory of value has been far-reaching.
Indeed, he has stood as a pivotal figure whose teachings and writings have shaped both the analytic and continental traditions. In the
continental tradition, two of the many students Brentano taught,
Husserl (through the development of the phenomenological movement) and Ehrenfels (through the development of Gestalt psychology), have had an extraordinary influence on twentieth-century perceptions of art. Moreover, in the analytic tradition, G. E. Moore, in
his widely publicized review of *The Origins of Our Knowledge of
Right and Wrong*, accords Brentano the highest esteem for the content as well as the methodology of his ethics. He says:

This is a far better discussion of the most fundamental principles of Ethics
than any other with which I am acquainted. Brentano himself is fully conscious that he has made a very great advance in the theory of Ethics . . . and
his confidence both in the originality and value of his own work is completely justified. In almost all points in which he differs from any of the
great historical systems, he is in the right; and he differs with regard to the
most fundamental points of Moral Philosophy. . . . It would be difficult to
exaggerate the importance of this work. (p. 115)

Moore's statements should serve to remind us that anyone who is
serious about constructing a value theory should begin by studying
Brentano.

11   Brentano on religion and natural theology

BACKGROUND AND ORIENTATION OF BRENTANO'S THOUGHT

Although Brentano broke with organized religion in the late 1870s, he remained a traditional theist all his life and was still writing (by dictation) on subjects in natural theology in 1917. His interests connected with this topic ranged from Darwin's theory of natural selection and Laplace's theory of probability to Comte's critique of causal knowledge and Cuvier's zoology. At every turn he showed himself to be conversant with scientific and philosophical developments of his day, as well as with relevant ancient and medieval philosophical speculations. Brentano's respect for the natural sciences and for the history of philosophy is nowhere more evident than in his discussions of the existence of God, the immortality of the soul, and the ultimate triumph of good over evil. These themes were dear to his heart, and he championed the traditional view not only that they are accessible to philosophy but that their discussion constitutes philosophy's highest achievement.

The best way to understand Brentano's natural theology is to see it in the context of Aristotelian empiricism as modified by the somewhat Cartesian outlook of Brentano's philosophical psychology. Thus both scientific data and psychological reflections are brought to bear. There are four main sets of arguments to which he devoted attention: (1) arguments against skepticism, which include refutations of the view that it can be known a priori that God's existence is impossible to prove; (2) arguments for God's existence based on empirical data from the sciences (especially including empirical evidence of teleology in nature); (3) arguments for the immateriality of the human soul, based on internal perception; and (4) arguments in favor of optimism, the view that the existence of evil in the world is not necessarily inconsistent with the existence of an infinitely good God. Because of the sublime nature of its subject, Brentano considered natural theology to be the pinnacle of philosophy, and his work in this area is intimately connected to his work in psychology, metaphysics, and ethics. His lectures on the proofs of God's existence also provide a good sense of how Brentano saw his own philosophy in relation to the thought of Descartes, Leibniz, Locke, Hume, Kant, and Mill, among others. Brentano's lectures on natural theology were very well attended and highly regarded, moving at least one famous skeptic, Sigmund Freud, to admit that he had found Brentano's arguments *almost* convincing.[1]

The published works by Brentano that are chiefly occupied with questions of religion and natural theology (all posthumous) include *Die Lehre Jesu und ihre bleibende Bedeutung* (Leipzig, 1922), *Religion und Philosophie* (Bern, 1954), and *On the Existence of God: Lectures given at the Universities of Würzburg and Vienna, 1868–1891* (Nijhoff, 1987; German edition, *Vom Dasein Gottes*, Leipzig, 1929). The four topics mentioned above are explicitly dealt with in the lectures included in *On the Existence of God* (EG). The present discussion, however, is focused on a dictation of 1915, "*Gedankengang beim Beweise für das Dasein Gottes*" ("Train of Thought on the Proof of God's Existence," hereafter referred to as *Gedankengang*), which is included after the lectures at the end of EG. This dictation provides not only a synopsis of the lecture material but also the most mature and definitive treatment of natural theology that we have from Brentano, including fresh arguments not to be found in the lectures. In what follows I shall adhere closely to the order of presentation in the *Gedankengang* (occasionally including points taken from the lectures). The reader should bear in mind that this is a late work, representing Brentano's natural theology as it emerged during the reistic phase of his philosophical development which is notoriously difficult to understand and for explorations of which the reader is referred to *The Theory of Categories* (TC), to Parts Three and Four of *The True and the Evident* (TE), and to *Philosophical Investigations on Space, Time, and the Continuum* (STC). The first two sections below will require patience on the part of the reader, but they are short and immediately followed by a discussion whose terms may be more familiar.

THERE IS NOTHING WHICH IS ABSOLUTELY ACCIDENTAL

For Brentano it is a matter of principle that everything that exists is necessary, and this principle serves to form the foundation of his natural theology. Like all fundamental principles, it is mainly to be defended by consideration of the impossibility of its opposite, namely, the impossibility of anything being absolutely accidental or existing purely by chance. It is also a principle which is revealed to us with the evidence of inner perception. That is to say, it is an ontological or metaphysical principle arrived at by close attention to psychological fact. The psychological foundations of Brentano's metaphysics should not be mistaken, however, for mere subjectivity in the pejorative sense. On the contrary, for Brentano as for Descartes the absolute certainty of some subjective truths is what lends objective reliability to conclusions drawn from them about reality outside the mind.

In addressing the question whether anything could be absolutely accidental, Brentano considers first temporal things, then spatial things, and then mental and physical things. He begins by pointing out that every presentation and every judgment has a temporal mode, therefore everything that exists exists in time. Now, if a finite temporal thing could be absolutely accidental, then at any moment it would be as likely to pop out of existence as to persist. But for a finite temporal thing to exist it would also be necessary that the moments of such persistence be infinitely more frequent than the moments of such popping out of existence. And this is a contradiction. Therefore no temporal thing is absolutely accidental. But since everything that exists is temporal, it follows that nothing at all is absolutely accidental.

Brentano then proves this general conclusion to hold also in the specific case of spatial things. For these require spatial continuity in the same way that temporal things require temporal continuity. But if a spatial thing, for instance, a line, were absolutely accidental, then the probability of its existing at a given point would be equal to the probability of its not existing at that point. Yet at the same time, for the spatial thing to exist, there must be infinitely many more points at which it does exist than points at which it does not exist, which is a contradiction. Therefore no spatial thing is absolutely accidental.

Further, in the physical world generally the probability that a given place is occupied would be equal to the probability that it is unoccupied. Yet Brentano holds that necessarily, in the whole of infinite space, more space remains unoccupied than occupied, due to the impossibility of infinite filled space, what he calls an actually (as distinct from potentially) infinite extension. In this connection Brentano devises further supportive arguments reminiscent of Zeno's paradoxes, but we will not enter into those details here. Suffice it to say that the physical world, both in its parts and as a whole, is such that its existence cannot be attributed to absolute accident or pure chance.

Likewise in the mental realm Brentano shows that things exist necessarily or not at all. For if we suppose that potentially there are infinitely many souls, and that the actual number of souls must be finite, then each soul that might exist accidentally to eternity will be such that its non-existence is equally possible, but at the same time infinitely many more souls must not exist than exist. But this is a contradiction because the infinite probability of non-existence is not compatible with an equal probability of existence or non-existence.

In this way, very concisely, Brentano demonstrates that nothing that exists is absolutely accidental, or, stated positively, everything that exists is necessary.

NOTHING WHICH WE EXPERIENCE IS DIRECTLY NECESSARY

Brentano's next step is to show that nothing within our experience is directly necessary, but rather everything in our experience is indirectly necessary. He shows this with regard both to bodies (physical things) and to our mental life (non-physical things). The key idea concerning bodies is that it is part of their essence to have a location in space. But each location in space is such that its being occupied is just as probable as its being empty. Therefore the body itself which exists at a given location cannot account for its own being there. Yet its being there is necessary, and not absolutely accidental, as was previously proved. Therefore its being there is indirectly and not directly necessary, or, in other words, it is due to something other than itself.

The key idea concerning the indirect necessity of mental life is that it is always conditioned by things other than itself. Thus in sense perception, in judgment, and in choice there are always determining factors of one kind or another. If the subject of sense perception (the perceiver) is physical, then it has already been proved to be indirectly and not directly necessary. Besides, its activity is under the steadily renewed causal influence of physiology. Similarly, if the subject of sense perception is taken to be mental, it will follow, as we have seen, that reasons beyond the given mental thing itself account for its existence. Further, in making judgments we are aware of the causal influence of our thoughts about the premises, and in choice we are aware that there are motives behind it. In other words, judgment and choice are experienced as being the result, not of themselves alone, but of outside causal factors. And sense perception must exist in a subject which is not directly necessary. Hence the necessity of sense perception, judgment, and choice (like all mental things they have already been proved to be necessary and not absolutely accidental) is indirect necessity and not direct necessity.

THERE IS A DIRECTLY NECESSARY, CREATIVE INTELLIGENCE

Thus in the *Gedankengang* Brentano arrives very quickly, but admittedly by means of dense and difficult argumentation, at the conclusion that there must be something directly necessary to account for our universal experience of indirect necessity. In one sense this all presupposes the chief tenets of his mature philosophy, for instance, that everything which really exists is an individual, that what counts as an individual is every substance (thing or being), every part of a substance, and every accident (attribute, or characteristic), that mental phenomena or accidents are divisible into presentations, judgments, and emotions. Various Brentanian speculations concerning the nature of physical bodies are likewise presupposed. So in one sense, to understand the foregoing arguments one would need to be well-versed in Brentano's philosophy generally. In another sense, however, the reader may take heart because the definitive account of natural theology that Brentano produced near the end of his life is understandable, too, as an exercise in classic philosophical reasoning about the "highest" things. Thus any familiarity with writings on these topics by Aristotle, Aquinas, Descartes, or Leibniz will be good preparation for Brentano's version. There is a quality of axiomatic derivation in some of his arguments that is even reminiscent of Spinoza. An appreciation of the elegance of presentation that Brentano strove to perfect in his last years will surely count as understanding him at an important level, even if the more obscure features of his thought remain less than perfectly clear or convincing.

Let us forge ahead, then, to explore the concept of the directly necessary being. According to Brentano it is first of all *transcendent*. The indirect necessity of all things in our experience, that is to say, cannot be accounted for by any indirectly necessary thing in the series, no matter how far back we go and even if we go back infinitely far. For even the whole infinite series of indirectly necessary beings, each determined by another, will just exist by accident unless it is brought into existence by a being whose necessity is brought about not by some other being but by itself. This directly necessary being is therefore outside the series of indirectly necessary beings, and transcends them.

The directly necessary being is also a *creative principle* in the sense that it can produce something out of nothing. In this way, too, it transcends the world of our experience, for although we can distinguish transformation or alteration from coming-to-be (shaping something out of clay is different from combining sodium and chlorine to produce salt, for instance), still we always presuppose a subject out of which something is made. But the directly necessary being requires no such subject and its creative activity is wholly undetermined by anything external to it. This will be equally true, Brentano tells us, whether the creative activity of the directly necessary being has a beginning in time or not.

It will be remembered in this connection that Brentano holds that everything which exists is temporal, however, and the directly necessary being is no exception. He even tells us that the directly necessary being could just as easily be thought of as a directly necessary *process*. In any event, its being in time has the important consequence for Brentano that the directly necessary being is *not changeless*. Two considerations shed light on this. First of all, as the productive cause and first principle of all motion and change, it must be active in the fullest sense and not static or changeless itself. Secondly, as the first productive cause of all things the directly necessary being must know all things, and what it knows must, of course, be true. But because things change, what was true in the past may not be true now, and what is true now may not be true in the future. The knowledge which the directly necessary being has, then, must likewise change over time. Otherwise, Brentano points out, the directly necessary being would be no better than a bachelor planning to get married in a year who, when the year is up, still plans to get married in a year.

That the directly necessary being exists in time, that it changes, and that its knowledge also changes over time leads Brentano to add that the directly necessary being is an *intelligence*. It does not act blindly. With this result, Brentano finds himself in a position to articulate four proofs of the existence of a creative intelligence. First of all, it is not plausible that the various parts of space are filled at random, rather some intelligent being has chosen that certain places be filled rather than others. Secondly, if the directly necessary being which creates everything out of nothing were a physical being itself acting blindly, then it would have to be as complex as its product is. But this is implausible, and besides we have already established that what is physical is not directly necessary. Therefore the directly necessary being is an intelligence acting intelligently and able to comprehend the whole complexity of its creation in itself. Thirdly, its comprehension or understanding is in tune with its creation and so the directly necessary being is an intelligence always in harmony with itself, affirming what is true even as the truth about creation changes over time. Finally, despite the well-known objections of David Hume, we discern an order and design in the physical universe which naturally leads us to acknowledge the intelligence of its original creator and designer. The attempt of Darwinism to explain away the appearance of teleology, or purposefulness, in nature fails. Taken together, these are the four arguments in the *Gedankengang* on which Brentano rests his case for the existence of a creative intelligence.

It is a case based on high probability, indeed the very highest probability, Brentano would say. He thus ascribes what he calls *physical certainty* to his proofs of God's existence, and not deductive or logical certainty. The ontological argument, which Brentano rejects as involving some equivocation or other depending on the version of it, was supposed to have provided deductive certainty of God's existence based on a correct understanding of the concept of God. But Brentano holds that only an infinitely perfect being could have an adequate concept of an infinitely perfect being, and so he sides with Aquinas and others who reject the ontological argument and accept only a posteriori or empirical proofs of God's existence. It is important to recognize, then, that even though they sometimes appear to be parts of an axiomatic system, Brentano's proofs of God's existence are intended by him to be grounded in empirical fact. It is a consequence of his philosophical psychology that some aspects of the empirical data (such as the impossibility of a spatial or temporal continuity existing by chance) have an apodictic character.

Brentano rejects any a priori proof of God's existence, then, but he also rejects proofs intended to show a priori that God does not exist, or that God's existence is impossible to prove. He rejects skepticism in this regard, too, including ancient forms of skepticism and the skeptical arguments about proving God's existence that we have inherited from Hume and Kant (both of which he discusses at considerable length in the lectures). In the course of refuting various varieties of skepticism he also develops in the lectures a positive defense of the causal law, that no real thing comes to be without a cause. It is not possible to do justice to that defense here, but it is worth noting both that the causal law is fundamental to Brentano's proofs for God's existence and also that he understands it to be established in terms of the highest probability, not in terms of deductive certainty. Thus the causal law is a genuinely empirical proposition for Brentano and not a mere regulative principle of thought as in Kant.

Brentano claims infinite probability in favor of each of the four theistic proofs in the *Gedankengang*, which probability exceeds what he says the physical scientists claim for the so-called laws of nature. Thus he takes each of these proofs to have the force of a real law of nature and not merely the force of a highly reliable predictor as in the case of the scientific laws of nature.

Thus with regard to the first theistic argument, which shows that the places in space which are occupied have been filled as the result of intelligent choice by the directly necessary being, Brentano says it all rests on the demonstration that an actual infinitude of material things (or spiritual things, for that matter) cannot exist, although a possible infinitude cannot be denied. This he says we can know with the same certainty as we know there is an external world. From the non-existence of such an infinitude, together with the possibility for each of an infinitude of things that it might exist, we can conclude with infinite probability that the things that do exist could not exist except as a result of intelligent choice. Therefore the directly necessary being is a creative intelligence.

The second theistic argument, which shows that the directly necessary being must be not a physical thing acting blindly, but rather an intelligence acting intelligently, rests on the assertion that if it were a physical thing then it would have to have as many parts as its physical creation has. It would be a physical thing extended in space, producing different parts of the cosmos out of different parts of itself automatically. But if so, it would not be directly necessary, as was established earlier in the discussion of the indirect necessity of physical things. Yet that conclusion was arrived at with infinite probability, and so the second proof, too, has more than finite probability. Therefore the directly necessary being does not act blindly.

The third theistic argument, to the effect that the directly necessary being is actively aware of its creation at every moment, rests on two facts: first, the first principle of change and motion cannot itself be wholly changeless; and second, we do encounter change and motion in our experience. Each of these points is *evident* to us, or in other words, each is in principle unquestionable. Then upon consideration it becomes obvious that, although it may appear that its direct necessity would rule out the directly necessary being's capacity to change, this is not so. In fact, a directly necessary being whose knowledge undergoes a steady, infinitesimal change over time, as things in its creation change, is actually more constant and more self-consistent than a changeless, directly necessary being would be. According to Brentano, this conclusion, too, carries more than finite probability. Therefore the directly necessary being is a dynamic intelligence.

When he comes to the fourth proof, the teleological proof, both in the lectures and in the *Gedankengang*, Brentano takes time to relish the details. Other arguments are presented in terse, almost axiomatic form, but the facts of teleology (technically, the facts of its appearance, and the infinite probability of its reality based on the appearance) charm him and provide him with the opportunity to display his considerable knowledge of scientific lore concerning inorganic and organic nature.

It is an innovation on Brentano's part to find indications of teleology among non-living things. Not only does he call on the fact of increasing entropy to support the claim that the created universe had a beginning and will come to an end after having existed for a finite period of time, which in turn supports the claim that the universe has a first mover as its creative cause. Brentano also focuses on well-known features of inorganic matter and calls attention to their apparently teleological nature. Among other facts he points out that it is, as he says, infinitely many times infinitely improbable that two particles should collide, that their paths should intersect and that they should be at the intersection at the same time. That this should happen very frequently is all the more improbable, and yet it does. Moreover, that so many atoms should be identical in form, that is, that there should be identifiable kinds of atoms, is just as highly improbable, and yet not only are atoms divisible into kinds within which all atoms are identical but this is what makes possible the regular formation of chemical bonds including those required for organic compounds. Brentano sees teleological regularity in all of this, a purposeful ordering of matter suitable for the development of living things.

The appearance of teleology in the organic realm is all the more striking; this is where most philosophers have called attention to it, but here, too, Brentano adds his unique observations. In his lectures especially the details are elaborated, and the objections carefully laid to rest. Quoting extensively from authorities on both sides, Cuvier in favor of teleology, Lange, Littre, and others against, Brentano develops a thoroughly reasoned and richly illustrated account of the purposeful design of living things. Undaunted by the flightless wings of an ostrich, the blind eyes of a lizard, the teeth of whales, nipples on human males, and the rabid dog's impulse to bite, not to mention tapeworms and other parasites, and sickness, suffering, and death, Brentano sifts the apparently anti-teleological facts, like an archaeologist, until the bits of teleology that explain them come to light. Among the most interesting points he makes is that the seeds and originary cells of things show a capacity for several possible courses of development even though only one such course is ultimately evident in the resulting adult organism. For example, human zygotes and early embryos are alike, he says, but distinctively male or female features first emerge in the course of development beyond that stage. When vestigial organs are apparent in a given species or sex, then, that counts as evidence for intelligent design, not as evidence against it. Not only zygotes and embryos, but also parts of some kinds of mature organisms are capable of more than one line of future development. Thus Brentano says certain *annelids* (segmented worms) when cut in two are capable of growing a new head or a new tail, and some will grow new heads at intervals along their length and then spontaneously divide into several organisms. All this seems to anticipate what we now know about stem cells and about gene expression, which Brentano would surely take for further evidence of intelligent design as showing forethought regarding future contingencies.

The evolution of species, too, is evidence of teleology for Brentano and Darwinian attempts to explain it away fail. That is to say, Brentano accepts Darwin's account of the facts of evolution but rejects the explanation of those facts in terms of random mutation and natural selection. It is not possible here to do justice to Brentano's arguments, except to say that he anticipates the hypothesis of "punctuated equilibrium," in part, and insists that in addition to abrupt emergence of certain organs and species there must also be an intelligent principle operating to assure that a sufficient number of mutations are favorable and that those that are favorable persist. Otherwise what you would have is an infinite preponderance of unfavorable accidental mutations and insufficient time to establish the favorable ones that might appear. Brentano's treatment of teleology is far more complex and scientifically knowledgeable, for his day, than are standard, clichéd suggestions that, for instance, it would be highly improbable, if all the letters in Homer's *Iliad* were scattered at random, that they would land in the order familiar to us. He is not talking about monkeys at typewriters, or even about the intelligent origin of "clockworks." Rather, in the spirit of Aquinas's "fifth way," he is reasoning *from* the fact that in nature mindless things regularly reach advantageous goals *to* the fact that if they do so they must be guided in their activity by an intelligence that is aware of, and does know how to achieve, those goals. He concludes that it is infinitely improbable that mindless things would regularly achieve any goals or desirable outcomes without the guidance of a creative intelligence – far more improbable, in other words, than the finite improbability that a randomly generated assemblage of letters would assume the form of the *Iliad*.

With this we have further confirmation that the directly necessary being is an intelligence and not a physical, extended thing. In fact, even our human intelligence, though it is dependent on physical organs, cannot be assigned to any single organ as its physical subject. In the lectures, Brentano argues at length against psychological materialism, and then uses the established, non-material nature of the human soul as a further proof of God's existence on the grounds that no material cause could account for the existence of the non-material soul or mind. This so-called psychological proof rejects the semi-materialism of Aristotle, who took the human intellect to be the "form" of the body, in favor of a semi-Cartesian conception according to which the human soul is present in but not identical with a physical body (such as the brain). Unlike Descartes, Brentano held that animals have souls, too, and that their souls (not only ours) are immortal.

Although the human soul is an indirectly necessary being and has need of bodily organs, the creative intelligence is a directly necessary being, absolutely undetermined by things outside itself, and thus cannot be thought to be physical or extended in space. In sharp contrast to all embodied minds, then, the creative intelligence is to be conceived of as a substance without any accidents. The embodied minds, such as human minds, are *substances* (things, or beings) whose existence is enriched, as Brentano sees it, by a multitudinous variety of *accidents* (attributes, or characteristics) over time. Many of these accidents involve sense perception, as when one becomes a taster, or hearer, or seer of something. Other accidents involve judgment and still others the emotive phenomena of love, hate, and desire. For Brentano, one who sees is actually an accident containing a substance, a thinking thing, as a one-sidedly separable proper part. Thus the thinking thing continues to exist while various accidents of perception, judgment, and feeling come to be and pass away. Unlike other theories of substance and accident, Brentano's theory treats each accident as a distinct individual, yet retains human individuality and identity by locating them in the mental substance which participates (literally is a part of) many different accidents over a lifetime. Brentano even claims, in disagreement with Descartes, that the human embodied mind can continue to exist while unconscious, that is while having (strictly speaking, being a part of) no accidents at all. The creative intelligence, however, so far from being asleep or unconscious when it has no accidents, is actually always actively thinking and never has any accidents whatsoever. For the thinking of the creative intelligence, of the directly necessary being, is a substantial determination, not an accidental one. Thinking constitutes its very being, whereas for us thinking comes and goes. So all the characteristics we might attribute to the creative intelligence – including thinking, knowing, willing, and the steady infinitesimal change in knowledge mentioned above – are substantial determinations. Having established this, Brentano agrees with traditional theists in holding that the directly necessary, creative intelligence is "impassible," that is, it never suffers any external influence.

According to Brentano, there could not be more than one directly necessary, creative intelligence. If there were a second one, it would have to be either active or inactive. Now if it is active, then either it is intelligent or it acts blindly. But if both directly necessary beings are intelligent and impassible, then they could not know about each other, which is absurd, since by hypothesis each is somehow in charge of all that is. Moreover, if one of them is a non-intelligent principle that acts blindly, then its activity could not affect the intelligent one, again due to the latter's impassibility. This leaves only the possibility of a second directly necessary, creative intelligence that is wholly inactive. Whether we say that the first one knows about the second one, or that it does not know about the second one, we are equally led to absurdity, according to Brentano, because both the knowledge and the ignorance in such a case contradict the direct necessity of a directly necessary being. Therefore there is *at most* one directly necessary, creative intelligence. (It has already been shown, of course, that there is *at least* one directly necessary, creative intelligence.)

Finally, Brentano establishes in keeping with traditional natural theology that the directly necessary, creative intelligence is infinitely perfect. Thus its knowledge, love, power, and happiness are all complete and flawless. There must be no truth that it does not know, no good that it does not love, and no logically possible being that it cannot produce. "But joy depends upon the ability to unite with one's love the consciousness of the reality of what one loves."[2] Therefore the infinitely perfect creative intelligence enjoys complete felicity, and as Aristotle had said,[3] what our life is in the best of moments its existence is always.

THEODICY

There remains to be discussed the defense of God's justice, traditionally called "theodicy" (from the Greek, "*theos*," god, and "*dike*," justice). For even if it is true that there is no good that the directly necessary being does not love, still the evils in the world of our experience seem to prevent our concluding that the world has been produced by an infinitely perfect being. Or if the directly necessary being did produce this world, then it would seem to be a flawed product in many respects, given the amount of suffering, immorality, error, ignorance, crime, mental illness, and so forth, that we find here.

In one sense, the teleological argument on which Brentano relies more than any other argument for proving God's existence is itself a theodicy. For the orderly design of the created universe would provide a context in which the apparently disorderly elements of it could find their teleological place. Thus, according to Brentano, many things may serve good purposes even though considered in themselves they are not preferable to their opposites.

In another sense, however, Brentano's theodicy goes beyond the teleological argument for God's existence. For it is oriented around the fundamental question whether there is any existing thing such that we can be sure that the world would be better if that thing did not exist. Against the backdrop of Brentano's later metaphysics this becomes a question with regard to any substance, any part of a substance, any accident, and any sum of accidents or substances, up to and including not only the whole created universe but also the created universe taken together with its directly necessary creator. Brentano does not claim to possess the definitive answer to this question in every possible case. With regard to individual things in the world, he points out that we have to ask whether the thing is such that its existence is preferable to its non-existence. If we consider that being, life, perception, knowledge, and what he calls

correct emotion (love of the good and hatred of the bad) are all intrinsically good considered in themselves, it is not as obvious as might
be thought that any existing things (including animals and human
beings) are so thoroughly evil that they ought never to have existed.
Stated another way, it is more possible than we might initially think
that for each thing that exists the directly necessary being has had
good reason to prefer its existence to its non-existence. With regard
to the world as a whole, however, some questions seem to be impossible to answer. Why does this world exist, rather than its mirror
image? Why not a world with no beginning, or a world with a different beginning in time? Still, it is not obvious that a mistake has
been made in either case. Of course, it also is not obvious that this
is the best of all possible worlds. But Brentano's theodicy does not
require either that we be able to prove that the creator has made no
mistakes, nor that we be able to prove that this is the best of all possible worlds. It suffices for Brentano's purposes if we concede that
we cannot prove that mistakes have been made, and if we concede
that it is possible that this world, *taken together with the existence
of its creator*, results in a greater sum of goods than some other world
would even if *taken by itself* it is a better world. These conclusions,
in other words, leave open the possibility of hope, of optimism that
the evils in the world are or will be outweighed by the good in it.
This is all Brentano aims at in rejecting pessimism and defending
God's justice.

Brentano's natural theology in general, and his theodicy in particular, are unique and distinct from other philosophers' accounts,
then, in the following ways. First, the emphasis on empirical data
used to support theistic conclusions is greater than usual. Second,
and as a result of this, the conclusions themselves are drawn with
a very high degree of probability, not with deductive certainty, as
in more dogmatic natural theologies. Third, the nature of God is
conceived by Brentano as including process and change. And fourth,
the defense of God's justice, rather than explaining away the evil
we experience, encourages us to hope that as the history of the created universe unfolds the good will tend to outweigh the evil overall.
Brentano's natural theology is thus an empirical, experiential, prob-
abilistic, and optimistic world view intended to be compatible with
a scientific outlook and with active rational inquiry in general.

THE SPIRIT OF BRENTANO'S NATURAL THEOLOGY

As a traditional part of philosophy, natural theology is decidedly eclipsed in our day by less audacious philosophical projects. On the one hand, as scientific specialization has narrowed, so too philosophical analysis has focused on finer and finer details rather than on the big picture. On the other hand, as the horrors of the twentieth century have begun to make their enormity felt, many philosophers have decided that humanistic and ethical concerns should occupy us and that metaphysics and cosmology should be set aside. Brentano died in the middle of World War I, notoriously a watershed period marking the end of a traditional or classical era in the history of the West and the beginning of a skeptical and fragmented era that has lost its bearings by comparison with an earlier time. Does Brentano's somewhat antique enterprise of natural theology have anything to say to us today?

The answer is yes, but not only because of its connection to earlier philosophical theologies. Rather the innovative and forward-looking aspect of Brentano's natural theology should also recommend it to us. One might think that skepticism about the theistic proofs and about theodicy has reached such a pitch in the twenty-first century that any energy spent in that direction would be wasted. But in fact, such skepticism was already well formed in the eighteenth century, long before Brentano was born. Hume and Kant had put the finishing touches on it, and philosophical discussions of such topics had become quaint, minority interests long before Brentano left the scene. Brentano was as well aware of this as we are. Why, then, did he continue to work in the area? And what is there to be found in his work that could be of value to us?

Besides being a time of skepticism and fragmentation, our era is also characterized by intense political ideology and fierce religious fundamentalism,[4] not only in the West but all over the world. We may leave it to sociologists and historians to figure out the causes of this, and simply note that philosophy has not escaped unscathed. One result has been that people's beliefs, especially in religion and ethics, have been allowed to elude rational scrutiny on the grounds of pluralism (we will never all agree anyway) or unimpugnable sincerity (we must respect others' dearly held views no matter how unfounded). Thus the power of rational inquiry to shed light on these areas has been lost except as an exercise in apologetics. Apparently the days are gone when getting an education meant facing challenges to one's beliefs. On the contrary, secular and religious institutions of higher learning alike take in as students and send forth as graduates people who have arrived and departed in a frame of mind harmonious from the outset with the prevailing secular or religious world view there. How common is it that a secular institution takes religion seriously, or that a religious institution takes religious skepticism seriously, in our day? Like medieval theologians, who labored to prove that in any case the doctrines of the Trinity and the Incarnation cannot be proved *not* to be true, many on both sides abdicate the throne of free inquiry to marry a commoner, blind belief.

By contrast, Brentano held that it is a mistake to grant knowledgeable assent to propositions that cannot be known to be true, or that are not in fact known by the one who gives assent. He specifically rejected any duty to believe, or alleged virtue of faith, that would claim to supersede rational grounds for giving assent.[5] It was this commitment that had led to his break with the Catholic Church and prevented his adopting any other religious faith. Whatever one's opinion about the value of organized religion, it can hardly be denied that Brentano set a good example of intellectual integrity, one which in our day we certainly could profit by emulating, for it would signal a rebirth of open-minded rationality. It was because he could see the opposing view clearly, and take the objections to his own view seriously, that Brentano was able not to convince but to challenge the atheistic materialist, young Sigmund Freud.

Beyond this, it is also true that, somewhat like Spinoza, Brentano was a "god-intoxicated" and deeply spiritual man. Just pause to consider what it must be like to view the spatial and temporal world as filled at every point and at every moment with beings that have been put there by God. This goes beyond simple wonderment at the fact that things exist and persist, and it goes beyond the ancient question, why there should be something rather than nothing. For Brentano, space and time positively shimmer with divine influence, always and everywhere. Likewise his natural theology radiates a confidence in human curiosity and in the power of contemplative thought that calls to mind Whitehead's assertion, "the purpose of philosophy is to rationalize mysticism."[6] There is a sense in which Western philosophy, inherited from the ancient Greeks and passed on by thinkers like Brentano, is one of the world's great religions, perhaps the only one to recommend, not so much the belief in any set of propositions thought to be true, but rather faith in the search for truths, even for truths about things like the nature of the divine that remain beyond our reach. Brentano's willingness to stretch into that realm, on the strength of probability and hope that extend beyond deductive logic, sets a pattern for a philosophical future flexible enough to let the oldest questions live.

NOTES

1. See Peter Gay, *Freud: a Life for our Time* (New York: W. W. Norton and Company, 1988), p. 29. Freud is quoted from his letters to Silberstein as having referred to Brentano as a "damned clever fellow," and a "genius." "Temporarily," Freud wrote, "I am no longer a materialist, also not yet a theist."
2. EG, p. 330.
3. Aristotle, *Metaphysics*, Bk. XII, ch. 7.
4. See Karen Armstrong, *The Battle for God* (New York: Ballantine Books, 2000).
5. RP, pp. 85–9.
6. Whitehead, *Modes of Thought* (New York: Macmillan, 1958), p. 237.

12 Brentano and Husserl

INTRODUCTION

Though Brentano is a highly significant philosopher in his own right as well as the teacher of various outstanding philosophers, he is most widely known as the teacher of the founder of phenomenology, Edmund Husserl. After Husserl had received his doctorate in mathematics in 1882, he made a career shift to philosophy in 1884 when he decided, under the influence of Thomas Masaryk,[1] to attend lectures of Brentano in Vienna. He continued to do so until 1886, when Brentano recommended Husserl as a diligent student of philosophy to Carl Stumpf[2] in Halle where Husserl was to join the staff in the following year. In the course of the 1890s, however, Husserl changed his philosophical orientation until he finally made his "breakthrough" to phenomenology with the *Logical Investigations* (1900/1). In later years, in spite of his repeated admissions of Brentano's profound influence on him,[3] he only distanced himself more and more from Brentanian philosophy, while Brentano himself was rather dismayed with Husserl's innovations.

In the present chapter the relationship between Brentano and Husserl will be discussed as follows. Brentano's philosophical orientation will be exposited only insofar as this was familiar to Husserl. This is not to say that only Brentano's views during the period from 1884 to 1886 will be taken into account here. Husserl was indeed an enthusiastic collector of notes from Brentano's lectures. Moreover, Husserl took special interest in his mentor's "psychognostic investigations," as Brentano indicates in a letter to Husserl (circa May 1891).[4] Developments that occur in Brentano's thought in the later 1890s and especially his reism of the last couple of decades of his life, however, fall outside Husserl's sphere of familiarity. As regards Husserl's philosophical orientation, his work prior to the transcendental turn (circa 1905) will be emphasized. The approach to philosophical problems that results from this turn, with its special method of a phenomenological reduction, becomes in large measure alien to the one that he had learned from his mentor. There are nonetheless certain features of Husserl's philosophy which were inherited from Brentano and endured to the end of his life. After the pretranscendental Husserl is discussed in relation to Brentano, the common features of their philosophies will be briefly indicated. The results of the chapter will in large measure be a summary of what has been said before in greater detail,[5] but it should be kept in mind that an entire volume could be written on the topic under discussion.[6]

BRENTANO'S PHILOSOPHICAL ORIENTATION

Though Brentano's philosophical views certainly went through various phases of development, what is clearly present in all phases is the conviction that philosophy can and must be scientific. It was precisely this feature of his philosophy that attracted Husserl,[7] the young mathematician who had been scientifically educated under Carl Weierstrass in Berlin. There is, however, a great problem in finding reliable sources for the discussion of Brentano's philosophy. Unfortunately Brentano published very little from the wealth of ideas he conveyed through lectures and letters and worked out in manuscripts, many of which he dictated after he had become blind. His most philosophically significant publication is certainly *Psychology from an Empirical Standpoint*, though this was only the first volume (the first and second books) of a larger project, to be followed by a second volume (the third, fourth, fifth and sixth books) which never appeared.[8] In the discussion of Brentano's relation to Husserl, however, we need not rely solely on this work and a few other philosophically significant ones which Brentano published in his life-time, for some notes from lectures of Brentano also prove helpful.[9]

By far the most widely discussed concept of Brentano's philosophy is that of intentional reference or inexistence.[10] Such reference obtains whenever an act of consciousness has something as its object. If something is imagined, for example, there obtains intentional reference to the imagined object. Alternatively it could be said that what is imagined exists in the act of imagining or is the content of this act. Accordingly Brentano introduces the term "immanent object" in contrast with the real one.[11] The formulation of intentional reference in terms of such concepts as "inexistence," "content," and "immanent object" (or the equivalent "intentional object") turned out to be of considerable difficulty for Brentano's students, including Husserl, as will be seen later.

It is important to note the often-overlooked context in which Brentano presented his concept of intentional reference. This concept was primarily to serve the purpose of distinguishing mental (or "psychical") phenomena, e.g. imagining, judging, and willing, from physical ones, e.g. colors and sounds (whether these be really perceived or merely imagined). Brentano's thesis of intentional reference is simply the statement that mental phenomena intentionally refer to objects whereas physical ones do not. It is not in any way to be construed as an attempt to distinguish mind from matter.[12] By means of intentional reference the subject matter of Brentano's descriptive psychology could be identified. All other phenomena, namely the physical ones which do not intentionally refer to objects, are to be left to natural science, albeit in a highly qualified way which will not concern us here.[13]

It may be asked why Brentano was so interested in psychology and what sort of psychology it was which he took pains to develop. The answer to the first question is to be seen in the fact that Brentano maintained that psychology was to provide the theoretical basis of practical philosophy, as will be seen below. This is not to say that theoretical philosophy for Brentano was to consist only of psychology. In fact he saw metaphysics as the more important concern of philosophy. While metaphysics is to prove the existence of God,[14] it is nonetheless impossible to conceive of God without an analogy to the mind we ourselves directly experience. Psychology is accordingly not irrelevant to metaphysics. Moreover, psychology was to provide the foundations for the answer to the question of immortality, which Brentano actually wanted to discuss in the final book of *Psychology from an Empirical Standpoint* which unfortunately never made its way into print.

As to the type of psychology Brentano attempts to develop, the title of the work just mentioned already tells us that this psychology is to be empirical and accordingly one that is based on experience. Brentano's empirical orientation, according to which concepts are to be derived from either inner or outer intuition, naturally makes him a close ally with the empiricist tradition. It also makes him an enemy of the inflationary philosophy that established itself in Germany in the wake of Kant and eventually discredited philosophy itself for many in the second half of the nineteenth century. The psychology we find in Brentano therefore sets out from what we actually experience, i.e. mental phenomena, and not from more speculative notions such as "soul" or "spirit."[15] The task of Brentano is thus to describe the phenomena of mind and at first to abstain from any hypotheses about their causes or effects until the descriptive foundation is secured. Accordingly Brentano's psychology is not only empirical, but also descriptive rather than "genetic."[16] This empirical descriptive endeavor, however, does not exclude a certain "ideal intuition" of its subject matter.[17] Here we are reminded of Hume's attempt to let experience have its say and at the same time to allow for knowledge of relations of ideas.

The investigations that concerned Brentano in psychology were given various names. In the winter semester of 1887/8 he presented lectures under the title of "descriptive psychology," part of which has been published.[18] The term "descriptive phenomenology," however, was used in the title of the lecture given in the winter semester of 1888/9.[19] Again, only a small part of these lectures has been published. The discipline in question was called "psychognosy" in the lectures that Brentano gave in the winter semester of 1890/1. These lectures have been published in their entirety.[20] Brentano's lecture notes, however, are extremely sketchy. If lecture notes from his students were published, a fuller understanding of his philosophical endeavors could be obtained.

In the above-mentioned lectures Brentano attempts to differentiate his concerns not only from the unfettered speculations of philosophers, but also from contemporaries such as Wilhelm Wundt, who were all too quick to provide causal explanations on the basis of experiments without an adequate descriptive foundation. It is widely known that Brentano had great respect for Aristotle and accordingly saw classification as one of the main tasks of science. In his descriptive psychology the phenomena under consideration were divided into three different classes depending on the way in which these

phenomena refer to their respective objects.[21] These classes are presentations, judgments, and love or hate. This threefold division of
mental phenomena, which will soon be discussed more thoroughly,
allowed Brentano to order the subject matter of practical philosophy, which for him consisted of aesthetics, logic, and ethics. The
first of these disciplines, on his view, is to be based on the theory of
presentations,[22] whereas the theory of judgments is to provide the
basis for logic.[23] Ethics, on his view, has its theoretical foundation
in the theory of love and hate.[24] Further discussion of this three-
fold division of practical philosophy would unfortunately take us
too far afield here, but it is nonetheless mentioned because it gives
us a notion of the philosophical application of Brentano's descriptive
psychology and its concomitant division of the modes of intentional
reference.

The term "presentation" is used here to translate *Vorstellung*.[25]
Brentano employs this term in a very broad sense to cover instances
in which an object appears in thinking, imagining, or sensation.
He in fact regards presentations as the founding acts of consciousness. All acts which are not themselves presentations are founded on
presentations.[26] A judgment, for example, is not itself a presentation,
but it is possible only if the object that is judged about is presented in
consciousness. There are various distinctions which Brentano makes
regarding presentations. He maintains that they can vary in their degrees of intensity. A sensation, for example, is of greater intensity
than a phantasy presentation.[27] Moreover, some presentations are
concrete, while others are abstract. The abstract ones are concepts.
Finally, presentations can be authentic or inauthentic. The inauthentic presentations occur whenever mere symbols must somehow be
substituted for the proper object of the act. Our presentations of extremely large integers, irrational numbers, contradictions, and God
are all examples of inauthentic presentations.

It has already been mentioned that judgments are for Brentano acts
of consciousness which are not themselves presentations, though of
course founded on presentations. In this regard he opposes the view
that a synthesis of concepts is all that is needed for a judgment.[28]
As far as Brentano is concerned, such a synthesis will result only
in another presentation, albeit a conceptual one. If, for example, the
concepts of green and tree are brought together in a synthesis, the
result is the presentation "green tree," but not the judgment that is

expressed by saying that a tree is green or that a green tree exists. What must be added to the presentation "green tree" in order to bring about such a judgment is the acceptance or rejection of what is presented. If one judges that a green tree exists, the presented object is accepted. If one judges that a green tree does not exist, the presented object is rejected. Moreover, Brentano allows for judgments which need not involve concepts. The acts of perception, according to him, are judgments, for they are obviously instances in which objects are accepted.[29] Yet, they are not conceptual.

In *Psychology from an Empirical Standpoint* Brentano proceeds without the slightest mention of propositions, which are for some philosophers regarded as special objects of judgment, not to be identified with sentences as expressed in language. The judgment which is expressed by the sentence "a green tree exists," for example, is for Brentano an act of consciousness whose object is simply a green tree and not the proposition *that a green tree exists*. The rejection of propositions, as will be seen, is in fact one of the main reasons why Brentano found Husserl's *Logical Investigations* unacceptable.

Judgments, on Brentano's view, differ from presentations not only insofar as judging is an acceptance or rejection, but also insofar as judgments are (1) either true or false and (2) evident or blind. As to the conception of truth and falsehood, Brentano advocated a version of the correspondence theory, which he later rejected for another view that will not concern us here.[30] Concerning evidence Brentano finds it present in both certain perceptions and certain conceptual judgments. In any case in which there is evidence, he insists, this is not to be identified with a certain feeling.[31] The perceptions to which he ascribes evidence are only inner perceptions whereas outer perceptions are said to be blind.[32] When we see colors and hear sounds, we accept the objects in question as belonging to the external world, but Brentano follows the line of modern philosophy which will not allow for this acceptance as evident or even true. This is not to say, however, that Brentano denies the existence of the external world. As it turns out, he regards it as a legitimate hypothesis in natural science. The vibrations of air and the waves of light that exist quasi-spatially and quasi-temporally, however, are not the sounds and colors which appear in time and space.[33]

Be this as it may, he says that inner perception, as opposed to outer perception, is fully and indubitably evident. My own presentations, judgments, and acts of love and hate are perceived and cannot be doubted by me while they are present. In addition Brentano thinks that evidence is possible in certain judgments, which can be called a priori. These are to be found not only in logic and mathematics, but also to some extent in descriptive psychology. Brentano's conception of the judgments in question is comparable with the Leibnizian conception of *vérités de raison* and (as already mentioned) Hume's conception of relations of ideas, though the synthetic judgments a priori of Kant do not meet with a warm reception from Brentano.

Since Husserl came to see Brentano's distinction between inner and outer perception as a very problematic one, it is advisable to consider this distinction a bit more here. It is already clear enough that inner perception for Brentano has greater evidence than outer perception, which is nothing more than blind instinctive belief. Moreover, inner perceptions have mental phenomena as their objects, while the objects of outer perception are physical phenomena. In the nineteenth century, however, doubts arose whether it was possible to perceive present mental phenomena. Auguste Comte argued that this would require something impossible, namely that consciousness would be both that which observes and that which is observed.[34] Though Brentano concedes that Comte was right about the impossibility of inner observation (i.e. attentive perception), he maintains that in inner perception the present acts of consciousness are perceived only secondarily and not primarily.[35] If an outer perception, for example, occurs, this act is primarily directed at the outwardly perceived object such as a color or a tone, but the act is secondarily directed at itself. The threat of infinite regress of inner perceptions is thereby avoided, for such a threat only arises if the inner perception of a mental act is an additional mental act. Moreover, Brentano maintains that all mental acts are perceived while they are conscious. Otherwise it would be necessary to accept the notion of an unconscious consciousness, which for him is not contradictory (in spite of what the combination of words may suggest), but unnecessary for the explanation of anything that occurs in consciousness.[36] In this regard it is ironic that Freud attended lectures of Brentano.

It is highly significant that Brentano does not include the future and past among perceivable objects.[37] His restriction of perception to present objects is indeed emphasised by him to such an extent that he is willing to say that motions and changes cannot be perceived. Since they require temporal duration, part of the motion or change must be in the past or future. The concept of change and also the concept of time, however, are given by means of an "original association" which takes place in imagination.[38] That is to say, during a perception the immediate past is associated with the present and creates the impression of the temporal continuum. This view of time consciousness was indeed not the only one that Brentano formulated, but it was the one that was familiar to Husserl.

Thus far we have looked at Brentano's view of two of the classes of mental phenomena: presentations and judgments. The third of these consists of acts of love and hate, which includes not only emotions but also volitions.[39] In this class there is also acceptance and rejection, though obviously in a different sense from the acceptance and rejection in the class of judgments. When I love something, I accept it as pleasant, useful, or good, and not merely as existent as in the case of affirmative judgment. Likewise, when I hate something I reject it as unpleasant, useless, or bad, and not merely as nonexistent as in the case of negative judgment. Moreover, Brentano maintains that, though truth and evidence in the strict sense apply only to judgments, they have their analogs in acts of love and hate. The love of knowledge, for example, is not merely something that all human beings love by nature, as Aristotle asserted at the outset of the *Metaphysics*, but also something that another species would hate incorrectly if there were such a species.[40] In this way Brentano develops his ethics as a kind of objectivism.

There are many other aspects of Brentano's philosophy which are of great interest and have unfortunately been all too often neglected, but in the present context only two more should receive attention. The first of these is Brentano's theory of wholes and parts, once again as this was familiar to Husserl and not its later developments. According to this theory, there are four basic ways in which we may speak of the parts of a whole: (1) physical, (2) metaphysical, (3) logical and (4) collective. Physical parts are separable from the whole, whereas metaphysical ones are not. A patch of red, for example, can be divided into two halves, each of which is a physical part of the whole. The extension of the patch of red and the hue, saturation, and brightness that this particular instance of red has are metaphysical parts. Color is also part of red, but this is a logical part rather than a physical or metaphysical one. Logical parts, like metaphysical ones and unlike physical ones, are inseparable from the whole. Finally, collective parts are exemplified in such objects as an army, in which the soldiers are parts of the whole. These are like physical parts in that they are separable from the whole.

In closing this discussion of Brentano's philosophy, mention should be made concerning his view of *irrealia*. Though his later philosophy is in large measure a concerted effort to eliminate these from ontology, his earlier view was very different in this regard. In his reply to Christoph Sigwart's attempt to equate existence with perceivability, Brentano says, "Now everyone sees at once that this concept of existence is too narrow, as it could well be claimed, for instance, that there is much that is imperceivable, such as a past and a future, an empty space and any privation, a possibility, an impossibility, and so forth and so on."[41] Accordingly, Brentano did at one time allow for the existence of various non-real objects. It will be seen below that in the *Logical Investigations* Husserl advanced the thesis that in some manner such objects are perceivable.

HUSSERL'S PHILOSOPHY OF ARITHMETIC

Husserl's first book, based partly on the thesis that he wrote to join the faculty in Halle,[42] was published in 1891 under the title *Philosophy of Arithmetic*[43] and dedicated to Brentano.[44] It was to be followed by a second volume under the same title, but this second volume never did appear. The task Husserl first set for himself was to work out the Brentanian philosophy of arithmetic. Such an attempt had been made by Benno Kerry, another student of Brentano, in a series of articles.[45] Kerry, however, died when he was only 30 years old in 1889 before he could fully realize all the investigations he planned in this regard and in the philosophy of mathematics in general. He had proceeded in his work on this topic under the assumption that all of mathematics arises from inauthentic presentations (thus by means of symbols), whereas Husserl takes a very different route in his philosophy of arithmetic by allowing for authentic presentations of cardinal numbers up to three.[46]

Authentic presentations are intuitions. Accordingly, Husserl maintains in his *Philosophy of Arithmetic* that there is an intuitive foundation of arithmetic. While he leaves it open whether cardinal numbers are the ultimate objects of arithmetic, he begins his psychological investigations of these precisely because some of them can be authentically presented. Husserl insists that his main concern is a psychological characterization of cardinal numbers and not a definition of them.[47] Hence the subtitle of the work in question is *Psychological and Logical Investigations*.[48] In this regard Husserl proceeds in philosophy as he had learned to do so from Brentano: by making descriptive psychology his starting point.

The intuitions from which the concepts of cardinal numbers are derived, Husserl maintains, are to be found in instances of collective combinations.[49] In this respect as well he exhibits the influence that Brentano had on him, as is also evident in his distinction of collective combinations from the three other whole–part relations. Yet, Husserl's additional assertion that the concept of cardinal number is reached by means of an attentive reflection on intuitively presented collections is his own innovation which was in fact to meet with criticism from at least one other student of Brentano, Alexius Meinong.[50]

It is interesting to note that Husserl had little to say about judgments in *Philosophy of Arithmetic*. The investigations are carried out almost entirely in the realm of presentations. The distinction between concrete and abstract presentations is of course of great importance here, for arithmetic as a conceptual enterprise is in need of abstraction. More important for Husserl, however, is the distinction between authentic and inauthentic presentations. Though a few cardinal numbers can be intuitively presented, the rest of them can be presented and operated on in addition, subtraction, multiplication, and division by symbolic means. The second volume of *Philosophy of Arithmetic* was in fact to give extensive treatment of symbolic presentations in arithmetic.[51] This volume, however, never appeared because it became increasingly apparent to Husserl that the problems under consideration could only be dealt with by investigating the horizons and origins of logic.

HUSSERL'S TURN TO PHILOSOPHY OF LOGIC

The 1890s

Husserl was working on problems in the philosophy of arithmetic at a time when mathematics and logic were being closely linked. It was accordingly only natural that he made a transition in the 1890s to the philosophy of logic. As already indicated, *Philosophy of Arithmetic* was to include "logical" as well as "psychological" investigations. In 1894 (November 22) Husserl wrote to Meinong that he must devote his attention to the completion of the second volume of *Philosophy of Arithmetic*, which he characterizes as "investigations in the logic of deductive sciences."[52] Instead of accomplishing this task, however, Husserl turned to philosophy of logic as such without special consideration of arithmetic.

In 1894 he published an article which was meant to be the first and second parts of "Psychological Studies in Elementary Logic."[53] The first of these concerns the distinction between the abstract and the concrete, while the topic of the second article is intuitions and representations. While the study of the abstract and the concrete develops ideas which were already developed in the school of Brentano, most notably by Carl Stumpf, Husserl maintains in a posthumously published treatise of 1893 that intuitions and representations are presentations in totally different senses.[54] Such a conception of them does, to be sure, suggest a divergence from the Brentanian one of presentations, for Brentano had conceived of these as belonging to a single class of psychical phenomena without ambiguity or equivocation. Nevertheless, the very title "Psychological Studies in Elementary Logic" suggests a strong allegiance to the Brentanian philosophical undertaking, not only by the fact that the studies in question are called "psychological," but by the fact that Husserl had attended lectures of Brentano in Vienna on the very topic of elementary logic.

In Husserl's philosophy of logic one of the towering figures was Bernard Bolzano, who had in large measure been neglected for decades until Brentano lectured on his *Paradoxes of the Infinite*[55] and certain pupils of his turned their attention to other works of Bolzano, especially his four-volume *Theory of Science*.[56] In 1894 one of Brentano's students, Kasimir Twardowski, published a book in which the Bolzanian conception of "objectless presentations" was discussed.[57] These are presentations such as "round square" and "golden mountain," i.e. ones that refer to non-existent objects. Such presentations were of course problematic for Brentanian philosophy, for they are apparent counterexamples of the thesis of intentional reference. Husserl responded to Twardowski's book by writing a review (which was left unpublished) and also an extensive essay entitled "Intentional Objects."[58] As Husserl understands Twardowski's position,[59] it amounts to the assertion that so-called objectless presentations do in fact refer to objects, namely to objects which exist only in consciousness. Though Husserl misunderstands Twardowski in this regard, his attempt to solve the problem posed by the presentations in question is nonetheless an interesting one.

According to Husserl's view that is presented in "Intentional Objects," presentations such as "round square," "golden mountain," and "Zeus," strictly speaking, do not refer to objects, but there is an improper mode of speech in which it is acceptable to say that the presentations in question do refer to objects. In such cases there is an "assumption" or "hypothesis" at work, though not actual judgment or belief. If the assumption or hypothesis were true, the presentation would have objective reference. The presentation of Zeus, for example, refers to an object insofar as we "assume" Greek mythology (without of course actually believing in it) when Zeus is presented. In opposition to the thesis of intentional inexistence, however, Husserl flatly denies that there exists in consciousness an object called "Zeus." Thus Husserl's conception of intentional reference does not always allow for intentional inexistence, though he still allows for such inexistence in the case of the objects of intuition.

In "Intentional Objects" it is also noteworthy that Husserl speaks of objective presentations and thereby draws on a notion that was introduced by Bolzano. In his *Theory of Science* (1837) Bolzano had maintained that elementary logic is not concerned with subjective presentations and sentences in expression, but rather with objective presentations (presentations in themselves) and objective sentences (sentences in themselves). While their subjective counterparts come and go in the mind, the objects of logic are in no way bound to temporal and spatial conditions. In the essay of 1894, however, Husserl does not yet apply the concept of objective presentations to logic. This is done two years later in his lectures in Halle[60] and then for the wider public in the first volume of his *Logical Investigations*,[61] which will now be discussed.

Pure logic

In 1900 the first volume of Husserl's *Logical Investigations* was published under the title *Prolegomena to Pure Logic* where psychologism comes under attack. By "psychologism" Husserl means the view that psychology is the only theoretical foundation for logic as a practical discipline. By "pure logic" Husserl means a theoretical discipline that is altogether a priori and also a foundation for the practical discipline of logic. Husserl argues that psychology can only provide us with inexact and inductively derived laws of thought, while the laws of logic are both exact and not inductively derived.[62] In his defense of pure logic Husserl indicates that Bolzano is among those who have influenced him.[63] Here the important concept for Husserl is especially that of the "sentence in itself," though he is content to speak of propositions (*Sätze*). That to which truth is ascribed in logic and ultimately in any theoretical endeavor, Husserl maintains, is not something that comes and goes, but rather something that is altogether timeless.[64] Such bearers of truth are propositions and not our acts of judgment. While logic as a practical discipline is indeed concerned with how to form correct judgments, this is done on the basis of a pure logic that tells us under what conditions propositions can be true and false. The consequence of viewing only psychology as the basis of logic, Husserl argues, is relativism.[65]

The *Logical Investigations* were not at first widely received in the professional academic community. In Munich, however, they attracted the attention of some of the pupils of Theodor Lipps. By 1905 many of these young men and women were flocking to Göttingen, where Husserl had been a professor since 1901, to hear his lectures. Already in the autumn of 1904 Brentano had become aware of the resonance that Husserl was enjoying and asked him by letter to explain in what ways Husserl diverged from Brentano's teachings.[66] Though Husserl attempted to do this in more than one letter, Brentano remained unconvinced that it was necessary to posit propositions and other Bolzanian "thought-things" in order to rescue logic from relativism.[67] The question remains whether Brentano fell prey to psychologism and thus to its most undesirable consequences, namely relativism. Nowhere in the *Prolegomena* is Brentano regarded as a proponent of psychologism. Nonetheless, the issue of psychologism was first on his agenda when Husserl visited him in Florence in 1907. According to Brentano's account of this meeting, Husserl gave him every assurance that his views were not psychologistic.[68] Yet, it is difficult to see how such assurances could be legitimately made and the notion of a pure logic in the Husserlian sense could be upheld at the same time. If Brentano found a way to avoid psychologism without positing the thought-things of pure logic, Husserl's argument in the *Prolegomena* can only be regarded as unsound. Thus it seems that Husserl could have well been insincere in exonerating Brentano from the charge of psychologism.

PHENOMENOLOGY OF LOGICAL MENTAL PROCESSES.[69]   In 1901 Husserl published the second volume of the *Logical Investigations* which consist in large measure of descriptive psychology (or phenomenology) in application to the logical mental processes.[70] It is by no means possible here to summarize all six of the investigations which make up the volume (and each of which will henceforth be referred to as a "Logical Investigation"), but some of the crucial points on which Husserl diverges from Brentano in this volume may be indicated. In this regard it will be seen that Husserl differed from Brentano not only in the conception of the subject matter of logic, but also in various issues of descriptive psychology. To be sure, Husserl retracted his characterization of phenomenology as descriptive psychology soon after the publication of the *Logical Investigations*.[71]

Accordingly, the passage in which this characterization occurs was removed and replaced by another one in the second edition of the work (1913).[72] Such a shift, however, only can be intelligible, if indeed it is intelligible at all, in the light of the development of transcendental phenomenology. Here we must restrict the discussion to phenomenology as descriptive psychology. Given Husserl's well-known assertion that the results of transcendental phenomenology run parallel to those of descriptive psychology, there will be no harm done in restricting the discussion in the way suggested.

Great caution is recommended in attributing a different method to the phenomenology of the *Logical Investigations* as compared to Brentano's empirical descriptive method. Such an attribution can be found Theodor Celms's assertion that Brentano was concerned with "types" and Husserl with laws of essence.[73] It must be emphasized, contrary to Celms and other important phenomenologists,[74] that this distinction is not at all to be found in Husserl.[75] To be sure, Husserl came to distinguish between typical and exact essences,[76] but his phenomenology, just like Brentano's descriptive psychology, concerns the former rather than the latter. In both cases an "ideal intuition" is sought regarding the same subject matter, namely consciousness. It is also doubtful if Husserl's later transcendental point of view can be read into his *Logical Investigations* without further ado, as Celms and others have attempted to do.[77] The ways in which Husserl's views in this work differ from Brentano's in fact have little to do with method. Rather, they are differences in ontology and descriptive psychology.

As already seen, Husserl had rejected the notion of the immanent or intentional object in 1894. While this rejection continues in the *Logical Investigations*,[78] Husserl also arrives at a different conception of consciousness in other important respects. In the fifth "Logical Investigation" he is particularly concerned with intentionality, but there he allows for psychical processes ("contents of consciousness") which are not intentionally directed.[79] These include the sensations, which are "interpreted," "apprehended," or "apperceived" in the acts of outer perception. Among the non-intentional psychical processes are also phantasms, which undergo the same apperceptive operation in acts of imagination. In this theory Husserl goes against the grain of Brentano's view that the intentionally directed and the psychical are the same. Nonetheless Husserl's qualification that a being devoid of intentional processes cannot be legitimately regarded as a psychical being[80] appears to be a significant concession to Brentano.

Far more doubt is raised by Husserl concerning another one of Brentano's ways of distinguishing psychical from physical phenomena, namely concerning Brentano's thesis that only a psychical phenomenon is either a presentation or founded on a presentation. A good part of the fifth "Logical Investigation" (chapters 3 to 6) is in fact a critique of this particular thesis. Husserl's argument against it, however, is extremely complex and can hardly be treated adequately here. Suffice it to say that for Husserl there are acts, e.g. perceptions and judgments, which are not founded on presentations in the sense of acts which could occur independently. Suppose, for instance, something is taken to be a young lady and then on closer inspection it becomes clear that the object in question is a wax figure rather than a young lady.[81] Brentano's analysis would suggest that a young lady is presented throughout the change and that the change is essentially a transition from the acceptance of this object to a rejection thereof together with an acceptance of a wax figure. While Husserl certainly concedes that something remains constant throughout this change, he insists that it would be wrong to characterize it as a mere presentation, which could subsist alone. It is rather the "matter" of the act, which requires a "quality" in order for it to be a concrete act. That is to say, the part of the act that endures in the case under discussion is for Husserl not a whole act, whereas the presentations on which non-presentational acts are founded for Brentano are indeed whole acts. This is not to say that Husserl rejects the very notion of one act being founded on another. As it turns out, the fifth "Logical Investigation" results in a two-fold classification of acts that are said to be in a relation of founding and being founded. One class consists of objectifying acts, e.g. perceptions and judgments as well as mere presentations, while the other consists of non-objectifying acts, e.g. emotions. The non-objectifying acts, according to Husserl, are founded on objectifying ones.

In the sixth "Logical Investigation" Husserl introduces his notion of categorial intuition, which can again be viewed as an innovation to solve an *aporia* that arises in Brentano's philosophy. Categorial intuition, according to Husserl, stands in contrast with sensory or straightforward intuition.[82] If, for example, I see white paper, this is an instance of the latter, whereas a categorial intuition occurs when I see *that* a piece of paper is white. If we now recall that Brentano was reluctant to equate existence with perceivability because he acknowledged unperceived *irrealia*, it is of considerable interest that in Husserl's copy of the book in which this reluctance is expressed Husserl wrote "categorial perception!" next to the passage in question.[83] Accordingly, Husserl thought of categorial intuition as a type of perception that would allow him to avoid the conclusion that existence and perceivability are not equivalent. While it is plausible, however, to say that perception occurs whenever one sees that a piece of paper is white, it becomes much more difficult to see how such *irrealia* as past and future could ever be regarded as perceivable. To be sure, Husserl developed a notion of time-consciousness that includes retention (about the past) and protention (about the future).[84] However, no matter how much evidence he ascribes to retention and protention, it would be far-fetched to say that the distant past or the distant future are perceivable.

In the *Logical Investigations*, Brentano's conception of inner perception is also subject to criticism. While inner perception is among the references of "consciousness" which Husserl identifies in the fifth "Logical Investigation," he dismisses Brentano's view that such perception is only secondarily directed at its object as a dubious theoretical artifice which does not effectively avoid an infinite regress.[85] In the Appendix of the work Husserl rejects the view that all those perceptions which are directed at the psychical are in fact as evident as Brentano claimed.[86] The problematic cases for Husserl are the ones in which inner perceptions are bound up with outer ones. If, for example, the object of perception is pain in a tooth, the perception is at least in part an outer one and therefore not a matter of absolute certainty.[87] For this reason Husserl prefers to avoid the Brentanian term "inner perception," though he still thinks that the acts and other elements of consciousness can be given adequately.

There are other points of disagreement between Brentano and Husserl that arise in the *Logical Investigations* and closely related texts. Husserl's concession to the synthetic a priori[88] is of course one way in which he prefers Kant to Brentano. In the area of value-theory Husserl again showed signs of assimilating Kantian notions which were alien to Brentano.[89] In Husserl's early 1904/5 lectures on imagination, he was moreover very critical of Brentano's views on this topic, however much respect he shows for his mentor.[90] In the same lectures Husserl attacks the theory of original association.[91] While all these and other topics are of great interest, they would require a much more extensive treatment of the relation between Brentano and Husserl than is possible in the present volume. There is moreover a danger in focusing on the disagreements between these two, because what they had in common certainly must not be over-looked.

PHILOSOPHY AS THE SCIENCE OF CONSCIOUSNESS

The current of philosophy which Husserl started, the so-called "phenomenological movement," has drifted far away from the ideal of scientific philosophy that he first found expressed in the lectures of Brentano and was meant to be realized in his own phenomenological investigations. The sharing of this ideal sets their philosophical endeavors light years apart from most of what is called "phenomenology" today, which is of course in large measure shaped by the anti-scientific tendencies of Heidegger and his French followers. If we look at Brentano's four-phase theory of the history of philosophy, three types of decay are identified: (1) the preference for the practical over the theoretical, (2) skepticism and relativism, and (3) mysticism.[92] It is, of course, obvious that Husserl sought to develop his phenomenology first and foremost as a theoretical enterprise. Moreover, his rejection of skepticism and relativism was already strongly pronounced in his critique of psychologism. His rejection of mysticism in philosophy is also to be found throughout his comments on Heidegger, Scheler, and Steiner as well as others.[93]

While the striving for scientific philosophy is of course something that Brentano and Husserl have in common with other philosophers, such as the logical positivists, it is to be noted that they differ from many of these others insofar as they see consciousness as the subject matter of such philosophy. When we speak of science in English, what is primarily meant is natural science. It may accordingly be difficult to understand how Brentano and Husserl could have advocated or advanced scientific philosophy without seeing natural science as its foundation. As difficult as this is for the contemporary Anglo-American understanding, it must time and again be emphasized that consciousness, completely devoid of any sort of physicalistic reduction, is an object of science for Brentano and Husserl. This science, moreover, they regard as absolutely central to all the concerns of philosophy.

It thus turns out that Brentano and Husserl offer us something that we cannot find among the two main streams of contemporary philosophy, generally classified as continental and analytic. Roughly speaking, the continentals reject the very ideal of philosophy as a science and perhaps even science itself, whereas the analytic philosophers do not as a rule allow for any other kind of science besides that which is exemplified in its finest form in physics. It is, to be sure, of great importance not to allow philosophy to decay into the dogmatism, relativism, and mysticism of the continentals. It is, however, of equal importance not to overlook a whole dimension of scientific inquiry. In spite of the many disagreements between Brentano and Husserl, their common concerns may well be the only ones that will ultimately prevail in a genuinely scientific philosophy.

NOTES

1. See Robin D. Rollinger, *Husserl's Position in the School of Brentano* (Dordrecht, Boston, MA, London: Kluwer Academic Publishers, 1999), pp. 2–3, 15–16.
2. See *ibid.*, pp. 83–123.

3. See, for example, Edmund Husserl, *Aufsätze und Vorträge (1911–1921)*, in *Husserliana* xxv, 1987, pp. 304–15 and Maria Brück, *Über das Verhältnis Edmund Husserls zu Franz Brentano, vornehmlich mit Rücksicht auf Brentanos Psychologie* (Würzburg: Triltsch, 1993).
4. Husserl, *Briefwechsel* I, p. 6.
5. See Rollinger, *Husserl's Position*, pp. 1–67.
6. Much more needs to be done than what can be found in Maria Brück, *Über das Verhältnis*.
7. Husserl, *Aufsätze und Vorträge*, p. 305.
8. PES-E, p. xv.
9. See Rollinger, *Husserl's Position*, p. 22.
10. PES-E, pp. 88–91.
11. *Ibid.*, pp. 24 and 139.
12. Dermot Moran, "The Inaugural Address: Brentano's Thesis,"1996.
13. PES-E, pp. 98ff.
14. See EG.
15. PES-E, pp. 3–8.
16. *Ibid.*, pp. 3–11.
17. *Ibid.*, p. xv. The translator renders Brentano's *ideale Anschauung* as "ideal point of view," but this translation deprives his term of its epistemic importance.
18. DP-E, pp. 129–36.
19. *Ibid.*, pp. 137–42.
20. *Ibid.*, pp. 1–87.
21. PES-E, pp. 194–264.
22. GA 1988.
23. PES-E, pp. 230–1.
24. USE.
25. The translators of Brentano 1973 render this term "sometimes . . . as 'presentation,' and sometimes as 'idea,' or 'thought'" (Brentano, p. xiv). While the reading of the text is thereby made somewhat easier, this approach has the disadvantage of missing Brentano's point that there is indeed one class under consideration here. The term "presentation" also has the advantage of being grammatically related to the verb "present" as the German noun *Vorstellung* is related to the German verb *vorstellen* (which is also translated in different ways by the translators of the work under consideration).
26. PES-E, pp. 201–34.
27. See Robin D. Rollinger, "Husserl and Brentano on Imagination," *Archiv für Geschichte der Philosophie*, 75, 1993, pp. 195–210.
28. PES-E, pp. 80–5.
29. DP-E, p. 36.
30. TE.

31. USE, p. 58.
32. PES-E, pp. 91–2.
33. Ibid., pp. 98–9.
34. Ibid., p. 32.
35. Ibid., pp. 29ff.
36. Ibid., pp. 104–26.
37. See Rollinger, Husserl's Position, pp. 29–32.
38. See Robin D. Rollinger, "Brentano and Meinong on Time-Consciousness," in, eds., Hans-Reiner Sepp and Toru Tami, Zeit in der Phänomenologie (Freiburg-München: Karl Albert Verlag, forthcoming).
39. PES-E, pp. 235–64.
40. See Rollinger, Husserl's Position, pp. 42–3.
41. USE, p. 62.
42. Edmund Husserl, Philosophie der Arithmetik. Mit ergänzenden Texteni (1890–1901), in, ed., Lother Eley, Husserliana XII (The Hague: Martinus Nijhoff, 1970), pp. 287–339.
43. Ibid., pp. 1–283.
44. Ibid., p. 3.
45. See Rollinger, Husserl's Position, pp. 125–37.
46. Husserl, Philosophie, p. 339.
47. Ibid., 1970, pp. 20–1.
48. Edmund Husserl, Philosophie der Arithmetik. Psychologische und logische Untersuchungen, p. i.
49. Husserl, Philosophie, pp. 65–76.
50. Rollinger Husserl's Position , pp. 166.
51. See Husserl, Philosophie, p. 7 and pp. 340–73.
52. Edmund Husserl, Early Writings, p. 134.
53. Ibid., pp. 139–70.
54. Ibid., p. 327.
55. See Brentano's letter to Hugo Bergmann (June 1, 1909), as translated and quoted in Rollinger, Husserl's Position, pp. 70–1.
56. See Bernard Bolzano, Theory of Science: Attempt at a detailed and in the main novel Exposition of Logic with constant Attention to earlier Authors, trans. Rolf George (Berkeley, CA: University of California Press 1972).
57. See Kasimir Twardowski, On the Content of object of Presentations: a Psychological Investigation (Dordrecht, Boston, MA, London: Kluwer Academic Publishers, 1977).
58. This essay has been published in Husserl 1979 and again in an improved edition in Husserl 1990/1. The older edition is translated in Husserl, Early Writings, pp. 345–87, whereas a translation of the newer edition appears as an appendix in Rollinger, Husserl's Position, pp. 251–84.

59. As pointed out in Jens Cavallin, *Content and Object: Husserl, Twardowski and Psychologism* (Dordrecht, Boston, MA, London: Kluwer, 1997), Husserl misunderstands Twardowski. For a discussion of this lecture, which was crucial for Husserl's philosophical development and his growing distance from Brentano, see Rollinger, "Husserl's Elementary Logic: The 1886 Lectures in their Nineteenth Century Context," *Studia Phaenomenologica: Romanian Journal for Phenomenology*, forthcoming.

60. See Edmund Husserl, *Logik Vorlesung 1896*, in, ed., Elisabeth Schumann (Dordrecht, Boston, MA, London: Kluwer, 2000).

61. Husserl, *Einleitung in die Logik und Erkenntnistheorie. Vorlesungen 1906/1907*, ed. Ulrich Melle (The Hague: Martinus Nijhoff, 1984), p. 57.

62. Husserl, *Logical Investigations* (London: Routledge and Kegan Paul, 1970), pp. 98ff.

63. *Ibid.*, pp. 222ff.

64. *Ibid.*, p. 184.

65. *Ibid.*, pp. 145ff.

66. See Husserl, *Briefwechsel* I, p. 24.

67. See *ibid.*, pp. 24–44.

68. See Rollinger, *Husserl's Position*, pp. 19–20.

69. The term "mental processes" is here a translation of *Erlebnisse*. While it leaves much to be desired, it avoids certain confusions which arise in Findlay's translation of this term as "experiences."

70. Husserl, *Logical Investigations*, pp. 262–3 .

71. Husserl, *Early Writings*, pp. 250ff.

72. Husserl, *Logical Investigations*, p. 261–2.

73. Theodor Celms, "Der Phänomenologische Idealismus Husserls," *Acts Universitatis Latviensis*, 19, 1928, p. 283.

74. See Oskar Becker, "Beiträge zur Phänomenologischen Begründung der Geometrie und ihrer physikalischen Anwendung," *Jahrbuch pür Philosophie und phänomenologische forschung*, 6, 1923 and Alfred Schutz, *Collected Papers III: Studies in Phenomenological Philosophy*, ed., I. Schutz (The Hague: Martinus Nijhoff, 1970), pp. 92–115.

75. See Rochus Sowa, "Typus," in, ed., Helnut Vetter, *Lexikon der Phänomenologie* (Stuttgart: Kröner, forthcoming).

76. Husserl, *Ideas Pertaining to a Pure Phenomenology and to Phenomenological Philosophy* (The Hague, Boston, London: Martinus Nijhoff, 1982), §§ 73–4, pp. 164ff.

77. Celms, *Phänomenologische Idealismus Husserls*, pp. 283–4.

78. Husserl, *Logical Investigations*, pp. 557–8, 595–6.

79. *Ibid.*, pp. 565ff., 740ff.

80. *Ibid.*, p. 556 n.

81. *Ibid.*, pp. 609–10.

82. *Ibid.*, pp. 773–802.

83. Rollinger, *Husserl's Position*, p. 58.

84. Husserl.

85. Husserl, *Logical Investigations*, p. 543.

86. *Ibid.*, pp. 852–69.

87. *Ibid.*, pp. 859–60.

88. *Ibid.*, pp. 456ff.

89. Rollinger, *Husserl's Position*, pp. 63–6.

90. *Ibid.*, pp. 201–10.

91. *Ibid.*, pp. 29ff.

92. See B. Mezei and B. Smith, *The Four Phases of Philosophy, with an Appendix: The Four Phases of Philosophy and its Current State by Franz Brentano* (Amsterdam: Rodopi, 1998).

93. See, for example, Husserl, *Briefwechsel* II, p. 184 and Husserl, *Briefwechsel* III, pp. 24–5.

13 Brentano's impact on twentieth-century philosophy

If we look at Brentano's publications, we quickly see that they cover a wide variety of topics, ranging from the experimental psychology of visual perception, through specialized studies on Aristotle and the juridical intricacies of Austrian marital law, to extra-scientific pieces about chess and riddles. In view of this unusual situation, it seems clear that Brentano must have exerted his undoubted and far-reaching philosophical influence almost exclusively through his lecture courses. Through those courses he attracted many gifted students, and they constituted a school whose members came to hold important chairs not only in Austria, but also in Germany. Although these students, in their publications, often refer to Brentano's *Psychology from an Empirical Standpoint* published in 1874, they do so for the simple reason that his lecture courses were (and remained) unpublished and could not be quoted directly, and this was therefore the only published work which they could cite.

Add to this the fact that in preparing these courses, which he delivered without exception in eloquent and polished language, Brentano usually jotted down only a few disconnected notes, and we can see why even after his death it was impossible to publish a set of ten to twenty volumes documenting the full content of these courses. Nor should we forget that the texts of Brentano's major works published earlier by Oskar Kraus and Alfred Kastil and also more recent publications are, for different reasons, notoriously unreliable. A detailed and complete picture of Brentano's courses can emerge only from the comprehensive shorthand notes taken by his students on the spot. This too, however, is problematic. The most extensive notes were taken by Brentano's immediate pupils Anton Marty, Carl Stumpf, and Edmund Husserl, who donated their treasures to the Brentano

Archives in Prague.[1] All these materials were, however, lost in 1939
when the Archives were hastily evacuated to England. As a result, it
is very difficult – and I will not attempt it here – to describe in detail
the role Brentano's ideas played among his immediate followers and
heirs. This is why people have spoken of a certain "invisibility" that
Brentano has had in twentieth-century philosophy.[2] Since his impact
on this philosophy, for the reasons just mentioned, was often chan-
neled through that of his direct disciples, it is worth looking at them
first. Brentano's problems and questions went through many meta-
morphoses and to a large extent determined the agenda of twentieth-
century philosophy, but philosophers are often unaware of the fact
that they do indeed originate with him.

PSYCHOLOGY

The first distinctive characteristic of Brentanism is the view that
philosophy should be based on psychology. True, the psychology in
question is "descriptive" psychology, but that is only half of the
discipline, the other half of which is experimental (psychophysical)
psychology. Therefore not only Brentano himself, but also his disciples Stumpf and Alexius Meinong, though in their own estimate
genuine philosophers, devoted a large amount of their time to experimental work and founded schools of experimental psychology. When
Husserl, in the first volume of his *Logical Investigations* (1900),
branded this Brentanist conception "psychologistic," we should
note that this verdict concerns above all the empirical character of
Brentano's descriptive psychology, and not the conception as such.
Husserl himself successfully replaced this psychology with what he
termed "phenomenology," which aimed at an intuitive description
of the essential features of our experiences and of the essences of
what we experience. Husserl always remained convinced that phenomenology and (phenomenological) psychology are distinguished
from each other only by a "nuance," and that phenomenology leaves
the status of real existence out of consideration. Thus, even in his
last work, the *Crisis of European Science* (1936), he can state that
the best way into phenomenology is through psychology, for both
are "sisters."[3]

The cultivation of this close link between philosophy and psychology remained a central concern of the later phenomenological

movement,[4] and psychologists such as Karl Jaspers, Ludwig Binswanger,[5] Frederik J. Buytendijk,[6] Medard Boss,[7] Erwin Straus, Carl Rogers, or Rollo May, and even Jacques Lacan readily integrated phenomenological conceptions into their psychologies. At the same time, most mainstream phenomenologists held the view that psychology is the science closest to phenomenology and that phenomenology should be informed by it. Jean-Paul Sartre, early in his career (*L'imagination*, 1936, *Esquisse d'une théorie des émotions* 1939), published on psychological topics, and Maurice Merleau-Ponty's *La Structure du comportement* (1942) and *Phénoménologie de la perception* (1945), and Paul Ricœur's *De l'Interpretation: essai sur Freud* (1965) draw heavily on psychology. A figure of special importance on the borderlines of philosophy and psychology is Stumpf's disciple Aron Gurwitsch (*The Field of Consciousness*, 1979), whose non-egological conception of consciousness as a "field" centering around a thematic object, but surrounded by the spheres of the thematic and finally the marginal field, is still influential in the United States.

The first major attempt to introduce Brentano's conception of psychology into the English-speaking world was George F. Stout's *Analytic Psychology* (1896).[8] In this work, he follows Brentano in treating judgment as a mental activity of its own, but diverges from him in his interpretation of presentations, which he understands not as modifications of consciousness but rather as sense-data (meaning thereby material, though not physical entities, which for this very reason cannot be identified with real objects). This conception met with sharp opposition from George Dawes Hicks, who countered it with Brentanian (and Meinongian) arguments which he preferred to read in a realist fashion. From 1891 to 1920 Stout was editor of *Mind*, a journal that was to publish most of the key articles by the young representatives of analytic philosophy, such as George E. Moore (from 1921–47 Stout's successor as editor of *Mind*) and Bertrand Russell. It was Stout who paved the way for their more or less critical adaptation (and even for their explicit rejection) of Brentanist tenets. It is worth mentioning that in his review of the English translation of Brentano's *The Origin of the Knowledge of Right and Wrong*, Moore explicitly hailed this work as being of major importance in the field of ethics,[9] and that Russell developed his own theory of definite descriptions in direct response to Meinong's theory of objects, which itself is simply an ontological application of the principles of Brentano's psychology.[10]

But the true revival of Brentano's idea of a descriptive psychology did not take place until around 1970, under the influence of the later Wittgenstein, when the so-called "philosophy of mind" became a central issue.[11] As John R. Searle, a major representative of this new development, has stated, since that time philosophy of mind has become for a great many philosophers genuine First Philosophy.[12] Against the background of new developments in cognitive science, artificial intelligence, and the neurosciences, the basic problem dividing philosophers concerns the question whether, and to which degree, mind or consciousness can and should be maintained as a category of its own, or whether an eliminative programme of "naturalization," reducing it to material and more specifically biological categories, looks more promising. The most forceful proponents of the second type of approach are Paul and Patricia Churchland (*Neurophilosophy*, 1986; *The Engine of Reason, the Seat of the Soul*, 1995), who plead in favor of a revision, and ultimately a replacement, of our (folk) psychological concepts to keep pace with the constant progress of the neurosciences. So we may in the end look forward to a neurocomputational perspective on mind. Daniel C. Dennett's functionalism (*The Intentional Stance*, 1987; *Consciousness Explained*, 1991) distinguishes between three levels of description of behavior: the physical stance which describes the physical properties of the system in question, the design stance, which involves the function a system exerts in its environment, and the intentional stance of behavioral patterns, in which a system is considered as a reasonable agent. As there are no "facts of the matter" that would render such a system intrinsically intentional, the attribution of such states to a system can be justified only instrumentally. As a consequence, there is no fundamental difference between the non-conscious and conscious processing of information, and correspondingly consciousness cannot be understood as a private inner sphere, a Cartesian theatre, that is accessible to us in some privileged way. Donald Davidson (*Essays on Actions and Events*, 1980) holds a more modified position, according to which the behavior of a person can be described using the causal vocabulary of physics but also interpreted in psychological language, according to the explanatory context applied. He not only underlines the coherence of and interaction between the mental and the material, but at the same time affirms a certain irreducibility of the mental. Closest to Brentano's original position is perhaps Searle, with his realist, albeit non-ontological view of consciousness (*The Rediscovery of Mind*, 1992; *The Mystery of Consciousness*, 1997). In all these cases, it seems as if recent progress in physiology, brain research and neurology is a major factor behind the divergences between Brentano's own original conceptions and those of more recent philosophers. In connection with this, we should remember that Brentano himself deeply deplored the rudimentary state of those sciences in his own time.

INTENTIONALITY

Brentano's view of the centrality of philosophy of mind has won increasing support in recent decades, all the more so since Husserl's attack on "psychologism" has somewhat lost its persuasive momentum, and his emphasis all along on intentionality as a key feature of the mind has not only kept this concept at the forefront of the debate but has also ensured that it is indissolubly linked with his name. Indeed, his reintroduction of the Scholastic term "intentional," and especially his specific interpretation of it, constitute what is probably his most successful contribution to recent and contemporary philosophy. Mental phenomena, Brentano holds, refer to or are directed upon something. This feature is both the universal "mark" of all mental acts and applies exclusively to them, and in this sense it is the distinctive element characterizing mental phenomena *tout court*. This is why Stumpf (*Erscheinungen und psychische Funktionen*, 1907) preferred to speak of mental functions rather than mental acts. For mental acts are not entities closed upon themselves, but rather relate to, vary with, and are in that sense dependent upon what appears in them. In fact we owe the most influential refinement of this concept of intentionality to Husserl, according to whom all consciousness is essentially consciousness-of. For Husserl, this is the basic fact of phenomenology, and the task of phenomenology is to elucidate the nature of the correlation between the act and what this act refers to. In this respect, intentionality turns out to be not just the mark of isolated individual acts, say, of perception, thanks to which something that is given to experience (sense-data) in such mental acts can be interpreted as presenting external objects. Rather,

Husserl believes, every act of perception both points back to itself and forward to other acts of the same kind which have presented or will present the same thing. In this way, the intentionality of an act of perception constitutes the "horizon" of the given act, looking beyond itself to another act and another, without end. Intentional acts additionally serve to establish the identity of a perceived object, when it appears in different aspects or from different sides; they allow us to identify this thing as the same object of different acts of perception with different perceptual qualities. Thus, the same object, say, a house with which we are familiar, may be given in acts of perceiving, remembering, imagining, doubting, thinking, and the like.

This Husserlian doctrine was developed mainly along two different lines. Sartre (L'Etre et le néant, 1943) stressed above all the capacity of consciousness to transcend itself toward a world of things existing in themselves. Consciousness is not about itself, but necessarily refers to a being that differs from it. Consciousness is alterity, non-identity, negativity. It does not coincide with itself and is that which it is not; it is consciousness of objects without ever being an object itself. In a comparable way, Emmanuel Levinas (Totalité et infini, 1961; Autrement qu'être ou au-delà de l'essence, 1974) also posits the irreducible alterity of that which consciousness is related to, but in his case this radical element of otherness is the other person as (s)he is disclosed in the sight of a person's countenance.

Such views, which have Husserl's notion of consciousness as their central axis, were contested by Martin Heidegger (Sein und Zeit, 1927), who incidentally decided on philosophy as a career after reading Brentano's dissertation, On the Manifold Senses of Being, while he was in secondary school. According to Heidegger, the most basic mode of our existence is not so much a conscious relation to things, but rather our factual being in a factual world. This being-in consists in the actual practice of handling things and communicating with other people according to our purposes. The mode in which this attitude discloses things to us is that they appear as utensils that are ready-to-hand and are arranged in zones of nearness and distance. Only when this non-thematic way of using things is disrupted (when the hammer is not in its usual place or is broken), do things turn into objects that are simply before-our-hands.[13] It is this deficient manner of presentation that is wrongly considered primary by

Husserl and others. In a comparable vein, Merleau-Ponty (*Phéno-ménologie de la perception*, 1945) argued that the primordial form of experience is that of embodied perception, thanks to which we are present at the world. The body opens up a world for us, even if only in a limited perspective, and thus is the true basis of all cognition. The subject is a body-subject. In his later work (*Le Visible et l'invisible*, 1964) Merleau-Ponty makes the foundation even more basic. There is continuity between the flesh of the incarnate subject and "the flesh of the world"; both are inextricably intertwined and they interlock in the manner of a "chiasm." This basic texture of the world is the true meaning of intentionality.

An ingenious attempt to dispense with intentionality was launched by Bertrand Russell in his book *The Analysis of Mind* (1921). Following Ernst Mach, he tried to show that the concept of mind is derivative from non-mental phenomena, and that intentionality is not an irreducible character at all. Mental acts are fictions; instead of saying "I think," it would be more correct to say that there is a thought in me. My mental acts come into being only by establishing relations between thoughts and a body, and the person is not an ingredient in a given thought, but rather vice versa. However, this model was definitively refuted by Roderick M. Chisholm, who is largely responsible for the influence of Brentano in analytic philosophy (*Perceiving*, 1957; *Brentano and Meinong Studies*, 1982). Chisholm argued that the referential character of language can be understood only on the basis of the presupposed intentionality of thought. This leads him to posit the primacy of the person as the individual substance which entertains intentional attitudes. As a consequence, linguistic usage can be analyzed in terms of its intentionality, for which he develops an adverbial theory of object-directedness. To say "I see a star" does not of necessity require an act-object-analysis, and neither does the expression "I dance a waltz." Just as the latter means dancing in a certain way ("waltzily"), the former means a manner of seeing ("starrily"). The attribution in question is therefore to be made directly to ourselves, and the person is the primary object of all intentional attitudes. Searle (*Intentionality*, 1983) agrees with Chisholm that philosophy of language is a branch of philosophy of mind, and that the relation of the mind to the world is to be described in terms of intentionality. This does not preclude the possibility that consciousness is biologically based: mental phenomena are both caused by brain activity and realized in the structure of the brain. But this non-ontological understanding of intentionality still insists on the specificity of the phenomenon, which requires in each case an intentional (representative) content that is satisfiable, thanks to its inherent direction of fit, by some object, as well as an intentional (psychological) mode such as a belief or desire. Searle also insists that intentional states are parts of networks of such states and can be satisfied only relative to their position in this network; such networks, moreover, include a background of nonrepresentational mental capacities (biological and cultural resources such as practices and preintentional stances).

A last modification of Brentano's intentionality thesis rejects the term "directedness" as a spatial metaphor in favor of the more appropriate notion of aboutness. This is no doubt a feature of mental experiences, but it is not necessarily restricted to them: linguistic and computer phenomena are also about something. The close relation between this aboutness and the basic notions of representation and symbol processing underlying cognitive science and artificial intelligence will be obvious.

CONTENT AND OBJECT

Thus far we have skirted the question of what intentionality is directed at or about. First we must distinguish between the objects of presentations, the fundamental category of acts in Brentano's classification, and the objects of judgments. As regards presentations, Brentano is of the opinion that they are structured wholes made up, on the one hand, of the act moment proper, and on the other of something that this act moment necessarily refers to. This something, insofar as it is an integral and constitutive element of the complete act, is the content of this act; insofar as the act is directed at it, it is its object. It is the act moment which has empirical and real existence here; the content or object only coexists with it. The object is therefore an immanent object, not a transcendent reality, which for this reason may also be called an intentional object existing only in the presenting act. It must be emphasized that this is merely a description of the structure of the psychological act, and not an attempt to determine the ontological status of this object/content. However, such an ontological turn became inevitable in Brentano's school, once it was confronted with Bolzano's ontological thesis that there are objectless presentations. In order to reconcile this view with the intentionality thesis, Brentano's disciple Kazimierz Twardowski[14] (*Zur Lehre vom Inhalt und Gegenstand der Vorstellungen*, 1894) differentiated between the presentation's internal content which he identifies with its meaning, and its transcendent object. Presentations essentially refer to both. In a case where there is such an object, to call it "presented" by the presentation is to distinguish it from all other objects not presented by a presentation, i.e. to determine this object as an object that is presented. However, in a case where no such object exists, to speak of a presented object means that it is merely presented, i.e. that it is an "object" only in a modified sense of the term: merely presented objects can no more be considered objects than painted horses in an artwork can be considered real horses.

This view, that for a presentation to have an object it is not necessary for the object to exist in some genuine sense, was extensively developed by Meinong (*Über Gegenstandstheorie*, 1904). According to him, to be an object and to exist are widely different predicates. The object as such is beyond being and non-being; it is to be defined simply as that which can be grasped by an act. Intentionality is essential to the act. To be graspable is, however, merely an extrinsic feature of the object it is not essential that the object actually be grasped. In this way not only existing objects, but also facts and factually non-existing objects or ones that are by nature impossible (such as round quadrangles) can be presented and grasped and therefore must count as objects. This very comprehensive theory of objects met with strong opposition not only from Russell,[15] but also, in the version developed by Twardowski, from the early Husserl (*Logische Untersuchungen*, vol. II, 1901). Intentional objects, Husserl declares, are not shadowy objects of some "modified" kind: they are no objects at all. Just as painted horses are paintings, intentional objects are intentions. If acts do have objects, they really do; if not, they simply don't. In other words, there exists no special realm of objects which are called intentional objects and can be distinguished from real ones, for only one world exists. The city of London which I present exists out there, but there exists no replica of it in my thought; the god Jupiter, on the contrary, exists neither out there nor in my mind: it does not exist at all. Husserl also objects to Twardowski's interpretation of act-contents as meanings. Acts are empirical entities, and so must be their constitutive parts, including their contents. Meanings, in contrast, are ideal.

Later Husserl (*Ideen I*, 1913) preferred to call the real act a noesis, to which he opposes a "noema" as its correlate. Noemata are irreal, ideal, and therefore no part of the act. On the one hand, they are the identical poles of meaning which different acts will refer to; on the other, they are the unitary and phenomenologically constituted object of the act and as such they are distinguished from the real object. The tree-noema cannot burn down (for it is the meaning of my tree-perception); the real tree can. Such Husserlian characterizations of the noema led – especially in America – to two widely diverging interpretations: the noema as percept vs. the noema as concept. The first line of interpretation goes back to Gurwitsch, according to whom the noema is an object's perceptual appearance; the object itself is nothing but the ideally realizable totality of noemata presenting it. On the other hand, Dagfinn Fóllesdal has proposed a Fregean reading of the noema as *Sinn*. He understands it as an abstract intensional entity which is the intentional, albeit not the intended object; it brings the mind into contact with this very object. For this reason the noema is not a perceivable thing, but is accessible only in reflection. In short, the question is whether the noema is or is not the intentional object of an act.

The philosopher who most thoroughly eradicates all talk of intentional objects and the like is, apart from the "reism" of the later Brentano himself, undoubtedly Twardowski's disciple Tadeusz Kotarbinski (*Elementy teorii poznania, logiki formalnej i metodologii nauk*, 1929).[16] In his "somatism" he rejects not only universals and sets or classes, but also such putative particulars as processes, events or states of affairs, limiting himself strictly to the admission of real individual and concrete things which in every case are physical bodies. Correspondingly talk of intentional objects or immanent contents (images), which by definition are not three-dimensional, is purely fictitious. There are no acts, contents or objects, say, of hearing, thinking, or desiring; there are only hearers, thinkers, or desirers.

STATES OF AFFAIRS

Whereas the tripartite distinction between the act, the content, and the object of a presentation was worked out gradually by Brentano's followers, Brentano himself had very early on established a comparable distinction in the field of judgment. Certainly, acts of judging are founded on presentations, but these furnish no more than the judgment's matter. A judgment also has a specific judgmental content. Thus to judge "God exists" includes, in addition to the act of judging, the presentation "God" as its matter, but in addition has God's existence as its content. On the other hand, the judgment "God does not exist" is about exactly the same presentation or judgmental matter "God," but its content is God's non-existence. Such judgment contents can also be expressed by that-clauses ("that God exists," "that God does not exist"). In consequence, Stumpf, who introduced the technical name *Sachverhalt* (state of affairs) to denote the judgmental content, understood these states of affairs not only as the proper and direct correlates of acts of judging, but also as immanent to these acts. Out there in the world there may be *Sachen* (affairs), but no *Sachverhalte* (states of affairs). This immanent character allows Stumpf also to accept negative states of affairs. There are no negative things in the world, but negative states of affairs may be thought of. A comparable immanentist position is defended also by Nicholas Rescher,[17] who sees states of affairs as mind-dependent, because there are not only actually conceived states of affairs, but also potential and merely conceivable ones which depend for their being on the capabilities of the mind (as well as on given language systems that allow for the construction of such possibilities). An intermediary position is defended by Meinong (*Über Annahmen*, 1902), who, however, prefers his own term "the objective" to the term "state of affairs." Meinong uses this term, which has nothing to do with the word taken in its ordinary sense, to designate the objects of propositions. On the one hand, these "objectives" are the bearers of truth and of logical modalities such as probability or possibility (there are no probable objects, but it may be probable that an object exists or has a given property); on the other, all objects are minimally comprehended in one "objective" (any object either exists or does not). In the first respect "objectives" resemble propositions; in the second they are ways in which the world is structured.

As with the concept of the object, so also the concept of *Sachverhalt* in Brentano's school underwent a fundamentally objectivist and non-psychological metamorphosis. This was mainly the work of Husserl, who took over the term directly from Stumpf.

According to Husserl, states of affairs are to be distinguished not only from acts of judgment and their possible immanent contents, but also from propositions in the sense of the meanings of judgments. Rather, they are the transcendental ground of judgments and as such constitute, next to the category of objects (things), a second ontological category. They serve as the identical correlate of different acts of judging. Moreover, the same state of affairs may appear in different ways as the acts of judging become modified. The same state of affairs will be given differently according to whether we simply affirm that "S is P" or whether we state that the P-being of S is desirable, doubtful, etc. The claims "a is greater than b" and "b is smaller than a" both express one single state of affairs. Again, the state of affairs as an identical entity cuts across the distinction of acts of different classes. A state of affairs can not only be judged, it can also be merely presented or desired, it can be assumed, put into question or into doubt. This shows that states of affairs are the object not only of judging, but also of presenting and even of emotive acts (in Brentano's terminology, "acts of love and hate"). Indeed, if I wish that the knife should lie on the table, I neither wish the knife nor the table, but am interested in the knife's lying on the table, i.e. that this be the case.

The philosopher who developed the most comprehensive theory of states of affairs was Husserl's student Adolf Reinach,[18] who held that every judgment has its own corresponding state of affairs. The judgment "the rose is red" is true, if there is a red rose there, and the judgment that it is not yellow is true if it is a fact that this rose is not yellow. Thus the world consists of both positive and negative states of affairs. Correspondingly, states of affairs stand in the relation of complementary positivity and negativity: wherever a state subsists, its contradictory opposite will not subsist. Reinach agrees with Meinong that states of affairs are also the bearers of logical modalities. In addition, only states of affairs, not objects, stand in relations of ground and consequent: things themselves do not entail anything, at most their existence or non-existence does. The logical laws of inference therefore derive from the law-governed relations between states of affairs. The principle of non-contradiction as applied to judgments is certainly not a primitive principle, because any judgment (including this principle itself) depends for its truth on some state of affairs or other. Indeed, two contradictory judgments cannot both be correct, because two contradictory states of affairs cannot both subsist.

Ludwig Wittgenstein (*Tractatus*, 1921) countenances only positive states of affairs, be they subsistent or non-subsistent. Objects do not constitute an ontological category next to that of states of affairs, but are the substance of the world that are chained together in the changing and unstable configurations of given states of affairs. However, the variability of these states of affairs is prefigured in and predetermined by the very nature of the objects; and for the objects it is essential to be potentially constitutive parts of some states of affairs, to the exent that it is their defining feature (in much the same way, Meinong insists on the relation between objects and "objectives" whereby objects are parts of or contained in objectives or states of affairs). Wittgenstein clearly distinguishes between facts (the subsistence or non-subsistence of states of affairs) and states of affairs themselves. In contrast with states of affairs, which he regards as always positive, facts may be both positive or negative. States of affairs are the correlates of elementary propositions, in that they are true whenever the simple objects signified by simple names are connected in a way that is mirrored by the structure of the elementary proposition. Since the truth values of such elementary propositions are supposed to be mutually independent, the corresponding states of affairs are too. In contrast with Reinach, Wittgenstein therefore affirms that it is impossible to infer the (non-)existence of one given state from that of another.

A position that oscillates somewhat between the older internalist and the more recent externalist view of states of affairs has been developed more recently in the situation semantics of Jon Barwise and John Perry (*Situations and Attitudes*, 1983).

LANGUAGE

Brentano distinguishes three classes of mental acts: presentations, judgments, and phenomena of interest. Each of these can be expressed by certain linguistic means. Presentations are expressed by names, and names serve, as Twardowski was to point out, a three-fold function. Using a name makes the listener know that we entertain the corresponding presentation. But this name also names something and in addition is meant to awake in the listener the presentation we entertain ourselves; if this process succeeds, then the name is said to have a meaning. This model was extended by Marty to judgments (*Untersuchungen zur Grundlegung der allgemeinen Grammatik und Sprachphilosophie*, vol. I, 1908). Affirmative sentences indicate that in me there occurs a certain state of mind, i.e. a corresponding act of judging. Moreover, my judgings have a certain judgment content, and the second function of the sentence uttered is to represent this content. However, the primary aim of speaking is to influence and direct the mental life of the interlocutor and to call forth a similar judgment in him. For Marty also, this third aspect of judging shows that a sentence is meaningful only if it is understood.

Marty's model was almost entirely taken over by Karl Bühler (*Sprachtheorie*, 1934), although he begins by stating that all investigation of language must start with the concrete "speech event." Following Fernand de Saussure's distinction between *langue* and *parole*, he distinguishes two elements in this event: speech action (*Sprechhandlung*) and linguistic formation. The latter is the ideal system of signs presupposed by and applied in the former. Speech actions are structured after the "organon model": they have the three functions of expression, representation, and appeal. The transmitter, when uttering linguistic noises, produces symptoms that allow the listener to read his mind. As for the listener, speech appeal has the function of signaling to him that the speaker wants to make him behave in certain ways (the rhetorical aspect of language). And finally, to speak means to use symbols which refer to objects and states of affairs respectively. A view very close to Bühler's is that of Alan H. Gardiner (*The Theory of Speech and Language*, 1932), who distinguishes between the act of speech (whose unit is the sentence) and language (whose unit is the word). Words have meanings, but these are nothing but a multitude of ways in which a speaker may legitimately employ a word when he speaks. Language is thus a product of speech, and the meaning of a word derives from the meaning of the sentence in which it occurs.

Marty's account of the expression of the third category of Brentanian mental phenomena, the acts of interest, does not differ from his general view on names and sentences. These acts, which he calls "emotives," differ from judgmental sentences only in that they seek to arouse in the listener not a cognitive act (a judgment), but an emotion or an interest instead. These latter terms should be broadly defined as comprising both acts of feeling and acts of willing. Examples of emotives are therefore not only questions or requests, but also consolations, reproaches, and encouragements – which, in contrast with judgments, can be neither true nor false. However, in view of the fact that states of affairs are the correlates of such acts, too, Husserl declared that these supposed emotives are nothing but judgments: the question "Is S P?" (does object S have property P?) may after all be reformulated as the categorical statement, "I ask, whether S is P."

Husserl's view was fundamentally opposed by Reinach (*Die apriorischen Grundlagen des bürgerlichen Rechtes*, 1913), who, following Marty among others, developed a comprehensive theory of "social acts," i.e. of acts that are of a non-judgmental sort and which for that reason stand beyond the alternative values of true and false. Other kinds of acts, such as taking a decision, entertaining a conviction, judging, even forgiving someone's wrongdoing, can take place internally in the mind without being expressed vis-à-vis a second person; such an expression is accidental to them. Social acts, by contrast, can be performed only if a second person is explicitly addressed and, moreover, if the act in question is understood by that person.

The structure of the social act is as follows. A person, A, must be in a certain state of mind (if you prepare to utter a command, you must have the will that something be done; if you are to ask a question, you must be uncertain about something). However, it is not this state of mind which is expressed in the social act, for this would be no more than a judgment about yourself. The state in question is the necessary basis of the social act, which consists in an externally perceivable communicative action, be it a gesture or – in most cases – a linguistic utterance. The social act *is* the very act of speaking and cannot be detached from it. In the social act we identify three elements. First there is its "body," i.e. the utterance itself, which is not to be confused with involuntary expressions such as cries of pain or reports about mental acts which have just taken place ("I am afraid," "I just gave a command"). Secondly, social acts also have a "soul," which determines whether a given perceivable expression is meant, for example, as a communication, a command, or whatever. After all, these can be couched in the same words, but have different meanings ("The door is open" can be meant as a statement, or as a request to shut the door). And finally, for a social act to be performed it is essential that there be a second person, and that this person understands and responds to the act. This basic structure of the social acts can be modified in various ways. Social acts may be performed by many persons together (A may give a command together with B and C) or be addressed to a collective of persons (D, E, and F together should carry away the table). Somebody may perform a social act on his own authority or by proxy, or a social act may be addressed to a person who is only representing the real addressee. Most important among these modifications are the merely apparent pseudo-performances of going through the motions of such acts that render them deficient. Thus, the required internal state of mind may be lacking (an assertion without a corresponding conviction is a lie, a command given by somebody lacking any authority is at best a stage performance). And a command not heard by the person concerned cannot count as having been given at all. Finally, social acts often are non-repeatable; they can be executed only once in the present tense and in the first person ("I promise"), to be amplified by the term "hereby" ("I hereby promise"). On the other hand, this execution can be reported many times and also in other tenses ("I will promise," "I have promised").

Reinach's theory of social acts was practically forgotten when, half a century later, John L. Austin published his theory of speech acts, *How to Do Things With Words* (1962), which was in many ways comparable. Although there exists no direct link between the two theories and an indirect one has not been proved, Austin's work was developed in a way similar to Reinach's, where only statements as verifiable descriptions of states of affairs, or "constatives," were deemed to be philosophically admissible. To such "constatives" Austin opposes the "performatives" which do not describe anything and cannot be true or false. In order to enact them successfully, you need the appropriate circumstances, correct execution, and certain thoughts or feelings in the persons involved (Reinach's theory omits the second of these three conditions). Infelicities, that is deficiencies (see Reinach's pseudo-performances), may affect all three conditions: in the first case the act will only be purported rather than actually executed, in the second its effect will be undermined, in the third it will be insincere. Austin also recognizes the unique character of performatives in the first person singular present indicative active and also the unique character of the "hereby" formula. In general, speech acts need a locutionary act (an utterance) and an illocutionary act (the intended way in which the utterance is used: informing or warning a person, asking or answering a question, pronouncing a sentence). These are of course close to Reinach's "body and soul" of the social act. In most cases, however a further perlocutionary act is associated with the other two: by uttering certain words, we aim to convince, deter, surprise, mislead, etc. the person to whom we speak. A more comprehensive version of this theory was developed by Searle (*Speech Acts*, 1969), and it is largely in reaction to his work that Reinach's theory has received continuing attention in the Anglo-American world.

PARTS AND WHOLES

Brentano had been confronted with problems about the relations between parts and wholes not only in his analysis of the composite nature of the act, but also when he analyzed the relation between the single act and the unity of consciousness as a whole. He mainly distinguished between a thing's physical (separable) and metaphysical (inseparable) parts. Husserl (Third *Logical Investigation*, 1901) expanded this theory from consciousness to objects at large, developing a comprehensive theory that pertains to (formal) ontology. Objects in general are divided into simple ones without parts and complex ones that have parts. Parts are either independent, that is, detachable from the whole, or dependent and non-detachable. In the first case, they are pieces, in the second, they are moments. The latter are established as features of other parts of the whole, which they require as their metaphysical foundation, whether this foundation be one-sided (acts of judging depend on acts of presenting, but not vice versa) or mutual (extension is unthinkable without color, just as color is without extension). Moreover the metaphysical foundation of a part in another part may be a direct (color and extension) or an indirect one (intensity of the color and extension). Wholes may consist of parts which have their metaphysical foundation, either directly or indirectly, in each other, so that the whole is the same as the totality of its parts, or they will all of them together constitute something new, even though the parts are relatively independent of each other. This is the case, for example, with a flock of geese as compared with the individual geese, or a pattern as compared with the dots it consists of.

This latter type of wholes – consisting of something different from the sum of their parts – had first been introduced by Brentano's disciple Christian von Ehrenfels, in an article which was to secure him pride of place in the history of psychology.[19] Entities such as melodies cannot be the sum of the notes they consist of, for in that case, transposing a melody would mean creating a new one. What you in fact need is the (memory) presence of the successive, temporally distributed notes; the complex of these foundational presentations then allows for a presentation to be founded upon them that is not reducible to the presentations on which they are founded. This is the *Gestalt*. Though the Gestalt is one-sidedly dependent on its foundation, it is also a presentation of its own that may remain invariable notwithstanding certain alterations in its foundation – at least, as long as the most important relations between the elements constituting this foundation are kept intact. Among Meinong's students, the ontological question concerning the status of Gestalts vis-à-vis their foundations was answered by a "production theory." On a production theory of Gestalts, it does not necessarily follow from the fact that the foundations, also referred to as "inferiora" or objects of lower order, are given, that the Gestalt itself is thereby given. Rather, the Gestalt must be actively produced by the act of thinking. The Gestalt, therefore, is an object of thought, in contrast with its inferiora which in most cases are objects of sensation. This relation makes the Gestalt a "superiora" or "object of higher order," whose existence depends on the inferiora or foundations from which it arises. Experimental work along these lines was carried out above all by Meinong's Italian pupil Vittorio Benussi and his followers (Cesare Musatti, Gaetano Kanizsa). However, according to Stumpf's Berlin school (comprising psychologists such as Max Wertheimer, Kurt Koffka, and Wolfgang Köhler), Gestalts occur whenever their foundations occur; all we have to do is to notice them. A Gestalt, therefore, is a concrete structure of elements mutually supporting each other, not an object of thought added to sense data. As an example, we may think of the interchangeability of figure and ground in certain visual images, such as the Neckar cube, in which first one surface and then the other appears to lie in the foreground. On this view of Gestalts, sensations and their configuration do not occur separately. As a result, the "constancy hypothesis" was rejected which implies that stimulation of the sense organ in one certain way would predetermine the corresponding sensation. The "egological approach" to sensation proposed by J. J. Gibson (*The Egological Approach to Visual Perception*, 1979) in some degree harks back to this conception, just as does more recent Gestalt linguistics.

EPILOGUE

By way of epilogue, let us consider Brentano's famous fourth habilitation thesis, in which he states that the method of natural science is also the method of philosophy. Philosophy, in other words, is a scientific enterprise. This has been cashed out in terms of the necessity of logical argument, exact language, and the orientation toward narrowly circumscribed, well-defined, and therefore solvable problems. Such virtues were considered to be the hallmark of "Austrian" philosophy, as distinct from its German counterpart, which indulges in the construction of holistic systems, employing profound and therefore obscure language. This is not the place to discuss the merits of such a thesis. Suffice it to point out that the young mathematician Husserl was won over to philosophy by Brentano, who had convinced him that philosophy, too, could be done in a scientific way.[20] Wherever in twentieth-century philosophy this spirit of science survives, one may suppose that it is at least not alien to Brentano's aspirations, and this is true not only of the Vienna circle, founded in the city where Brentano had taught for so long. However, the members of the Vienna circle went considerably beyond Brentano in identifying not only the methods, but also the positive content, of natural science and philosophy, so that for the Vienna circle there remained only the negative task of showing that beyond the limits of science there was nothing to be known. Analytic philosophy, which from the very beginning had been in contact with and influenced by Brentanism, shared this spirit of science and rationality. It is precisely in this Brentanian spirit, and often with explicit reference to Brentano, that many contemporary thinkers oppose all forms of irrationalism.

NOTES

1. Husserl in 1935 gave the Archives no less than 28 notebooks. Cf. Oskar Kraus, "Brentano-Gesellschaft in Prag," *Philosophia*, 2, 1937, pp. 402–5.
2. Cf. Roberto Poli, "The Brentano Puzzle: an Introduction," in, ed., Roberto Poli, *The Brentano Puzzle* (Aldershot, Brookfield USA, Singapore, Sydney: Ashgate, 1998), p. 1.
3. *Husserliana* VI, 209.
4. For a survey see Herbert Spiegelberg, *Phenomenology in Psychology and Psychiatry* (Evanston, IL: Northwestern University Press, 1972).
5. His *Daseinsanalyse* is, however, primarily based on Heideggerian thought.
6. He is the best-known representative of a Dutch group of phenomenological psychologists. Cf. Joseph J. Kockelmans (ed.), *Phenomenological Psychology. The Dutch School* (Dordrecht: Martinus Nijhoff, 1987).
7. Also his *Daseinsanlytik* mainly draws on Heidegger.
8. This work on the classification of conscious attitudes was followed in 1898 by Stout's *Manual of Psychology*, a genetic exposition of psychology, which became a standard text-book for generations of students in British universities.
9. G. E. Moore, "*The Origin of the Knowledge of Right and Wrong* by Franz Brentano," *International Journal of Ethics*, 14, 1903, pp. 115–23.
10. It was apparently because of this anti-Brentanist stance that Stout initially refused to publish Russell's "On Denoting" (1905) in which this theory was first developed. An attempt to reconcile the seemingly contradictory positions of Meinong and Russell is to be found in Hector-Neri Castañeda's "guise theory" which admits only properties (relations) and operators such as quantifiers, which generate complex objects from simpler ones.
11. For a survey cf., e.g. Samuel Guttenplan (ed.), *A Companion to the Philosophy of Mind* (Oxford: Blackwell, 1994); Jaegwon Kim, *Philosophy of Mind* (Boulder, CO: Westview Press, 1996); Georges Rey, *Contemporary Philosophy of Mind* (Oxford: Blackwell, 1997).
12. John R. Searle, *Mind, Language and Society* (New York: Basic Books, 1998).
13. Only recently it has become clear that Heidegger's distinction between things ready-to-hands and before-our-hands is comparable to Gilbert Ryle's famous distinction in *The Concept of Mind* (1949) between knowing-how and knowing-that. In Brentanist terms, both are modalities of intentionality.

14. Later he later was to become the "father of Polish logic"; best known among the members of his Lvov–Warsaw school are Jan Łukasiewicz, Kazimierz Ajdukiewicz, and Alfred Tarski.

15. Russell took exception to the fact that impossible objects violated the principle of non-contradiction. Meinong agreed, but could not see a problem here. This principle applies, after all, only to objects that can exist or obtain. Impossible objects by definition cannot, and therefore are exempt from the principle. Still, they function as truthmakers of true and wrong statements: it is correct to state that the round quadrangle is round, but it is wrong to state that it is elliptic.

16. It will not come as a surprise to learn that Kotarbinski has written an important article on later Brentano: "Franz Brentano comme réiste," *Revue internationale de philosophie*, 20, 1966, pp. 459–76.

17. Cf. his "The Ontology of the Possible," in, ed., M. J. Loux, *The Possible and the Actual* (Ithaca, NY: Cornell University Press, 1979), ch. 8.

18. Cf. Reinach's article "On the Theory of the Negative Judgment," in, ed., Barry Smith, *Parts and Moments* (Munich, Vienna: Philosophia, 1982), pp. 315–77.

19. "Über Gestaltqualitäten," *Vierteljahrsschrift für wissenschaftliche Philosophie*, 14, 1890, pp. 249–92.

20. It should be remembered that in certain surveys Husserl figures as the fountainhead of "postmodern" philosophy.

BIBLIOGRAPHY

WORKS BY BRENTANO

German Texts (Monographs, books and pamphlets)

Von der mannigfachen Bedeutung des Seienden nach Aristoteles (Freiburg i. Br.: Herder, 1862).

Ad disputationem qua theses gratiosi philosorum ordinis consensu et auctoritate pro impetranda venia docendi in alma universitate julio-maximiliana defendet (Aschaffenburg: J. W. Schipner, 1866).

Die Psychologie des Aristoteles, insbesondere seine Lehre vom Nous Poietikos (Mainz: Franz Kirchheim, 1867).

Psychologie vom empirischen Standpunkt (Leipzig: Duncker and Humblot, 1874); second edition, Oskar Kraus (Leipzig: Felix Meiner Verlag, 1924).

Über die Gründe der Entmutigung auf philosophischem Gebiete (Vienna: Braumüller, 1874).

Was für Philosophie manchmal Epoche macht (Vienna, Pest and Leipzig: Hartleben, 1876).

Alte und neue Logik. Lecture notes, 1877. Houghton Library, Harvard. Formerly filed with EL72.

Die elementare Logik und die in ihr nötigen Reformen. Lecture notes for 1879, re-used with modifications 1884–5. Houghton Library, Harvard.

Neue Rätsel von Änigmatias (Vienna: Carl Gerolds Sohn, 1879); second edition, *Änigmatias: Neue Rätsel* (München: Oskar Beck, 1909).

Logik. Lecture notes, late 1880s. Houghton Library, Harvard.

Über den Creatianismus des Aristoteles (Vienna: Carl Gerolds Sohn, 1882).

"Miklosich über subjektlose Sätze". In VE 1925, pp. 183–98 (This additional essay was not translated for the English edition of the *Psychology*).

Offener Brief an Herrn Professor Eduard Zeller aus Anlass seiner Schrift über die Lehre des Aristoteles von der Ewigkeit des Geistes (Leipzig: Duncker and Humblot, 1883).

Vom Ursprung sittlicher Erkenntnis (Leipzig: Duncker and Humblot, 1889); second edition, Oskar Kraus (ed.) (Leipzig: Felix Meiner Verlag, 1922); third edition (Leipzig: Felix Meiner Verlag, 1934).

Das Genie (Leipzig: Duncker and Humblot, 1892).

Das Schlechte als Gegenstand dichterischer Darstellung (Leipzig: Duncker and Humblot, 1892).

Über die Zukunft der Philosophie (Vienna: Alfred Hölder, 1893), Oskar Kraus (ed.) (Leipzig: Felix Meiner Verlag, 1929); second edition (Hamburg: Felix Meiner Verlag, 1968).

Die vier Phasen der Philosophie und ihr augenblicklicher Stand (Stuttgart: Cotta, 1895), Oskar Kraus (ed.) (Leipzig: Felix Meiner Verlag, 1926); (Hamburg: Felix Meiner Verlag, 1968).

Meine letzten Wünsche für Österreich (Stuttgart: Cotta, 1895).

Noch ein Wort über das Ehehinderniss der höheren Weihen und feierlichen Gelübde (Vienna: Manz, 1895).

Zur eherechtlichen Frage in Österreich: Krasnapolski's Rettungsversuch einer verlorenen Sache (Berlin: J. Guttentag, 1896).

Krasnapolski's letzter Versuch (Leipzig: J. J. Arndt, 1896).

Neue Vertheidigung der Spanischen Partie (Vienna: Verlag der Wiener Schachzeitung (Georg Marco), 1900); *Neue Vertheidigung der Spanischen Partie: Zweiter Artikel* (Vienna: Verlag der Wiener Schachzeitung, Georg Marco, 1900).

Untersuchungen zur Sinnespsychologie (Leipzig: Duncker and Humblot, 1907); second edition, Roderick M. Chisholm and Reinhard Fabian (ed.) (Hamburg: Felix Meiner Verlag, 1979).

Aristoteles und seine Weltanschauung (Leipzig: Quelle and Meyer, 1911).

Aristoteles Lehre vom Ursprung des menschlichen Geistes (Leipzig: Veit and Comp, 1911); second edition (Hamburg: Felix Meiner Verlag, 1980).

Von der Klassifikation der psychischen Phänomene (Leipzig: Duncker and Humblot, 1911).

Die Lehre Jesu und ihre bleibende Bedeutung, Alfred Kastil (ed.) (Leipzig: Felix Meiner Verlag, 1922).

Versuch über die Erkenntnis, Alfred Kastil (ed.) (Leipzig: Felix Meiner Verlag, 1925); second enlarged edition (Hamburg: Felix Meiner Verlag, 1970).

Vom sinnlichen und noetischen Bewußtsein (Psychologie III), Oskar Kraus (ed.) (Leipzig: Felix Meiner Verlag, 1928); second edition, F. Mayer-Hillebrand (ed.) (Hamburg: Felix Meiner Verlag, 1968).

Vom Dasein Gottes, Alfred Kastil (ed.) (Leipzig: Felix Meiner Verlag, 1929).

Wahrheit und Evidenz, Alfred Kastil (ed.) (Leipzig: Felix Meiner Verlag, 1930).

Kategorienlehre, Alfred Kastil (ed.) (Leipzig: Felix Meiner Verlag, 1933).

Grundlegung und Aufbau der Ethik, F. Mayer-Hillebrand (ed.) (Bern: A. Francke, 1952).

Religion und Philosophie, F. Mayer-Hillebrand (ed.) (Bern: A. Francke, 1954).

Die Lehre vom Richtigen Urteil, F. Mayer-Hillebrand (ed.) (Bern: A. Francke, 1956).

Grundzüge der Äesthetik, F. Mayer-Hillebrand (ed.) (Bern: A. Francke, 1959); second edition (Hamburg: Felix Meiner Verlag, 1988).

Geschichte der Griechischen Philosophie, F. Mayer-Hillebrand (ed.) (Bern: A. Francke, 1963).

Die Abkehr vom Nichtrealen, F. Mayer-Hillebrand (ed.) (Bern: A. Francke, 1966).

Philosophische Untersuchungen zu Raum, Zeit und Kontinuum, with commentary by Alfred Kastil, Stephen Körner and Roderick M. Chisholm (eds.) (Hamburg: Felix Meiner Verlag, 1976).

Geschichte der mittelalterlichen Philosophie, Klaus Hedwig (ed.) (Hamburg: Felix Meiner Verlag, 1980).

Deskriptive Psychologie, Roderick M. Chisholm and Wilhelm Baumgartner (eds.) (Hamburg: Felix Meiner Verlag, 1982).

Über Aristoteles, Rolf George (ed.) (Hamburg: Felix Meiner Verlag, 1986).

Geschichte der Philosophie der Neuzeit, Klaus Hedwig (ed.) (Hamburg: Felix Meiner Verlag, 1987).

Über Ernst Machs "Erkenntnis und Irrtum" (aus dem Nachlaß), Roderick M. Chisholm and Johann C. Marek (eds.) (Amsterdam: Rodopi, 1988).

Briefe an Carl Stumpf (1867–1917), Gerhard Oberkofler and Peter Goller (eds.) (Graz: Akademische Druck- und Verlagsanstalt, 1989).

English Translations

The Origin of the Knowledge of Right and Wrong, trans. Cecil Hague (London: Archibald Constable and Co. Ltd., 1902); trans. Roderick M. Chisholm and E. Schneewind (London: Routledge and Kegan Paul, 1969).

The True and the Evident, trans. Roderick M. Chisholm and E. Politzer (London: Routledge and Kegan Paul, 1966).

The Foundation and Construction of Ethics, trans. E. Schneewind (London: Routledge and Kegan Paul, 1973).

Psychology from an Empirical Standpoint, trans. Linda L. McAlister (London: Routledge and Kegan Paul, 1973); second edition with an introduction by Peter Simons (London: Routledge, 1995).

On the Several Senses of Being in Aristotle, trans. Rolf George (Berkeley: University of California Press, 1975).

The Psychology of Aristotle: in particular his Doctrine of the Active Intellect, trans. Rolf George (Berkeley, CA: University of California Press, 1977).

Aristotle and his World View, trans. Rolf George and Roderick M. Chisholm (Berkeley, CA: University of California Press, 1978).

Sensory and Noetic Consciousness: Psychology from an Empirical Standpoint III, trans. Linda L. McAlister and Margarete Schattle (London: Routledge and Kegan Paul, 1981).

The Theory of Categories, trans. Roderick M. Chisholm and Norbert Gutterman (Boston and Dordrecht: Martinus Nijhoff, 1981).

Descriptive Psychology, trans. and ed. Benito Müller (London and New York: Routledge, 1982).

On the Existence of God: Lectures Given at the Universities of Würzburg and Vienna (1868–1891), trans. Susan F. Krantz (Dordrecht: Martinus Nihhoff Publishers, 1987).

Philosophical Investigations on Space, Time, and the Continuum, trans. Barry Smith (London: Croom Helm, 1987).

Essays and Articles

"Geschichte der kirchlichen Wissenschaften," in, eds., Johann Adam Möhler, Kirchengeschichte, P. R. Grams, Band II, 526–84; Band III, Part Two, 103–4 (Regensburg: Georg Joseph Mans, 1867).

"August Comte und die positive Philosophie," *Chilianeum: Blätter für katholische Philosophie, Kunst, und Leben*, Neue Folge, 2, 1869, pp. 15–37.

Review of Friedrich Kampe, *Die Erkenntnistheorie des Aristoteles*, *Zeitschrift für Philosophie und philosophische Kritik*, 59, 1872, pp. 219–38 and 60, 1872, pp. 81–127.

"Thomas von Aquin" (review of Johannes Delitzsch, *Die Gotteslehre des Thomas von Aquino*), *Theologisches Literaturblatt*, F. H. Reusch (ed.), 5, 1872, pp. 459–63.

"Herr Horwicz as Rezensent: Ein Beitrag zur Orientierung über unsere wissenschaftlichen Kulturzustände," *Philosophische Monatshefte*, 4, 1875.

"Über ein optisches Paradoxon," *Zeitschrift für Psychologie und Physiologie der Sinnesorgane*, 3, 1892, pp. 349–58; 5, 1893, pp. 61–82.

"Der Brief an Anton Marty (März 1895)" in Kraus, "Zur Phänomengnosie."

"Zur Lehre von der Empfindung," *Dritter internationaler Congress für Psychologie in München* (Munich: Lehmann, 1897), pp. 112–33.

"Von der psychologischen Analyse der Tonqualitäten in ihre eigentlich ersten Elemente," *Atti del V. Congresso Internazionale di Psicologia* (Rome: Forzani, 1905), pp. 157–65.

"Aristoteles," in, ed., E. V. Aster, *Grosse Denker*, Band I (Leipzig: Quelle and Meyer, 1911), pp. 155–207.

"Zur Lehre von Raum und Zeit," *Kant-Studien*, 25, 1920, pp. 1–23.

"Religion und Philosophie," *Philosophie und Leben*, Band I, 1925, pp. 333–9, 370–81, 410–16.
"La Rivelazione Soprannaturale ed il dovere di crederla," trans. Mario Puglisi, *Il Progresso Religioso*, 2, 1926, pp. 3–22.
"Über Prophetie," in, ed., Oskar Kraus, *Jahrbuch der Charakterologie*, Band II–III, 1926, pp. 259–64.
"Gegen entia rationis, sogenannte irreale oder ideale, Gegenstände," in, ed., Oskar Kraus, *Philosophische Hefte*, 2, 1929, pp. 257–74.
"Briefe Franz Brentanos an Hugo Bergmann," *Philosophy and Phenomenological Research*, 7, 1946, pp. 83–158.
"Das Franz Brentano-Gutachten über die päpstliche Infallibilität," in, ed., Ludwig Lenhart, *Archiv für mittelrheinische Kirchengeschichte*, Band V, 1955, pp. 295–334.

SELECTED WRITINGS ON BRENTANO

Albertazzi, Liliana, "Brentano and Mauthner's Critique of Language," *Brentano Studien*, 2, 1989, pp. 145–59.
"Brentano, Meinong and Husserl on Internal Time," *Brentano Studien*, 3, 1990–1, pp. 89–109.
"The Phenomenon of Time in the Brentanist Tradition: Enzo Bonaventura", *Brentano Studien*, 8, 2000, pp. 163–92.
Albertazzi, Liliana and Libardi, Massimo and Poli, Roberto (eds.), *The School of Franz Brentano* (Dordrecht, Boston, London: Kluwer Academic Publishers, 1996).
Albuqerque, Daniel, "Machian Positivism versus Brentanian Psychological Descriptivism," *Brentano Studien*, 8, 2000, pp. 211–18.
Anasvili, Valerij, "Rezeption Franz Brentanos in Russland (einleitende Materialen)," *Brentano Studien*, 8, 2000, pp. 219–31.
Antonelli, Mauro, "Franz Brentano und die Wiederentdeckung der Intentionalität: Richtigstellung herkommlicher Missverstandnisse und Missdeutungen," *Grazer Philosophische Studien*, 58–9, 2000, pp. 93–117.
Seiendes Bewusstsein, Intentionalität im Frühwerk von Franz Brentano (Freiburg-München: Karl Albert Verlag, 2001).
Baumgartner, Elisabeth and Baumgartner, Wilhelm, "Von Brentano zu Külpe: Die deskriptive Psychologie Brentanos und die 'Würzburger Schule' der Denkpsychologie," *Brentano Studien*, 7, 1997, pp. 31–52.
Baumgartner, Wilhelm, "Die Begründung von Wahrheit durch Evidenz: Der Beitrag Brentanos," in *Gewißheit und Gewissen: Festschrift für Franz Wiedmann zum 60. Geburtstag* (Würzburg: Königshausen und Neumann, 1987), pp. 93–116.

"Mills und Brentanos Methode der beschreibenden Analyse," *Brentano Studien*, 2, 1989, pp. 63–78.

"Objects Analysed Brentano's Way Toward the Identity of Objects," *Topoi*, Supplement, 4, 1989, pp. 20–30.

"Brentano, Franz," in, eds., Hans Burkhardt and Barry Smith, *Handbook of Metaphysics and Ontology* (Munich: Philosophia Verlag, 1991), vol. I, pp. 104–7.

"Act, Content and Object," in, eds., Albertazzi, Libardi, and Poli, 1996, pp. 235–8.

"On the Origins of Phenomenology: Franz Brentano," in, eds., Elisabeth Baumgartner, Wilhelm Baumgartner, Bojan Borstner, Matjaz Potrc, John Shawe-Taylor, and Elizabeth Valentine *Handbook of Phenomenology and Cognitive Science* (Dettelbach: Verlag Josef H. Röll, 1996), pp. 25–35.

"Franz Brentano (1838–1917): Philosoph und Lehrer Sigmund Freuds," in, ed., Bernd Heidenreich, *Geist und Macht: Die Brentanos* (Wiesbaden: Westdeutscher Verlag, 2000), pp. 117–30.

Baumgartner, Wilhelm, and Simons, Peter, "Brentanos Mereologie," *Brentano Studien*, 4, 1992–3, pp. 53–77.

Becker, Oskar. "Beiträge zur phänomenologischen Begründung der Geometrie und ihrer physikalischen Anwendung," *Jahrbuch für Philosophie und phänomenologische Forschung*, 6, 1923, pp. 285–560.

Bell, David, *Husserl* (London and New York: Routledge, 1990).

Bergmann, Gustav, *Realism: a Critique of Brentano and Meinong* (Madison, WI: University of Wisconsin Press, 1967).

Bergmann, Hugo, *Untersuchungen zum Problem der Evidenz der inneren Wahrnehmung* (Halle: Niemeyer, 1908).

"Brentano's Theory of Induction," *Philosophy and Phenomenological Research*, 5, 1944, pp. 281–92.

"Unbekannte Manuskripte Franz Brentanos," in, eds., James Frank, Hermann Minkowski, and Ernst J. Sternglass, *Horizons of a Philosopher: Essays in Honor of David Baumgardt* (Leiden, 1963), pp. 34–49.

"Brentano on the History of Greek Philosophy," *Philosophy and Phenomenological Research*, 26, 1965, pp. 94–9.

"Franz Brentano," *Revue internationale de Philosophie*, 20, 1966, pp. 349–72.

Binder, Thomas, "Die Brentano-Gesellschaft und das Brentano-Archiv in Prag," *Grazer Philosophische Studien*, 58–9, 2000, pp. 533–65.

"Die Prager Brentano Gesellschaft," *Brentano Studien*, 8, 2000, pp. 259–86.

Bolzano, Bernard. *Theory of Science: Attempt at a detailed and in the main novel Exposition of Logic with constant Attention to earlier Authors*, trans. Rolf George (Berkeley, CA: University of California Press, 1972).

Brandl, Johannes, "Vorwort zu Franz Brentanos 'Von der Natur der Vorstellung,'" *Conceptus*, 21, 1987, pp. 19–23.
"Brentano's Theory of Judgement," *Stanford Encyclopedia of Philosophy*
   (http://plato.stanford.edu/entries/brentano-judgement/), 2000.
Brentano, J. C. M., "The Manuscripts of Franz Brentano," *Revue Interna-
   tionale de Philosophie*, 20, 1966, pp. 477–82.
Brown, Deborah, "Immanence and Individuation: Brentano and the Scholas-
   tics on Knowledge of Singulars," *The Monist*, 83, 2000, pp. 22–47.
Brozek, Josef and Hoskovec, Jiri, "Psychology, T. G. Masaryk and Franz
   Brentano, with Special Reference to Their Correspondence," *Brentano
   Studien*, 8, 2000, pp. 115–19.
Brück, Maria, *Über das Verhältnis Edmund Husserls zu Franz Brentano,
   vornehmlich mit Rücksicht auf Brentanos Psychologie* (Würzburg:
   Triltsch, 1933).
Buzzoni, M., "Brentano, Sprache, Ontologie und Person," *Brentano Studien*,
   1, 1988, pp. 153–87.
Campos, Eliam, *Die Kantkritik Brentanos* (Bonn: Bouvier Verlag Herbert
   Grundmann, 1979).
Carroll, L., *Symbolic Logic*, ed., W. W. Bartley III. New York: Potter, 1977.
Cavallin, Jens. *Content and Object: Husserl, Twardowski and Psychologism*
   (Dordrecht, Boston, London: Kluwer, 1997).
Celms, Theodor. "Der phänomenologische Idealismus Husserls," *Acts Uni-
   versitatis Latviensis* 19, 1928, pp. 249–441.
Chisholm, Roderick M., *Perceiving: A Philosophical Study* (Ithaca: Cornell
   University Press, 1957).
"Brentano's Theory of Correct Emotion", *Revue Internationale de
   Philosophie*, 20, 1966, pp. 395–415.
"Brentano on Descriptive Psychology and the Intentional", in, eds., Lee
   and Mandelbaum, *Phenomenology and Existentialism* (1967), pp. 1–23.
"Franz Brentano," in, ed., Paul Edwards, *Encyclopedia of Philosophy* (New
   York: Collier-Macmillan, 1967), pp. 365–8.
"Brentano's Descriptive Psychology", *Akten des XVI. internationalen
   Kongresses der Philosophie*, 2, University of Vienna, Herder, 1968,
   pp. 164–74.
"Brentano als analytischer Metaphysiker," in, ed., Marek, *Österreichische
   Philosophie* (1977), pp. 77–82.
"Brentano's Analysis of the Consciousness of Time," *Midwest Studies in
   Philosophy*, 6, 1981, pp. 3–16.
Brentano and Meinong Studies (Atlantic Highland, NJ: Humanities
   Press, 1982) ("Brentano's Theory of Substance and Accident," pp. 3–16;
   "Brentano's Theory of Judgement," pp. 17–36).

Brentano and Intrinsic Value (Cambridge: Cambridge University Press, 1986).

"Brentano's Theory of Pleasure and Pain," *Topoi*, 6, 1987, pp. 59–64.

"Brentano and Marty on Content: a Synthesis Suggested by Brentano," in, ed., Mulligan, 1–9.

"Spatial Continuity and the Theory of Part and Whole: a Brentano Study," *Brentano Studien*, 4, 1992–3, pp. 11–23.

"Brentano on 'Unconscious Consciousness,'" in Poli (ed.), 1993, 153–9.

Chisholm, Roderick M. and Haller, Rudolf (eds.), *Die Philosophie Franz Brentanos: Beiträge zur Brentano-Konferenz* (Amsterdam: Rodopi, 1978).

Chrudzimski, Arkadiusz, "Die Theorie der Intentionalität Franz Brentanos," *Grazer Philosophische Studien*, 57, 1999, pp. 45–66.

"Die Theorie des Zeitbewusstseins Franz Brentanos aufgrund der unpublizierten Manuskripte," *Brentano Studien*, 8, 2000, pp. 149–61.

Intentionalitätstheorie beim frühen Brentano, Phaenomenologica Series 159 (Dordrecht, Boston, MA, London: Kluwer Academic Publishers, 2001).

Dölling, Evelyn, "Kritik der Urteilslehre: Land versus Brentano, mit Blick auf Frege," *Brentano Studien*, 7, 1997, pp. 123–46.

DuBois, James M., "Investigating Brentano's Reism," *Brentano Studien*, 6, 1996, pp. 283–95.

Eaton, H. O., *The Austrian Philosophy of Values* (Norman, OK: University of Oklahoma Press, 1930).

Fabian, R. and Simons, P., "The Second Austrian School of Value Theory," in, eds., W. Grassl and B. Smith, *Austrian Economics. Historical and Philosophical Background* (New York: New York University Press, 1986), pp. 37–101.

Føllesdal, Dagfinn, "Brentano and Husserl on Intentional Objects and Perception," in, eds., Chisholm and Haller, *Philosophie Franz Brentanos*, 1978, pp. 83–94.

Fürth, Rheinhold, Kraus, Oskar, Kastil, Alfred, Strohal, Richard, Link, P. F., and Rogge, Eberhard (eds.), *Naturwissenschaft und Metaphysik: Abhandlungen zum Gedächtnis des 100. Geburtstages vom Franz Brentano* (Brünn and Leipzig: Röhrer, 1939).

Galewicz, Wlodzimierz, "Substanz und Individuation in Brentanos Kategorienlehre," *Brentano Studien*, 4, 1992–3, pp. 79–88.

"Brentano und der epistemologische Fundamentalismus," *Brentano Studien*, 8, 2000, pp. 95–106.

George, Rolf, "Brentano's Relation to Aristotle," in, eds., Chisholm and Haller, *Philosophie Franz Brentanos*, 1978, pp. 249–66.

Gilson, Etienne, "Franz Brentano's Interpretation of Medieval Philosophy" *Medieval Studies*, 1939, pp. 1–10.

Gilson, Lucie, *La Psychologie Descriptive selon Franz Brentano* (Paris: Vrin, 1955).

Méthode et métaphysique selon Franz Brentano (Paris: Vrin, 1955).

"Science et Philosophie selon Franz Brentano," *Revue Internationale de Philosophie*, 20, 1966, pp. 416–33.

Haller, Rudolf, "Brentanos Sprachkritik oder daß 'man unterscheiden muß, was es (hier) zu unterscheiden gibt,'" in, eds., Chisholm and Haller, *Philosophie Franz Brentanos*, 1978, pp. 211–14.

"Franz Brentano, ein Philosoph des Empirismus," *Brentano Studien*, 1, 1988, pp. 19–30.

"Bemerkungen zu Brentanos Ästhetik," *Brentano Studien*, 5, 1994, pp. 177–86.

Hedwig, Klaus, "Der scholastische Kontext des Intentionalen bei Brentano," in, eds., Chisholm and Haller, *Philosophie Franz Brentanos*, 1978, pp. 67–82.

"Intention: Outlines for the History of a Phenomenological Concept," *Philosophy and Phenomenological Research*, 39, 1979, pp. 326–40.

"Brentano's Hermeneutics," *Topoi*, 6, 1987, pp. 3–10.

"Über das intentionale Korrelatenpaar," *Brentano Studien*, 3, 1990–1, pp. 47–61.

Hillebrand, F. *Die neuen Theorien der kategorischen Schlüsse (NTKS)* (Vienna: Hälder, 1891).

Höfler, Alois (in collaboration with Alexius Meinong), *Logik* (Vienna: Tempsky Verlag, 1890).

Howarth, J. M., "Franz Brentano and Object-Directedness," *The Journal of the British Society for Phenomenology*, 2, 1980, pp. 239–54.

Husserl, Edmund. *Philosophie der Arithmetik. Psychologische und logische Untersuchungen*. First edition. (Halle a. S.: C. E. M. Pfeffer Robert Stricker, 1891).

"Erinnerung an Franz Brentano," in, ed., Kraus, *Brentano*, 1919, pp. 151–67.

Philosophie der Arithmetik. Mit ergänzenden Texten (1890–1901), in, ed., Lother Eley, *Husserliana XII* (The Hague: Martinus Nijhoff, 1970).

Logical Investigations. Trans. F. Findlay, 2 vols. (London: Routledge and Kegan Paul, 1970).

Vorlesungen zur Phänomenologie des inneren Zeitbewusstseins (Tübingen: Niemeyer, 1980).

Ideas pertaining to a Pure Phenomenology and to Phenomenological Philosophy in *Collected Works*, Vol. II. Trans. F. Kersten (The Hague, Boston, London: Martinus Nijhoff, 1982).

Einleitung in die Logik und Erkenntnistheorie. Vorlesungen 1906/1907, ed. Ulrich Melle (The Hague: Martinus Nijhoff, 1984).

Aufsätze und Vorträge (1911–1921) in, eds., Thomas Nenon and Hans-Rainer Sepp, *Husserliana XXV* (Dordrecht: Martinus Nijhoff, 1987).

"Husserls Abhandlung 'Intentionale Gegenstände'. Edition der ursprünglichen Druckfassung," ed. Karl Schuhmann, in *Brentano–Studien*, 3, 1990/1, pp. 137–76.

On the Phenomenology of the Consciousness of Internal Time (1893–1917), trans. John Barnett Brough (Dordrecht, Boston, London: Kluwer, 1991).

Briefwechsel, 10 volumes, in, ed., Karl Schuhmann in collaboration with Elisabeth Schuhmann, *Husserliana Dokumente* III (Dordrecht, Boston, London: Kluwer, 1994).

Early Writings in the Philosophy of Logic and Mathematics, trans. Dallas Willard (Dordrecht, London, Boston: Kluwer, 1994).

Logik. Vorlesung 1896, in, ed., Elisabeth Schuhmann, *Husserliana Materialienbände* I (Dordrecht, Boston, London: Kluwer, 2001).

Jacquette, Dale, Review of Roderick M. Chisholm, *Brentano and Intrinsic Value*, The Journal of Value Inquiry, 22, 1988, pp. 331–4.

"The Origins of *Gegenstandstheorie*: Immanent and Transcendent Intentional Objects in Brentano, Twardowski, and Meinong," *Brentano Studien*, 3, 1990–1, pp. 277–302.

"Brentano, Franz," in, ed., Robert Audi, *The Cambridge Dictionary of Philosophy* (Cambridge: Cambridge University Press, 1995), pp. 86–87; second edition (1999), pp. 100–1.

"*Fin de Siècle* Austrian Thought and the Rise of Scientific Philosophy," History of European Ideas, 27, 2001, pp. 307–15.

"Brentano's Scientific Revolution in Philosophy," Spindel Conference 2001, *Origins: the Common Sources of Analytic and Phenomenological Traditions*, Southern Journal of Philosophy, Spindel Conference Supplement, 40, 2002, pp. 193–221.

Review of Arkadiusz Chrudzimski, *Intentionalitätstheorie beim frühen Brentano*, The Review of Metaphysics, 46, 2002, pp. 163–7.

Johnston, William M., *The Austrian Mind: an Intellectual and Social History 1848–1938* (Berkeley, CA: University of California Press, 1972).

Kamitz, Reinhard, "Acts and Relations in Brentano," *Analysis*, 22, 1962, pp. 73–8.

Kastil, Alfred, *Die Philosophie Franz Brentanos: Eine Einführung in seine Lehre* (Bern: A. Francke, 1951).

Katkov, G., "Bewußtsein, Gegenstand, Sachverhalt: Eine Brentano-Studie," *Archiv für die gesamte Psychologie*, 75, 1930, pp. 462–544.

Kent, O. T., "Brentano and the Relational View of Consciousness," *Man and World*, 17, 1984, pp. 19–51.

Körner, Stephen, "Über Brentanos Reismus und die extensionale Logik," in, eds., Chisholm and Haller, *Philosophie Franz Brentanos*, 1978, pp. 29–43.

"On Brentano's Objections to Kant's Theory of Knowledge," *Topoi*, 6, 1987, pp. 11–19.

Kortooms, Toine. *The Phenomenology of Time. Edmund Husserl's Analysis of Time-Consciousness* (Dordrecht, Boston, London: Kluwer, 2002).

Kotarbinski, Tadeusz, "France Brentano comme réiste," *Revue Internationale de Philosophie*, 20, 1966, pp. 459–76.

"Franz Brentano as Reist," in, ed., McAlister, *Philosophy of Brentano*, 1976, pp. 194–203 (trans. from French as "Franz Brentano as Reist," Linda L. McAlister and Margarete Schättle, and reprinted from *Revue Internationale de Philosophie*, 20, 1966, pp. 459–76).

Krantz, Susan, "Brentano's Arguments Against Aristotle for the Immateriality of the Soul," *Brentano Studien*, 1, 1988, pp. 63–74.

"Brentano on 'Unconscious Consciousness,'" *Philosophy and Phenomenological Research*, 50, 1990, pp. 745–53.

"Brentano's Revision of the Correspondence Theory," *Brentano Studien*, 3, 1990–1, pp. 79–87.

"Brentanian Unity of Consciousness," *Brentano Studien*, 4, 1992–3, pp. 89–99.

"Brentano's Empirical Aesthetics," *Brentano Studien*, 9, 1999, pp. 215–28.

"Brentano: Intentionality and Consciousness," in *The Edinburgh Encyclopedia of Continental Philosophy* (Edinburgh: Edinburgh University Press, 1999), pp. 261–9.

Kraus, Oskar, *Franz Brentano: Zur Kenntnis seines Lebens und seiner Lehre, mit Beiträgen von Carl Stumpf und Edmund Husserl* (Munich: Beck, 1919).

Brentanos Stellung zur Phaenomenologie und Gegenstandstheorie (Leipzig: Felix Meiner Verlag, 1924).

"Zur Phänomenognosie des Zeitbewußtseins," *Archiv für die gesamte Psychologie*, 75, 1930, pp. 1–22.

Land, J. P. N., "Brentano's Logical Innovations," *Mind*, 1876, pp. 289–92.

Lee, E. N. and Mandelbaum, Maurice (eds.), *Phenomenology and Existentialism* (Baltimore, MD: Johns Hopkins University Press, 1967).

Leśniewski, Stanisaw, *Collected Works*, 2 vols., eds., S. J. Surma, J. T. Srzednicki, D. I. Barnett and V. F. Rickey (Warsaw, Dordrecht, Boston, MA, London: PWN and Kluwer, 1992).

Libardi, Massimo, "Franz Brentano (1838–1917)," in, eds., Albertazzi, Libardi, and Poli, School of Franz Brentano, 1996, pp. 25–79.

MacNamara, John and Boudewijnse, Geert-Jan, "Brentano's Influence on Ehrenfels's Theory of Perceptual Gestalts," Journal for the Theory of Social Behaviour, 25, 1995, pp. 401–18.

Marek, J. C. (ed.), Österreichische Philosophie und ihr Einfluß auf die analytische Philosophie, Conceptus, 1, 1977.

Margolius, H., Die Ethic Franz Brentanos (Leipzig: Felix Meiner Verlag, 1929).

Marras, Ausonio, "Scholastic Roots of Brentano's Conception of Intentionality," in, ed., McAlister, Philosophy of Brentano, 1976, pp. 128–39.

Mayer-Hillebrand, F., "Franz Brentanos ursprüngliche und spätere Seinslehre und ihre Beziehungen zu Husserls Phänomenologie," Zeitschrift für philosophische Forschung, 1959, pp. 313–39.

"Remarks Concerning the Interpretation of Franz Brentano: a Reply to Dr. Srzednicki," Philosophy and Phenomenological Research, 23, 1963, pp. 438–44.

McAlister, Linda L., "Franz Brentano and Intentional Inexistence," Journal of the History of Philosophy, 4, 1970, pp. 423–30.

"Chisholm and Brentano on Intentionality," The Review of Metaphysics, 28, 1974–5, pp. 328–38.

The Development of Franz Brentano's Ethics (Amsterdam: Rodopi, 1982).

(ed.), The Philosophy of Brentano (London: Gerald Duckworth and Co. Ltd., 1976).

Mezei, Balázs M., "The Brentano-School and Hungarian Philosophy," Existentia, 1–4, 1993–4, pp. 647–57.

"Brentano and Psychologism," Psychologia, 2, 1994.

"Brentano, Cartesianism, and Jan Patocka," Brentano Studien, 7, 1997, pp. 69–87.

"Brentano and Husserl on the History of Philosophy," Brentano Studien, 8, 2000, pp. 81–94.

Mezei, Balázs M. and Smith, Barry, The Four Phases of Philosophy, with an Appendix: the Four Phases of Philosophy and its Current State by Franz Brentano (Amsterdam: Rodopi, 1998).

Moore, G. E., "Review of Franz Brentano, The Origin of Our Knowledge of Right and Wrong," International Journal of Ethics, 14, 1903, pp. 115–23.

Moran, Dermot, "The Inaugural Address: Brentano's Thesis," Inaugural Address to the Joint Session of the Aristotelian Society and the Mind Association, Proceedings of the Aristotelian Society Supplementary Volume 70, 1996, pp. 1–27.

"Heidegger's Critique of Husserl's and Brentano's Account of Intentionality," *Inquiry*, 43, 2000, pp. 39–66.

Introduction to Phenomenology (London, New York: Routledge, 2000).

Morrison, James C., "Husserl and Brentano on Intentionality," *Philosophy and Phenomenological Research*, 31, 1970, pp. 27–46.

Morscher, Edgar, "Brentano and his Place in Austrian Philosophy," in, eds., Chisholm and Haller, *Philosophie Franz Brentanos*, 1978, pp. 1–9.

Most, Otto, *Die Ethik Franz Brentanos* (Münster: Helios, 1931).

Müller, Robert, *Franz Brentanos Lehre von den Gemütsbewegungen*, ed. E. Otto (Brünn, München, Wien: Verlag Rudolf M. Röhrer, 1943).

Mulligan, Kevin, "Judgings: Their Parts and Counterparts," *Topoi*, Supplement, 2, 1989, *La Scuola di Brentano* (Bologna Brentano Conference 1984), pp. 117–48.

"Exactness, Description and Variation – How Austrian Analytic Philosophy was Done," in, ed., Nyíri, *Von Bolzano zu Wittgenstein*, 1986, pp. 86–97.

"The Expression of Exactness: Ernst Mach, the Brentanists and the Ideal of Clarity," in, ed., Pynsent, *Decadence and Innovation*, 1989, pp. 33–42.

"Genauigkeit und Geschwätz – Glossen zu einem paradigmatischen Gegensatz in der Philosophie: Brentano und die Brentanisten," in *Wien – Paradigme der Moderne* (Amsterdam: J. Benjamins, 1990), pp. 209–36.

"Marty's Philosophical Grammar," in, ed., Mulligan, *Mind, Meaning and Metaphysics*, 1990, pp. 11–28.

"Sur l'Histoire de l'approche analytique de l'historie de la philosophie: de Bolzano et Brentano à Bennett et Barnes," in, ed., J.-M. Vienne, *Philosophie analytique et Histoire de la philosophie* (Paris: Vrin, 1997), pp. 61–103.

(ed.), *Mind, Meaning and Metaphysics: the Philosophy and Theory of Language of Anton Marty* (Dordrecht, Boston, London: Kluwer Academic Publishers, 1990).

Mulligan, Kevin, and Smith, Barry, "Critical Notice of F. Brentano, 'Deskriptive Psychologie,'" *Philosophy and Phenomenological Research*, 45:4, 1984, pp. 327–44.

"Franz Brentano on the Ontology of Mind," *Philosophy and Phenomenological Research*, 45, 1985, pp. 627–44.

"Parts and Moments: Pieces of a Theory," in, ed., Smith, *Parts and Moments*, 1982, pp. 15–109.

Münch, Dieter, "Brentanos Lehre von der intentionalen Inexistenz," in, ed., Nyíri, *Von Bolzano zu Wittgenstein*, 1986, pp. 119–27.

"Brentano and Comte," *Grazer Philosophische Studien*, 35, 1989, pp. 33–54.

Intention und Zeichen: Untersuchungen zu Franz Brentano und zu Edmund Husserls Frühwerk (Frankfurt am Main: Suhrkamp, 1993).

"Die Einheit von Geist und Leib: Brentanos Habilitationsschrift über die Psychologie des Aristoteles als Antwort auf Zeller," *Brentano Studien*, 6, 1996, pp. 125–44.

Nyíri, J. C. (Christoph) (ed.), *Von Bolzano zu Wittgenstein: zur Tradition der österreichischen Philosophie* (Vienna: Hölder-Pichler-Tempsky, 1986).

"Ungarn und die Brentano-Schule: Ein Überblick," *Brentano Studien*, 5, 1994, pp. 13–23.

Orth, Ernst Wolfgang, "Brentanos und Diltheys Konzeption einer beschreibenden Psychologie in ihrer Beziehung auf Lotze," *Brentano Studien*, 6, 1996, pp. 13–29.

"Metaphysische Implikationen der Intentionalität: Trendelenburg, Lotze, Brentano," *Brentano Studien*, 7, 1997, pp. 15–30.

Park, Chan-Young, *Untersuchungen zur Werttheorie bei Franz Brentano*, Brentano Studien Sonderband (Dettelbach: Josef Röll, 1991).

Pasquerella, Lynn, "Brentano and the Direct Attribution Theory," *Brentano Studien*, 1, 1988, pp. 189–97.

"Kotarbinski and Brentano on Truth," *Topoi*, Supplement (The Object and its Identity), 4, 1989, pp. 98–106.

Pavlik, Jan, "Franz Kafka and Franz Brentano," *Brentano Studien*, 8, 2000, pp. 121–47.

Philipse, Herman, "The Concept of Intentionality: Husserl's Development from the Brentano Period to the 'Logical Investigations,'" *Philosophy Research Archives*, 12, 1986–7, pp. 293–328.

Poli, Robert, "Brentano in Italy," *Brentano Studien*, 8, 2000, pp. 233–57.

Poli, Roberto (ed.), *Consciousness, Knowledge and Truth* (Dordrecht, Boston, London: Kluwer Academic Publishers, 1993).

The Brentano Puzzle (Aldershot: Ashgate Publishing, 1998).

Potrc, Matjaz, "Brentano and Veber," *Brentano Studien*, 8, 2000, pp. 193–209.

Prior, A. N., *Formal Logic*, 2nd edn. (Cambridge: Cambridge University Press, 1962).

The Doctrine of Propositions and Terms (London: Duckworth, 1976).

Pynsent, Robert (ed.), *Decadence and Innovation: Austro-Hungarian Life and Art at the Turn of the Century* (London: Weidenfeld and Nicolson, 1989).

Rancurello, Antos C., *A Study of Franz Brentano: his Psychological Standpoint and His Significance in the History of Psychology* (New York: Academic Press, 1968).

Richardson, Robert, "Brentano on Intentional Inexistence and the Distinction Between Mental and Psychical Phenomena," *Archiv für Geschichte der Philosophie*, 65, 1983, pp. 250–82.

Rinofner-Kreidl, Sonja, "Zeitbewusstsein, innere Wahrnehmung und Reproduktion: die phänomenologische Zeitlehre in der Auseinandersetzung Husserl-Brentano," *Brentano Studien*, 6, 1996, pp. 193–227.

Rojszczak, Artur, "Wahrheit und Urteilsevidenz bei Franz Brentano," *Brentano Studien*, 5, 1994, pp. 187–218.

Rollinger, Robin D., "Husserl and Brentano on Imagination," *Archiv für Geschichte der Philosophie*, 75, 1993, pp. 195–210.

Husserl's Position in the School of Brentano (Dordrecht, Boston, MA, London: Kluwer Academic Publishers, 1999).

"Brentano and Meinong on Time-Consciousness," in, eds., Hans-Rainer Sepp and Toru Tami, *Zeit in der Phänomenologie* (Freiburg-München: Karl Albert Verlag, forthcoming).

Runggaldier, E., "On the Scholastic or Aristotelian Roots of 'Intentionality' in Brentano," *Topoi*, 8, 1989, pp. 97–103.

Sanchez-Migallon, Sergio, "Die Rezeption Brentanos in den spanischsprachigen Ländern," *Brentano Studien*, 6, 1996, pp. 315–22.

Sauer, Werner, "Erneuerung der Philosophia Perennis: Über die ersten vier Habilitationsthesen Brentanos," *Grazer Philosophische Studien*, 58–9, 2000, pp. 119–49.

Schuhmann, Karl, "Der Gegenstandsbegriff in Brentanos 'Psychognosie,'" *Brentano Studien*, 5, 1994, pp. 167–76.

Schutz, Alfred. *Collected Papers III: Studies in Phenomenological Philosophy*, ed., I. Schutz (The Hague: Martinus Nijhoff, 1970).

Simons, Peter, "A Brentanian Basis for Leśniewskian Logic," *Logique et Analyse*, 27, 1984, pp. 297–307.

"Brentano's Reform of Logic," *Topoi*, 6, 1987, pp. 25–38.

"Brentano's Theory of Categories: a Critical Appraisal," *Brentano Studien*, 1, 1988, pp. 47–61.

The Doctrine of Propositions and Terms (London: Duckworth, 1976).

"Tree Proofs for Syllogistic," *Studia Logica* 48, 1989, pp. 539–54.

Parts (Oxford: Clarendon Press, 1987).

Philosophy and Logic in Central Europe from Bolzano to Tarski (Dordrecht, Boston, London: Kluwer Academic Publishers, 1992).

"Logic in the Brentano School," in, eds., Albertazzi, Libardi, and Poli, *School of Franz Bretano*, 1996, pp. 305–21.

"Bolzano, Brentano and Meinong: Three Austrian Realists," in, ed., Anthony O'Hear, *Philosophy since Kant* (Cambridge: Cambridge University Press, 1999).

Simons, Peter and Woleński, Jan, "*De Veritate*: Austro-Polish Contributions to the Theory of Truth from Brentano to Tarski," in, ed., K. Szaniawski, *The Vienna Circle and the Lvov-Warsaw School* (Dordrecht, Boston, London: Kluwer Academic Publishers, 1989), pp. 391–442.

Skrbensky, L., *Franz Brentano als Religionphilosoph* (Zürich: Verlag der freigeistigen Vereinigung der Schweiz, 1937).

Smith, Barry, "The Substance of Brentano's Ontology," *Topoi*, 6, 1987, pp. 37–47.

"The Soul and its Parts: a Study in Aristotle and Brentano," *Brentano Studien*, 1, 1988, pp. 75–88.

"The Primacy of Place: an Investigation in Brentanian Ontology," *Topoi*, 8, 1989, pp. 43–51.

"On the Phases of Reism," in, ed., Jan Woleński, *Kotarbinski: Logic, Semantics and Ontology* (Dordrecht, Boston, London: Kluwer Academic Publishers, 1990), pp. 137–84.

"Sachverhalt," in, eds., J. Ritter and K. Gründer, *Historisches Wörterbuch der Philosophie*, vol. 8 (Darmstadt: Wissenschaftliche Buchgesellschaft, 1992), pp. 1102–13.

"The Soul and its Parts II: Varieties of Inexistence," *Brentano Studien*, 4, 1992–3, pp. 35–51.

Austrian Philosophy: the Legacy of Franz Brentano (Chicago, IL: Open Court, 1994).

"Boundaries: an Essay in Mereotopology," in, ed., L. H. Hahn, *The Philosophy of Roderick Chisholm* (Chicago, IL and LaSalle, IL: Open Court, 1997), pp. 534–61.

"Brentano and Kafka," *Axiomathes*, 8, 1997, pp. 83–104.

"On Substances, Accidents and Universals: in Defence of a Constituent Ontology," *Philosophical Papers* 26, 1997, pp. 105–27.

"Boundaries: a Brentanian Theory: Zeno's Paradox for Colours," *Brentano Studien*, 8, 2000, pp. 107–14.

Smith, Barry (ed.), *Parts and Moments: Studies in Logic and Formal Ontology* (Munich: Philosophia Verlag, 1982).

Sorabji, Richard, "From Aristotle to Brentano: the Development of the Concept of Intentionality," in *Aristotle, the Later Tradition, Oxford Studies in Ancient Philosophy*, Supplementary Volume, eds., H. Blumenthal and H. Robinson, 1991, pp. 227–59.

Sowa, Rochus, "Typus," in, ed., Helmut Vetter, *Lexikon der Phänomenologie* (Stuttgart: Kröner, forthcoming).

Spiegelberg, Herbert, "Der Begriff der Intentionalität in der Scholastik bei Brentano und bei Husserl," *Philosophische Hefte*, ed., Maximilian Beck, 5, 1936, pp. 72–91.

"'Intention' and 'Intentionality' in the Scholastics, Brentano and Husserl," trans. Linda L. McAlister, in, ed., McAlister, *Philosophy of Brentano*, 1976, pp. 108–27.

"On the Significance of the Correspondence Between Franz Brentano and Edmund Husserl," in, eds., Chisholm and Haller, *Philosophie Franz Brentanos*, 1978, pp. 95–116.

The Phenomenological Movement: a Historical Introduction, 2nd edn., 2 vols. (The Hague: Martinus Nijhoff, 1978).

The Phenomenological Movement. A Historical Introduction, 3rd rev. and enlarged edn. (The Hague: Martinus Nijhoff, 1981).

Srzednicki, Jan, "Remarks Concerning the Interpretation of the Philosophy of Franz Brentano," *Philosophy and Phenomenological Research*, 22, 1962, pp. 308–16.

Franz Brentano's Analysis of Truth (The Hague: Martinus Nijhoff, 1965).

"Some Elements of Brentano's Analysis of Language and their Ramifications," *Revue Internationale de Philosophie*, 20, 1966, pp. 434–45.

Stumpf, Carl, "Erinnerungen an Franz Brentano," in, ed., Kraus, *Franz Brentano*, 1919, pp. 89–149.

Tanasescu, Ion, " 'Der Vorstellungsgegenstand': Zu Twardowskis Rezeption der Psychologie Brentanos," *Brentano Studien*, 8, 2000, pp. 53–66.

Terrell, D. B., "Brentano's Argument for Reismus," in, ed., McAlister, *Philosophy of Brentano*, 1976, pp. 204–12.

"Quantification and Brentano's Logic," *Grazer Philosophische Studien*, 5, 1978, pp. 45–65.

Thomasson, Amie L., "After Brentano: a One-Level Theory of Consciousness," *European Journal of Philosophy*, 8, 2000, pp. 190–209.

Tiefensee, E., *Philosophie und Religion bei Franz Brentano* (Tübingen und Basel: A. Francke, 1998).

Twardowski, Kasimir (Kazimierz), "Franz Brentano und die Geschichte der Philosophie," *Prezlom*, 11, 1895.

On the Content and Object of Presentations: a Psychological Investigation (Dordrecht, Boston, London: Kluwer Academic Publishers, 1977).

Zur Lehre vom Inhalt und Gegenstand der Vorstellungen: Eine psychologische Untersuchung [1894] (Munich and Vienna: Philosophia Verlag, 1982).

Utitz, E., "Erinnerungen an Franz Brentano," *Zeitschrift für philosophische Forschung*, 1959, pp. 102–10.

Vallicella, William F., "Brentano on Existence," *History of Philosophy Quarterly*, 18, 2001, pp. 311–27.

Velarde-Mayol, Victor, *On Brentano* (Belmont: Wadsworth/Thomson Learning, Inc., 2000).

Volpi, F., "War Brentano ein Aristoteliker? Zu Brentanos und Aristoteles Auffassung der Psychologie als Wissenschaft," *Brentano Studien*, 2, 1989, pp. 13–29.

Wagner, J., *Die Kritik an Kants Philosophie bei Bolzano, Brentano, ihren Schülern und Max Scheller* (1923).

Weiler, Gershon, "In Search of What is Austrian in Austrian Philosophy," in *Von Bolzano zu Wittgenstein: Zur Tradition der österreichischen Philosophie*, ed. J. C. Nyíri (Vienna: Hölder-Pichler-Tempsky, 1986).

Weingartner, Paul, "Brentano's Criticism of the Correspondence Theory of Truth and the Principle *"Ens et verum convertuntur,"* in, eds., Chisholm and Haller, *Philosophie Franz Brentanos,* 1978, pp. 183–95.

Werle, J. M., *Franz Brentano und die Zukunft der Philosophie: Studien zur Wissenschaftsgeschichte und Wissenschaftssystematik im 19. Jahrhundert* (Amsterdam: Rodopi, 1989).

Werner, Alfons, *Die psychologisch-erkenntnistheoretische Grundlagen der Metaphysik Franz Brentanos* (Hildesheim: Franz Borgmeyer, 1931).

Woleński, Jan, "Brentano's Criticism of the Correspondence Conception of Truth and Tarski's Semantic Theory," *Topoi,* 8, 1989, pp. 105–10.

"Brentano, the Univocality of Thinking, 'Something' and 'Reism,'" *Brentano Studien,* 5, 1994, pp. 149–66.

"Reism in the Brentanist Tradition", in, eds., Albertazzi, Libardi, and Poli, *School of Franz Brentano,* 1996, pp. 357–75.

Zelaniec, Wojciech, "Franz Brentano and the Principle of Individuation," *Brentano Studien,* 6, 1995–6, pp. 145–64.

"Am Rande der Transzendentalphilosophie: Auseinandersetzung Brentanos mit dem Zeno-Paradox," *Brentano Studien,* 7, 1997, pp. 447–54.

"Disentangling Brentano: Why did he get Individuation Wrong?," *Brentano Studien,* 7, 1997, pp. 455–63.

Zimmer, Alf, "On Agents and Objects: Some Remarks on Brentanian Perception," in, ed., Poli, *Consciousness, Knowledge and Truth,* 1998, pp. 93–112.

INDEX